Innovations in Labour Market Policies

THE AUSTRALIAN WAY

OECD

ORGANISATION FOR ECONOMIC CO-OPERATION AND DEVELOPMENT

ORGANISATION FOR ECONOMIC CO-OPERATION AND DEVELOPMENT

Pursuant to Article 1 of the Convention signed in Paris on 14th December 1960, and which came into force on 30th September 1961, the Organisation for Economic Co-operation and Development (OECD) shall promote policies designed:

- to achieve the highest sustainable economic growth and employment and a rising standard of living in Member countries, while maintaining financial stability, and thus to contribute to the development of the world economy;
- to contribute to sound economic expansion in Member as well as non-member countries in the process of economic development; and
- to contribute to the expansion of world trade on a multilateral, non-discriminatory basis in accordance with international obligations.

The original Member countries of the OECD are Austria, Belgium, Canada, Denmark, France, Germany, Greece, Iceland, Ireland, Italy, Luxembourg, the Netherlands, Norway, Portugal, Spain, Sweden, Switzerland, Turkey, the United Kingdom and the United States. The following countries became Members subsequently through accession at the dates indicated hereafter: Japan (28th April 1964), Finland (28th January 1969), Australia (7th June 1971), New Zealand (29th May 1973), Mexico (18th May 1994), the Czech Republic (21st December 1995), Hungary (7th May 1996), Poland (22nd November 1996), Korea (12th December 1996) and the Slovak Republic (14th December 2000). The Commission of the European Communities takes part in the work of the OECD (Article 13 of the OECD Convention).

Publié en français sous le titre :
DES POLITIQUES DU MARCHÉ DU TRAVAIL NOVATRICES
La méthode australienne

Foreword

This review examines labour market policy and industrial relations reform in Australia. It is part of a series on the Public Employment Service and labour market policies in OECD countries, with 19 countries covered since the early 1990s. Other recent publications in this series have been *The Public Employment Service in the United States* [OECD (1999e)] and *Pushing Ahead with Reform in Korea: Labour Market and Social Safety-net Policies* [OECD (2000h)].

The volume draws upon information collected by Secretariat staff during a visit to Australia in October 2000 and submissions by the Australian government. It has been prepared by David Grubb, Douglas Lippoldt and Peter Tergeist from the OECD's Directorate for Education, Employment, Labour and Social Affairs.

A draft of the review was discussed by the Employment, Labour and Social Affairs Committee in April 2001. In late May 2001, shortly before going to press, the Australian government announced a package of measures which are summarised in a box that appears after the Summary and Conclusions section, but are not otherwise reflected in the text.

This volume is published on the responsibility of the Secretary-General of the OECD.

Table of contents

Boxes

Tables and Charts

Chapter 1

7|

Introduction

This report examines labour market policy in Australia, with attention to both workplace relations and the functions of job-broking, benefit administration and referral to and administration of labour market programmes which typically make up the Public Employment Service (PES). However, Australia has been among the first OECD countries to introduce market-type mechanisms into job-broking and related employment services. Since the introduction of Job Network in 1998, employment services are mainly offered by independent providers from the private and community sector. The remaining government body is offering services on the same terms and conditions as the private providers, and has retained only a relatively minor market share in the market. This radical transformation of employment service delivery is without parallel in OECD countries, and it shows that the delivery of publicly-financed employment services by private and community providers is a viable option.

Another significant recent development has been the government's intention of retaining only the most cost-effective active labour market programmes. This led to the abolition of the main long-term training and subsidised employment programmes for the unemployed, although many smaller programmes for particular target groups were retained or introduced. A third development has been an increased emphasis on the principle of "Mutual Obligation" in the benefit system which requires some people who have been unemployed for some time to take up one of a number of options (including part-time and voluntary work), or participate in a new job-creation programme called "Work for the Dole". Against a background of rapid economic growth, unemployment fell rapidly during the early years of these new policies.

Industrial relations can make an important contribution to labour market efficiency. Australia's industrial relations system is exceptional in that most workers are covered by "awards" set through a quasi-judicial system of conciliation and arbitration operating through industrial tribunals at both state and Commonwealth levels. Awards, which originated as a response to industrial disputes, set wages and other conditions of work for a large proportion of workers. Over the last decade, the system has been undergoing a paradigm shift in that awards are rapidly losing in importance in favour of bargained agreements at enterprise and workplace level. Arbitration has nevertheless remained important with a vital role in such matters as setting minimum wage levels for some workers. The search for avenues to further reform continues, but it has been difficult to find a political consensus for a particular future model.

The report is organised with a Summary and Conclusions section appearing first, followed by a summary of the Australians Working Together package announced in the May 2001 budget. Chapter 1 then gives an overview of the Australian labour market and Chapter 2 presents the institutions involved in labour market policy and employment services. Chapters 3 to 5 cover Job Network and placement issues, unemployment and related benefits, and labour market programmes, while Chapter 6 considers workplace relations and wage determination. To ease the flow of the main text, material on payment mechanisms for competitive employment service provision and three major areas of labour market programmes is presented in final annexes.

Summary and Conclusions

A. Overview: the recasting of labour market policy and labour market institutions

Australia was one of the first OECD countries to introduce market-type mechanisms into its employment services. Its strategy for tackling unemployment has been based on a new system for delivering employment services through private and community providers (the "Job Network"), and on a range of options which younger adults are obliged to participate in to receive benefit ("Mutual Obligation"). The Howard government, since taking power in 1996, sought to retain only the most cost-effective active labour market programmes. Disability programmes and the CDEP scheme for indigenous workers were maintained, and spending on apprenticeships and traineeships was increased. But there were major budget reductions in funds for training and subsidised employment programmes for the unemployed, prior to the cashing out of the remaining funds into a flexible pool of funding for employment services. As a result, total spending on active labour market programmes declined from 0.8% of GDP in 1995/96 to just over 0.4% of GDP in 1998/99.

Australia has established a network of contracted employment service providers, and new obligations for unemployed claimants. Services have been overhauled, funds pooled, and spending on active programmes nearly halved.

The introduction of Job Network (JN) in 1998 was preceded by the establishment of a new public body, Centrelink. Centrelink processes claims and payments for a range of benefits such as age pensions, disability and unemployment assistance on behalf of the Department of Family and Community Services (FaCS). It refers jobseeker clients to JN services and other labour market programmes on behalf of the

Centrelink is a single access point, processing claims and payments and also referring to Job Network and other services.

Department of Employment, Workplace Relations, and Small Business (DEWRSB) and other Departments. Centrelink is thus a kind of "first-stop shop" for employment services, but not a "one-stop shop" in the sense used in some other OECD Member countries because its role in job-broking is limited to providing access to vacancy listings and career information through computerised touchscreens.

This review looks at job-brokerage, benefit payment and labour market programmes – all areas where issues arise for Job Network – and then at workplace relations reform.

The OECD Secretariat's reviews of the Public Employment Service (PES) in Member countries focus on its three main functions of job-brokerage, income support, and referral to and management of labour market programmes. This summary devotes a section to each of these functions. Job Network accounts for only about a third of the "active" side of spending on labour market programmes, but some issues for Job Network arise under each heading. Two final sections consider policy processes and workplace relations reform.

Australia has performed well against recent OECD Jobs Strategy criteria...

OECD *Economic Surveys* in 1995 and 1996 made only four country-specific recommendations for the implementation of the OECD Jobs Strategy, in the area of labour market policies and institutions, to Australia, suggesting that it has been among the OECD countries complying best with this Strategy. Later *Surveys* commented favourably on the 1996 Workplace Relations Act and supported further developments along the same lines.

...and it served as a model for some policies, but the various functions of the PES have remained fragmented.

Australia has complied with – and perhaps partly inspired – several of the original recommendations in the 1994 OECD *Jobs Study*, notably concerning the individualisation of assistance benefit (separate entitlements for both members of a couple) and making long-term benefits conditional on participation in programmes – as well as some policy proposals later developed by OECD concerning profiling new benefit claimants and experimentation with the contestability of the PES. However it did not move towards integration of the three basic functions of the PES (FaCS and DEWRSB both develop and manage strategies for tackling unemployment), and discrepancies may also exist concerning in-work benefits for low-paid workers (the Australian strategy, which promotes part-time work by the unemployed, diverges somewhat from the recommendations), for example. This review does not focus further on assessing implementation of the OECD *Jobs Study* recommendations, although elements of the underlying philosophy may often be detectable. It aims primarily to assess current policy in detail and on its merits, while also allowing international readers to learn from Australia's many remarkable experiences and innovations in labour market policy.

B. Job Network

1. *General description*

Private-sector and community-based organisations were contracted to provide training and to organise job clubs for clients registered with the Commonwealth Employment Service in the 1980s. In 1994 "contracted case management" was introduced, making public provision of this service "contestable". The incoming government in 1996 opted to establish a "fully contestable" market and the Job Network started operation in May 1998. The remaining government-owned provider (Employment National) offers services on the same terms and conditions as the private and community providers under the principle of "competitive neutrality", and since 2000 it has retained only a relatively minor market share. This radical transformation of employment service delivery is without parallel in OECD countries.

The residual government-owned provider now has only a minor role in an open employment services market: an unparalleled change.

How does Job Network operate in practice? First, the government sets the range and broad nature of employment services to be provided. The Job Matching service provides vacancy referrals and related services and is open to nearly all unemployed people. Job Search Training (JST) requires attendance at a minimum of 15 days' assistance, to which unemployed people are referred by Centrelink after they have remained unemployed for some time

The government defines the services that Job Network must provide for those referred to it by the public body, Centrelink...

(between 2 and 12 months). Intensive Assistance (IA) is a programme of individualised case management in which participation can continue for up to 12 to 21 months. Centrelink refers clients to Intensive Assistance if their score on the Job Seeker Classification Instrument (JSCI) is above a certain threshold, and they have a capacity to benefit. This results in some clients being referred at the start of their unemployment spell, while others are referred only at review a year or more later.

...and then puts these services to tender, a process that offers considerable flexibility but can cause uncertainty and disruption.

Second, a tender process, managed by DEWRSB, determines which organisations will be contracted to provide JN services. Some of the fees that will be paid to providers are defined in advance while others are determined by competitive tender. IA providers are financially rewarded on the basis of client intake (commencements) and the employment and training outcomes they achieve: they are free to pay for measures such as training on behalf of their clients, but are not reimbursed directly for these costs, nor (in contrast to the earlier contracted case management model) are they generally able to place clients in other government programmes. Tender decisions may take into account not only the prices bid but also factors such as the tendering organisation's track record and its intended strategy for the service for which it is bidding. Tender decisions allocate to providers a maximum number of jobseekers that they can assist (specified in terms of paid placements for Job Matching, jobseeker caseload at a point in time for Intensive Assistance, and both flows and stocks for JST). So far, two tender rounds have been organised, in 1997 and 1999. Each tender has been supervised by a probity advisor. Each tender has involved a huge work load both for DEWRSB and individual providers, and many existing providers lost business in the second round decisions. There is a need for arrangements under which provider contracts can be renewed with less uncertainty and disruption.

In the second contract period (stretching from 2000 to 2003), over 200 providers try to attract jobseekers to their services offered on over 2000 sites throughout Australia. Providers come from a wide variety of backgrounds, including charitable organisations, recruitment consultants, private placement agencies and the former public service itself. OECD Secretariat estimates suggest that about 16 000 staff are employed by DEWRSB, Centrelink and the JN providers together in providing employment services. Relating these numbers to the potential number of clients or to actual workload indicators such as unemployed jobseekers or the inflow of notified vacancies, it appears that employment services in Australia are fairly well resourced in international comparison, in contrast to other types of active labour market spending.

With a total of 16 000 staff across the different organisations involved, employment services are well resourced by international standards.

Many providers offer assistance in all principal service categories. About 80% provide Job Matching while 60% provide Intensive Assistance. Within Intensive Assistance, a significant proportion focus on specialist services for particular client groups, such as indigenous Australians, the disabled or persons with a non-English-speaking background.

Job Network providers are engaged in different combinations of services...

In the second tender round, for Intensive Assistance not only past performance but also a Declaration of Intent, describing strategies and services that the tenderer expected to provide (*e.g.* maximum caseloads per case manager or the expected frequency of contact with jobseekers) were taken into account. Service standards and expectations are also detailed in the Job Network Code of Conduct which, to a certain extent, resembles operational guidelines for PES offices in other countries. The focus on service standards and monitoring has thus partly replaced the initial "black box" concept that the government could pay for employment outcomes without needing to know the service strategies adopted to achieve those outcomes. This implies that the employment services "market" operates in different ways from other markets for goods or services. Organisations from the community sector, which may have paid attention less to profitability

...and are now being judged partly on service standards and processes, as well as outcomes. This has favoured quality community sector providers.

considerations during the first contract period, gained business in the second tender round owing to the quality of their service provision and good outcomes.

2. Operational issues

One challenge is to ensure that jobseekers and employers have enough information about the services available.

DEWRSB client surveys and some research papers using data from the first JN contract period provide insights into areas for improvement. One issue is the on-going challenge to ensure that clients understand the opportunities that Job Network provides. For jobseeker clients, choosing a JN provider has been difficult, although a report presenting comparable performance information was recently released. The 1999 employer survey indicated an insufficient awareness of the working of Job Network among most employers. It may be that awareness has increased (*e.g.* through DEWRSB-supported efforts by providers, word-of-mouth advertising and a recent high-profile advertising campaign), but continued efforts and follow-up monitoring are needed.

Jobseekers sometimes find it difficult to get complete information on vacant jobs.

A key issue for some jobseekers is the perception of fragmentation in the Job Matching system. Although the AJS Internet site and DEWRSB self-service kiosks offer clients an opportunity to review vacancies system-wide, the fact that a large majority of vacancy listings are semi-open (*i.e.* are listed without all the available information, in particular the employer's name and address) means that clients may need either to enrol with a number of Job Matching providers to get more complete information, or to consider their options based on the partial information available publicly.

The fact that training and assistance are often not taken up remains a concern...

For JST and Intensive Assistance, a substantial share of jobseekers who are referred do not commence. This issue has been partly addressed through improvements in information systems and clarification of procedures for reporting and sanctioning non-attendance, but it remains a concern. Acceptable reasons for non-commencement include leaving income support (with many finding employment) and being exempt from assistance (including those who have commenced other programmes or have personal reasons such as ill-health for not attending). Those who do not commence and are not in these categories are likely to be sanctioned.

In the case of Intensive Assistance, the content of the services rendered is a further issue. In the 1999 jobseeker satisfaction survey, less than one-half of IA clients reported they had been sent to a job interview or to speak with an employer about a job. Apparently, providers hesitated to refer jobseekers they believed not to be job-ready. Also, in some cases contact with clients became infrequent after a while. As noted in DEWRSB's stage one evaluation of Job Network, very few providers appeared to be offering effective services to address the underlying barriers to employment. The caution of IA providers in referring clients to vacant jobs appears to some degree to be merited in light of DEWRSB's 1999 employer survey, which indicated that, among the minority of dissatisfied employer clients, a main reason for dissatisfaction was referral of applicants who were of poor quality, not interested or did not even turn up. Changes to conditions in the second tender sought to ensure that providers would offer substantial assistance and improve the job readiness of clients, and these efforts should continue.

...as does the content of the assistance provided to the hardest-to-service clients.

3. Initial results

The reaction among the jobseeker and employer clientele to Job Network has largely been favourable. Jobseeker satisfaction and employer surveys conducted in 1999 indicate that the majority of surveyed clients who participated in Job Matching, JST or Intensive Assistance were satisfied with the services they received (with satisfaction rates of more than 75%). Moreover, among Job Matching clients who entered paid employment, most characterised the assistance of the provider as having played an important role. Similarly, JST clients characterised their providers as having improved their job prospects. Most employers also assessed the Job Network favourably, notably with respect to key aspects of the jobseeker referral process.

Jobseekers and employers have generally been happy with Job Network...

...while in terms of job placement the reformed service achieves similar results to its predecessor...

However, popularity with clients does not in itself imply that Job Network is effective. Concrete results in terms of labour market outcomes are also an essential element of an assessment. Here, the available statistics indicate that Job Network has delivered results that are not dramatically different from those obtained under the Working Nation programme of the previous government. For example, Job Network has broadly maintained the market share of placements by employment service providers as a percentage of hirings. Total unemployment fell considerably in 1998, 1999 and 2000, but this could be due to number of factors. In administrative data, the evidence that various active labour market policy measures were having an impact was limited in 1999, but emerged more clearly during 2000 and early 2001.

...though at less cost, albeit in a more favourable economy.

In sum, the results of the Job Network approach during its first years of operation might be considered mixed. On the one hand, the system delivered results comparable to those of the previous approach, but at significantly less cost overall. On the other hand, as some observers have noted, it may have been possible to improve some results (*e.g.* concerning the reduction of long-term unemployment) faster during the recent period of economic upswing. It is important, however, to recognise that this mixed assessment is based largely on the performance of the system under the first round of JN contracts. It will take quite some time before one can make a full assessment of the effectiveness of Job Network in terms of helping jobseekers into work – at least a complete economic cycle.

4. Potential system adjustments

The system for identifying individuals' need for Intensive Assistance could be enhanced: it may be worth referring all long-term unemployed.

The available qualitative information and outcomes data suggest a number of areas for potential adjustments, which might best be developed on the basis of future field trials, research or evaluation work. Some jobseekers when interviewed by Centrelink do not disclose all information about their personal characteristics that is needed for JSCI. Measures to encourage initial disclosure and facilitate reclassification as new information becomes known might be developed. Another step may be to refer people who have been on benefit for a year automatically to Intensive Assistance, because when a person has not found work yet appears to be highly employable in all other respects, this in itself can indicate a need for intensive intervention which is not of a nature to be picked up by JSCI. Also, since referrals to JST now usually occur after six or fewer months of unemployment, a long break in intensive service provision occurs if the person is not referred after a year of unemployment.

The system of payments to providers is a critical determinant of their behaviour and the resulting outcomes. Job Matching provision is generally regarded as an unprofitable activity. This seems paradoxical as an outcome from a competitive tender process. One possible explanation is that the lowest tender bids for the Job Matching placement fee may correspond to the costs for providers who specialise in particular client groups or types of vacancy, which are below the costs of servicing an average client or vacancy. Another possible explanation is that IA providers are prepared to cross-subsidise their own Job Matching services on a permanent basis, to ensure access to vacancies, which is central to IA performance. This may make Job Matching-only operations structurally unprofitable in a competitive market. Another issue in Job Matching is that, while the "hoarding" of vacancies may be desirable when it gives disadvantaged clients priority of access to them, efforts by individual providers to gain exclusive access to vacancies are subject to a negative externality – these efforts do not improve overall system performance. Possible changes to the fee system for Job Matching include: to introduce relatively lower fees for short-term repeat placements (already, placements of a jobseeker more than twice a month with the same employer do not qualify for a fee); to encourage the "selling" of certain vacancies suitable for IA clients to the highest bidder (giving an incentive to advertise and distribute rather than hoard such vacancies); and to

Payment systems are important: Job Matching services do not seem to be profitable...

split the Job Matching fee into two parts, one for the provider who first lists a vacancy and another for the provider who places a client into it, with increased payments for vacancy listings which provide detailed information and/or that are frequently accessed by other providers.

...while for Intensive Assistance:

The system of payment for Intensive Assistance raises some complex issues. Some key points in the Secretariat analysis are:

Maximum outcome fees would need to rise to reflect the full potential social gain from time spent in employment and off benefits;

• Outcome fees should reflect a total value attached by society to each week or month that the client spends in employment rather than in unemployment, and not the average cost of assistance provided or the result of a competitive tender. This total social value should be taken as the net government budgetary impact of employment outcomes, plus a valuation how the utility of the jobseeker is affected (taking into account the gain in earnings, the loss of benefit, and the utility or disutility of work) and various externalities (*e.g.* reduction in crime or public health spending costs). The latter two components are probably positive and in any case cannot reasonably be supposed to be strongly negative. The maximum payment available, where an IA provider achieves an early, stable placement of a client which lasts for 12 months and is likely to continue (or perhaps preferably, is known to have continued) even after this, should therefore be well over the cost of a year's benefit payments. In the case of less-disadvantaged (level A) clients, this is about five times the maximum payment that providers can currently get for employment outcomes (partly because outcomes are only tracked for six months). Yet if providers can devise programmes that generate net employment impacts, sustained for at least 12 months, at an average cost of about $10 000 – and experience suggests this may be possible – the use of them should be profitable, whereas fees for level A clients are currently too low to permit this.

- Many employment outcomes from Intensive Assistance would have occurred even in the absence of any significant service provision. For this reason, it is important to pay outcome fees only at the margin, *i.e.* only for the increase in outcomes that is caused by IA assistance. This could be achieved in various ways, but a competitive mechanism is possible whereby the government invites providers to continuously bid (*e.g.* every month or three months) for referrals of a certain flow (or proportion of the total flow) of jobseekers in an area. Bidding would take place in terms of a threshold rate of employment outcomes, with the winning provider subsequently only being paid for employment outcomes above the threshold rate it specified in its bid. This system would allow maximum outcome fees to be much higher than they are at present, while not necessarily costing much more in total than the current system does – unless and until much higher service levels and outcome rates emerge, as a result of the increased incentives.

But higher fees need not cost more, if they are paid only for the increase in outcomes that is due to the services provided;

- The payment system outlined here is more highly leveraged on outcomes, and thus exposes providers to greater financial risk. It may be desirable, and perhaps necessary in order to ensure that a wide variety of small organisations are willing to participate in the market, for government to bear a substantial proportion of this risk. This could be done by reducing outcome fees in a certain large proportion and simultaneously subsidising providers' input costs (including salary costs) by the same proportion. Such an arrangement would require additional auditing of providers' finances and operations and in a sense bring the whole employment services market partly back into government sector, but it is in other respects

Although in doing this, the government may need to pay some core costs so as to reduce providers' exposure to financial risk.

23

consistent with maintaining both genuinely competitive market conditions, and incentives for spending on service provision that are in line with the principles of a cost-benefit analysis.

The current fee structure for Intensive Assistance, with an up-front commencement fee, makes it necessary to supplement the financial incentives with government monitoring...

In the current IA fee structure, a large proportion of provider income comes from the payment of a positive up-front "commencement" fee for each client. Because of this feature, the profitability of IA work is guaranteed if not too much is spent on ongoing service provision, and this probably explains why Intensive Assistance is generally regarded as a profitable activity. These features of Intensive Assistance make active surveillance necessary in order to ensure that income from commencement fees is spent appropriately. This involves monitoring costs, and may jeopardise the efficiency gains that should arise from competition. Also, entry to and exit from the market need to be determined by DEWRSB's assessments of provider performance although the technical basis for such assessments is liable to be uncertain, *e.g.* when there is only one provider with a particular disability specialisation. The market cannot be a competitive one in the sense that some providers leave because they are losing money and other providers are free to enter wherever they see a business opportunity.

...although this might not necessarily create serious problems, if the government gets the cost, benefit and incentive issues right.

It is possible that none of these potential problems with current arrangements are too serious, *i.e.* that government supervision of service provision adequately reinforces financial incentives to achieve employment outcomes, and the government's preferences about placement strategies, its decisions about the overall level of spending, and its techniques for assessing provider performance and managing entry and exit from the market, mimic quite well the outcomes that would arise from theoretically optimal arrangements. But policy in these areas should, at a minimum, be informed by close attention to the cost/benefit and incentive features outlined above. Incentives for placing jobseekers who have intermediate levels of employability deserve particular attention, because the potential impact of employment services may be largest for this client group. There clearly might be advantages in fully adopting a system where market forces can be left to operate relatively freely, subject to minimum standards and a regulatory framework.

Previous contracted case management arrangements were supervised by a separate regulatory agency. A separate regulatory body for Job Network might, *inter alia*, provide an external check that the government is keeping the playing field as level as possible across providers and safeguard their interests when the government modifies parameters of the system. However currently Job Network is directly managed by DEWRSB, an arrangement which may increase effective control while reducing costs: DEWRSB goes to significant lengths to ensure probity in the tender process and equal treatment of all JN members, and the Competition and Consumer Commission would also be concerned by any restrictive practices in the market.

This type of market sometimes has an independent regulator.

C. Unemployment benefits

1. *Benefit entitlements*

Australia's benefit system relies upon reasonably generous assistance benefits. These fall into two main categories: allowances, which are reduced by 70% for each dollar of earnings (above a free area) and traditionally have covered short-term contingencies, and pensions which are reduced by 40% for each dollar of earnings (above a free area), and are paid in particular to the disabled and sole parents, *i.e.* groups with restrictions on availability which may often allow them to work at most part-time. For unemployment allowances, the 70% taper on earnings replaced a 100% taper (above a free area and a 50% taper in some ranges) in 1995. One unemployment beneficiary in six is now working part-time. Another important change in 1995 was the individualisation of benefit entitlements, which has improved equity, reduced the dependence of one partner's income and incentives upon the

Under arrangements which allow claimants to retain a large proportion of their earnings, one unemployment beneficiary in six now works part-time; incentives for partners in a couple have also improved with the individualisation of entitlements...

25

earnings of the other and in general required both members of a married couple to be available for work in order to claim full benefits.

...but facilitating part-time work while claiming benefits might be counterproductive, if some people prefer this to full-time work...

Some entitlement arrangements, such as the United Kingdom's system of in-work benefits and Canada's SSP experiment, provide additional incentives only for a transition to full-time (or high-hours part-time) employment. In Australia by contrast, net income varies continuously as status varies between unemployment and full-time work. This leaves increased scope for high-hour workers to reduce hours in order to become more dependent on benefits. It can also make co-ordination with active labour market policies difficult, since the process of moving jobseekers first into part-time work with low hours and from there into full-time work is too complex to be easily assisted or made effectively obligatory for benefit eligibility purposes. The latter problem arises as an issue in the practice of recent years when some jobseekers, by temporarily taking part-time work, still draw a nearly full benefit yet avoid participation in activation measures such as Work for the Dole. The Mutual Obligation framework, which is now applied six months a year to the long-term unemployed, defines a minimum work requirement of 16 hours each fortnight for at least 8 out of 13 fortnights. Nevertheless this amount of work does not in itself greatly reduce benefit costs (perhaps by about 17%, in the case of a single adult). Success in terms of transitions to permanent full-time work remains crucial.

...and loss of medical benefits remains a significant work disincentive.

Loss of the Health Care Card, which gives access to a range of health and other benefits granted by different levels of government, is high on the list of disincentives for taking up work as perceived by the unemployed themselves. Although transitional arrangements exist and some families can get such a card on grounds of low income, for individuals who use the card heavily its loss could be a real disincentive to taking permanent work. This issue arises in a range of OECD countries, and seems to be difficult to tackle except by further extending the coverage of medical benefits.

2. Eligibility conditions

General availability requirements for unemployment benefits in Australia are strict in the sense that work in any occupation, whether part-time or temporary, must be accepted. A less strict definition of suitable work, allowing restriction of job search to a worker's customary type of occupation in the first few months of unemployment, might be appropriate, with more attention to how suitable work criteria in general can realistically be applied. In the 1990s, there was a widespread view among expert Australian observers that the "activity test" had replaced the "work test". This was not correct, in legal terms. However, if people who satisfy the activity test (*e.g.* through job search, voluntary work or part-time work) are rather often in administrative practice understood to have satisfied requirements for receipt of benefit and as a consequence are no longer actively expected to take any suitable full-time paid work that becomes available, unemployment may be increased. In many countries, there is a more single-minded focus on the requirement to leave benefit for full-time paid work.

In recent years, job-search reporting requirements have been applied more systematically and in 2000 the maximum requirement was increased to 10 applications per fortnight. However, in 1999/2000 still less than a quarter of the unemployed at a given point in time had a Job Search Diary to fill out: job-search reporting appears to be required mainly for the short-term unemployed.

Under the principle of Mutual Obligation, young people aged 18 to 34 years who have been unemployed for six or twelve months are required to choose between a number of options, *e.g.* part-time work, voluntary work (including Green Corps and Volunteer Defence Reserves) and education or training. Those who do not start in any of these options are referred after six weeks to Work for the Dole. In opinion surveys, a large majority of respondents support the application of this principle to young people and middle-aged groups of workers, but

Australia may have, de facto, a less stringent requirement to seek full-time work than many OECD countries...

...and job-search requirements are unevenly enforced...

...but Mutual Obligation requiring 18 to 34 year-olds to take up some activity enjoys wide public support...

27

support falls to two-thirds or less when a general question about older workers (*e.g.* all workers aged over 50 years) is asked.

...and has in practice caused many to leave unemployment.

FaCS longitudinal data show that the first cohort of 18 to 24 year-old people affected by Mutual Obligation in 1998 had sharply increased rates of exit from unemployment, starting shortly before the nominal date of entry to Mutual Obligation and continuing for some weeks after this. This suggests that it has a "deterrent» or "motivation" effect. The changes were large enough to reduce inflows to long-term unemployment status for the age group concerned considerably, by 20% to 25%.

Up to 1999, the activation measures apparently reduced only short-term unemployment...

For several years prior to 2000, the ratio of beneficiary unemployment to labour force survey unemployment stayed close to 110%. In 1998 and 1999, the long-term share in total beneficiary unemployment, which was already far higher than the long-term share in labour force survey unemployment, continued to rise. Activation measures are delivered to beneficiaries rather than to people in labour force survey unemployment, and this pattern might suggest that they were not very effective for the long-term unemployed. Centrelink-managed activation measures (*i.e.* job-search monitoring and Mutual Obligation) and JST seem to have provoked exits from short-term unemployment, whereas the long-term unemployed were generally not concerned by these measures, and the frequency of IA provider contact with some clients was not high enough to increase their rate of exit from unemployment. The fact that the Centrelink-managed activation measures cease to apply when clients enter Intensive Assistance may be a continuing problem for IA performance.

...but their impact on the unemployment beneficiary total seems to have come through in the statistics for 2000 and 2001.

After changes in the second JN contract period (starting early 2000), placements of IA clients increased significantly, and since the impact of other activation measures was increasingly feeding through, the beneficiary total fell relative to labour force survey unemployment. Also the long-term share fell below 60%. But it remains – even allowing for definitional peculiarities – high, suggesting that there is considerable scope for activation measures to reduce long-term unemployment further.

3. Benefit sanctions

The number of benefit sanctions (called "breaches" in Australia) has increased significantly with the introduction of Job Network and the intensification of various activation measures. Many of these sanctions relate to failure to attend JST and Intensive Assistance. Sanctions for administrative or procedural reasons of this kind appear to be more frequent in Australia than in most other countries, which use sanctions mainly in relation to substantive labour market behaviour (*e.g.* refusal of a suitable job). The "breaching process", which involves a rigorous process of evidence-based decisions assuring natural justice, seems overly complex and costly when applied to situations where the issue is a person's failure to be contactable or to attend an interview. When a fortnightly Application for Payment is submitted to Centrelink without the Job Search Diary or Mutual Obligation Diary being returned as required, Centrelink simply makes no payment and this procedure ensures a high level of compliance, usually without sanctions, giving the Centrelink activation measures a head start as compared to JN activation measures. Upon referral to Intensive Assistance, benefit payments should be made to depend on attendance at the IA provider premises in line with common procedures for the placement service in other countries, and most of the current concern with non-commencement and non-attendance would disappear.

Centrelink enforces compliance with its activation measures in a straightforward and effective way: for Intensive Assistance, it would be easier if benefit payments were made conditional on attendance...

Because unemployment benefits in Australia are assistance benefits, beneficiaries include many people who elsewhere (*e.g.* in European countries) would be case managed primarily by municipal social workers. Although some benefit claimants are identified as eligible for the Community Support Program, others may not be identified and nevertheless have or develop behavioural, housing and other problems

...while when more complex issues arise, case managers have a role to play in applying sanctions.

which are identified by IA providers. Case management thus should identify not only situations where sanctions are needed but also factors which may justify the non-application of sanctions. The need for IA case managers to supply relevant information raises general issues about whether it is appropriate for private providers to have such a role, and whether private providers themselves are willing to play this role. Current arrangements, where Centrelink takes the final decision, ensure a reasonably uniform application of the law, and private providers will probably have to recommend sanctions in appropriate cases if they are to survive in the business. There is no particular case for rewarding providers who recommend sanctions, since effective providers may establish a clear framework for their clients and then not need particularly high sanction rates. General efficiency does require, however, that evidence about inappropriate behaviour by clients should be acted upon at reasonable cost to the provider: late in 1999 the government issued new guidelines about the interpretation of "reasonable excuse" for failing to attend JN services, and these have helped to reduce problems in this area.

4. The role of Centrelink

There is scope for more case management in relation to Centrelink activities...

Centrelink has only very limited resources for individual case management. However, currently benefit sanctions may arise before any case management contact with a client and this may result in inappropriate application of sanctions or non-application of sanctions (when the person presents an excuse, and Centrelink has no track record to tell whether this is genuine). More case management assistance might also improve outcomes from Mutual Obligation, helping people to find regular work before they are referred automatically to Work for the Dole, or to otherwise choose the most appropriate option, and tackling "loopholes", *e.g.* identifying use of sickness certificates to avoid Mutual Obligation requirements and targeting it for further follow-up. Some co-ordination of Job Network with Mutual Obligation might help. Job Matching providers could be notified in advance that jobseekers will soon enter Mutual Obligation, and encouraged to target them for job referrals.

Intensive Assistance lasts for a maximum of between 12 months (level A, without extension) and 21 months (level B, with maximum permitted extension). However, about 40% of the unemployed people have been on benefit for over two years. For many, participation will be just one episode within a longer spell of unemployment. Policies for handling such situations are not very well defined, in terms of whether people exiting Intensive Assistance are issued with Job Search Diaries or Mutual Obligation Diaries or should be referred directly to Work for the Dole, for example. There has been a risk that many workers would fall through the gaps, although the recently-established principle that Mutual Obligation applies six months out of every twelve may now be leading to clarification of the issues. By default, responsibility for longer-term case management lies with Centrelink. However, Centrelink does not maintain individual case management records which might, for example, include the outcomes of a psychological assessment, remedial training undertaken and jobs applied for during Intensive Assistance. Thus, a type of "carrousel" effect may arise as people "go back to zero" in the terms of the system's case management expertise concerning their individual barriers to employment. Better arrangements for managing the very long-term unemployed, whose barriers to employment should have been relatively well identified by this stage, are needed.

...and Centrelink needs to deal more coherently with the needs of very-long-term claimants, who risk revolving through the system.

D. Active labour market programmes

1. The Intensive Assistance case manager's "tool kit"

Australia's reduction in spending on longer-term training, wage subsidy and job creation programmes except for particular target groups may be justified, given doubts as to whether many of these labour market programmes were cost-effective. However, open vacancies suitable for long-term unemployed people

Intensive Assistance providers could make more use of short courses as part of their "tool kit" to activate the unemployed.

31

are in short supply, judging by the limited proportion of IA clients that is sent to a job interview, and referrals to short training and related courses or work experience could be a useful additional activation tool. Government provision of standardised packages can offer some advantages such as economies of scale (in developing manuals, etc.) although since Australia's training market is active and should be well able to develop packages tailored to the needs of Job Network, the case for government provision is not very clear. The government does encourage IA providers to offer training, and some providers that do so seem to be getting good results although recent evidence suggests that standardised provision of short job-specific skills training may not be enough, and that less tangible factors such as the appropriateness of training and its contribution to self-confidence are important. At the same time significant external training or other courses do cost money; increased outcome fees at the margin are one factor that might motivate providers to be more active in this area.

2. Work for the Dole

The compulsory Work for the Dole programme has brought community benefit and does not seem to be as harsh as some feared, or to undercut wages...

Upon its introduction in 1997, the Work for the Dole (WfD) programme in which participants undertake community work in return for unemployment benefit plus a small supplement ($20.80 per fortnight) was attacked as a form of compulsory labour which fails on principles of human rights, echoing criticisms of workfare which have arisen in other countries. In practice, WfD projects are appreciated by sponsoring community organisations, and working conditions do not seem particularly rigorous compared with those in many low-wage jobs. Hours of work are low enough to ensure that unemployment benefit divided by hours worked is no less than the minimum wage, and on this basis similar workfare programmes in other countries seem to be surviving human rights criticisms. Economic theory suggests that such arrangements can offset the disincentive impact of benefits, because the hours/income combination is no longer more favourable than in open employment (as it can be when unemployment benefits are paid in return only for job-search activity).

It is, however, uncertain whether WfD participation in itself has a positive impact on employment prospects. As discussed above, there is evidence that Mutual Obligation has an impact and thus the "motivation" impact of WfD on jobseekers who do not ultimately participate in it seems clearer than its direct impact. Because WfD participants must remain available for other work and continue job search, many workers leave projects before completing them: this may be frustrating for project managers, but it ensures that the "lock-in" effect (a reduction in the rate of entry to unsubsidised work) of participation in this programme is minimised, or even reversed.

...and while its direct impact on employment is uncertain, its existence has contributed to incentives to take other options...

Within the "activation" strategies of Denmark and the United Kingdom, subsidised employment in the private sector is one of the options. Although experience in OECD countries suggests that large schemes with high subsidy rates can cause excessive displacement and distort labour markets, some provision can be sustainable, and it is natural to consider whether some Mutual Obligation option in this area could be provided. In urban areas WfD projects already often offer a wide variety of activities, but there may be various means of introducing further "programme" options.

...and there is some scope for also using subsidised private-sector jobs to "activate" workers.

3. New Apprenticeships

New Apprenticeships have been extremely successful in bringing state-supervised forms of employment-based training into a wider range of industries and non-trade occupations – ranging from labourers to managers and professionals – where it was previously very largely absent, and in bringing prime-age workers and firms' existing employees into training. This expansion has built on structures that were put into place from 1985 to 1996, but the current government's New Apprenticeship Centres (NACs) and its general strategy of promotion, responsiveness to employer needs and willingness to finance expansion have done much to drive it forward. At the same time, completion rates for traineeships in the new areas are

The present government has built successfully on earlier measures which established traineeships; the push for volume growth should now be pursued alongside steps to raise completion rates and assure portable qualifications that certify high quality training.

33

low, and reviews conducted in three states have reported fears that employer freedom in specifying training modules is leading to non-portable qualifications and concerns with the quality of training, particularly on-the-job training. Steps probably needed include improving the incentives for completing training; separating the delivery of training more clearly from the certification of its quality; and more enforcement of uniform assessment and certification criteria on individual employers and apprenticeships, while also strengthening the role of sectoral employer representatives in defining these criteria and otherwise trying to ensure that the qualifications gained will be valued in the relevant labour market.

4. The CDEP *scheme for indigenous workers*

When remote indigenous communities were given control of welfare funds, they restricted income of some who did not work...

The CDEP scheme, introduced in 1977 for a small number of remote indigenous communities, involved a community decision to give up entitlements to unemployment benefits. The funds were then transferred to community leaders, who could use them to pay people to do work of value to the community. The incentives for work arose from wage differentials: as late as 1997, up to a third of CDEP participants were being paid as little as $30-$40 per week under "no-work-no-pay" rules set by project managers. However, social security offices came under increasing pressure to pay unemployment benefits to individuals in these situations.

...but when the government insisted that participants be paid at least normal unemployment benefit, the scheme started to look more like an unconditional income transfer – for those who have been able to enter it...

In line with the recommendations of the 1997 Spicer review, official government policy is now that project managers should pay each CDEP participant at least the equivalent of the unemployment benefit that would otherwise be received, and should ensure that all participants work enough hours to earn this wage. But CDEPs have not been expelling participants and participants now appear to be entitled to a wage which is the equivalent of an unemployment benefit, without a clear obligation to work in return for it. Hours of attendance are required and are monitored, but not necessarily hours of work of value to the community. This gives the scheme something of the character of a relatively unconditional transfer payment to participants, although the government recently introduced changes to remove from the scheme those who have not participated for five weeks. Government funding restrictions have – despite announcements of additional funding from time to time – become part of the picture, and there are signs that CDEP participant status has become a vigorously-defended privilege, with participants rarely leaving the programme.

A more modest conclusion from the observations of the Spicer review would have been that no-work-no-pay situations within CDEPs should be subject to appeal, to ensure that a no-work-no-pay principle is applied only where the option of doing more work and earning a correspondingly higher salary is really available to a person. The recent declaration that CDEP participation is voluntary for purposes of entitlement to unemployment benefits may make it difficult to insist that CDEP participants must work in return for the equivalent of unemployment benefits within the programme, and is likely to lead to a continuation of the incentive issues within projects.

...leaving incentives within the scheme confused.

CDEPs also undertake commercial activities which provide additional income and additional wages for participants (CDEP wages are not reduced when participants have additional earnings in the way that unemployment benefit is). While this is a positive development in itself, it may be putting government under pressure to separately fund services which the community has previously provided for itself through the non-commercial activities of the CDEP. It will be necessary to maintain overall funding equity between communities with and without CDEPs.

Commercial activities supplementing CDEP income are welcome but raise funding equity issues...

It also seems that CDEP commercial operations might exploit the key business opportunities in a particular area (because CDEP participants in effect have a permanent wage subsidy, equivalent to unemployment benefit) and thus undermine the

...and they may displace other commercial activity, including subsidised open employment...

35

potential viability of unsubsidised indigenous business activity. This is quite serious since the government's Indigenous Employment Policy, which aims at achieving entries to open employment, is having some success but only for individuals who are not entitled to CDEP. Although CDEP locations are often remote, it seems hard to maintain that there is no potential for open employment locally, when CDEPs are engaged in significant commercial operations.

...and create a conflict of interest when it comes to encouraging CDEP participants to move on.

In the area of disability employment services, the recent "Business Services Review", noting that transitions from supported employment (sheltered workshops) to open employment are very infrequent, recognised that a requirement on providers to promote transitions into open employment may create an inherent conflict of interest for organisations whose dual purpose is to provide long-term supported employment and operate a commercially viable business. The same issue arises for CDEPs: it is against the interests of a CDEP which has commercial operations to promote, as the government wishes, transitions of the best workers into open employment. In both cases, an obvious conclusion is that individuals should only be allowed to enter these programmes, which can involve a relatively high rate of subsidy to participants on a near-lifetime basis, if there is little chance that they could ever retain unsubsidised or little-subsidised open employment. Since assessments looking far into the future are often uncertain, this implies that policy towards entry should be restrictive. But this conclusion has by no means been clarified and established as a formal principle of government policy in these two areas.

5. Statistical evaluation of labour market programmes for the unemployed

Australia has a useful system for follow-up monitoring of programmes, but:

The Australian Employment Department has a longstanding programme of labour market assistance evaluations. A key data collection element of this process is a post-programme monitoring (PPM) survey which tracks outcomes from employment programmes and services by sending a questionnaire to participants three months after they leave assistance. The PPM method has advantages in terms of providing basic programme monitoring information with little delay. However in some cases, a comparable group of unemployed people is identified from the register, and the same questionnaire is sent to them three months later. Comparing outcomes – defined, for example, as the percentage of questionnaire respondents who are employed – between the group that has left a programme and the control group then provides an estimate of the "net impact" of programme participation. This definition of "net impact" – based on the percentage people who have a certain outcome three months after leaving a programme – is also being applied in analysing administrative data for "off-benefit" outcomes. There are two issues with this procedure:

- While PPM outcome rates (or other three-month outcome rates) might be useful for comparisons across two programmes in which participation has the same fixed duration, they do not mean much when comparing relative performance across quite different types of programme or with a control group. For example, a high employment (or other) outcome percentage among individuals who left a programme three months previously can arise – quite independently of whether the programme actually makes any difference to the employment prospects of its participants – merely because the programme rules allow participants to leave in order to take up work but not in other circumstances.

  It does not really measure the net impact of programmes, relative to each other or to a control group...

- Estimates of the impact of a programme on participants do not in any case capture "motivation" or "deterrent" effects: the tendency for people who have been referred to a programme, or are liable to be referred to a programme in the future, to enter market work before their participation starts. DEWRSB's

  ...and does not capture indirect effects, which can be large: the existence of programmes can affect the behaviour of non-participants.

recent net impact evaluation of JST and Intensive Assistance has for the first time included an estimate of this effect (calling it a "compliance" effect). It is reported to be large in the case of JST, but the methodology used is, so far, not very clear.

Some programmes have negative effects by "locking in" participants...

Attention should instead focus on the rate at which people who have entered (or were referred to) a programme subsequently enter (and remain in) ordinary employment, as compared to people who entered other programmes, or no programme. On this criterion, the impact of many Working Nation programmes is believed to have been negative (because of the "lock-in" or "retention" effect of programmes *i.e.* the tendency for rates of entry to market work to fall after participants start in a programme) and there is also no clear published evidence for recent programmes. Data through to November 1999 suggest that 13% of IA participants left with a positive (employment or education) outcome (as later assessed by the PPM questionnaire) during the first three months of participation, and this rate probably did not much increase later in the participation period: it seems rather low, although no really comparable information (using the same measure of "outcome") is available for a control group.

...tracking data would give a clearer picture of outcomes...

The public would be better informed if basic tracking information in terms of off-benefit outcomes month by month, after referral to programmes and commencement in programmes, were published alongside similar tracking information for matched control groups (DEWRSB's relatively simple matching procedures for defining a control group appear to give adequate results). In general, the necessary information is already available, or potentially available, from internal systems. Publication of it should be supplemented by information on employment and education outcomes when available, although this requires special surveys in addition to administrative data. Once appropriate tracking data from programmes is available, energies can be better focused on wider issues of interpretation, in particular understanding what services, exactly, were typically delivered to programme participants and control groups.

It is always important to know the details of programmes and of the data relating to them. Highly positive PPM outcomes from the JobStart programme have frequently been cited as evidence that wage subsidies are the most effective type of programme and that they would be more effective than current programmes. Yet in this case the programme environment was complex (under Working Nation, employers using the Jobstart subsidy were required to retain employees for three months after the subsidy had ended) as were measurement procedures (the outcomes reported for certain participants were measured three months after the employer's potential eligibility – which itself arose some months after the main subsidy period had ended – for a one-off bonus payment). So statistics cited for this programme are not really comparable with those for other programmes, or for a control group.

...but it is always important to know how programmes operate and how data were collected.

E. Labour market policy and the process of government

1. *Tendering and contracting processes*

Not only Job Network and WfD but also many smaller labour market programmes are implemented by tender and contract procedures, notably the Jobs Pathway Programme (JPP), Jobs, Placement, Employment and Training (JPET) and NACs for youth, and the Community Support Program (CSP), Literacy and Numeracy Training and Return to Work programmes for other target groups. Also under the "case-based funding trial", FaCS is imposing near-zero growth on the block-grant funding of disability providers, where the level of funding per client is historically based and not linked to outcomes, but is allowing some of them to take on new clients on the basis of fees related to individuals serviced and

Subcontracting of employment services is well developed in Australia, through application to a range of different programmes. It is running smoothly...

outcomes achieved. Thus, general contract terms with payments based in varying degrees on services provided, key performance indicators, and outcomes, and procedures for choosing providers by tender, are now very well developed in Australia. The network of existing providers will often make acceptable bids when a Request for Tender document for a new programme is released, and the whole system works flexibly and smoothly, compared to the way it might initially operate in countries where the market is not so well-developed.

...and is particularly helpful where innovation is needed while retaining equitable provision, which can be built into the contract conditions.

The tendering and contracting approach to labour market programmes appears to be particularly successful where an innovative, entrepreneurial or promotional approach is needed, as is the case for JPP, NACs and WfD, and when the needs of special target groups have to be addressed, as is the case for JPET and the CSP. A major advantage is often that, by tying payments to services provided for individuals, pressures for broad and equitable provision are created. Providers have every incentive to attract and serve as many of the potential clients within their local area as possible, while at the same time not spending more on an individual client than the fee level can justify. In the alternative model where similar services are funded by a block grant (as used to be common in many countries with government-owned training centres), there is a risk that programme managers will attract and concentrate resources on particular client groups, resulting in inequitable provision.

2. Information, evaluation and the openness of government

In general, public information on labour market programmes is very good...

Public information about labour market policies is in many respects very open. Government websites provide access to information of a factual nature about various programmes, in some cases (*e.g.* New Apprenticeships) also marketing and promoting the measures. Websites also provide easy access to policy documents such as official evaluations and reviews of programmes and Request for Tender conditions.

These, particularly when read in combination with information from lobby groups and academic experts, give citizens good access to basic information about most contracted and tendered programmes, their management structure and objectives, and the policy issues arising. Speeches and media releases by government ministers and their aides, including archives, are also readily available, so the intentions of politicians at various times can be clearly seen.

However, information about the details of government-run processes (*e.g.* operational guidelines for when Centrelink will issue a Job Search Diary and make referrals to Job Search Training) is sometimes thin. Statistical information is increasingly available, but one partial gap is a lack of regular access to basic administrative series which exist on official computer or reporting systems. Monthly statistics for unemployment benefit payments are published but not available on websites. DEWRSB now regularly publishes on the Internet annual, but not quarterly or monthly, information on commencements in and exits from its main labour market assistance programmes.

...but with some gaps in the case of activities managed directly by government.

As noted above, background information is often needed to adequately interpret statistical information about the impact of programmes. Moreover for programmes of considerable size and importance such as CDEP, statistical evaluations of overall programme impact will not much help the policy decision process, because with any set of statistical controls a rate of entry into open employment of 0.5% per year will remain relatively low: the case for the CDEP programme focuses on different objectives. DEWRSB's broader evaluation reports on Working Nation and Job Network have provided information on the practical content of the programmes and the services they deliver, and procedures for referral, the profile of participants, incentives influencing both programme providers and participants, the history of programme growth and policy adjustments and the general institutional background. Such wide-ranging evaluation studies, as well as programme reviews, are valuable

Australia's broad evaluations and programme reviews are valuable, both for interpreting statistical information and for the general policy decision process.

41

and essential for interpreting statistics and for the general policy decision process.

Private operators must be required to provide some information about their operations...

The widespread use of purchasing and contracting arrangements raises some specific issues for evaluation and access to information. Particularly when payments are made on the basis of outcomes, the government may not know much about the services that are being provided. This has led to criticisms that researchers lack sufficient access to data on Job Network, partly because of confidentiality requirements. Restrictions on JN members supplying information are probably no stricter than those applying to civil servants, and in practice, JN members seem to be free to provide interested researchers with access to data. However, openness to outside evaluation is not enough in itself. Private sector employers are legally required to respond to official statistical surveys (*e.g.* wage surveys) about their practices and, since Job Network is publicly financed, there is a particular duty towards parliament and citizens to document how the money is spent, *i.e.* the services purchased and provider profitability.

...for example, via a regular "census" ...

To create comprehensive data while distributing the information burden fairly across providers, a Job Network census, counterpart to the Disability Services Census conducted by FaCS, should be conducted occasionally, with researchers allowed access to results with as much detail as possible. Questions could be selected for inclusion on the basis of interest to potential users and pre-research of their operational viability. Some of the data on JN processes which rests on departmental computer systems might also be published.

...and should also remain open to research and analysis of best practice, which can be hard in a competitive environment.

DEWRSB may be able to facilitate access to JN providers for independent researchers as a way of leveraging its own research effort. The need to diffuse information to JN members on best practices is receiving increasing attention within DEWRSB, but such efforts can face a natural reticence by providers to engage managerial time or to share information in a competitive environment. Job Network contracts permit access to information for evaluation purposes, and it might be possible to engage in a rolling programme of audits, or contract for independent evaluation studies on particular issues covering a sample of providers. Possible research outputs relating to Job Network include, for example, off-benefit hazard rates for IA clients between referral and commencement, and for successive months after commencement; correlations between employment outcomes and the type of service offered by the provider; qualitative information from interviews with clients and managers; and detailed descriptions of best practice in specific areas of work. Quite a lot of information of this kind in fact exists or is in preparation, but some of the information is not published and some of it remains soft (*e.g.* did good services as perceived by jobseekers cause good outcomes, or did good outcomes lead jobseekers to assess services favourably?), so continuing efforts are needed.

F.   Issues in workplace relations reform

Industrial relations reform has been a key component on the Agenda of all major Australian political parties over the past two decades. The current government has integrated the previously separated policy areas relating to employment policies and workplace relations in one Department (DEWRSB). This recombination of the portfolio signals the enhanced focus on the nexus between employment opportunities and good labour-management relations. Accordingly, recent reform measures have been designed with a view to improving labour market efficiency and increasing employment, productivity and living standards. These outcomes are to be achieved mainly through determining wages and conditions of employment by means of collective and individual bargaining at workplace or enterprise level. However, this "paradigm shift" in Australian labour relations has been a partial one so far, and the evidence as to what extent it has contributed to the above goals remains inconclusive.

The present government has brought employment and workplace relations into a single department and sought to combine improvements in employment opportunities with better labour relations.

43

1. Australia's exceptionalism

Australia is unique in its tradition of settling disputes and setting wages through tribunals...

Australia is exceptional among OECD Member countries in that most workers are covered by awards set through a quasi-judicial system of conciliation and arbitration operating through industrial tribunals. This system dates back to the very founding of the country itself, when the Constitution empowered the federal government to set up machinery for settling interstate industrial disputes. Consistent with the federal character of the country, arbitration occurs through both state and federal tribunals. Up until recently, "National Wage Cases" heard by the federal Australian Industrial Relations Commission (and the flow on of these to state jurisdictions) were the principal means through which wage increases were provided to wage and salary earners (although for many workers overaward bargaining has also been important).

...a system which in the 1980s was criticised for being rigid, detached from the workplace and fragmented, yet not bringing industrial peace...

This Australian industrial relations system, although exceptional through its arbitration focus, thus belonged to the group of OECD countries characterised by "highly centralised, highly co-ordinated" wage determination systems. The main points of critique, which intensified since the 1980s, addressed, in particular:

- The reliance on centralised settlement of disputes by outside actors which served to undermine direct forms of negotiation and bargaining (the main method of conflict resolution and wage determination in other OECD countries).

- The failure of the award system to deliver industrial peace, which it had originally set out to guarantee.

- The "lowest-common-denominator" basis of awards which did not sufficiently take into account the particular needs of a workplace, and which hampered organisational flexibility and company productivity.

- The continuing existence of half a dozen separate workplace relations systems, where large numbers of worksites have some employees covered by the federal system and others by the relevant state system, implying that many employers are forced to deal with two distinct systems of labour regulation.

2. Recent reforms and their impact

Since the 1980s, the shortcomings of the industrial relations system have been increasingly recognised. Reform was initially set in motion under the series of Accords between the trade unions and the Labor Government after 1983. The emphasis subsequently shifted from centralised incomes policy arrangements towards decentralisation of wage-setting and the encouragement of productivity-related enterprise bargaining. Awards started to focus more on issues such as flexible working-time, multi-skilling and the removal of certain restrictive work practices. Legislative changes facilitated the conclusion of enterprise agreements, with or without trade union involvement.

...and thereafter was decentralised, with an enhanced focus on enterprise-level bargaining...

The most recent wave of workplace reform began with the adoption of the Workplace Relations Act (WRA) under the Liberal/National coalition in 1996. This Act, as well as reform measures undertaken since, has further enhanced enterprise and workplace bargaining and has scaled back the compulsory award system, without, however, abolishing arbitration altogether as New Zealand had done in 1991.

...a process taken further by the 1996 government...

Instead, a mixed system remains characteristic for Australia, with most employees covered by "safety-net" awards setting their minimum terms and conditions, *and* by bargaining agreements determining actual pay. However, for many low-paid workers in certain industries, such as wholesale and retail trade, restaurants and accommodation services, the minimum awards continue to set actual pay rates. Bargaining agreements in the federal jurisdiction are certified by the Australian Industrial Relations Commission (AIRC), based on a test as to whether the agreement, when considered as a whole, does not disadvantage affected employees compared with the relevant award. Awards thus still provide a framework for enterprise-level

...but retaining arbitration and minimum awards to provide a minimum safety-net, especially important for lower-paid workers.

45

negotiations and continue to restrict employer discretion at the bottom of the wage scale.

Direct formal agreements between employers and individual employees, introduced in 1996, remain controversial.

In a break with Australia's "collectivist" legacy, the 1996 Act introduced a new category of formalised individual agreements, the Australian Workplace Agreements (AWAs), which are made directly between employers and employees. Both AWAs and the increased availability of certified collective agreements without trade union involvement are evidence of the intention of the current government to give employees and employers more choice between different models of agreement-making, and to increase the scope for direct employee participation. AWAs, in particular, have become an important political symbol both for the government and opposition (if elected, the latter is likely to abolish them).

As a result of these changes, today:

A number of statistical indicators give an impression of the impact of the institutional shift in patterns of labour relations and wage determination:

Awards determine the pay of one-quarter of employees, down from two-thirds a decade ago;

• Less than a quarter of current employees still have their actual pay determined by awards; a decade ago, this figure was over two-thirds. For 35% of employees, pay is determined by registered collective agreements, and for an additional 2% by registered individual agreements. The rest either receive informal over-award payments or remain outside the award system.

Only a quarter still belong to unions, down from one-half 25 years ago;

• The trade union density rate has declined from over 50% in the mid-1970s to about 25% currently. Although changes in the composition of employment can explain part of the decline, the legislative changes and the associated trend towards decentralised bargaining seem to have played an important role. The decline in density has been more rapid than in most other OECD countries.

Strike rates have considerably decreased in the evolving system of decentralised settlements;

• The Australian strike rate (number of workdays lost per 1 000 employees) is much lower today than in the 1980s or early 1990s, suggesting that the compulsory arbitration system with its binding settlements was more prone to industrial conflict than the evolving system of decentralised settlements, underpinned by safety-net awards. The major part of the decline occurred during, or even before, the Accord years, and strike rates have been stagnant since 1997, so that the reduced legal protection for strikes not related to single-business bargaining introduced by the WRA is not likely to have played a major role in the decline.

- Wage dispersion has increased since the 1970s, although at a more modest pace than, for example, in the United States, the United Kingdom or New Zealand. The trend, which began during a period of more centralised wage-fixing, partially reflects the higher growth in employment of high-skilled, high-paid occupations. However, there is some evidence that changes in bargaining structure have been associated with rising differentials; for example, there is a growing dispersion in rates of wage increase set in certified agreements, which seems to reflect a stronger link of remuneration with enterprise performance. The ratio of federal minimum wages, as set through safety-net reviews, to average wages remains high in international comparison (at around 50%), although some employers outside the federal jurisdiction can in fact pay less than the federal minimum.

And wages have become more unequal, but remain less so than in many other OECD countries.

- Evidence from certain industries, and in particular low-productivity workplaces, points to beneficial effects of the changing workplace relations environment on labour productivity growth, which has turned around from relatively sluggish performance during the 1970s and 80s to exceed the OECD-average performance in the 1990s, and which has facilitated strong growth in average real wages.

Labour productivity has grown faster than the OECD average.

47

3. Options for the future

Further emphasis on bargaining rather than awards would bring Australia into line with other countries...

Have the reforms gone far enough? Although change is impressive when comparing the current workplace relations system with that of two decades ago, there is definite scope for further reducing the complexity of the system, and for enhancing the primacy of agreements over awards. If, as seems the case, Australia does not intend to follow the New Zealand example and completely abolish its arbitration system, a further tilting of the balance in favour of bargaining, restriction of tribunal powers, and a further reduction in the share of employees whose terms and conditions of employment are completely reliant on awards would help to bring it in line with labour relations systems prevailing in other OECD countries.

...and the system needs simplifying: reforms have made it even more complex.

While aiming for simplification, the reforms have in some sense added to the complexity of the system by putting a layer of registered and certified agreements on top of arbitrated awards. Furthermore, it is expected that even after the current drive for "award simplification" is completed, over 4 000 awards at federal and state levels will remain in force. In addition, a significant number of employees are still working in enterprises bound by multiple (federal and state) jurisdictions, and this is hampering efficiency. Social partners and the federal government should be encouraged to pursue more vigorous discussions about realistic alternatives.

One way to reduce complexity would be to increase direct labour legislation, by using different powers under the Constitution.

The government has been promoting debate on the possibility of rebasing the country's federal labour relation system on the constitutional "Corporations Power" (instead of the current conciliation and arbitration power which largely prevents direct legislation), and this could be one of several ways to reduce complexity. It would largely remove dual coverage, bring a large majority of employees under the federal umbrella, and allow awards covering all constitutional corporations and their employees in a particular industry, instead of being limited to employers that are signatory to the award.

The powers of industrial tribunals, in particular of the AIRC, have already been greatly curtailed in recent years, and awards have become less prescriptive. However, in line with an approach giving primacy to agreement-making, their role could be further narrowed. For example, it is not immediately evident why the AIRC should continue to arbitrate on all 20 currently "allowable" matters, which appear to represent an unnecessarily long and detailed list. Concerning the Commission's role in dispute settlement, the option of reshaping it into a *voluntary* conciliation body should be seriously considered – currently it is a type of "compulsory conciliation" body, as employers are still required to notify the AIRC of pending disputes, after which conciliation procedures are normally initiated.

The role of industrial tribunals could be narrowed further, with the AIRC arbitrating on a smaller range of issues, acting as a voluntary conciliation body for dispute settlement...

The role of the AIRC in setting federal minimum wages for industries and occupations is an important one. However, the very process of setting the minima does not quite seem to correspond to the avowed "minimum safety-net" approach, in that minima are not only set for low-skilled, low-pay workers, but there is a whole ladder of minima including for high-skilled workers with above-average pay. Again in line with the approach giving primacy to agreement-making while focussing awards on minimum conditions, there is a case for putting a cap on such award rates and limiting these to low-wage workers. The AIRC, which has so far rejected proposals along these lines, should be encouraged to rethink its position.

...and its safety-net powers limited to basic pay for low-paid workers...

It is important to note that the Australian "federal minimum wage" is not based on any legislation and only applies to less than half of the workforce (*i.e.* those under AIRC jurisdiction). In fact, a certain number of employees are not affected by safety-net adjustments and remain paid at rates below the federal minimum wage. While the States also set their specific minimum wages, it needs to be kept in mind that close to 15% of dependent employees are not covered either by the award safety-net or by bargaining agreements. Although it is regarded by many as currently unrealistic

...a process which could be helped if Australia moved to a legislated and universal minimum wage, which it now lacks.

49

(both from a political and a legal point of view), it may nevertheless be fruitful to discuss avenues for developing a *legislated* minimum wage (based for example on the External Affairs power in the Constitution) which would fill these gaps and apply to *all* Australian wage and salary earners. The AIRC could then take over the role of determining the minimum pay level, or making recommendations about it to the Commonwealth government, along the lines of the UK Low Pay Commission.

Despite controversy over the present wave of reforms, the overall change in approach since the late 1980s is unlikely to be reversed: it has contributed to economic success.

The coalition government has introduced an array of "second-wave" workplace reform proposals to Parliament. Some of these (such as the requirement for secret ballots before industrial action) conform to regulations in other OECD countries, while others (those further facilitating individual bargaining agreements, or removing legal protection from "pattern bargaining", for example) are unique and may lead to further criticism for violation of ILO Conventions. Should it achieve office, the current opposition will probably attempt to preserve, or restore, some elements of industry-wide bargaining. However, a return to the previous, highly centralised system of pay determination is unlikely. After all, the principles of workplace reform between 1988 and 1996 were widely accepted throughout the political spectrum – not the least on the premise that previous arrangements had not been conducive to maximising economic performance and productivity.

Australians Working Together[1]

As part of the 2001/02 Budget released on 22 May 2001, the Australian Government announced a comprehensive $1.7 billion package of reforms to labour market assistance and income support arrangements over the next four years. This package – Australians Working Together: Helping people to move forward – responds to the findings of the Final Report of the Reference Group on Welfare Reform (the McClure Report) and the results of programme evaluations which have identified ways of enhancing the performance of the Job Network, Work for the Dole and other existing labour market programmes. Among the aims are to better sequence and link various forms of assistance, such as Intensive Assistance and Job Search Training provided by the Job Network, and Work for the Dole, to maximise employment outcomes.

There will be about $400 million of additional spending over four years on Work for the Dole and community work, Job Network services, the Personal Support Program and Training Credits, another $500 million on Working Credit, and a further $800 million on other targeted measures, mainly assistance for parents, mature age people, people with disabilities and indigenous Australians.

Mutual Obligation requirements, Work for the Dole and community work

Mutual Obligation requirements will be extended to 35-49 year-olds and standardised, so that unemployed people aged from 18-49 years will be required to undertake an activity, in addition to job search, for six months starting after six months on unemployment payments, and for six months of each later year that they remain on unemployment payments. (There is no change to activity requirements applying to jobseekers 50 years and over.)

Work for the Dole will be the default activity with a requirement for 390 hours of work over six months for 18-39 year-olds if another activity is not chosen. A lesser Mutual Obligation requirement for 150 hours of community work over six months will apply for people aged 40–49 years. Community Work Coordinators, who currently manage Work for the Dole, will provide a greater range of assistance including facilitation of community (voluntary) work placements. At the end of Work for the Dole or equivalent community work, Community Work Coordinators will update participants' job resumes, references and job search skills.

Pathways to Independence

Australians Working Together articulates four pathways by which those of working age on income support may move forward greater independence, with Centrelink as the gateway.

Job Search Support Pathway

Jobseekers who are job ready will use Job Matching services and job vacancy touch screens in Centrelink offices. They will all be referred to Job Search Training after three months on unemployment payments (unless they are in another programme). People (up to age 49) who remain unemployed after six months will need to choose a Mutual Obligation activity. Most jobseekers will follow this pathway until they find a job, or need to move to the Intensive Support Pathway.

Australians Working Together (*cont.*)

Intensive Support Pathway

Jobseekers who are most at risk of remaining unemployed without assistance will be referred to Intensive Assistance. The duration of participation in Intensive Assistance will generally be limited to 12 months, as 99% of employment outcomes are achieved in this period. Intensive Assistance providers will conduct up-front assessments of new clients over a four-week period to identify those who would benefit from taking up other services – such as Work for the Dole, Literacy and Numeracy Training, or the new Personal Support Program – before they commence Intensive Assistance. This link with other programmes should ensure that jobseekers are better able to benefit when they commence Intensive Assistance.

Community Participation Pathway

For people with severe or multiple non-vocational barriers to employment (*e.g.* drug or alcohol addiction) a new Personal Support Program will replace the Community Support Program, assisting three times as many people and with funding increased by over 50% per participant. This will enable participants to better stabilise their lives and should help some of them to prepare better for Intensive Assistance. Participants will be able to undertake Intensive Assistance activities for up to 18 months while continuing to receive support from their Personal Support Program provider to ensure sustained recovery.

Transitional Pathway

A new Transition to Work programme will help parents, carers and mature age people returning to the workforce (either after a lengthy absence or as first time entrants). It will be created from the current Return to Work programme and the pre-vocational training component of the existing Jobs, Education and Training programme. The assistance will include career counselling, job search skills training, and work related skills training such as basic computing courses.

Support for training

People attending approved literacy and numeracy training will be eligible for a fortnightly supplement, similar to the supplements already paid to WfD and CDEP participants, of $20.80. Training Credits of up to $800 will be offered for mature age (age 50 and over) and indigenous participants in Job Search Training (following participation) and in Intensive Assistance, to meet the cost of accredited training (on or off-the-job). Participants in Work for the Dole or community work will be offered a Training Credit of $500 after 240 hours of work rising to $800 after 390 hours of work which should be used within six months, with Community Work Coordinators advising on the choice of suitable training and administering the payments.

Working Credit

The Working Credit incentive encourages greater take-up of work. Each income support recipient will accumulate (up to a maximum of $1 000) a credit of

Australians Working Together (*cont.*)

up to $48 per fortnight (reduced by any paid income) when they are not in work or earn very little. In any fortnight that earned income exceeds the current free area (for single persons, this is $62 per fortnight for allowees and $106 for Disability Support Pensioners), this credit can be drawn down allowing earnings to be retained in full until the credit is exhausted. This provides a benefit to people continuing on income support who undertake part-time or irregular work, as well as a return to work bonus for people moving into full-time work.

Assistance and requirements for people on other types of income support

Australians Working Together also encourages more active participation in the labour market by people on what currently are passive forms of income support. There will be no new entrants to Mature Age Allowance and Partner Allowance from July 2003. These people will have to claim unemployment payments.

People receiving Parenting Payment with a youngest child in school (aged 6 or over) will meet for annual interviews with Centrelink Personal Advisers to consider economic or community participation options. Parents with their youngest child in high school (aged 13-15 years) will be required to participate in appropriate levels of part-time activity (150 hours over six months) from July 2003, from a range of activities, with financial penalties as a last resort. People who apply for Parenting Payment (as well as those attending the annual interviews) will be provided with a Participation Pack containing information about the advantages of work, assistance available to help them return to work, financial incentives and local support services.

Improved assistance and assessment for people with disabilities

People at high risk of claiming a Disability Support Pension will be referred to early intervention and assistance, including encouraging continuing activity, to slow or reverse any deterioration in their condition and to give them maximum chance of finding appropriate employment. There will be more thorough assessment of work capacity for claims for Disability Support Pension and Newstart (Incapacitated) through more extensive use of external assessors, in addition to the ongoing reports on medical impairment by the claimant's treating doctor and independent medical advisers. There will be a very substantial extension of disability employment assistance places, rehabilitation places and vocational education and training places.

Improved assistance for indigenous people

A number of steps will be taken to address the high unemployment rates experienced by indigenous people. Centrelink will establish remote area servicing centres employing local staff. Community Development Employment Project (CDEP) organisations will act as Indigenous Employment Centres, assisting 10 000 CDEP participants to find paid work outside CDEP, in areas where jobs are available. Greater assistance will be given to indigenous students in high school and in vocational education and training.

53

Australians Working Together *(cont.)*

Centrelink Personal Advisers

Centrelink Personal Advisers will provide better case-by-case assessment and referral to assistance for people with special needs, particularly people who are of mature age, on Parenting Payment, indigenous jobseekers, those on Newstart allowance exempt from the activity test, or temporarily incapacitated and people recently released from prison. Individual assistance will be provided to refer people to service providers, link them to other community support and monitor their progress.

Outcomes sought

The Australian Government aims through this package to help those of working age move from welfare to work or contribute to community life, and to give them the assistance and incentive to do so, supported by fair requirements. The Government expects the initial investment of $1.7 billion to achieve savings of $924 million over the next four years, virtually all of which will flow from people moving off income support or reducing their reliance on it. This will reduce the net cost of the package to below $800 million.

---

1. Information on the Australians Working Together package is available on www.together.gov.au.

Chapter 1
Setting the Scene:
an Overview of the Australian Labour Market

A. Introduction – land, population and economic development

Australia is an immense country with a population that is concentrated along the temperate coasts (Figure 1.1). As of June 2000, its population amounted to 19.16 million [ABS (2000*g*)]. The average population density of about two people per square kilometre is the lowest among the OECD Member countries [OECD (2000*g*)]. Only five cities have populations exceeding one million: Sydney (4.0 million); Melbourne (3.4 million); Brisbane (1.4 million); Perth (1.3 million); and Adelaide (1.1 million). At the same time, about 85% of the population is concentrated in urban areas, a rate of urbanisation that is roughly 8 percentage points higher than the average OECD country [ABS (2000*j*) and WDI (2000)].

In recent years, the Australian population has grown at a rate of about 1.2% annually, in part due to significant inflows of immigrants [ABS (2000*j*)]. Since the 1960s, immigration from Asia in particular has boosted the diversity of the population. During the years from 1995 to 1998, net overseas migration accounted for roughly 40% of population growth. Overall, in 1998, foreign-born individuals accounted for 23% of the population resident in Australia, the second highest share among OECD countries for which data are available (after Luxembourg) [Hugo (2001) and OECD (2000*g*)]. Those born in the United Kingdom, Ireland and New Zealand together accounted for over 8% of the total population. The share of the Australian population born in the main Asian sending countries (China, Hong Kong/Macao, Vietnam and the Philippines) amounted to 2.6%. In contrast, the indigenous people comprise only about 2.1% of the total population (Box 1.1).

In 1999, Australia ranked twelfth among OECD Member countries in terms of per capita GDP on a purchasing power parity basis (Table 1.1). Between 1980 and 1999, real GDP nearly doubled in size and per capita real GDP rose by just over 50%. Chart 1.1 highlights two periods of expansion, one running from March 1983 to March 1990 and the other from June 1991 through the year 2000 and continuing. Over the past eight financial years (which run from July to June), real GDP grew at an annual rate of about 4.4%, well above its 30-year average of roughly 3½% [OECD (2000*a*)].

Figure 1.1.

Box 1.1. **Official statistics on the indigenous population**

The coverage of indigenous people in Australia's official population statistics dates from the 1971 Census onwards. Prior to this, people considered to be more than 50% aboriginal (based on a series of questions about race in earlier Census questionnaires) were excluded from the figures. Now, the main sources of statistics include the five-yearly Census of Housing and Population and ad hoc ABS surveys such as the 1994 National Aboriginal and Torres Strait Islander Survey. Self-nomination is the primary criterion now

Box 1.1.   **Official statistics on the indigenous population** (*cont.*)

used to identify members of the indigenous population. For example, the 1996 and 2001 censuses include a standard question, "Are you of Aboriginal or Torres Strait Islander origin?" Administrative data sources can also sometimes be used to generate statistics on the indigenous population (*e.g.* concerning health issues). The labour force survey has not been used to provide regularly-published information on the indigenous population, but ABS recently published experimental estimates based on the survey and intends to publish such estimates annually in the future.[1]

According to census-based estimates, as of 30 June 1996 the indigenous population was estimated at about 386 000 [ABS (2000*j*)]. New South Wales and Queensland had the largest indigenous populations in absolute terms (each over 100 000). The Northern Territory had a relatively large proportion of indigenous population, amounting to over 25% of its total resident population, whereas the other states and territory had shares less than 4%. For the period 1991 to 1996, the annual growth rate of the indigenous population was nearly twice the rate of the total population.

An ABS statistical profile of the Aboriginal and Torres Strait Islanders based on the 1996 census provides some details on their situation [ABS (1999*c*)]. The indigenous population was comparatively young, with a median age of 20 years as compared with a median age of 34 years for the total resident population. Some 73% lived in urban areas (centres of 1 000 or more people), some 12 percentage points fewer than the average for the nation as a whole. About 13% spoke an indigenous language at home, with particular concentrations among the older indigenous population and in the Northern Territory and the northern half of Western Australia. Indigenous Australians had relatively low enrolment rates in full-time education. For example, only about 74% of indigenous 15-year-olds were in full-time education as compared with about 92% in the total population.

The most comprehensive data on the labour force status of indigenous Australians are also drawn from the census. As the table below indicates, the indigenous population has lower labour force participation and lower employment rates than the total population.[2] At the same time, they have higher rates of unemployment.

Labour force status of the Indigeneous population, 1996 (percentages)[a]

	Aboriginal and Torres Strait Islanders	Total Resident Population in Australia
Participation rate	52.7	61.9
Employment/population ratio	40.7	56.2
Full-time employment as a share of the total	56.6	67.8
Unemployment rate	22.7	9.2

a)   Population aged 15 years and older
Source: ABS (1999*c*).

---

1. The labour force survey estimates for indigenous people are considered experimental due to the very small sample of indigenous people and concerns about data quality. See ABS (2000*e*).
2. In 1996, participants in Community Development Employment Projects (CDEP) accounted for nearly 30% of the employed indigenous population. See Chapter 5 for a detailed discussion of the role CDEP plays in indigenous employment.

57

Table 1.1. **GDP per capita at current market prices, 1999**
Using current PPPs[a]

	US $	Index, OECD Average = 100
Australia	24 400	110
Austria	24 600	110
Belgium	24 300	109
Canada	25 900	116
Czech Republic	13 100	59
Denmark	26 300	118
Finland	22 800	102
France	21 900	98
Germany	23 600	106
Greece	14 800	66
Hungary	10 900	49
Iceland[b]	27 300	122
Ireland	25 200	113
Italy	21 800	98
Japan[b]	24 500	110
Korea	15 900	71
Luxembourg	39 300	176
Mexico	8 100	36
Netherlands	25 100	112
New Zealand[b]	18 000	81
Norway	27 600	124
Poland	8 100	36
Portugal	16 500	74
Spain	18 100	81
Sweden	23 000	103
Switzerland[b]	27 500	123
Turkey[b]	6 300	28
United Kingdom	22 300	100
United States	33 900	152
G7	**27 500**	**123**
EU-15	**22 000**	**99**
Total OECD	**22 300**	**100**

a) Purchasing Power Parities (PPPs) are the rate of currency conversion which eliminates the differences in price levels between countries. They are used to compare the volume of GDP in different countries. PPPs are obtained by evaluating the costs of a basket of goods and services between countries for all components of GDP; PPPs are given in national currency units per US dollar.
b) Countries still using the System of National Accounts (SNA) 1968.
Sources: Secretariat estimates based on OECD, *Main Economic Indicators*; and the OECD National Accounts database.

B. The labour force and employment

Overall, as of 1999, some 9.4 million individuals were in the labour force, including 8.7 million in employment. The labour force participation rate of the working-age population (persons aged 15 to 64 years) was about 2½ percentage

Chart 1.1. **Real GDP, Australia**
Indices, 1980 = 100

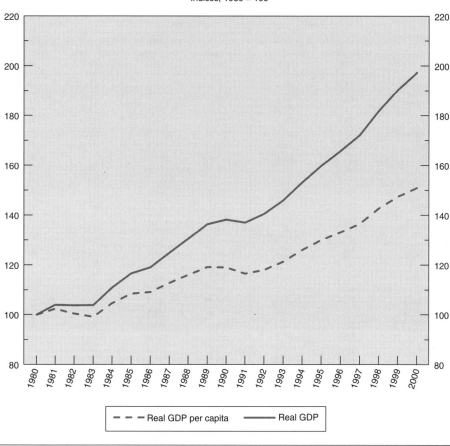

Real GDP per capita ─ ─ ─   Real GDP ──────

Source: OECD Economic Outlook, No. 69, June 2001.

points above the OECD average (Table 1.2). This rate in Australia tended to be higher in the 1990s than in the 1980s, with an increase of 3 percentage points between 1980 and 1999. This change was associated with a gradual, long-term decline in male participation rates and a strong long-term rise in female participation rates (Chart 1.2*a*). The share of the Australian working-age population in employment in 1999 was also higher than the OECD average, in this case by two percentage points. In Australia, the tendencies in this indicator were similar to those with respect to labour force participation (Chart 1.2*b*). Women have

59

Table 1.2. **Labour force participation and employment in OECD countries, 1999**
Percentages of the population aged 15 to 64 years old

	Total		Women		Men	
	Labour force participation rate	Employment/ population ratio	Labour force participation rate	Employment/ population ratio	Labour force participation rate	Employment/ population ratio
Australia	72.9	67.7	63.6	59.3	82.1	76.1
Austria	71.6	68.2	62.7	59.7	80.5	76.7
Belgium	64.6	58.9	56.0	50.2	73.0	67.5
Canada	75.9	70.1	69.8	64.7	82.0	75.5
Czech Republic	72.2	65.9	64.1	57.4	80.2	74.3
Denmark	80.6	76.5	76.1	71.6	85.0	81.2
Finland	73.6	66.0	71.2	63.5	75.9	68.4
France	67.8	59.8	61.3	52.9	74.4	66.8
Germany	71.2	64.9	62.3	56.5	79.7	73.1
Greece[a]	62.5	55.6	48.5	40.3	77.1	71.6
Hungary	59.9	55.7	52.3	49.0	67.8	62.6
Iceland	85.9	84.2	82.3	80.2	89.4	88.2
Ireland	66.2	62.3	54.3	51.3	78.2	73.4
Italy	59.6	52.5	45.6	38.1	73.7	67.1
Japan	72.4	68.9	59.5	56.7	85.3	81.0
Korea	63.9	59.7	50.8	48.1	77.1	71.5
Luxembourg	63.1	61.6	50.2	48.5	75.7	74.4
Mexico	62.5	61.2	40.7	39.6	86.4	84.8
Netherlands	73.6	70.9	64.4	61.3	82.6	80.3
New Zealand	75.2	70.0	67.4	63.0	83.2	77.3
Norway	80.6	78.0	76.1	73.8	85.0	82.1
Poland	65.9	57.5	59.8	51.6	72.3	63.6
Portugal	70.6	67.3	62.8	59.4	78.7	75.5
Spain	63.9	53.8	49.9	38.3	78.3	69.6
Sweden	78.5	72.9	76.0	70.9	80.9	74.8
Switzerland	82.2	79.7	74.5	71.8	89.6	87.2
Turkey	56.2	51.9	34.4	32.0	77.9	71.7
United Kingdom	76.3	71.7	68.4	64.9	84.1	78.4
United States	77.2	73.9	70.7	67.6	84.0	80.5
Total OECD[b]	**70.2**	**65.6**	**59.4**	**55.2**	**81.1**	**76.1**

a) 1998 instead of 1999.
b) Unweighted averages for above countries using 1998 figures for Greece.
Sources: OECD, Labour Force Statistics, 1979-1999, Part III, 2000. For Austria, Belgium, Denmark, Greece, Italy, Luxembourg and the Netherlands, data are from the European Labour Force Survey.

substantially increased their employment rate, while the rate for men has tended to decline.

The labour force participation and employment rates for younger workers (i.e. those aged 15 to 24 years) are among the highest in the OECD. For prime age workers (i.e. those aged 25 to 54 years) Australia's performance is similar to the OECD average, while for older workers aged 55 to 64 years it is below the OECD

Chart 1.2.*a*. **Labour force participation rates, Australia, 1980-1999**
Percentage of population aged 15 to 64 years old

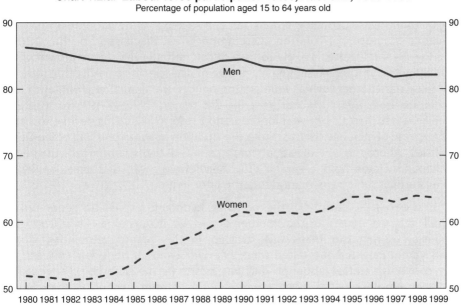

Chart 1.2.*b*. **Employment/population ratios, Australia, 1980-1999**
Percentage of population aged 15 to 64 years old

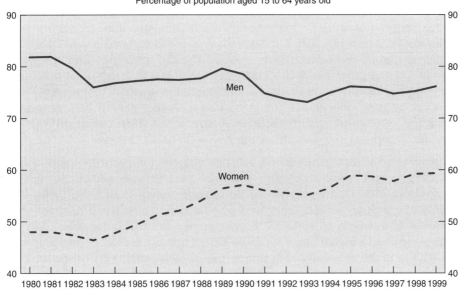

Source: OECD, *Labour Force Statistics, 1979-1999*, Part III, 2000.

average (Table 1.3). The result is that, in comparison to most OECD countries, Australia's workforce age-structure is somewhat younger. Nevertheless, as in other OECD countries, Australia's labour force is ageing, a development that will influence its future evolution. One impact, as discussed in the OECD's 1998 *Employment Outlook*, is likely to be a deceleration in the rate of growth of the Australian labour force. Assuming no change in age-specific participation rates (or other key parameters such as immigration policy), the annual rate of growth may decelerate from about 2% per year for the period 1970 to 1995 to a rate of somewhat less than 1% per year for the period 1995 to 2020. This decline to a still-positive rate of increase contrasts with the situation in about one-half of the OECD countries, where the size of the labour force may actually contract if age-specific participation rates hold constant. (The deceleration will, of course, be less if workers adjust their participation to retire later in life.)

Between 1991 and 2000, the on-going economic expansion generated an overall increase of 19% in the number employed in Australia (Chart 1.3).[1] The expansion during the 1980s was stronger in this regard, generating steady employment growth that totalled some 25% over a shorter period. In contrast, the pace of average annual labour productivity growth (as measured by change in real GDP per employee) has been greater in the current expansion than in the previous one.

In recent years, Australia has experienced a shift in the sectoral composition of employment. As in many OECD countries, the share of employment in the service sector has grown while the shares in industry and agriculture have declined. As shown in Chart 1.4, Australia has come to have a relatively large service sector in comparison with most of the G-7 countries and the OECD average. On the other hand, the Australian employment structure is notable in that it has a relatively small share of employment in industry.[2, 3] (Among all OECD countries in 1998, only the Netherlands had a smaller share.) With respect to agriculture, the employment share in Australia was larger than all the G-7 countries except for Italy and Japan, but below the OECD average.

Australia has also experienced substantial growth in part-time employment and casual work (Box 1.2).[4] The share of part-time employment in total employment increased by about 3½ percentage points during the 1990s. With roughly one in four workers employed part-time, Australia has a relatively high incidence of this type of working.[5] In 1999, among the OECD countries, only the Netherlands had a higher rate [OECD (2000e)]. A notable feature of part-time work in Australia is the relatively high proportion of men working part-time. In 1999, over 14% of male employment in Australia was part-time, the highest share among OECD countries. At the same time, over 40% of female employment in Australia was part-time. More than two-thirds of the part-time workers in Australia worked short hours (*i.e.* less than 21 hours per week) [OECD (1999d)] and the overall

Table 1.3. **Labour force participation rates and employment/population ratios by age, 1999**

Percentages of the corresponding population group

	Australia		Total OECD[a]	
	Labour force participation rate	Employment/population ratio	Labour force participation rate	Employment/population ratio
15 to 24 years	68.4	59.2	52.3	45.9
25 to 54 years	79.6	75.3	80.4	75.9
55 to 64 years	46.9	44.2	51.1	48.4

a) The total is for OECD countries excluding Greece and the Slovak Republic.
Sources: OECD, *Labour Force Statistics*, 1979-1999, Part III, 2000. For Austria, Belgium, Denmark, Italy, Luxembourg and the Netherlands, data are from the European Labour Force Survey.

Chart 1.3. **Civilian employment, Australia, 1980-2000**
Index 1980 = 100

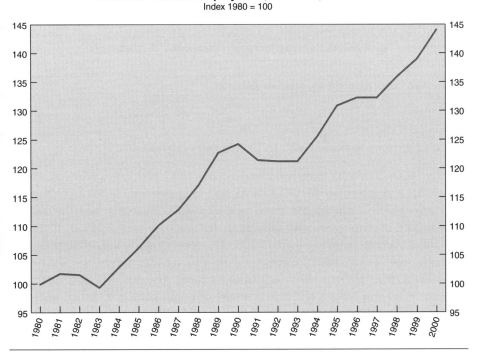

Source: OECD, *Labour Force Statistics, 1980-2000*, Part I and Part II, 2001, forthcoming.

63

Chart 1.4. **Civilian employment by industry, selected OECD countries, 1999**

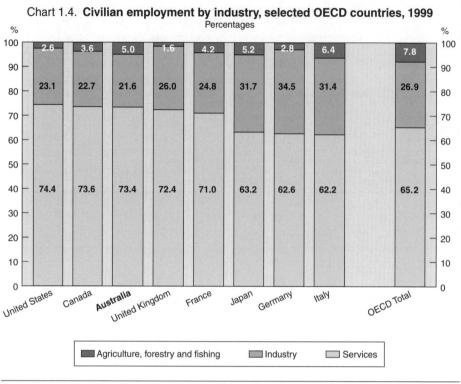

Percentages

Source: OECD, *Labour Force Statistics, 1979-1999*, Part I, 2000.

average part-time workweek was 16.7 hours [ABS (2000a)].

The Australian work force has had relatively low job stability as measured by job tenure and retention. An OECD analysis found that among the ten countries for which roughly comparable data were available, Australia had the second largest share of employees with tenures under one year (about 25% in 1996) and the lowest average tenure (6.4 years) [OECD (1997c)].[6] Moreover, while there was some fluctuation over time, the tenure figures did not vary widely over the period considered (from 1979 to 1996, in Australia's case). The analysis also compared five-year retention rates (*i.e.* the percentage of employees in a certain year who were still with their current employer five years later). Australia had the lowest retention rate (41.3%) among nine OECD countries during the first half of the 1990s.[7] At the same time, data cited in the OECD analysis indicate that in 1996 a majority of Australian workers were satisfied with their job security.

Box 1.2. Casual employment

There is considerable misunderstanding about data on the extent and nature of "casual" employment in Australia. Under Australia's industrial relations system, most federal and state awards give "casual" employees wage premia (wage loading) instead of certain employment conditions such as paid sick leave and paid annual holidays. The Australian Bureau of Statistics (ABS) relies on this feature of the award system to define casual employees as those "who were not entitled to either paid holiday leave or paid sick leave" [ABS (2000c)]. Such employees could work part-time or full-time schedules and could, in practice, be employed for long periods.[1] According to the ABS definition, such casual employment increased by 70% between 1988 and 1999 and came to total nearly 2 million workers or about 23% of total employment.[2]

While in the popular perception casual employment is often linked with the notion of precarious employment, this is not necessarily a characteristic of casual employment according to the ABS definition. As Murtough and Waite (2000a) note, the "ABS definition of 'casual employee' includes: many workers who do not have a casual employment contract; a large group whose work is not casual (in the sense of being occasional, irregular or short term); and aggregates across distinct groups of casual contract employees who have very different entitlements and work arrangements." For example, according to the ABS definition of casual employees many owner-managers of incorporated enterprises are classified as casual employees of their own business; they have chosen not to have paid sick or annual leave.[3] There has been substantial growth in this category of employment in Australia over the past two decades and by August 1999 such owner-managers comprised one-in-ten casual employees.

An alternative to the use of "casual" employment as a statistical concept might be to focus instead on "temporary" employment (i.e. employment intended to be of a fixed duration).[4] One problem with this alternative is that Australian awards do not distinguish between permanent and temporary employment in general. Although in individual cases employers may indicate that a particular post will be of a short duration, this is legally little more than advanced notice. While it is possible retrospectively to distinguish short-term from long-term employment, it is difficult to do so prospectively. Nevertheless, focusing on such an alternative may provide an indicator that is closer to the popular understanding of precarious employment and closer to concepts used in international comparisons.

---

1. Some awards use conversion clauses to place restrictions on how long an individual may remain a casual employee before the employment must cease or become permanent. In December 2000, the Australian Industrial Relations Commission ruled that casual employees in the manufacturing metals industries have the right to elect to convert to permanent status (i.e. to forgo the wage premia paid in lieu of certain entitlements) if they have been employed for more than six months on a systematic and regular basis with a particular employer.

2. The ABS also tracks a group called "self-identified casuals" who are essentially those without leave entitlements who consider themselves as casual employees. There were nearly 1.5 million self-identified casuals in 1998, corresponding to 18% of total employment.

Box 1.2.   Casual employment (*cont.*)

3. Potentially, a similar problem with the definition could arise as a result of the introduction of enterprise agreements and individual Australian Workplace Agreements (AWA's, discussed in more detail in Chapter 6). Under these agreements, the ABS definition could become outmoded if leave entitlements begin to be bargained away completely in return for other improvements in employment conditions. The statistical definition of "casual" employment would then include some employment that is both permanent in intention and not consistently "casual" over time in terms of the award system either. To date, there is no evidence that leave entitlements are being bargained away completely, although there is some 'cashing out' of a portion of sick leave or annual leave.

4. According to OECD correspondence with the Australian authorities, in August 1998 around 5% of Australians in employment had temporary or seasonal work situations. Such an estimate can be derived, for example, based on data from the Forms of Employment Survey [ABS (2000c)]. If temporary employment is interpreted to include employees on fixed-term contracts, in seasonal or temporary jobs, who are completing their current jobs or who are working for employers that have announced closure or down-sizing, then such workers accounted for 5.1% of total employment in August 1998.

A supplement to the Australian Labour Force Survey (ALFS) in February 2000 provides more recent information on job tenure and labour mobility [ABS (2000f)]. The survey found that about 24% of those in employment had short job tenures (*i.e.* they had been in their current jobs for less than one year). Among those with short tenures, about one-third had not had a previous job during the year, while two-thirds were job changers. Among those who had changed jobs during the year, 42% changed industry and 34% changed occupation. Job mobility was highest among young adults (aged 20 to 24 years).

The Australian population also exhibits an above-average geographic mobility. An OECD analysis of internal migration of the population covering 17 OECD countries found that in 1995 only four had higher shares of the population changing region of residence over a one-year period.[8] That year, the gross flow of persons changing region amounted to 1.9% of the population.[9]

Educational attainment is an important contributing factor to the human capital of a nation. Australia's labour force has at least two notable characteristics in this regard. First, among the adult population, Australia has an above-average share of individuals that have attained at least tertiary education (Table 1.4). Second, a large share of the adult population has not completed upper secondary education.[10]

The existence of a sizeable population with low educational attainment in Australia is partly due to the traditional engagement of large shares of the population aged 15 to 19 years in full-time employment and relatively low educational enrolment rates for them. However, participation of teenagers in education and the labour market has changed substantially over the past 15 years [DEWRSB (2000*h*)]. During this period, the share of this age group in full-time education increased by nearly 20 percentage points, while the share in full-time

Table 1.4.   **Educational attainment and literacy**[a]

	Percentage of the population aged 25 to 64 years, 1998			Percentage of the population scoring at IALS literacy levels 3 or higher, 1994-1995[b]	
	Primary/Lower secondary	Upper secondary	Tertiary	16 to 25 years old	46 to 55 years old
Australia	44.0	30.6	25.4	62	49
Austria[c]	26.7	62.6	10.6	..	..
Belgium[d]	43.3	31.4	25.3	76	52
Canada	20.3	40.8	38.8	67	46
Czech Republic	14.7	74.9	10.4	..	..
Denmark	21.6	53.2	25.2	..	..
Finland[c]	31.7	38.9	29.4	..	..
France	39.3	40.1	20.6	..	..
Germany	16.2	60.8	23.0	66	58
Greece[c]	54.5	30.0	15.5	..	..
Hungary	36.7	50.1	13.2	..	..
Iceland	38.1	41.0	20.9	..	..
Ireland	48.7	30.2	21.1	50	34
Italy	56.4	34.9	8.7	..	..
Japan	20.1	49.5	30.4	..	..
Korea	34.6	43.3	22.1	..	..
Mexico	78.8	7.7	13.4	..	..
Netherlands	35.7	40.1	24.2	77	52
New Zealand	27.3	46.1	26.6	53	45
Norway[c]	17.0	57.2	25.8	..	..
Poland	21.7	67.4	10.9	35	17
Portugal	79.9	10.8	9.3	..	..
Spain	66.7	13.4	19.8	..	..
Sweden	23.9	48.1	28.0	80	73
Switzerland	18.5	58.5	23.0	67	45
Turkey	82.3	11.5	6.1	..	..
United Kingdom	19.2	57.2	23.6	56	47
United States	13.5	51.6	34.9	45	51
Total OECD[e]	**36.8**	**42.2**	**20.9**	**61**	**47**

..   Data not available.
a)   The categories of educational attainment are defined as follows: primary/lower secondary includes pre-primary, primary and lower secondary education; upper secondary includes upper secondary and post-secondary non-tertiary education; tertiary includes non-university tertiary and university-level education.
b)   IALS = International Adult Literacy Survey. Level 3 refers to a scale from 1 to 5 and involves ability to perform such tasks as searching texts to match information using low-level inferences or conditional information. For details see: OECD and Statistics Canada (1995), *Literacy, Economy and Society*, Paris and Ottawa.
c)   For educational attainment, 1997.
d)   Literacy scores apply to Flanders only.
e)   Unweighted average of shares in OECD countries shown above.
Source: OECD, *Education at a Glance*, 2000.

Chart 1.5. **Education and employment participation of teenagers, Australia, 1986-2000**[a]
Shares of population aged 15 to 19 years old

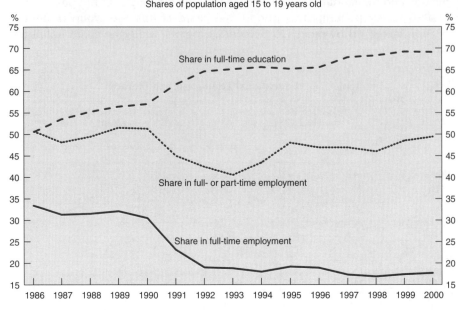

a) Data refer to April of each year.
Sources: ABS, *Labour Force, Australia*, Catalogue Nos. 6203.0 and 6291.0, various issues.

employment decreased by about 16 percentage points (Chart 1.5).[11] Roughly one in four in this age group was engaged in both part-time employment and full-time education [ABS (1999*b*)]. Also, members of this age group engaged in full-time education accounted for nearly 15% of Australia's casual employment [ABS (2000*c*)].

With respect to literacy, the International Adult Literacy Survey (IALS) provides a useful indicator: the shares of adults scoring at IALS literacy level 3 or higher where level 3 was the minimum level considered by experts to be necessary for functioning satisfactorily in today's economy and society. Table 1.4 provides these data for twelve OECD countries and two age groups. Australia scores close to the OECD average for each age group. As for most of the other countries, the share of the younger age group at level 3 or higher was substantially greater than for the older age group.

C. Unemployment

Chart 1.6 presents the evolution of the number of unemployed and the number of unemployment benefit recipients as percentages of the labour force. The chart highlights both the increases in the unemployment rate as a consequence of recessions in the early 1980s and again early in the 1990s, and the persistence of unemployment during the following periods of expansion. During the early 1990s, unemployment rose to a higher peak than was experienced in the 1980s and, as of 2000 had still not quite returned to the low levels seen at the beginning and end of the 1980s. A similar pattern can be seen among unemployment benefit recipients. However, in the 1990s, the rate of unemployment benefit receipt actually came to exceed the unemployment rate due, in part, to changes in eligibility criteria. While a number of changes were introduced, two of the more significant ones included: 1) *individualisation of benefit eligibility* in the case of married couples, such that where both partners were unemployed, each would need to file a claim separately (previously one partner was, in effect, assumed to be dependent and exempted from the activity test); and 2) *easing of benefit withdrawal rates*, thereby enabling more benefit recipients with occasional or part-time work to retain a portion of their benefits (see Chapter 4 for a detailed discussion of eligibility issues).

The persistence of long-term unemployment has been even more pronounced than that of total unemployment. As shown in Chart 4.1, the incidence

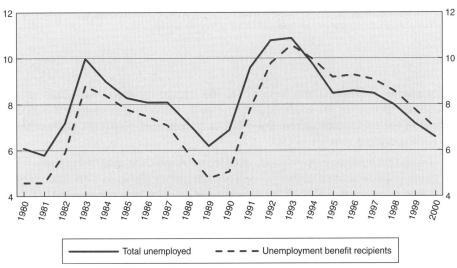

Chart 1.6. **Unemployment benefit recipients and total unemployed, Australia**
Percentages of the labour force

Sources: Direct submissions by national authorities for unemployment benefits recipients; ABS Web site accessed on May 09, 2001, spreadsheet 620201.wks, Table 1, and OECD Secretariat estimates, for total labour force; and Space-Time Research Website: www.str.com.au, Table 1: Unemployed persons by State (Aust), age and duration, from February 1978, accessed on May 09, 2001, for total unemployment.

Table 1.5.   **Unemployment rates for selected demographic groups**
Percentages

	Australia				European Union	OECD
	1989	1992	1996	1999	1999	1999
Total	**5.7**	**10.5**	**8.4**	**7.0**	**9.3**	**6.4**
Youth						
15-24 years old	10.4	19.5	14.8	13.5	17.2	11.8
Prime-age workers						
25-54 years old	4.3	8.0	6.8	5.4	8.1	5.4
Older workers						
55-64 years old	4.8	9.5	7.7	5.8	8.6	5.2
Men	**5.4**	**11.3**	**8.8**	**7.2**	**8.2**	**6.0**
Youth						
15-24 years old	10.0	20.8	15.4	14.7	16.1	11.7
Prime-age workers						
25-54 years old	4.0	8.7	7.2	5.5	6.9	4.9
Older workers						
55-64 years old	5.6	12.2	9.5	6.3	8.4	5.6
Women	**6.2**	**9.5**	**7.9**	**6.7**	**10.9**	**6.9**
Youth						
15-24 years old	10.8	18.0	14.1	12.0	18.6	11.9
Prime-age workers						
25-54 years old	4.7	7.1	6.4	5.3	9.8	6.1
Older workers						
55-64 years old	2.6	2.7	4.2	4.7	9.0	4.6

Sources: OECD, *Labour Force Statistics*, 1979-1999, Part III, 2000, for **Australia**; and OECD, *Employment Outlook*, June 2000, Statistical Annex, Tables B and C, for **European Union** and **OECD** averages.

of long-term unemployment tended to be higher in the 1990s than in the preceding decade. In the fourth quarter of 2000, with the economic expansion in its tenth year, this indicator remained about 2½ percentage points higher than in the corresponding quarter of 1989.

Table 1.5 shows unemployment rates for selected demographic groups. While the overall rate remained about 1.3 percentage points higher in 1999 than in 1989, there was substantial variation by gender and age. Male youth experienced the largest increase in unemployment rate (4.7 percentage points) over this period. This group faced an unemployment rate 3.0 percentage points above the corresponding OECD average in 1999. For the other age and gender groups, the Australian unemployment rates were within one point of the corresponding OECD averages. All of the Australian averages were well below those for the European Union countries.

Table 1.6 highlights the variation over time in unemployment rates across the various states and territories. Tasmania and South Australia have had the highest

Table 1.6.   **Unemployment rates^a by state**
Percentages

	1989	1992	1996	1999	2000
Australian Capital Territory	5.2	7.7	8.2	5.8	4.9
Northern Territory^b	6.5	7.9	6.1	4.1	5.2
New South Wales	6.3	10.3	7.9	6.5	5.7
Queensland	7.0	10.5	9.3	8.1	7.8
South Australia	7.3	11.7	9.5	8.5	7.9
Tasmania	9.2	11.6	10.4	9.7	9.2
Victoria	4.9	11.6	8.9	7.4	6.5
Western Australia	5.9	11.0	7.7	6.8	6.3
Australia	**6.2**	**10.8**	**8.5**	**7.2**	**6.6**

a)   Twelve-month average of unemployed divided by twelve-month average of labour force multiplied by 100.
b)   Data for the Northern Territory refer only to mainly urban areas and are excluded from the comparisons in the text.
Source: ABS, *Labour Force, Australia*, Catalogue No. 6202.0, various issues.

unemployment rates in recent years, while the Australian Capital Territory (ACT), New South Wales and Western Australia have had the lowest.[12] While state capitals tended to have relatively low levels of unemployment, labour market problems tended to be concentrated in certain other local areas.

D.   Income inequality and poverty

While increases in per capita income are important to material well-being, the distribution of income is important for equity concerns. During the first half of the 1990s, there was an increase in the rate of government income support measured as a share of GDP.[13] (As shown in Chart 1.7, Government income support rose to 7.4% of GDP in 1994 and has remained at approximately 7% since.) While this may have been one factor contributing to improvements in certain income distribution and poverty indicators for Australia between the mid-1980s and mid-1990s, by these same indicators it also appeared that Australia continued to experience greater income inequality than many OECD countries and a poverty rate in the mid-range for OECD countries (Table 1.7).[14]

With respect to the Gini coefficient indicator presented in the table, Australia ranked eighth among the 21 OECD countries for which data were available.[15] During the period covered, Australia was among the five countries recording a decline in inequality as measured by this indicator. The Survey of Income and Housing Costs (SIHC) provides information on changes in income and its distribution in Australia for a more recent period [ABS (2000d)]. Data from the SIHC indicate that income inequality across all income units did not change substantially between the 1994/95 and 1997/98 survey rounds.[16]

71

Chart 1.7. **Share of Gross Domestic Product spent on income support, Australia**
Percentages

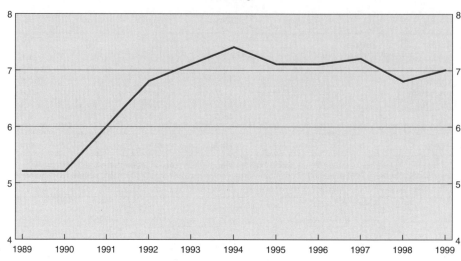

Source: ABS, *Australian Social Trends 2000*, Catalogue No. 4102.0.

According to the poverty rate indicator shown in Table 1.7, Australia ranked tenth among the 21 countries shown. As of 1994, about 9.3% lived in households with incomes below 50% of the median, adjusted for equivalency in family size and needs. At the same time, Australia succeeded in reducing the proportion of the population in relative poverty by nearly 3 percentage points over the decade, the biggest drop among the countries shown.

A more recent ABS study examined the incidence of poverty in Australia by age and type of income unit [ABS (1998a)]. In the case where the poverty line for income units was defined as income below 50% of the median equivalent income, the study found that some 10.2% of all income units were in poverty in the year ending 30 June 1996.[17] The poverty rates for couples with or without children were below the average, as they were for most one-person income units for persons aged 25 or older.[18] On the other hand, the incidence of poverty was much higher for one-parent income units, amounting to 17.2%.

E. Government

Australia's current system of government was established in 1901, when the Australian Constitution came into force. That document laid the foundation for the new nation state as a commonwealth with a federal system of government centred

Table 1.7.   **Indicators of income inequality and poverty, mid-1980s to mid-1990s[a]**
(Equivalency scale elasticity = 0.5)[b]

Country and period	Gini coefficient[c]		Poverty rate	
	Gini coefficient (end of period)	Absolute change in the coefficient during the period	Poverty rate (percentage with incomes below 50 % of the median income, end of period)[d]	Absolute change in the indicator during the period
Australia, 1984-1994	30.5	−0.7	9.3	−2.9
Austria, 1983-1993	23.8	0.2	7.4	1.3
Belgium, 1983-1995	27.2	1.2	7.8	−2.8
Canada, 1985-1995	28.5	−0.4	10.3	−1.3
Denmark, 1983-1994	21.7	−1.1	5.0	−2.0
Finland, 1986-1995	22.8	2.1	4.9	−0.2
France, 1984-1994	27.8	0.3	7.5	−0.5
Germany, 1984-1994	28.2	1.7	9.4	3.0
Greece, 1988-1994	33.6	0.0	13.9	0.4
Hungary, 1991-1997	28.3	−0.9	7.3	−1.3
Ireland, 1987-1994	32.4	−0.6	11.0	0.4
Italy, 1984-1993	34.5	3.9	14.2	3.9
Japan, 1984-1994	26.5	1.2	8.1	0.8
Mexico, 1989-1994	52.6	2.3	21.9	0.7
Netherlands, 1985-1994	25.5	2.1	6.3	3.2
Norway, 1986-1995	25.6	2.2	8.0	1.1
Sweden, 1983-1995	23.0	1.4	6.4	0.5
Switzerland, 1992	26.9	..	6.2	..
Turkey, 1987-1994	49.1	5.6	16.2	−0.2
United Kingdom, 1985-1995	31.2	2.5	10.9	4.0
United States, 1984-1995	34.4	0.4	17.1	−1.2

..   Data not available.
a)   Based on disposable income.
b)   Equivalence scale elasticity refers to the power by which needs increase as family size increases.
c)   The Gini coefficient is an indicator summarising the dispersion of income across the entire income distribution.
d)   This poverty rate, also known as the head-count indicator, refers to the number of persons in households below the poverty line, as a percentage of all persons. In this case the poverty line refers to income below 50 % of the median.
Source: FÖRSTER, M., assisted by PELLIZZARI, M., "Trends and Driving Factors in Income Distribution and Poverty in the OECD Area", Labour Market and Social Policy Occasional Papers, No. 42, OECD, Paris, 2000.

on a democratically-elected parliament. At both the federal and state levels there are legislative, executive and judicial arms of government, and a separation of power between the three arms.

The Constitution allocates specific legislative powers to the Commonwealth Parliament, which is responsible for defence, foreign relations, trade and many domestic issues of national concern.[19] The domestic jurisdiction of the Commonwealth Parliament covers, among other issues, key aspects of taxation (*e.g.* the income tax), regulation of interstate commerce, regulation of foreign and domestic trading or financial corporations, immigration, conciliation and

73

arbitration for the prevention and settlement of industrial disputes extending beyond the limits of any one state, as well as a variety of social protection measures including invalidity, old-age and widows' pensions, maternity and family allowances; and child endowment, unemployment, medical and student benefits [CCF (1999)].

The executive is established under a constitutional monarchy with the Queen's representative, the Governor-General, serving as head of state and performing both ceremonial and constitutional duties. In practice, the Governor-General is appointed on the advice of the Australian Prime Minister and generally acts on the advice of ministers.[20] Executive functions are guided by the cabinet comprised of senior government ministers under the Prime Minister. Key decisions of the cabinet are formally ratified by the executive council comprised of all government ministers, who must be members of parliament.[21] The implementation and administration of most federal government programmes are undertaken by senior public servants employed on a fixed-term basis and the Australian Public Service or the state and territory public services, which are comprised of career staff recruited on a permanent basis. Most major social welfare and benefit measures are exclusively administered by the Commonwealth.

The Constitution provides for the establishment of a High Court to serve as the supreme federal court (e.g. handling challenges to the constitutional validity of laws or appeals of state high courts). It envisages the establishment of lower federal courts as deemed necessary by the parliament, and a number of such have been established (e.g. the Family Court). There are also a number of specialised federal and state tribunals handling administrative review and industrial relations matters.[22]

The governments of the six states are based on parliamentary systems subject to both the Australian Constitution and their respective state constitutions. The two mainland territories – the Australian Capital Territory and the Northern Territory – also have legislative assemblies and self-government arrangements. In a manner similar to the federal level, the Queen appoints governors to serve as her representatives in each state. The legislative powers of the state-level parliaments cover all areas except those where the Commonwealth is assigned responsibility under the constitution. The result is that states have primary responsibility in some areas such as agriculture, education, health services, law enforcement and transport. In other areas, such as industrial relations, power is shared or split. Federal laws, duly enacted, take precedence over any state laws that are inconsistent in substance. The Commonwealth has used its power to provide financial assistance to the states as a means to extend its legislative competence in such areas as education and transport.

There are over 900 local government bodies at the city, town and municipal levels. Local government institutions are established via state and territory legislation and tend to have responsibilities for such functions as urban planning, local infrastructure, building codes, public health and sports facilities.[23]

In the post-World War Two decades, Australian Commonwealth governments have been led by either the Liberal Party or the Labor Party. Recent Prime Ministers have included Gough Whitlam (Labor, in office from 1972 to 1975), Malcolm Fraser (Liberal, in office from November 1975 until March 1983), Bob Hawke (Labor, in office from March 1983 until December 1991), Paul Keating (Labor, in office from December 1991 until March 1996) and John Howard (Liberal, in office from March 1996 onwards, in a coalition government including the Liberal Party and the National Party).

F. The post-war evolution of Australian labour market policy

1. The establishment of a public employment service

The establishment of a modern national public employment service (PES) can be traced to the period following World War Two. A 1945 government white paper entitled, "Full Employment in Australia" laid out the basis for the establishment of a PES system.[24] As one analyst commented, this white paper "signified the Commonwealth commitment to full employment as the primary economic, social and political objective which was supported by the full array of fiscal and monetary aggregate demand management tools, the creation of the Commonwealth Employment Service [CES] in 1945, and the 1947 Social Securities Act which established Unemployment Benefits" [Freeland (1998)]. Unlike the majority of OECD countries, Australia did not introduce a social insurance system (except for industrial injuries, which are governed by state law) that might have offered a guarantee of access to services or benefits to all labour market participants.

The nation-wide CES was set up by the government to be administratively under the Department of Labor (a predecessor to the current Department of Employment, Workplace Relations and Small Business, DEWRSB),[25] while unemployment benefits were the responsibility of the Department of Social Security (DSS, a predecessor to the Department of Family and Community Services, FaCS) [Finn (1997)]. The primary function of the CES was to improve labour market efficiency by matching jobseekers to vacancies. In view of relatively low levels of unemployment, few labour market programmes were developed. Unemployment benefits were established and made conditional on availability for work, willingness to accept suitable work and active job search. The Department of Social Security administered benefits and was responsible for setting the definition of "suitable work" and application of work and job search tests.

The employment security strategy was adjusted as needs changed, but until the early 1970s generally operated in an environment of relatively low unemployment. Pressures on the system increased, however, as a consequence of recession during the years 1973 to 1974 (and again during the recessions of 1981 to 1983 and 1990 to 1991). During the 1970s, unemployment grew in magnitude from tens of thousands to hundreds of thousands and chronic long-term unemployment emerged. These developments highlighted the need for more substantial adjustments in the system.

2. Development of labour market programmes

The Whitlam government introduced the first large-scale labour market programmes including measures to provide temporary public sector jobs, short-term training for adults and post-secondary vocational training for youth. There was a policy reversal under the subsequent Fraser government, whereby the pursuit of full employment was replaced by a commitment to fight inflation and abandonment of aggregate demand management for employment purposes. Labour market measures were scaled back and targeted largely on young unemployed. One new measure, introduced in 1977, was called "Community Development Employment Projects" (CDEP), which provided job creation and support for Aboriginal communities. The CDEP initiative has been modified over time and was considerably expanded during the 1990s (a detailed discussion is provided in Chapter 5).[26]

As the early 1980s recession abated, Labor returned to power. In the aftermath of the recession, a series of reviews of employment, education and training policies were conducted. Together, they contributed to the introduction of new approaches in the PES system and set the stage for the establishment of a reconfigured PES in the 1990s. One important review was conducted by the Committee of Inquiry into Labour Market Programs. Its findings were published in 1985 in the so-called "Kirby Report", criticising a lack of co-ordination across programmes and the confusing array of options that clients faced [DEWRSB (2000h)].[27] Other reviews were conducted focusing on training and education, while touching on issues related to the labour market such as school retention rates.[28]

In view of recommendations from these reviews, efforts were made to develop a co-ordinated set of policies covering education, entry-level training and labour market programmes. The Labor government rationalised programmes and gave greater emphasis to training. Provision of labour market assistance – including training – became more closely tailored to client needs and more targeted on labour market disadvantage [DEWRSB (2000h)].[29] In light of needs identified, a number of new measures were introduced including Jobstart (wage subsidies), the New Enterprise Incentive Scheme (NEIS, permitting unemployment benefits to be used in support of small business start-ups, which continues to operate), the Australian Traineeship System (combining on- and off-the-job training for young unemployed, but separate from the traditional apprenticeship system), Jobtrain (off-the-job training), and local or pilot initiatives to increase school-work linkages.[30] Other measures introduced toward the end of the 1980s included the SkillShare programme (offering community-based assistance for disadvantaged youth, long-term unemployed and others with multiple barriers to employment[31] and the Jobs, Education and Training (JET) programme for lone parents (that continues to operate and promotes re-entry into employment by providing assistance with matters such as locating child-care services and suitable education and training) [Finn (1997)].

The Labor government also oversaw the introduction of a number of benefit activation measures. In 1986, a drive was launched to enforce the requirement for claimants to register with the CES and a requirement for reporting job search efforts was introduced.[32] In 1988, unemployment benefits for youth under 18 years of age were repackaged as a Job Search Allowance with reporting and other requirements that reduced incentives to leave full-time education. In 1991, the Job Search Allowance was extended to cover all short-term unemployed. Also in that year, benefits for the long-term unemployed were shifted to the newly-established Newstart measure. This involved limited individual case management and needs-based jobseeker assistance. It introduced the requirement that the client enter into an "activity agreement" developed with the support of the case manager and including a plan for returning to work. Newstart could be open-ended in terms of duration, but provided for sanctions for those who "breached" benefit rules or the terms of the agreements. Through Newstart, the principle of reciprocal rights and obligations was explicitly embedded in the Australian employment security system.[33]

There were also changes in the industrial relation system during this period, beginning in 1983 with an accord between the Labor government and the Australian Council of Trade Unions (the peak union council). This accord helped to frame social and economic policy and was periodically adjusted. It served as a mechanism by which unions and the government of the day reached agreement on the size and basis of award wage increases that they would seek in wage cases before the Australian Industrial Relations Commission (AIRC). Under the accord, trade and finance were to be deregulated, while an increased emphasis on training was to promote the development of human capital needed to face expanded international competition [Finn (1997)]. Over time, the accord also addressed a range of social justice concerns such as the establishment of the Medicare system for national health insurance, reform of family allowances, introduction of a national superannuation pension scheme and improvement of child-care facilities [Botsman (1995)].

77

Early in 1992, the new Keating government introduced a package of labour market measures entitled "One Nation" [Finn (1997)]. Among other elements, this package foresaw an expansionary macroeconomic policy and an increase in labour market programme expenditure. Substantial additional resources were appropriated, in particular, for Jobstart, NEIS, Jobtrain and entry-level training (including apprenticeships and traineeships). New job creation measures were initiated with delivery mainly through community organisations and local government. These targeted adults over 21 years old (Jobskills) and youth aged 15 to 20 years (Landcare and Environment Action Programs). Despite these changes, continuing concerns with persistent unemployment led to the appointment of a Committee on Employment Opportunities to conduct a policy review. In December 1993, the Committee produced a discussion paper entitled "Restoring Full Employment" that laid the foundation for the major labour market programme reform in 1994.

3. *Working Nation*

In May 1994, a new white paper was published under the title "Working Nation" [Commonwealth of Australia (1994)]. It was intended to be a coherent package of policies to boost growth, including such elements as macroeconomic stability, microeconomic reforms (*e.g.* simplification of regulation), trade liberalisation, industrial development (*e.g.* improved productivity and competitiveness) and regional development. Labour market policy initiatives were an integral part of this strategy, covering employment services (including measures for programme monitoring and evaluation), training and unemployment benefits, as well as industrial relations (especially reinforcing a shift to enterprise-level bargaining).

Long-term unemployment was to be addressed on a priority basis because it was seen as impeding growth and the efficiency of the labour market. The Working Nation strategy regarded reductions in long-term unemployment as facilitating potentially-greater reductions in unemployment and reduced inflationary potential (*i.e.* yielding a lower NAIRU), with positive implications for growth.[34]

The centrepiece of the Working Nation package was the *Job Compact*, which was offered to clients at risk of long-term unemployment or in receipt of unemployment benefits for more than 18 months [OECD (1995a)]. At-risk clients were identified through a new targeting mechanism (discussed below). Eligible clients were served through a case management system, with a degree of client choice among public and private sector providers [Fay (1997)]. Once referred to a provider by CES, the client was evaluated by a case manager and entered into a Case Management Activity Agreement. The agreement was open-ended, included a return-to-work plan and required the client to accept a suitable offer of unsubsidised or subsidised employment or a place on a subsidised work experience project for 6 to 12 months. Through the agreement, case managers could tailor a package of activities designed to improve the individual's employability and prospects for sustained employment [OECD (1998d)]. A jobseeker who failed to abide by the terms of the agreement risked a benefit sanction.

Under the Job Compact, there were substantial numbers of placements into "brokered programmes", which were administered by contracted "brokers" outside of the CES. A new measure called New Work Opportunities (NWO) played an important role (e.g. 35 500 placements in the year ending 30 June 1996) by offering project-based work with an element of training to a substantial number of unemployed facing difficulties finding work because of a lack of suitable openings.[35] Concurrently, Jobstart wage subsidies, which required less government expenditure per client, were adjusted to link the level of subsidy to the duration of the individual jobseeker's spell of unemployment.

Contestability under Working Nation was introduced via the 1994 *Employment Services Act*. The Act created two new agencies with responsibilities for the implementation of the case management strategy. Employment Assistance Australia was established within the Department of Employment, Education and Training to serve as a public provider of case management services [DEETYA (1996)]. The Act also provided for an independent Employment Services Regulatory Authority which worked to establish a competitive market for case management services and which contracted for these services from private, non-profit and other government providers [DEETYA (1998b)].[36] Payments were linked to completion of activity agreements and to outcomes [Finn (1997)].

The new approach to case management was accompanied by a new approach to targeting [DEETYA (1998b)]. In order to facilitate early intervention, targeting based on simple categorical criteria (e.g. labour force status and age) was replaced with client assessment based on a weighted score of multiple characteristics. Under this targeting approach, personal, educational and locational characteristics were evaluated using a new Jobseeker Screening Instrument (JSI), with those scoring above a specific threshold being considered for case management. However, CES and DSS staff were permitted to override a JSI score using an alternative procedure based on a number of supplementary criteria intended to consider factors not directly measured by the JSI (e.g. poor motivation). In practice, most referrals took place based on the supplementary criteria. At the same time, special service channels were retained for certain groups including unemployed youth, lone parents and the disabled. Unemployed youth under 18 years of age remained a categorical priority group and were fast-tracked for intensive case management and referral to programmes. Lone parents continued to be assisted through the JET programme. The disabled continued to receive assistance through the Disability Reform Package.

It was under Working Nation that unemployment benefit eligibility was changed to consider individually the need for income support for each member of a couple. Benefit individualisation involved the replacement of the previous additional payment for beneficiaries with a dependent spouse with a parenting allowance for those with dependent children or, in the case of families without children, a Newstart allowance for spouses who applied separately. Benefit rates were also restructured in order to make part-time work a more attractive option (in particular, earnings disregards were made more generous) [OECD (1998d)]. Other changes involved the use of credits and advanced payments to assist with expenses linked to the return to work or education, increasing the range of activities available to long-term unemployed seeking to fulfil their benefit obligations, and attempts to simplify the benefit administration.

Training was given renewed emphasis under Working Nation. In addition to training provided under NWO, the Youth Training Initiative was launched to offer intensive assistance and case management for early school leavers under 18 years of age to assist in upgrading their skills through training or education and to help them to find suitable employment. Entry-level training was expanded to increase the number of traineeships and to better cover certain industries (e.g. finance, property and business). A National Training Wage was established with built-in employer subsidies intended to boost incentives to hire and train entry-level workers and unemployed adults. Moreover, in order to support school-to-work transitions, the Australian Student Traineeship Foundation (ASTF) was established by the Commonwealth Government in 1994. Managed by a joint industry, school and community management committee, the ASTF was intended to support the development of vocational education programmes targeting both workplace learning and the curriculum for upper secondary school.

Although an economic expansion had taken hold in 1991 and continued during the period of implementation of Working Nation, unemployment and, in particular, long-term unemployment fell more slowly than expected. Difficulties with implementation of Working Nation drew criticism. For example, relatively high client loads for case managers (averaging 130 clients per case manager in Employment Assistance Australia) and other pressures for quick placements into programmes may have led to fewer placements into sustained regular employment than might have otherwise been achieved [DEETYA (1996)]. Jobstart take-up was limited, while increasing numbers of unemployed were referred into more expensive programmes such as NWO. The persistent unemployment and the debate concerning the effectiveness of Working Nation became a factor in the elections of March 1996.

G. The current labour market policy framework

The newly-elected Howard government abandoned Working Nation and in August 1996 announced its first budget and plans for a deep restructuring of labour market policy. The changes were significant, particularly in the delivery of employment services and income security. The objectives included increasing work incentives, improving programme outcomes and substantially reducing expenditure (Box 1.3). In addition, there were changes and repackaging with respect to a number of training initiatives. Moreover, further industrial relations reforms were introduced that reinforced enterprise-level bargaining and established the option of negotiating individual agreements (discussed in detail in Chapter 6).

The **employment service** restructuring was largely accomplished under existing administrative authorities and was implemented with effect from 1 May 1998. Key aspects of the restructuring include [DEWRSB (2000d)]:

• The CES was shut down; most existing labour market programmes and the previous case management system were abolished.

• A contestable market for employment services was established with the contracted providers drawn from the private, community and public sectors and known collectively as "Job Network". The bulk of contracted services is delivered by private sector and non-profit providers. Clients referred to Job Network (JN) are offered a degree of choice among providers in their locality.

• A single point of initial contact, *Centrelink*, was established for most individuals wishing to access income support and employment services [DEWRSB (1999c)]. Incorporating resources from the former Department of Social Security and the CES network, Centrelink operates under a Business Partnership Arrangement with FaCS and DEWRSB to assess clients, administer claims for unemployment benefits, provide jobseekers with information about JN services and providers, classify jobseekers, make referrals to JN and other services, and offer access to a limited range of self-service job-search facilities, among other tasks. Centrelink uses the Job Seeker Classification Instrument (JSCI) to profile clients and, together with other criteria, determine the level of assistance that can be offered [DEETYA (1998a)].

• A *Community Support Program* (CSP) was established, outside of the Job Network, for jobseekers with severe barriers to employment. Centrelink assesses and refers clients to CSP based on the JSCI score, the number of identified barriers to employment (including personal factors such as substance abuse), and a Special Needs Assessment.[37]

Individual JN providers were contracted to deliver one or more key employment services:

• *Job Matching* consists of the provision of labour exchange services including obtaining available vacancy listings and assisting eligible jobseekers to find employment. It is available to all registered unemployed.

81

- *Job-Search Training* (JST) assists registered unemployed with a moderate degree of labour market disadvantage through services and training in such areas as job-search skills, interview techniques, motivation and confidence-building.
- *Intensive Assistance* (IA) provides individually-tailored assistance to the most disadvantaged registered unemployed at risk of long-term unemployment. Among other offerings, services can include training, work experience, employer incentives (*e.g.* wage subsidies), workplace modifications, post placement support, or subsidies for transportation, clothing or equipment to secure employment.
- *New Enterprise Incentive Scheme* (NEIS) and *Self Employment Development* provide support and training for selected registered unemployed persons to establish and run new businesses. (NEIS was a prior-existing measure that was integrated as a JN service.)
- *Project Contracting* provides labour exchange services for seasonal harvests and is available to all individuals entitled to work in Australia.

The restructuring scheme continued the practice of having an evaluation framework operated in-house at DEWRSB and included provision for consultation with other government departments and agencies. A three-stage evaluation of Job Network was set up to generate reports on implementation issues (released in May 2000), interim progress (released in May 2001), and effectiveness (due to be completed in December 2001). In addition, the framework provided for an independent review of Job Network which is scheduled to be carried out during 2001.

Income support for most unemployed was restructured to establish a single allowance under the Newstart programme with various supplements.[38] Important activity-tested income support changes were embodied in the Work for the Dole programme and the Mutual Obligation initiative:[39]

- The *Work for the Dole* initiative established new options for allowance recipients to satisfy activity requirements and gain work experience and for communities to accomplish projects that might not otherwise be carried out. Piloted in 1997, the programme was implemented in August 1998. Participation in a Work for the Dole project involves a six-month commitment of up to 30 hours per fortnight. Allowance recipients may be required to participate if they are subject to Mutual Obligation and in receipt of the full allowance rate, but without other activity under Mutual Obligation. It may also be required of unemployed youth aged 18 to 19 years who are in receipt of a Youth Allowance[40] for three months. Work for the Dole services are managed by Community Work Coordinators, who are contracted by DEWRSB to arrange projects with such partners as community groups or local government agencies. Community Work Coordinators refer and support jobseekers in their Work for Dole activities.

- *Mutual Obligation* introduced new activity requirements for unemployed youth aged 18 to 24 years (in receipt of Newstart or Youth allowances for six months or more) and, subsequently, also for other unemployed aged 25 to 34 years (in receipt of Newstart allowances for 12 months or more). Echoing the notion introduced in the 1980s that allowance recipients should be required to take actions to improve their labour market situation, Mutual Obligation makes benefit eligibility conditional on participation in an approved activity, in principle, designed to improve employability and contribute to the community.[41] Clients are given a degree of choice in the selection of an activity, but there is also a degree of compulsion in that those failing to choose may be automatically referred to a Work for the Dole project.

In part by drawing on previous reform initiatives, the Howard government also moved to advance change in the **vocational educational and training** sector, with the aim of improving the relevance, quality and portability of training, and to increase the volume of apprenticeship and entry-level training.[42] A National Training Framework was set up to move towards establishing standards for use by states and territories in registering training organisations, standards for trainee competency and supporting materials for trainers. In addition, a number of adjustments and changes was made to training programmes administered by the Department of Education, Training and Youth Affairs (DETYA):

- The *New Apprenticeships* programme was established, encompassing two different types of entry-level training: apprenticeships and traineeships. Building on earlier initiatives, this programme is trying to shift the emphasis from an experience-based approach to a competency-based approach with the possibility of earlier completion. The programme has increased flexibility in design of apprenticeships with respect to occupational categories and bolstered the competitive market for off-the-job training within apprenticeships. DETYA has funded community and other groups to operate New Apprenticeship Centres that act as one-stop shops to promote the New Apprenticeships programme and administer payments to employers.

- The *Literacy and Numeracy Program* was established in 1998 to provide basic literacy and numeracy training for eligible jobseekers whose skills are below the level considered necessary to get and keep a job. Initially, this programme only provided services to jobseekers subject to Mutual Obligation arrangements, but access was subsequently extended to other jobseekers such as participants in CSP.[43] Some 65 registered training organisations across Australia have been contracted to deliver assessment and training services under the Literacy and Numeracy Program (including community organisations, private providers, universities, colleges, and not-for-profit organisations).[44]

- *School-to-work transitions* are the focus of the DETYA Jobs Pathway Programme (JPP) and the Enterprise and Career Education Foundation (successor to the ASTF).[45] The JPP – based on a programme piloted in 1995 – seeks to assist youth (aged 15 to 19) who study vocational courses or who are at risk of dropping out or of long-term unemployment.[46] Through contracted providers, JPP offers advisory and placement services with post-placement follow-up; it is also classified as one of the approved Mutual Obligation activities. A related youth initiative is the Job Placement, Employment and Training (JPET) programme that aims to assist students and unemployed young people aged 15-21 years (with priority to be given to those aged 15 to 19), who are homeless or at risk of becoming homeless.[47]

Box 1.3. **Labour market programme indicators**

Chart 1.8 presents labour market programme indicators for the period 1989 to 2000, including: 1) participant inflows into active labour market programmes;[1] and 2) the combined expenditures on active labour market programmes and unemployment benefits. While changes in these indicators are influenced by a variety of factors including developments in the business cycle, policy decisions undoubtedly play an important role. The chart highlights the increased client inflows into active measures during the first half of the 1990s, including the expansion that followed the introduction of Working Nation. Although some decline might have been expected as the business cycle advanced, there is a notable decline following the shift in policy in 1996.[2]

In terms of the combined expenditure on active labour market programmes and unemployment benefits, shifts were somewhat more gradual over time, but nonetheless evident. This indicator had already begun to decline as the business cycle advanced in the middle of the 1990s, a trend that was reinforced by the implementation of policy changes during the second half of the 1990s. By 1999, Australia's expenditures had fallen to a share of GDP that was below 10 of the 17 OECD countries for which comparable data were available. A substantial share of the decline in the second half of the 1990s was due to steep cuts in Australia's spending on labour market programmes related to training for adults and subsidised employment. (A detailed discussion of programme expenditure can be found in Chapter 5.)

---

1. According to the OECD typology, active labour market programmes include: public employment services and administration, labour market training, youth measures (including apprenticeships and related forms of general youth training), subsidised employment and measures for the disabled.

2. The largest single component of the change between 1996 and 1997 was the reduction in inflows to labour market training programmes for adults, which fell from 4.8% of the labour force in 1996 to 2.1% of the labour force in 1997.

Chart 1.8. **Labour market programme indicators, Australia, 1989-2000**[a]
Percentages

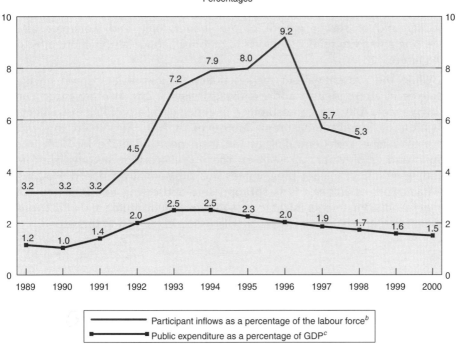

Participant inflows as a percentage of the labour force[b]
Public expenditure as a percentage of GDP[c]

a) Data refer to fiscal years ending on June 30.
b) Inflows refer only to active labour market programmes.
c) Expenditure includes active labour market programmes and unemployment benefits.
Source: OECD database on Active Labour Market Programmes.

H. Setting the scene

The preceding review of developments highlights certain strengths in the Australian labour market as well as persistent weaknesses. The economic expansion in the 1990s was associated with increases in real per capita GDP, substantial employment growth and declining rates of unemployment overall, for example. At the same time, some segments in the population (*e.g.* indigenous people, young males and some local areas away from the main urban centres) continued to experience relatively high rates of unemployment. Although the rate of long-term unemployment has decreased, it remains higher than at a similar point in the previous period of economic expansion. Job stability remains relatively low. International comparisons using standard measures reveal greater

85

income inequality than in many OECD countries and a poverty rate that is in the mid-range for OECD countries. In the Australian context, lone parents in particular experience a relatively high incidence of poverty. These difficulties occur against a background of slower growth of the labour force and workforce ageing, suggesting a need to reinforce efforts to mobilise labour supply more effectively in the future.

While the present labour market policy framework has drawn on earlier initiatives in attempting to address these issues, it has also advanced certain initiatives more fully (*e.g.* contestability, targeting using a profiling instrument and activation of benefit measures). Moreover, it has introduced innovations (*e.g.* establishment of Centrelink as the main point of intake for both income support and employment assistance). These changes were accomplished while spending on labour market programmes was substantially reduced. How well is this framework operating? Is it appropriately addressing needs in the labour market? What adjustments might lead to improved functioning and effectiveness? These and other related questions are discussed in the rest of this report.

Chapter 2

The Institutional Set-up of Labour Market Policy and Employment Services

A. Introduction

As the preceding chapter has shown in some detail, Australian governments have tried out a variety of policy approaches to labour market programmes and employment services. Above all, Australia is among the first OECD countries to introduce market-type mechanisms into its employment service framework, to contract out placement and individualised follow-up of jobseekers, and thus make its core PES activities "contestable".

After some experimentation in the first half of the 1990s with contracting out certain employment services, and in particular with competitive "case management" for the long-term unemployed, the incoming Howard government in 1996 opted for outsourcing the major part of the job matching and placement functions of the public employment service, and establishing a "fully contestable" market for the provision of these services.[48] Under the new arrangement, private, community and public sector organisations compete for funding, and the government's primary role in job matching and placement has changed from that of a provider to that of a purchaser. This chapter outlines the public and private labour market agencies and actors in the Australian placement market, their contractual relationships and internal operations. It also provides information on the relevant agencies' office structures and staffing levels.

B. Labour market agencies and actors

1. *From PES to contestable market*

The Commonwealth Employment Service (CES) functioned as Australia's PES agency from 1946 to 1998, operating about 300 local offices throughout the country under the general control of the Department of Employment (under its varying denominations). As in other OECD countries, it was given the tasks of matching supply and demand in the labour market and running, or referring clients to a variety of labour market programmes. However, it never reached particularly high levels of market share in reported vacancies and placements.[49] Also, it was never an integrated "one-stop shop", as the payment of unemployment benefits was handled separately by local offices of the Department of Social Security. Its main link to the benefit function was the requirement for the CES to notify social security offices of possible failure of the work test and instances of non-compliance with administrative obligations of unemployed benefit recipients.

The private sector has historically also been quite strongly involved in placement services. Commercial services were allowed early on and Australia never adhered to the ILO's recommendation of proscribing profit-oriented private employment agencies.[50] Private sector organisations were also contracted to provide training and organise job clubs for clients registered with the CES. However, a "qualitative leap" towards the involvement of the private sector in placement activities was reached with the introduction of "case management" (understood as individualised treatment of members of a target group), where contracted managers are drawn from the private sector and community groups and compete with their public counterparts.

The community sector in Australia has always had an important role in the provision of some government-financed social services, such as care for the disabled (see Chapter 5). Providers for the SkillShare training programme, which was introduced in 1988, soon developed quite detailed case management procedures [Ball (1996)]. Contracted case management specifically for placement purposes was initiated by the state government in Victoria, which in the late 1980s started to fund community organisations through grants paid out according to placement outcomes. At a later stage, private sector for-profit organisations were also allowed to compete for tenders. However, this was a small state programme and uptake was limited. The Federal government re-emphasised intensive counselling services under its 1994 *Working Nation* Program and started to outsource some of the case management previously handled exclusively by the CES. During 1995/96, about 300 providers of case management services from the private and community sector started operating in competition with CES local offices. This policy represented the first stage of what was to become a radical change in purchase/provider arrangements in the second half of the decade [OECD (1997d); Fay (1997); Webster and Harding (2000)].

The introduction of competitive case management required a number of administrative innovations. In particular, a regulatory framework had to be set up to introduce codes of conduct for private-sector case managers and award contracts as the outcome of a public tender process. A profiling mechanism (JSI, see Chapter 1) was created to assess jobseeker qualifications prior to their referral to case management providers. Also, changes in information technology were required to ensure adequate information-sharing between providers and the regulatory authority.

Under the new labour market policy strategy, two new bodies were set up: the Employment Services Regulatory Authority (ESRA); and Employment Assistance Australia (EAA). ESRA was charged with purchasing, regulating and monitoring private-sector case management and with managing the tender and accreditation process. EAA was established as the case management arm of the CES, *i.e.* the government provider in competition with private and community sector agencies. Contestability under this arrangement was somewhat constrained in that the operation of EAA within the CES may have influenced jobseeker decisions. Also, ESRA functioned in a broad policy framework set by the same government ministry that was overseeing the operations of EAA. Although jobseekers could choose among public, private and community-sector service providers, government provision remained dominant and the share of private providers increased only slowly.[51] It was the lack of a level playing field between the various providers that was criticised as a major failing of the case management set-up [Fay (1997); Golightly *et al.* (1996); Webster and Harding (2000)].[52]

The incoming Howard Government in 1996 announced a sweeping reorganisation and a substantial reduction in spending. It argued that the establishment of a fully competitive employment services market (subsequently termed "*Job Network*"), with the government no longer a direct provider, but rather a purchaser of services determined through competitive tendering, would provide a number of benefits to jobseekers and employers [Vanstone (1996*b*)]. A new incentive framework was to be set up with the intention of rewarding job assistance providers primarily for successful placement of jobseekers, while additional incentives would be introduced for placing the most disadvantaged among them.

In designing Job Network (JN), the government drew on lessons from the operation of Working Nation. These were based, in particular, on the experience under Working Nation with: screening and classification tools to target the most expensive assistance on those who were most at-risk of long-term unemployment; case management results indicating the effectiveness of job-search assistance as an alternative to vocational training for clients who were job-ready; and case manager observations on the need to focus employment assistance on those most able to benefit, while targeting other types of assistance on those with severe barriers to employment [DEWRSB (2000*d*)]. These lessons were applied, *inter alia*, through the introduction of the Job Seeker Classification Instrument (JSCI), abolition of most labour market programmes, renewed emphasis on early placements into employment and establishment of procedures to stream those experiencing the most severe barriers to employment into separate labour market programmes.

The coalition government introduced legislation in Parliament to support the implementation of the Job Network. However, after the draft bill encountered opposition in the Senate, the government decided to set up the scheme under

89|

existing legislation and administrative authority. Subsequently, all CES offices were closed in April 1998 and the provision of most employment services was contracted out to over 300 new JN-members operating from more than 1 400 sites, with the government-owned corporatised provider (drawn from the CES and newly established as *Employment National*) retaining only about one-third of available business. The first tender to select provider organisations was conducted in mid-1997 for a contract period running from May 1998 to February 2000. The second tender was undertaken in mid-1999, with the contract period to run for three years as from February 2000. Importantly, the tender process was monitored by an independent Probity Advisor and by the Australian National Audit Office [ANAO (1998, 2000); see Section C below for more detail].

Setting up the competitive market arrangements under Job Network involved the most significant reorganisation of labour market assistance since the establishment of the CES in the post-war period. However, as shown above, it also needs to be seen as the continuation of changes set in motion by previous Federal governments, as well as in the State of Victoria. Judging from an international perspective, the radical nature of the new arrangements is without parallel in OECD Member countries.

2. Structure and function of Government agencies involved in the Job Network

As shown in Chart 2.1, the main Commonwealth Government agencies involved in the employment services market are the Department of Employment, Workplace Relations and Small Business (DEWRSB), the Department of Family and Community Services (FaCS), and Centrelink. The Department of Education, Training and Youth Affairs (DETYA) is also of relevance for the job market through its responsibility for vocational education and training, higher education and its supervision of numeracy and literacy programmes, apprenticeship centres and other programmes to assist school-to-work transitions.

DEWRSB's wide portfolio encompasses the development of employment policies, supervision of the new employment services market through its Job Network Group, and administration of other labour market activities and programmes. Another part of the Department is concerned with the development of the workplace relations framework and labour relations practices in enterprises (see Chapter 6). Further, an Office of Small Business within the Department is focused on supporting and advancing small business interests, *inter alia* through a small business incubator programme. The portfolio also includes occupational health and safety and equal employment opportunity issues (via the National Occupational Health and Safety Commission, and the Equal Opportunity for Women in the Workplace Agency).[53]

The current set-up exists only since 1998 and brings together the previous Department of Workplace Relations and Small Business (DWRSB) with the

Chart 2.1. **Main actors in labour market policy and employment services, Australia**

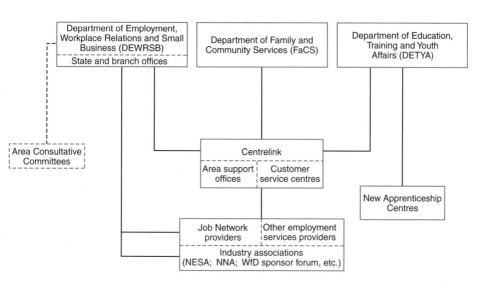

NESA: National Employment Services Association; NNA: National New Enterprise Incentive Scheme Association; WfD: Work for the Dole.

employment area of the previous Department of Employment, Education, Training and Youth Affairs (DEETYA). This recombination of the portfolio signals the enhanced focus of the current government on the nexus between employment opportunities and labour-management relations.

The Department has outsourced virtually all employment programmes and is responsible for ensuring that these services are delivered by several hundred private and community-sector organisations, particularly within the Job Network. It has developed contractual relationships with the private providers and pays them fees for contracted services, such as delivery of job search training and short- and medium-term job placements. DEWRSB staff, therefore, have had to develop expertise in contract management and performance monitoring. In this context, State and district offices, which employ one-third of departmental staff, are particularly important. Contract Mangers in many of these offices act as the first point of liaison to the employment service providers.[54]

FaCS was created in October 1998 as the successor to the Department of Social Security. It is responsible for implementing the Government's income security policies and managing, *inter alia*, support for the aged, childcare services, unemployment assistance and welfare housing. Its services are delivered, in

91

particular, through Centrelink offices (see below), the Child Support Agency and a vocational rehabilitation agency. The Social Security Appeals Tribunal – a large agency with over 200 staff, within the FaCS portfolio, but independent in relation to its powers of review – considers appeals lodged about decisions made by the service delivery agencies. FaCS also has a number of formal funding relationships with non-government agents at local and national level to deliver special and community services, with the largest single annual allocation going to the Australian Council of Social Services (ACOSS).

Centrelink is the principal service delivery agency within the FaCS portfolio. It was created in July 1997 by transferring staff from the service-providing elements of the former Department of Social Security and the jobseeker registration function of the CES to both administer the social security benefits determined by FaCS and channel jobseekers to JN providers. Some additional staff also joined Centrelink from the former CES when it closed down in 1998. Centrelink is financed by FaCS, DEWRSB, DETYA and several other Government Departments and agencies in a purchaser/provider arrangement governed by Business Partnership Arrangements. All of its income comes from services provided, implying that there is no direct funding for such activities as staff training and strategic planning.

Centrelink's 400-plus Customer Service Centres constitute the initial point of contact for jobseekers to access federally-funded employment services. They register unemployed jobseekers and determine their eligibility for unemployment benefits and Job Network services. Centrelink offices also administer unemployment benefits and may sanction benefit recipients for violation of the conditions attached to income support.[55] Finally, they provide all jobseekers, including those not in receipt of benefit, with access to job-search facilities, such as vacancy listings, touch screens, computers and printers, photocopiers, telephones, and other relevant job search and career information.

After classifying jobseekers by their relative difficulty of finding employment, using the JSCI, Centrelink refers them to JN providers or other appropriate assistance. It is thus a "first-stop-shop" for employment services, but not a "one-stop-shop" in the sense used in some other OECD Member countries, as it has no direct role in placement activities, which are the domain of the Job Network providers, and Centrelink has no influence over the make-up of these activities. It acts rather as a "gateway" to employment service providers and controls the flow of its clients to them (see Chapter 3 for more detail on JSCI and client flows).

3. *Partnership Arrangements*

Government Departments are linked with Centrelink through Business Partnership Arrangements (BPA). These specify what services Departments buy from Centrelink at what standard, provide for the necessary governance and consultation arrangements, and define performance indicators as a measure of whether Centrelink's services meet the agreed standards.

For example, Centrelink's BPA with DEWRSB is a three-year agreement negotiated between the Secretary of DEWRSB and the Chief Executive Officer of Centrelink. The term of the current BPA is between October 1999 and June 2002, with a review of the arrangement conducted annually. Based on the annual review, DEWRSB funds Centrelink annually for the provision of the agreed services. In comparison with funding by FaCS, funding of Centrelink for employment assistance activities by DEWRSB constitutes a relatively small share (about 10% of Centrelink's annual income).

Services to be provided by Centrelink to DEWRSB include:

- Registering jobseekers as unemployed, assessing them in relation to their eligibility for the various Job Network services, and signing them up for a Preparing-for-Work Agreement.

- Managing the referral of eligible jobseekers to Job Network providers and other employment programmes, ensuring that they are enrolled with at least one Job Matching provider and, when required, participate in JST and Intensive Assistance.

- Providing self-help facilities (computer terminals, etc.) for clients' active job search.

- Acting upon possible breach notifications from JN members and liaising with them for any necessary clarification of breach recommendations.

- Handling of jobseeker complaints, as well as referring them, where necessary, to DEWRSB's Job Network customer service line.

The BPA also specifies mechanisms for collaboration between the two agencies. In particular, the need for continuous liaison between functional areas in the Department and Centrelink is emphasised. Among the more formal co-operation arrangements, the DEWRSB Secretary sits on the Centrelink Management Board; a Business Partnership Review Group meets monthly to review Centrelink performance against agreed key performance indicators (KPIs) and discuss service delivery issues; a System Interface Strategic Committee aims to improve the interfacing of Centrelink's and DEWRSB's respective computer systems and facilities; and a Joint Operations Group meets as required to identify best practice for the delivery of services. In total, 14 KPIs and their accompanying benchmarks are laid down in the Arrangement, from jobseeker satisfaction with Centrelink services to the holding of JSCI interviews in the agreed timeframe, to sanction decisions following notifications submitted by service providers.

The functioning of Centrelink as a service delivery agency is highlighted by the stipulation that Centrelink keeps jobseeker records as required by DEWRSB and provides Department staff with access to such records upon request. Finally, 93 in the 2000/2001 financial year, the BPA includes a provision for piloting performance pay. This arrangement applies to the final quarter of the financial year and rewards Centrelink for exceeding KPI benchmarks. A predetermined amount is set aside from the agreed cost of services for the year and, depending on performance, Centrelink can earn as little as nil or as much as twice the amount set aside.[56]

4. The role of advisory bodies

In light of the importance of the decision to outsource the majority of employment services, it is not surprising that the corresponding government policies have involved substantial consultation with the actors involved. Both requests for tender were preceded by public consultation, and the government is holding regular meetings with peak representative organisations However, the National Audit Office has observed that, in the past, there was limited discussion with Job Network providers on strategic issues [ANAO (2000)].

The National Employment Services Association (NESA), established in 1997, is the representative industry association of provider organisations. NESA's Board of Management includes five members representing providers and two individual professionals. The government, *i.e.* mainly the Minister for Employment Services and key DEWRSB managers including the Secretary of the Department, now meets with the Board every other month, considering issues such as referrals of jobseekers to Job Network members, problems relating to chains of communication in the Job Network market, and issues relating to fees and purchasing policy. Similar consultative meetings are held with the National New Enterprise Incentive Scheme Association (NNA), the Work for the Dole sponsor forums, Jobs Australia – the peak body representing community-based providers – and other representative associations. In addition, groups such as ACOSS (Australian Council of Social Services) participate actively in the public debate and have met with DEWRSB to discuss Job Network issues.

Further consultative bodies of relevance for employment policies are the National Labour Consultative Council (NLCC) and decentralised Area Consultative Committees (ACCs). The NLCC, established in 1977, is a national body composed of 15 representatives from employer associations (7), the ACTU (7), and the Commonwealth Government (1) who jointly consider labour market and industrial relations matters. The Council is able to set up standing and *ad hoc* committees, with a view to making recommendations on issues of its own choice, such as pending legislation. It thus corresponds to the tripartite Social and Economic Councils operating in many European countries [ETUI (1990); Trebilcock *et al.* (1994)], although its influence seems to have been eroded over the more recent period.

The Area Consultative Committees were established in 1994 to advise the Minister for Employment, Workplace Relations and Small Business on ways to improve job and training opportunities in the regions. There are 56 ACCs operating throughout Australia, with approximately 850 members drawn from the business sector, community organisations and government agencies. Funding is through the Commonwealth Government under the Regional Assistance Program. The ACCs bring together community stakeholders to identify priorities for their respective regions, and are encouraged to develop regional employment strategies and project proposals for small business support, jobs generation and skills improvement. They also facilitate liaison between Job Network members at the regional level and advise the government on the extent to which Job Network providers are meeting the needs of local employers and jobseekers.

C. Job Network contracting, payment mechanisms and member profile

This section aims to provide more detailed information about the inner workings of the Job Network, including the range of services offered, selection of providers through the tender process, fee structures, as well as operational supervision through DEWRSB staff.[57]

1. Network profile and service provision

Currently about 200 contracted private, community and public providers compete with each other for the provision of placement and case management services. Job Network providers who have won contracts under a tender process compete to attract jobseekers to their service. The government sets the range and broad nature of employment services to be provided, and DEWRSB determines through the tender process which organisations qualify as providers for particular services. As outlined in Chapter 1, currently five key employment services are available under the scheme: Job Matching, JST, IA, NEIS and Project Contracting. During the initial contract period, New Apprenticeship Centres were included among the Job Network services. Since December 1999 these are operating under the responsibility of the Department for Education, Training and Youth Affairs.

DEWRSB allocates to providers, as specified in their contract, a maximum number of jobseekers that they can assist (in other words, fees that they can claim) under the Job Matching, JST, IA and NEIS schemes. High levels of outcomes achieved will increase the probability of being awarded additional contracts in the next tender round. They will also help to fill places as jobseekers, it is assumed, will turn to providers with a good performance rating.[58] Job Matching contracts do not provide any guarantee of a specific level of business, but for other types of contract the government has undertaken to try to make sufficient referrals to keep providers at a minimum proportion of their contracted "point in time" capacity as described in Centrelink's Business Partnership Agreement with DEWRSB (above 80% for JST providers, and above 85% for IA providers).

95

Job Network providers come from a wide variety of backgrounds, including charities initially specialised in providing assistance to the homeless, migrants or the disabled, training organisations, industrial psychologists and recruitment consultants, private placement agencies and the former public employment service itself. In the case of "non-profit" organisations, Job Network activities are often a separate profit-making arm with any profits remitted to the parent organisation.

Employment National, the main government provider, offers services on the same terms and conditions as other Network members. In order to match the requirement of full contestability and prevent any competitive advantage, Employment National has to fulfil stringent criteria of "competitive neutrality", such as full-cost pricing, regulatory and taxation neutrality [OECD (2000b)]. It also can be called upon as a provider of last-resort in areas where the tender process might fail to produce suitable providers of employment services. However, contrary to initial expectations, it has not been necessary so far to invoke this "community service obligation", as suitable service delivery agencies have been found even in remote areas.

Under the second tender period, there has been an increase in market share for the community and small business sectors. Community-based and charitable organisations that had comprised about 30% of the first Job Network now form around 47% of the market. The private sector also expanded from about 33% to 45% of contract volume. By contrast, the share of government providers fell from 37% to 8% in the second tender round. In particular, Employment National now has retained only 1% of the Intensive Assistance market, compared to 42% under the first contract. On the other hand, the agency was successful in its bid for Job Matching services and was contracted to provide an increased share for this service (from 18% to 22%), reflecting its good performance in Job Matching activities which is to some extent a carry-over from the traditional job brokerage business of the former CES.[59]

Tables 2.1 and 2.2 provide additional information on the profile of Job Network member organisations. Table 2.1 illustrates the number of providers active in each of the key Job Network services. Not all providers are active in all services simultaneously; they may have been awarded contracts in only one or two of these activities through the tender process, or may have applied for contracts only in what they consider their speciality. However, all JST and IA providers must also offer Job Matching services to the jobseekers registered with them. In all, about 80% of contracted providers provide Job-Matching services, while 60% (initially only 40%) provide Intensive Assistance to the most disadvantaged. The table also illustrates that the number of contracted providers has decreased in every category from the first to the second tender period, while the number of sites has greatly increased, from 1 400 to over 2 000, indicating that

Table 2.1. **Job Network members and sites by type of service, 1998-2000**

Service	Number of Job Network members		Number of sites	
	May 1998	October 2000	May 1998	October 2000
Job Matching	240	158	936	1 691
Job Search Training	117	92	419	664
Intensive Assistance	125	120	715	1 127
New Enterprise Incentive Scheme	64	51	194	339
New Apprenticeship Centres	59	–	200	–
Project Contracting^a	4	3	11	18
Total	**306**	**194**	**1 404**	**2 014**

– Not applicable.
a) Not all providers were fully in place in May 1998.
Source: DEWRSB (2000d; 2000g).

Table 2.2. **Number of Job Network services by sites and specialist services, May 1998**

Specialist service	Job Matching	Job Search Training	Intensive Assistance	NEIS
Long-term unemployed	23	5	17	–
Mature-aged people	12	1	12	3
Indigenous Australians	25	7	19	–
Non-English-speaking background	42	18	26	6
Persons with disability	48	12	34	3
Sole parents	5	1	3	1
Women	5	1	6	6
Youth	59	20	41	6
Other	15	8	11	1
Total	**234**	**73**	**169**	**26**

– Nil.
Source: DEWRSB (2000d).

services are being offered through an increasingly decentralised office network.[60] For example, outside the main metropolitan areas the number of sites has almost doubled, with an increase from about 600 to around 1 100. Thus, nearly 150 locations gained a Job Network site for the first time. This improved availability of services in non-metropolitan and thinly-populated regions reflects the substantial increase in the number of geographical purchasing areas under the second contract period, which allowed providers to take into account the cost of providing services in these areas.

Some providers have been contracted to provide services to all eligible jobseekers ("generalist services"), or to specific client groups ("specialist services"). Others deliver services under both tracks. Table 2.2, in combination with Table 2.1, illustrates that in the first contract period about one-quarter of Job Matching and Intensive Assistance sites, and one-fifth of Job Search Training sites offered services tailored to meet the needs of specific client groups (although they are also required to accept any jobseeker who is referred to them). In all of these categories, the largest number of sites offered services to youth, persons with a disability, and those with non-English-speaking background. Specialist services were fully introduced in the second tender, when IA providers were allowed to bid to specialise exclusively in specific client groups. Currently 110 sites offer specialist services; for example, there are 11 specialist providers for indigenous clients operating from 40 sites in areas where the indigenous population exceeds 5% of the total population [DEWRSB (2001b)].

2. Two tender rounds: 1997 and 1999

The purchase of Job Network services occurs through a national tender process organised by the Department, which invites organisations to tender for provision of one or more of the Job Network services in any one of many geographic tender areas. Two Job Network tenders have been organised so far. The selection criteria and indicative business levels are published and in each tender round a Probity Plan is put in place to ensure that tenders are assessed objectively and consistently.

The first, 1997 Job tender was the largest public tender of human services in Australia's history. More than 1 000 organisations submitted over 5 300 bids for a contract volume of $1.7 billion starting from May 1998. Only 300 of the 1 000 tenderers were awarded contracts.

Following a series of consultations, a draft of the second Employment Services Request for Tender was published on the Internet in April 1999 to provide the public and prospective tenderers with the opportunity to comment. The final version was released in June 1999 and the tender was closed on 30 July 1999. Tenderers could bid at regional level (19 regions), employment service area level (137 ESAs) or for particular postcodes, localities or towns. Subsequently conditional offers were announced for 205 tenderers. The second contract involves the delivery of employment services worth about $3 billion for three years from 28 February 2000. As funding for Job Network is a single line appropriation, allocation among the different JN services is flexible; however, the majority of funding is likely to be spent on Intensive Assistance. In budget year 1999/2000, a total of about $754 million was spent on Job Network, of which over two thirds was spent on Intensive Assistance.[61]

The fact that over 700 tenderers were unsuccessful in the first tender round led to some criticism of the tendering process (although, in accordance with the probity plan, feedback sessions had been made available to all tenderers). According to the Probity Adviser, there was no evidence of systematic bias, lack of objectivity, or ranking patterns, which advantaged or disadvantaged any particular bidder. An Australian National Audit Office report [ANAO (1998)] also concluded that the implementation of Job Network had been managed effectively and efficiently in accordance with announced Government policy and timeframe. Based on the experience of the first tender, the second Job Network tender process was also underpinned by a Probity Plan and monitored by an independent Probity Adviser.[62]

Among the risks when conducting a competitive tender are that tenderers may fail to conform with the basic tender requirements or get fundamental aspects of the tender, such as their price or business levels, wrong. To minimise these risks, tender documentation for both the first and second Job Network tenders clearly detailed the services the Government was to purchase and the process for deciding successful tenders. This was supported by information sessions conducted by senior DEWRSB staff, a telephone and Internet service to answer questions and, for the second tender, a guided electronic form that prompted tenderers to complete all relevant fields. The tender documentation pointed out that tenders would be excluded if they, for example, omitted certain key details or ignored certain instructions. In both Job Network tenders, some bids were excluded for these reasons.

3. Prices for services and outcomes

Payments by DEWRSB to providers are made according to the contracts established under the tendering process. The structure of payments is crucial in determining both the incentives influencing Job Network members and the economic viability of their operations.[63] It is set up to emphasise employment-related outcomes and to provide higher rewards in the case of successful outcomes for clients assessed as facing greater degrees of disadvantage or who are long-term unemployed. Under the Job Network Code of Conduct, jobseeker clients cannot be charged fees for employment services. Neither are employers usually charged for services, although some providers have experimented with charging them fees for Job Matching or special services.

For the second tender, fees and payment mechanisms for the three main services are outlined below.

- Job Matching: providers claim an outcome fee each time an eligible jobseeker is placed into a job.[64] The level of this outcome fee is determined by price-competitive tender (the average outcome fee under the second JN contract is $362). In addition, a fixed bonus payment ($268) may be claimed for long-term unemployed persons (twelve months or more), who are not being assisted through JST or IA. Where such jobseekers are in receipt of an unemployment allowance, they must maintain employment that generates sufficient income to reduce their basic rate of unemployment allowance by 70% or more over a period of 13 consecutive weeks; where they do not receive income support, they must work for an average of at least 15 hours per week over 13 consecutive weeks. Providers are contracted to make a certain number of job placements every six months. Part of the payment for anticipated placements is usually made "up-front", at the beginning of each six-month period, but the total paid depends only upon successful outcomes.[65]

• *Job-Search Training* (JST): for each commencement providers are paid a fee, which is determined by price-competitive tender. Placements of JST clients (as well as IA clients below) into a job engenders the regular Job Matching outcome fee. In addition, a fixed Job-Search Training Outcome fee ($268) is payable if the participant commences employment within 13 weeks of ceasing JST and stays in work for 13 consecutive weeks with an average reduction of benefit of at least 70% or, where jobseekers do not receive unemployment benefit, if they work on average 15 hours a week over 13 consecutive weeks. Providers are contracted to serve an agreed maximum caseload of clients (*contracted capacity*) and must also provide Job Matching services to them.

• *Intensive Assistance* (IA): fees paid are determined through a competitive tender, where bid prices are subject to a floor ($4 663 for level A and $9 219 for level B).[66] Thus, in the case of bids at the floor price, selection across tenders can be based entirely on the anticipated quality of service provision.[67] The fixed final outcome payment is subtracted from the contracted price and 30% of the remainder is paid on commencement. When a jobseeker achieves a primary interim outcome (*i.e.* enters and remains in employment for 13 weeks), the 70% balance is paid and after a further 13 weeks, the final primary outcome fee ($1 072 for level A and $2 144 for level B) is payable.[68] Placements into part-time employment which do not result in complete cessation of income support and into eligible education, are called "secondary outcomes"; for these, a smaller secondary fee of $536 is payable at 13 weeks and again at 26 weeks. As for JST, providers are contracted for a maximum caseload, and Centrelink will attempt to maintain referrals at above 85% of contracted capacity, although the exact level will depend on the availability of eligible jobseekers and also on jobseeker choice. IA providers (as well as JST providers) had to make a corresponding tender bid for Job Matching places. Where this bid was not accepted, they were still obliged to provide Job Matching at the weighted average fee level determined by the competitive tender outcome for this service in the region.

Job Matching outcomes can only be claimed for a placement if the vacancy has first been entered onto the National Vacancy Data Base and an eligible jobseeker has been registered with the provider. This does not preclude registration of a vacancy which is immediately filled and/or enrolment of a jobseeker who is immediately placed. Following a placement, a provider needs to confirm with the employer that the person has worked for 15 hours within 5 days of commencing the placement and electronically submit a claim to DEWRSB. To claim a Job Matching bonus payment, the JN member, using the information systems supplied by DEWRSB, must confirm that a jobseeker on unemployment benefit has achieved the required benefit reduction or, where a jobseeker is not on unemployment benefit, that the job obtained had the required characteristics.

In the case of Job-Search Training and Intensive Assistance, all entries to employment that reduce benefit by at least 70% over a period of 13 consecutive weeks are valid outcomes. For jobseekers who have found their own employment ("FOEs"), a Job-Matching fee is not payable, but to anchor an outcome, the provider must lodge the placement in the information management system (IES, see Box 2.2.) within 28 days of the start of the job, to be followed by a claim for payment within 28 days after the client's first 13 weeks on the job [DEWRSB (1999c)]. No payment is made in respect of late claims, which can arise if a provider has failed to maintain contact with the client and is unaware that he or she has found work. Some providers consider this arrangement harsh, but it creates incentives to have tight procedures for checking the status of clients as well as maintaining some post-placement contact with those who have started work. Providers can access the beneficiary status of their clients through computer systems. While the actual amount of benefit is not displayed, providers are able to use the IES to confirm that a jobseeker's benefit has been reduced and he/she may qualify for a JST or IA outcome payment.

There is a general requirement on providers to maintain documentary evidence that all conditions for claiming a payment have been met. For example, the provider could hold a signed copy of the Preparing-for-Work Agreement for the up-front fee and a statement from an employer that the jobseeker has been employed over a given period of time for the interim outcome payment. Computer system records do not constitute documentary evidence [DEWRSB (1999c)].

4. *Contract specifications and changes in service provision*

In the first tender round, selection criteria were relatively simple. Tenders were assessed as satisfying specified quality and performance standards and then ranked according to price within each tender region. In the second tender, there was an increased focus on the quality of services, measured partly on the basis of past performance, whether in Job Network or elsewhere. For Intensive Assistance, performance was assessed using administrative data for the proportion of jobseekers who had left benefits, with an adjustment for the composition of the client caseload and local labour market factors.[69] Providers received general advice on their relative performance in early 1999, a first regional comparison report in May shortly before the second tender submissions, and a final "star rating" (up to five stars) for performance in the first contract round.

In the second tender round, on top of past performance, the prospective strategies and interventions outlined by a tenderer were taken into account. In the case of Intensive Assistance, tender bids had to include a Declaration of Intent (DOI) summarising the services that the tenderer expected to provide. The service quality aspects accounted for 75% of the assessment outcomes, with price accounting for the rest. First performance information on second-round providers, using performance indicators laid down in provider contracts and focused on employment outcomes, were published in March 2001. Performance measurement took account of a range of factors known to influence employment outcome levels in the different regions. On a national basis, about one-third of providers rated "4 stars" or better [DEWRSB (2001c)].

The level of employment service places contracted in each region ("contracted capacity" for Job-Search Training and Intensive Assistance) is based on the number of jobseekers present. These data were published in the Request for Tender. In the first tender round, there were 29 labour market regions and bids were accepted from a minimum of five providers in each area.[70] In the second tender, the number of labour market regions was reduced to 19, but a second tendering layer was added with the creation of 137 smaller employment service areas. This change helped to create price differentials that could motivate the provision of services in more remote and difficult labour markets. That tenderers could take into account regional variations in the cost of service provision, encouraged them to bid to provide service points in areas outside of state capitals and the main metropolitan areas.[71] Also, the minimum number of providers was reduced from five to two or three which helped improve the economic viability of service providers in thinly populated regions. All of this contributed to an increase in the number of sites covered from 1 400 under the first JN tender to over 2 000. Box 2.1. provides some further detail on service changes decided under the first and second JN contract periods.

5. Operational management of contracts

DEWRSB contract managers, located in five District and seven State offices and overseen by a National office, support and monitor the operation of Job Network members. During the first contract period, contract management focused mainly on checking compliance with obligations, monitoring progress against contracted placement targets, making payments, and building relationships between Job Network members and DEWRSB.

In a change of strategy, the second contract period has seen a broadening of the focus of contract management by DEWRSB, in an attempt to refocus on the

Box 2.1.   **Service changes during the first and second tender periods of Job Network**

During the period of the first JN contracts, two sets of changes were introduced to enhance services for the unemployed and foster growth in the employment services market. Under the first set of changes, implemented in August 1998, the government decided to extend access to Job Matching to include certain unemployed jobseekers not on income support (Annex Table 3.A.1 presents the eligibility criteria for the various measures). Under this change, Job Matching providers became eligible to claim payments for placing this expanded group into jobs. Also in August 1998, the government made grants available to Job Matching providers in each labour market region for use in promoting their services in order to better inform employers and others about Job Network.

A further set of changes was introduced in December 1998. Eligibility for JST was expanded to include carers returning to the labour market after two years or more (regardless of the allowance status of the individual). However, the bulk of the changes were intended to improve the income and cash flow of JN members and to better promote the Job Network in the face of a degree of public confusion about the services available and a certain amount of negative press coverage [DEWRSB (2000d)]. Among other changes influencing incentives for providers, Job Matching outcome payments were increased by $100 for each successful placement with supplements for placements in rural and small-town labour market areas and for providers leasing touch-screen job-search facilities. Administrative changes were made to try and improve the flow of referrals to JN members and speed outcome payments. Also, further marketing grants were made available for each Job Matching site.

For the second Job Network contract period, changes were introduced concerning provider incentives, accountability,[1] service specialisation and points of service delivery, among other issues. A JST outcome payment was introduced in order to improve incentives for providers to strive for placement of participants into employment for at least 13 weeks. DEWRSB also raised interim and final outcome payments in relation to placement of the most disadvantaged clients. Accountability for delivery of IA services was increased through tendering rules that required a DOI from bidders concerning service provision. DEWRSB introduced a requirement for provider-client IA Support Plans (IASP) to be negotiated for clients not placed within a few months of commencing. Finally, IA providers were able to tender to provide specialised services for specific client groups (*e.g.* for the hearing impaired) where they could demonstrate a need. This change recognised that some groups of jobseekers experience particular needs best addressed by organisations with relevant skills and appropriately targeted strategies.[2]

---

1. Concerns about accountability were raised under the Job Network evaluation (stage one), which commented on the need to balance the flexibility granted providers against the need for accountability in their delivery of services [DEWRSB (2000d)].

2. DEWRSB also required providers to develop specific strategies for jobseekers of indigenous and non-English speaking background where those groups represented 5% or 10% respectively in the tendered employment service area.

103

process of service provision, not only on control of outcomes. In addition to incentives provided by the payment structure, the performance of Job Network members is regularly assessed (typically every six months) against key performance indicators (for outcomes, contractual compliance, and quality and equity of service). In the case of Intensive Assistance, contract managers also monitor the provision of the list of services anticipated in the DOI. In many cases, tenderers have specified in their DOI either a maximum caseload per case manager (as low as 40 in some cases and usually below 100) or a minimum frequency of contact between clients and their case managers (*e.g.* at least one contact per month). As DOIs were incorporated into the contract, these commitments represent contractual obligations. In the first tender round, a provider was only required to enter the initial Activity Agreement in respect of a client into the computer system (the commencement fee was conditional upon this). In the second round, the client's IASP must also be supplied and the provider must log every significant contact with a client. This allows DEWRSB contract managers to see whether contact with clients is being maintained.

Although there is now more active management of provider activity, DEWRSB continues to allow wide variation in the forms or level of provision of many services. However, any significant degree of contract management in a competitive environment does raise some delicate issues. For example, a perception that greater assistance or more latitude in relation to requirements is being given to one Job Network member over another, or that commercial information is being divulged to competitors, would be damaging.

The first two tender rounds each involved a huge work load both for the Department and for providers, which tended to divert management attention from regular operations and proved disruptive to business planning of JN members, to jobseekers whose providers did not win business in the new contract round, and to the Centrelink referral process.[72] For this reason, the government has consulted stakeholders on options for future contracting, where JN member companies are not made to tender for their entire business every three years. The currently (summer 2001) favoured model that has emerged from the consultations implies the extension of contracts for JN members who meet a performance benchmark, with remaining business (which could range from 30 to 60% of contract volume) being allocated through a pre-qualification/bidding process involving both existing providers and potential new entrants. It is currently planned to finalise the policy framework for the 3rd contract period by late 2001 and to publish the draft Request for Tender in early 2002 [DEWRSB (2001d)].

6. Code of Conduct and Complaint Procedures

The *Job Network Code of Conduct* forms part of the contract between the Commonwealth Government and Job Network members. Through the Code of

---

Box 2.2. Information technology support for Job Network

Efficient management information systems are essential to the successful operation of Job Network. They fulfil a number of crucial tasks including the management of job vacancy and jobseeker information, performance reporting and as a way for Job Network members to claim payments.

DEWRSB's mainframe computer system – the Integrated Employment System (IES) – supports the flow of information between Job Network members, DEWRSB and Centrelink. Through IES, Job Network members, DEWRSB and Centrelink can store information on jobseekers, employers, job vacancies and Job Network members, as well as the interactions that occur between them. Job Network members use IES to record details of job vacancies, match jobseekers against employer's requirements (and vice versa), record referrals to jobs, and substantiate commencements and outcome payments for Job Network services. Jobseekers are free to choose the Job-Matching provider(s) they prefer and can ask Centrelink to enrol them (*i.e.* to electronically link their personal records stored on IES) with all JN members in their local area (which may represent up to 30 different Job-Matching sites in metropolitan areas), to improve their opportunities of quickly getting a job. The jobseeker's name then appears on the provider's list of enrolled jobseekers.

The IES can be accessed by Job Network members via the Internet, or through a permanent or dial-up connection. Due to the increasingly common use of the Internet, the latter forms of connection will be phased out over the second contract. In addition, there are facilities which allow Job Network members to use their own computer systems to record and transmit information through a secure Internet link to IES.

Australian Job Search (AJS) is the public face of IES; it provides employers with a national vacancy distribution service and jobseekers with access to vacancies lodged by Job Network members, employers or government agencies. Users can access AJS by means of several thousand self-service touchscreen units in Centrelink offices, Job Network provider premises and other public locations, as well as through the Internet. AJS also displays information about the services provided by Job Network members, in order to facilitate client choice among providers.

Conduct, DEWRSB provides a "quality guarantee" to jobseekers and employers, by laying down detailed service standards for JN members and their staff that at times may resemble operational guidelines for PES offices. It also provides a review process which clients can invoke if they are not satisfied with the quality of the services delivered and specifies penalties for non-compliance.

The Code covers a number of items, including:

- The quality of the relationship with the customer: ensuring ethical and fair treatment of customers, organising, for example regular face-to-face contact with disadvantaged jobseekers, and providing them with the right kind of assistance to overcome their barriers to employment.

- The quality of information and assistance: providing accurate information and relevant advice to customers, for example, by ensuring that vacancies accepted are genuine, that they are shared immediately with other JN members by posting them on a nationally-shared vacancy data base, and by undertaking regular matching of jobseekers to available vacancies.

- Service standards: responding promptly to queries, agreeing on the frequency and duration of appointments with jobseekers and keeping to that commitment.

- Privacy requirements: conducting all interviews confidentially, ensuring that all staff receive training about their obligations under privacy law, and collecting only such information from customers that is relevant, necessary and consistent with existing privacy legislation.

JN members are also obliged to establish an internal complaints system and inform jobseekers and employers about complaints procedures. If conflicts cannot be settled through internal procedures, clients have the option of using the Job Network customer Service Line, a freecall service that puts clients in contact with DEWRSB representatives in their State or local area. As the Code of Conduct is administered and monitored by DEWRSB, a complaint may trigger a DEWRSB request to a JN member to address an issue or improve certain practices. The Department may also initiate quality audits of providers at its discretion, and has undertaken over 100 of these since the inception of the network. When there are continuous violations of the Code, penalties effected by DEWRSB may range from temporary suspension of referrals, to a reduction of contracted capacity, up to the termination of contract.

7. Current incentive structures

Extensive anecdotal evidence from the first Job Network contract indicates that certain Job Network members used funds from Intensive Assistance to pay for infrastructure expenses and to cross-subsidise other, in particular, Job-Matching, services, and that the profitability of Intensive Assistance work could be substantial. Anecdotal evidence also indicates that Job Matching has tended to be relatively unprofitable despite the fact that Job Matching fees were set by providers through a competitive tender process.[73] Possible explanations, and their implications, are:

- The lowest tender bids for the Job Matching placement fee may correspond to the costs for providers who indirectly specialise in low-cost client groups or types of vacancy, resulting in a fee level that is below the cost of servicing an average client or vacancy. To counter this, it might, for example, be desirable to pay lower fees for short-term repeat placements.

- Some Job Matching providers hoard vacancies that may be suitable for disadvantaged clients because they have operational links with an IA provider who needs such vacancies. Such hoarding may be a desirable outcome in that it gives disadvantaged clients priority of access to suitable vacancies. However, it results in IA providers being willing to cross-subsidise their own Job Matching services on a permanent basis.[74] This may make Job Matching-only operations structurally unprofitable in a competitive market. Their viability might be improved by formal recognition of hoarding, facilitating the "selling" of suitable vacancies to IA providers.

Another possibility may be to split the Job Matching fee into two parts, one for the provider who first lists a vacancy and another for the provider who places a client into it. This might encourage inter-provider referrals and the advertising of vacancies with contact details for the employer. However, additional tracking and monitoring might be needed to make such arrangements viable.

In the case of Intensive Assistance, there are indications that financial incentives – the fees paid for employment outcomes – in the first contract round were too low to motivate an optimal level of ongoing service to clients after commencement with the provider.[75] Several factors suggest that this is still the case:

- The combined fee for an interim and a final outcome for the least disadvantaged group (representing about two-thirds of IA clients) – $2 700 for Flex 3.1 clients under the first tender, and $3 586[76] for level A clients under the second tender – seems to be below a reasonable estimate of the average positive impact of such a placement on public finances.[77]

- Given that paid outcomes were obtained in the first tender round in respect of about 20% of commencements [DEWRSB (2000d), p. 82] and that the average fee per paid outcome must have been similar to the commencement fee,[78] it can be estimated that about 80% of provider income in the first tender round (about two-thirds in the second round, given that the fee structure has changed and the paid outcome rate has probably increased) came from commencement fees, not outcome fees. Because of this feature, the profitability of IA work is guaranteed, if not too much is spent on ongoing service provision. This probably explains why Intensive Assistance is generally regarded as a profitable activity, and it implies that the employment services market cannot be a competitive one in the sense that some providers leave because they are losing money and new entrants can enter wherever they see a business opportunity.

Where a paid outcome rate of 20% was achieved under Intensive Assistance, a large proportion of the paid outcomes (perhaps the first 15 percentage points[79]) would eventually have occurred even in the absence of any significant service provision. An exceptionally high level of ongoing service provision might be

107

expected to increase the paid outcome rate from 15% to 30%,[80] implying an increase of about 15% (increasing to 25% in the second tender round where outcome fees are larger) in total income. But providing a high level of ongoing services to clients after commencement probably increased costs proportionately more than this.

The considerations above suggest that incentives for service provision could be increased, possibly without increasing the total funds allocated to Intensive Assistance, by having higher outcome fees while at the same time paying only for outcomes achieved beyond a threshold which represents the level that would occur without significant service provision. This threshold can in principle be estimated on the same basis as the adjustments which DEWRSB applies when assessing relative provider performance, *i.e.* as a function of local labour market conditions and the characteristics of jobseeker clients [DEWRSB (2001*c*)], or it could be determined by competition between providers as described in Annex A.

Although good performance, as judged by DEWRSB's star rankings, has been highly correlated with a high rate of outcome payments, there is no evidence that it has been correlated with high levels of provider profitability. Indeed, the good performance of community sector providers in the first contract period could have been due to their principled commitment to providing good service regardless of its profitability.[81] This feature persists despite some tilting of the payment structure towards outcome payments in the second contract round. Current policy is to accept that short-term profitability considerations alone do not motivate optimal behaviour, and to rely on active surveillance of service provision (with administrative sanctions for poor performance and the threat of an eventual complete loss of the contract in a future tender round), in order to ensure that income from commencement fees is spent appropriately and that business goes to the best-performing providers. But this approach has its own problems:

- Monitoring of service provision involves administrative costs, reduces strategic flexibility and partly splits responsibility for the placement strategy that is finally delivered. (Providers have to stick to the strategy which was described in their tender submission, and the strategy itself had to win DEWRSB approval in the tender selection process.)

- Entry to and exit from the market need to be determined by DEWRSB's assessments of provider performance, although the technical basis for such assessments is liable to be uncertain, *e.g.* when there is only one provider with a particular disability specialisation.

- An ideal payment system would involve providers themselves in determining the level of spending on services and placement strategies which maximises social welfare. For example, providers would refer clients to training programmes when they find that the resulting employment outcomes are worth more than the cost of the programme. As it is, spending on employment services and (to some extent) placement strategies is still determined primarily by government rather than market arbitrage between costs and benefits.

Possibly, none of these problems are too serious, particularly if the government supervision of service provision adequately reinforces the financial incentives to achieve employment outcomes, and if its preferred placement strategies, decisions about the overall level of spending and techniques for assessing provider performance and managing entry and exit from the market are by and large correct. In this case, current Intensive Assistance arrangements may work quite well in the longer term. Comparative ratings of performance with "discontinuous" incentives (e.g. potential future loss of the contract, or prizes for the best performers) are often successfully used to motivate salesmen and subcontractors within long-term business relationships [McMillan (1992)].

Nevertheless, there is real risk that one of the possible problems remains quite serious, resulting in a significant shortfall in outcomes as compared to what could be achieved. What are the difficulties in trying to implement something closer to a theoretically optimal model, based on higher fees which are paid only for outcomes that would not have occurred without the service provision?

- Stronger incentives for providers might encourage strategies which generate artificial and unsustained entries to employment.

- Outcomes depend to a considerable extent upon factors such as linking jobseekers benefit eligibility to 'their attendance at case-management interviews and compliance with the terms of an Activity Agreement. Yet policy in these areas remains largely in the hands of government, particularly local Centrelink offices and DEWRSB contract managers (see Chapter 4 for further discussion of these issues). It may be unreasonable to make provider incomes depend heavily on factors which are outside their control.

- With a high level of outcome fees at the margin, while payments are made only for outcomes above a certain threshold level, a provider's profitability would depend strongly on how accurately the threshold is determined.

- In general, if outcome fees are larger, profitability will be more variable, exposing providers to higher levels of risk and in some cases, bankruptcy.

Annex A further discusses possible payment structures which could induce providers to choose an optimal level of spending on service provision, and permit a larger degree of competition with free entry of new providers to the employment services market, while also tackling the issues above.

D. Labour market programmes outside the Job Network

As detailed further in Chapter 5, Australia has a range of labour market programmes, administered by a variety of government agencies, which predate Job Network. Spending on Job Network remains less than the combined spending on three large and relatively longstanding programmes:

- The Aboriginal and Torres Strait Islander Commission (ATSIC) administers Community Development Employment Projects (CDEPs) which enable indigenous communities located in areas of limited employment prospects to exchange unemployment benefits against participation in public utility work and training projects. The CDEP scheme currently involves over 260 indigenous communities and over 30 000 participants. ATSIC is an independent statutory authority whose Board advises the Minister for Aboriginal and Torres Strait Islander affairs and liaises with DEWRSB and DETYA on employment and training matters [ATSIC (2000)].

- The Disability Employment Assistance Program is administered and funded by FaCS and seeks to assist jobseekers with permanent disabilities. Services include pre-vocational assistance, special employment sites for disabled workers, preparation for transiting from special employment to the open labour market, and wage subsidies. They are provided by about 440 non-governmental organisations and the Government's Commonwealth Rehabilitation Service (CRS) which has itself a national network of 160 service outlets. Access to disability employment services is again through Centrelink.

- The New Apprenticeship Program combines traditional apprenticeships with shorter courses and training above the normal apprenticeship-type level. Infrastructural support is provided by the New Apprenticeship Centres, which are managed directly by DETYA. The aim of ensuring school-to-work transition by appropriate skills-training is also pursued by several other targeted programmes in the DETYA portfolio, such as the Job Pathways Program and Job Placement, Employment and Training (JPET).

The current government has also created, roughly at the same time as Job Network, a number of new programmes, although these generally take over parts of the functions of earlier programmes. Some of the main ones are:

- The Community Support Program (CSP) for jobseekers with specific employment barriers, which is delivered by private, community and public sector organisations contracted through a competitive tender overseen by DEWRSB (previously Centrelink). In the second CSP tender, contracts were awarded to 83 organisations operating from 330 sites.

- Literacy and Numeracy Training (LANT), which is supplied by some 65 providers from a variety of backgrounds, including community organisations, private providers and Training and Further Education (TAFE) facilities, who were contracted through a tender process organised by DETYA.

- Work for the Dole projects (WfD), which are run by community sponsor organisations, while Community Work Coordinators, contracted to DEWRSB through a tendering process, provide assistance and liaison.

In addition to Commonwealth government programmes, there are fairly significant employment programmes in some States and Territories. For example, the Western Australian Government has funded community-owned employment services since 1985. In 2000 the government of Victoria announced spending of $100 million over four years to provide 27 000 apprenticeships, traineeships and jobs for the unemployed, through subsidies to local councils, community organisations and the private sector [Hannan (2000)].

In addition, most State and Territory governments provide payroll tax exemptions or rebates for trainees, apprentices and/or disadvantaged jobseekers. Nevertheless, overall expenditure out of State government funds for purposes other than education and training (where States are given prime policy responsibility) appears to be substantially lower than federal government expenditure [DEWRSB (2000*g*)].

E. Human Resources for employment services

Previous OECD labour market or PES reviews have tried to compare the resource intensity of public employment services among OECD Member countries. To calculate total staff involved in the three main PES functions (placement and counselling, benefit payment and referral to labour market programmes) has not been easy for any Member country, but in particular for those where one or the other of these functions is institutionally separate. For example, countries without a fully integrated PES often run separate social security offices where the payment of unemployment allowances takes up only a limited part of office resources among the range of benefit categories dealt with. This makes any calculation of "unemployment benefit staff" a difficult task.

In Australia, Centrelink staff poses the same kind of difficulty, as this service delivery agency combines a range of social security benefits, from pensions to family benefits, compensation for disability, and finally unemployment assistance. Moreover, the outsourcing of the public employment service and dissolution of previous CES offices means that the actual provision of placement and counselling services, as well as referrals to training or other labour market programmes and projects, is now undertaken by over 200 private and community-sector agencies of different firm size, and there is no registration of their staff numbers with any government authorities.

Despite the paucity of hard data, some estimates are possible which might throw some light on the total human resources involved in the provision of employment services in Australia. To start with DEWRSB, its annual report reveals a figure of slightly over 2 000 staff, of which 1 300 are in the national office and 700 work in decentralised area offices [DEWRSB (2000b)]. Within the national office, about 160 persons work for the Job Network Group, who undertake national co-ordination of the Job Network market and contract policy, and liaise with Centrelink and other stakeholders.

Contract Management offices are located in the seven State capitals and five additional regional centres. In these offices, DEWRSB has in place a network of over 200 staff who are responsible for managing the Employment Services Contracts with individual providers and for monitoring their performance. They are the primary point of contact for providers on operational and compliance aspects of service delivery, including payment issues, contract modifications requested by providers, etc. In all, therefore, about 400 persons are involved within the DEWRSB framework in employment services delivery and policy formulation.

Turning next to Centrelink, its staff work out of national headquarters, 15 area support offices, 25 national and regional call centres and over 400 regular Customer Service Centres (to which special family assistance offices, rural and veterans' centres would need to be added) [Centrelink (2000)]. The organisation employs over 20 000 staff (a bit less in full-time equivalents), of which about 12% are in the national office, 20% are in the call centre network and the remainder are in decentralised regional and local offices. Any regular Centrelink office has staff working on initial and follow-up interviews of jobseekers; jobseeker scoring through JSCI; unemployment benefit payment; and referrals to, as well as liaison with, Job network providers. These constitute clear and easily distinguishable employment services functions. Other staff will usually work on parenting payments and other family allowances, on disability support and on retirement pensions.[82] Based on several visits to Centrelink Customer Service Centres, a careful estimate would, nevertheless, put the share of office staff with full-time or part-time employment services-related functions at around 40%, i.e. 8 000 persons nation-wide. About 3 000 of these had changed over from the old CES office network.

This leaves the staff working with JN providers. Although there is no government authority registering staff numbers, one indication of the size of Job Network personnel is given by a recent ABS survey of businesses active in the employment service industry [ABS (2000b)]. The survey puts the combined number of employees in Job Network organisations and private placement offices at 11 300 (without short-term hires under temporary work agency contracts). Although it does not distinguish the number of employees at the two types of agencies, it may be possible to estimate their number by using other indicators from the survey. Considering that 28% of the income of the businesses surveyed is derived from employers, and that private placement agencies account for 36% of all permanent placements, it can be hypothesised that about two-thirds of employees (*i.e.* about 7 500 persons) are working for JN providers, and the remainder for private placement agencies. This would give a plausible average of three to four staff per site (considering that there are about 2 000 JN provider sites all over Australia).

These assumptions and adjustments can help determine the total number of staff working for employment services in Australia, which could be used for international comparison. Adding up the personnel at DEWRSB, Centrelink and JN providers, as estimated above, would result in a figure on the order of 16 000 staff.[83] Thus, Australia seems well resourced in international comparison, when relating staff numbers to the usual workload indicators. For example, there is one staff member in the employment services area per 1 200 Australians. Whether one regards the total labour force or wage and salary earners as the potential clientele of employment services, Australia seems to have a better staff/client ratio than most countries previously surveyed by the OECD [OECD (1996, 1998f, 1999e, 2000h)].

Among the most straightforward workload measures are the number of unemployed jobseekers registered with employment offices and the inflow of notified vacancies. Two figures are available for registered unemployment in Australia: a survey-based figure showing the proportion of self-declared unemployed who said that they registered with Centrelink (382 000 persons on 1 July 1999); and the number of all beneficiaries of unemployment benefit paid out by Centrelink, which includes many persons – such as part-time workers – who are not unemployed by the survey definition (682 000 on 2 May 2000) [ABS (1999a); DEWRSB (2000h)]. Again, whichever figure is being used, Australia has a better staff/client ratio than most other OECD countries. Finally, over 40 vacancies per employment services staff member were registered in 2000 by JN providers, a comparable figure to Germany, Sweden and the United Kingdom in the mid-1990s. This corresponds to an annual inflow of almost 100 vacancies per JN staff member, and an inflow of about 340 vacancies per Job Network site.

113

Chapter 3

The Job Network System and Placement Issues

A. Introduction

This chapter aims to provide a detailed overview of the functioning of the JN system with respect to placements into employment (aspects related to institutional set-up, benefit management and other labour market programmes targeting special needs are discussed in Chapters 2, 4 and 5, respectively). The presentation begins with a description of the main services, system components and jobseeker client flows. It then presents a brief overview of information flows, complaints procedures and vacancy acquisition. The available evidence on the actual accessing of services by clients is then considered. The chapter subsequently reviews monitored outcomes for clients, as well as the performance of the system as indicated by standard OECD market share indicators. It concludes by highlighting areas of concern for the future performance of the system.

B. Job Network services

Table 3.A.1 (annexed to this chapter) highlights the key features of each of the five main JN services. Job Matching, Job Search Training (JST) and Intensive Assistance (IA) account for the bulk of inflows of the unemployed into JN measures. The other two JN services include the New Enterprise Incentive Scheme (NEIS) and Project Contracting.[84] For each of these services, DEWRSB has specified the basic types of content that contracted JN members must provide to clients, but it has left providers flexibility in deciding how to achieve outcomes for these services as well as what additional services to offer in response to individual client needs. The requirements and incentives for providers have been adjusted several times since Job Network was introduced (as discussed in Chapter 2). Administratively, DEWRSB only tracks contractually-required services and the associated placements, commencements, client contacts, paid outcomes and client feedback [DEWRSB (2000d)].[85] In order to collect more detailed information on outcomes, service delivery and client satisfaction, it depends on other sources

---

such as the Post Program Monitoring Survey and the Service Quality Monitoring Program surveys.

1. Job Matching

Job Matching essentially consists of acquiring listings of vacancies from employers, facilitating jobseekers' access to vacancy information and assisting suitable candidates to apply for jobs. In most cases, JN members provide employers with related services such as applicant pre-screening. With respect to jobseekers, much of the emphasis in Job Matching goes to the provision of self-service facilities and access to staff for clients seeking advice concerning issues such as résumé preparation. Many providers report assisting some clients with preparing for the interview process through provision of supplementary information about the job vacancy as well as clothing, transportation allowances, business cards or other small items as needed.

A DEWRSB jobseeker satisfaction survey conducted in 1999 provides some additional information on the perceived quality of services delivered under Job Matching [DEWRSB (2000d)].[86] Overall, 79% of the respondents who enrolled with a Job Matching provider were satisfied with the services.[87] Over 90% of those who reported getting paid work considered that the provider played an important role in assisting them to get a job. Among the minority of clients who were dissatisfied, the main reasons given included a lack of assistance in finding employment, a lack of contact and poor staff service.

2. Job Search Training

JST offers services to jobseekers who have no major barriers to employment but who are in need of more substantial placement assistance than is available under Job Matching. In addition to basic labour exchange services, clients are interviewed and assessed in a short process leading to the negotiation of a Job Search Skills Plan. This plan lays out services to be provided and a timetable for their delivery over 15 full working days. These services might include training, supervision, role playing and practical job-search activities that help clients become motivated to look for work and learn how to apply for a job, interview and build employment-related networks.[88]

The DEWRSB jobseeker satisfaction survey found that about 86% of the respondents were satisfied with the services from their JST provider and 76% said they felt their participation had improved their job prospects [DEWRSB (2000d)]. Over 90% said their provider had discussed with them the skills they needed to develop, while a similar percentage said they had been given access to office equipment and material they required for their job search. Other services cited as being received by more than 70% of respondents included help with general job-search skills, preparing for interviews, writing job applications and preparing resumes. According to the stage two of the JN evaluation, both top- and bottom-performing JST providers were fairly consistent in offering the basic types of services [DEWRSB (2001*b*)]. However, there were substantial gaps between these two groups of providers in terms of assistance with job search, referrals to vacancies, interview preparation and overall quality of services. For example, over half of the participants served by the top-performing providers were either sent to a job interview or spoke with an employer about a job, whereas only one-fifth of those served by the bottom-performing providers had such contacts (see Chapter 5).

3. Intensive Assistance

IA offers the most substantial personalised service for jobseekers facing significant barriers to employment. Under the second JN request for tender process, DEWRSB imposed a basic framework for the delivery of this service. As noted in Chapter 2, providers were required to include in their tenders a Declaration of Intent that laid out their strategies and service options for each client group. JN members retained substantial freedom in designating the content of their strategies. In addition to basic Job Matching services, their declarations provided for such options as job-search assistance (including subsidies for the costs of applying for jobs), counselling, training, wage subsidies, paid or unpaid work experience, support for workplace modifications and post-placement support, among many others. (Programme services under Job Network are discussed in more detail in Chapter 5.)

Within a few weeks after Centrelink sends a client an initial referral notification letter, DEWRSB requires the provider to interview the client and negotiate a revised draft Preparing for Work Agreement (which DEWRSB must approve). The terms of these activity agreements must be consistent with the requirements of the Social Security Act of 1991 and lay out a client's commitments for actions to improve his or her job prospects and, hopefully, gain employment.[89] If a client has not achieved a placement within 13 weeks, the IA provider is required to negotiate an IA Support Plan with the client. This plan builds on the Preparing for Work Agreement and takes into account the approach and service options laid out in the provider's Declaration of Intent. It describes in more detail a framework for overcoming an individual's employment barriers including concrete support to be offered by the provider (such as payment for an accredited training course). While not a legally binding document, DEWRSB follows the providers' delivery of activities specified in the IA Support Plans as part of its contract monitoring activities.

Referrals to IA at Level A target those clients with significant labour market disadvantage and provide for an initial eligibility of up to 12 months of assistance.

Referrals at Level B target the most disadvantaged (with some exclusions, discussed below) and provide for an initial eligibility of up to 15 months of assistance. These periods may be extended by mutual agreement of the provider and the client, up to a total of 18 and 21 months, respectively, for Level A and Level B. DEWRSB does not provide additional up-front funding to providers for such extensions, but providers nevertheless have an incentive to seek extensions if it appears that they can place the client and obtain an outcome payment. During participation in IA, clients are exempted from Mutual Obligation and Centrelink job-search reporting requirements. Generally, if the clients have not found placement by the end of their assistance periods, they must exit IA for at least six months. Following exit, those jobseekers in receipt of activity-tested income support must again fulfil the requirements of Mutual Obligation. This may involve, for example, participation in a Work for the Dole project.

The 1999 DEWRSB jobseeker satisfaction survey again provides some insights into the services received [DEWRSB (2000d)]. Overall, the survey found that 83% of the IA respondents were satisfied that their providers had done everything they could to help them find work. The most common form of IA assistance reported was simply contact and personal support. Some three-quarters of respondents who had participated in IA said they had visited their providers on quite a few or several occasions and a comparable number said their provider had helped them to stay motivated. The most common frequency of contact was fortnightly or better. Nearly 9 in 10 respondents said that their IA provider was always available when they needed them. While some IA participants quickly found work, it is nevertheless notable that given the intended intensity of assistance, nearly one-quarter of those surveyed noted that they had visited their provider "only once or twice". Beyond basic contact and support, some 58% reported receiving one or more types of training. Most often this was training in job-search skills (43%), but also included job-specific skills training in areas such as computer skills (18%), unpaid work experience (4%), general math or reading courses (4%), or English-language training (4%).

Only about 37% of the respondents reported that they had been sent to a job interview or to speak to an employer about a job. As noted in the Job Network evaluation, stage one, "Providers appear reluctant to refer jobseekers who they believe are not job-ready to fill vacancies." Yet, the evaluation also reported that interviews with providers revealed that "very few [...] were offering services which would address underlying barriers to employment such as language classes, counselling or assistance with vocational training."

The Job Network evaluation, stage two, indicated greater variation in the types of basic services offered between the top- and bottom-performing IA providers than was the case with JST providers [DEWRSB (2001b)]. For example, more clients reported receiving training through the low-performing providers than through the best IA providers, but with the best providers they were more likely to find that the training improved their chances of getting a job. As with JST, clients of the top-performing providers were more likely to be sent to a job interview or to speak with an employer about a job (more than one-third) than clients of the bottom-performing providers (about one-fifth).

4. NEIS *and* Project *Contracting*

The two remaining JN measures are the NEIS and Project Contracting. As shown in Table 3.A.1, the inflows into these measures are much smaller than for the other measures. Under NEIS, JN providers assist interested registered unemployed in developing their self-employment options through screening of candidates, training, mentoring and on-going support. Project Contracting is essentially a job-matching programme for short-term, seasonal harvest jobs. It differs from the main Job Matching measure in that it is open to all jobseekers legally entitled to work in Australia. Intake into the programme is via the contracted JN providers and does not require registration through Centrelink. The Project Contracting providers market their services and placement opportunities through a variety of channels including DEWRSB's Australian Job Search (AJS) Internet site.[90]

5. Services *for employers*

DEWRSB's 1999 employer survey found that while 8 in 10 respondents had heard of Job Network, over one-half did not understand its working very well [DEWRSB (2000e)].[91] Many employers reported that they were content with their current recruitment methods or already had sufficient numbers of candidates such that they did not need to recruit actively. According to the survey, the most popular recruitment methods were advertising in newspaper, television or radio and use of head-hunting, recommendations and word of mouth (Table 3.1).

At the same time, about 38% of employers reported using Job Network to list at least one vacancy during the previous 12 months.[92] Among those who had used Job Network, 84% were satisfied with the services provided. Employers cited a variety of reasons for using JN members including: "previous experience with a Job Network member" (30%), "convenient location of the Job Network member" (18%), and "contacted by the Job Network member" (13%). JN members offer a range of services to employers in addition to the basic job-matching process. Among employers who responded to the DEWRSB survey and who used the Job Network, the additional services most often reported included: screening applicants (79%); setting up interviews (59%); reference checking (42%); interviewing applicants (37%); and advising unsuccessful applicants (30%).

Table 3.1.   **Method of recruitment used in previous 12 months**[a]
Percentages

	June 1999
Advertising in newspaper, television, radio	52
Head hunting/recommendations/word of mouth	50
Job Network[b]	38
Resumes sent in/cold callers	32
Employment agency	27
Employed family/friend/personal contact	26
Internal recruitment	19
Labour hire company	6
Advertising on the Internet	3

a)   Data are from a DEWRSB-contracted survey conducted by the Wallis Consulting Group, involving 6 500 interviews with employers who had recruited in the previous 12 months.
b)   This refers to employers who lodged *at least* one vacancy on the National Vacancy Database during the previous 12 months.
Source: DEWRSB, *Job Network evaluation, Key Findings from the 1999 Employer Survey,* Canberra, July 2000.

The DEWRSB survey found that employers who used Job Network tended to report that it was easy to contact, acted quickly, took account of business needs and provided high-quality service and assistance. About two-thirds or more of the employer-clients gave favourable responses to questions on the various aspects of referral including applicant suitability, motivation, candidate understanding of the job and follow-up. Most were also pleased with the speed of service in filling vacancies: nearly two-thirds of employers who had a vacancy filled via a JN member said their most recent JN vacancy had taken two weeks or less to fill. Where employers were dissatisfied, it was often in cases where vacancies had taken relatively long periods to fill (three weeks or more). Other reasons for dissatisfaction were cases where the applicants were of poor quality or not interested or did not even turn up (45%), the follow-up was poor or contact was lost (23%) or there were no referrals or a vacancy was not filled (19%). Nevertheless, among employers who had used both CES and JN services, roughly 7 out of 10 evaluated Job Network as the same or better in terms of quality of service, understanding of commercial reality, response time, responsiveness to individual business needs, quality of referrals and availability.

C.   System components and client flows

Under the Business Partnership Arrangement with DEWRSB, Centrelink registers jobseekers and assesses their eligibility for JN services and certain other employment-related services. Centrelink streams or refers eligible clients for services according to criteria laid out by DEWRSB (or in the case of the disabled, laid out by DEWRSB and FaCS). In order to be eligible for JST, IA and most Job Matching services, jobseekers must be registered with Centrelink and either: 1) in receipt of a Newstart or Youth Allowance (or certain other types of government-paid income support); 2) a youth aged 15 to 20 years and not in full-time education or training; or 3) an Aboriginal or Torres Strait Islander participating in CDEP. For clients benefiting from these JN services, Centrelink monitors their progress to ensure compliance with jobseeker obligations.

Some DEWRSB-supported employment services are available to all jobseekers, but the range of these services is limited. All jobseekers may use the self-service job search facilities located in Centrelink offices. They may access labour market information and the limited number of open vacancies listed in the National Vacancy Database through the AJS Internet site or using touch screen kiosks placed in over 2 400 locations across the country including Centrelink offices, JN member facilities and other sites. All jobseekers legally entitled to work in Australia may seek a short-term seasonal harvest job through the JN Project Contracting measure. They can also approach a Job Matching provider for referral to a semi-open vacancy (*i.e.* where employer contact details are not publicly displayed); however, only JN-eligible clients attract JN payments for the providers.

Chart 3.1 highlights the main components of the JN system and the pathways to employment for unemployed jobseekers who register with Centrelink. Table 3.A.1 describes the detailed client eligibility requirements and referral procedures. The JN services accessed via Centrelink include Job Matching, JST, IA and NEIS. The remaining service, Project Contracting, is operated independently by JN members, but clients can obtain information on this service through Centrelink and AJS.

Potential JN clients enter a Centrelink office and learn of their options at a reception counter. The counter personnel stream the clients according to the "life event" that has brought them to Centrelink. The unemployed are generally referred to a Centrelink counsellor for an interview and registration for access to employment services. During this interview, primary emphasis is given to early placement into employment rather than income-support issues. However, those who are potentially eligible for an allowance are assisted with filing a claim and informed of their responsibility to sign a Preparing for Work Agreement within seven days and link with a JN provider for Job Matching. Individuals in special categories, such as indigenous Australians, may be streamed toward targeted measures. Clients expressing an interest in self-employment are informed of the NEIS and encouraged to contact an NEIS provider for screening. However, most jobseekers proceed for classification of their level of disadvantage via a detailed interview aided by the computer-based JSCI and supplementary classification criteria. This procedure determines the eligibility of jobseekers for JST and IA.

JN-eligible clients are then issued a Job-Seeker Identity Number and a JN card and required to participate in an information seminar where they will learn about the operation of Job Network including the opportunity to choose a service provider.

Chart 3.1. **Job Network: flows of unemployed jobseekers**[a, b]

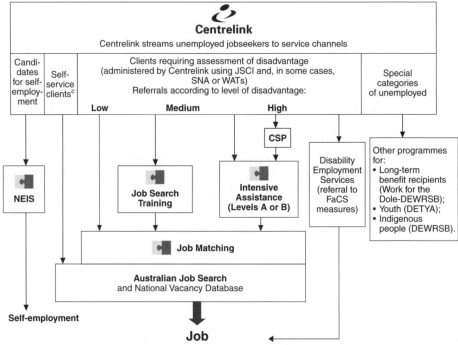

Unemployed jobseekers

a) Job Network providers are indicated with the symbol: ■
b) In addition to the elements shown in the chart, DEWRSB also underwrites a Job Network service known as Project Contracting. Through this service, a limited number of Job Network providers are contracted to recruit seasonal workers for harvest jobs. Providers market these short-term positions *via* a number of channels such as Australian Job Search (AJS) and the media.
c) All jobseekers, even unregistered unemployed or individuals currently in employment, can access the self-service job-search facilities of Centrelink, AJS and certain other services.
Source: DEWRSB (2000*g*).

D. Referrals of clients for service

1. Classification mechanisms and referral process

The JSCI is a profiling mechanism intended to provide an objective measure of a jobseeker's relative labour market disadvantage (defined as the risk of becoming or remaining long-term unemployed).[93] Centrelink applies it at the time of the jobseeker's initial registration and again at 12-month intervals as well as at the time a jobseeker finishes an approved activity. The JSCI was developed by DEETYA (and subsequently DEWRSB) drawing on previous experience under Working Nation with the Jobseeker Screening Instrument and Client Classification Level Questionnaire, but also taking into account substantial new inputs from: a jobseeker survey covering about 60 000 individuals that examined the association of various personal characteristics with long-term unemployment; a Classification Working Group consisting of case managers and experts from government and various non-government service providers; and other key stakeholders [DEETYA (1998a)]. It began operating in Centrelink in February 1998.

The JSCI calculates a score for each individual by summing points assigned for each of 18 risk factors based on the individual's characteristics.[94] Higher scores indicate greater probable difficulty in placement. The requisite information is collected largely through self-disclosure by clients in the course of Centrelink interviews and from forms and documents that clients submit [DEWRSB (1999c,f)]. This substantial dependence on self-disclosure means that Centrelink interviews play a critical role in the operation of the JSCI; a failure to encourage full disclosure may result in an inaccurate JSCI score and an inappropriate referral.[95]

As information is collected from the jobseeker it is entered into DEWRSB's Integrated Employment System (IES) database. Scores range from 0 (no apparent disadvantage) to 96 points (severe disadvantage).[96] JSCI scores, thus, provide an indication of the relative labour market disadvantage experienced by each jobseeker. They do not, however, provide an individual assessment of specific jobseeker needs, which instead is considered by DEWRSB to be the responsibility of the JN members. Clients are streamed or referred into appropriate labour market measures based on their JSCI scores, the availability of places and, where necessary, the results of supplementary procedures. The level of JN support made available to an individual depends on his or her relative level of need as assessed by the JSCI score.

As noted in Table 3.A.1, all JN-eligible clients can access Job Matching and they are offered the opportunity to enrol directly with a provider of their choice. Clients who have JSCI scores ranging from 0 to 23 points and who have been registered as unemployed for three months are generally eligible for JST, but must be referred to a provider by Centrelink.[97] Centrelink generally refers clients to

123

providers of their choice, subject to availability of places. Clients scoring 24 points or more and not participating in other labour market measures or FaCS specialist services are generally eligible for IA. Those with a significant level of labour market disadvantage (*i.e.* scoring in the band from 24 to 32 points) are eligible for IA at Level A. Those with a very significant level of labour market disadvantage (*i.e.* a JSCI score of 33 or more points) are generally eligible for more extensive IA support at Level B.[98] DEWRSB budgets 75% of IA places at Level A and 25% at Level B. It is notable that status as a long-term unemployed individual is not sufficient in and of itself to render the client eligible for IA (however, long duration of unemployment can add up to 15 points to an individual's score).

For some clients, the JSCI classification process is supplemented with a secondary process permitting inclusion of additional information or the results from two specially-designed instruments that are available for this purpose, the Special Needs Assessment (SNA) and secondary classification. A SNA may be triggered by a client recording three or more of eight specified factors that are part of the JSCI interview.[99] Secondary classification may be triggered by a client's particular responses to questions or other self-disclosure of special needs during the initial classification (*e.g.* concerning disabilities) or by behavioural triggers (*e.g.* aggressiveness). For the purposes of JSCI, a client can receive up to eight points through the secondary classification process. Centrelink uses SNAs and secondary classification to determine whether it is appropriate to refer a client to IA or whether the client may be better served through other measures.

Clients with particular barriers to employment that would greatly limit their ability to benefit from IA are considered for referral to special services outside of Job Network. These barriers, such as lack of stable accommodation, may become evident immediately due to self-disclosure by the client during the course of registration or JSCI assessment by Centrelink. Where necessary, clients are referred for a SNA with a professional (such as an occupational psychologist) to assist in identification of barriers such as psychological problems or substance abuse. One of the main referral destinations for clients experiencing substantial or multiple barriers to employment is the Community Support Program (CSP, discussed in more detail in Chapter 5). CSP is a DEWRSB-funded programme underwriting assistance through local organisations with a goal of helping individuals address such barriers, which, in turn, may enable them to subsequently benefit from participation in IA.

A second group generally streamed out of Job Network by Centrelink consists of the medium-to-severely disabled. Where a disability may constitute a substantial barrier to employment, Centrelink staff may request a secondary classification of the client by a Centrelink disability officer (or disability and carer team member) using the Work Ability Tables (WAT) instrument which takes into account nine aspects of the ability to work.[100] The request for such an assessment is made by the staff member based on guidelines that take into account certain triggers such as observing an apparently severe disability or receiving client-provided documentation of a disability. A low level of disability according to the WAT instrument generally results in streaming to a Job Network measure. A more severe level of disability, as evidenced by a WAT score above a threshold agreed by DEWRSB and FaCS, generally results in the client being streamed to the Disability Employment Services funded by FaCS.[101] In special cases, at the joint request of a client and a JN member, Centrelink may permit such a disabled client to participate in IA.

All clients who are eligible for IA may choose among generalist providers or, where appropriate, specialist providers who tailor their services to the needs of special groups such as the hearing impaired. As with JST, Centrelink seeks to refer clients to providers of their choice, subject to the availability of places. All Job Network clients who are in receipt of activity-tested income support and who fail to select a provider within a prescribed period are automatically referred to one. However, such automatic referrals are not made to specialist IA places. The actual referral to JST or IA has been facilitated by the introduction of an accelerated referral process in 1999 [ANAO (2000)]. Under this procedure, clients eligible for JST and IA are notified via letters generated through IES to register their provider preferences with Centrelink. The client can contact a Centrelink call centre to do this. Moreover, the IES system uses a "virtual waiting room" to help smooth client flows, sending out such letters only as availability of clients and capacity in a given area permit.

Under certain circumstances, a jobseeker or a JN member (with the jobseeker's permission) can request a review of a JSCI classification assigned by Centrelink. Such requests will only be considered by Centrelink in cases where the classification was based on information that was incorrect at the time the jobseeker was referred to the JN member. Circumstances that change after the time of referral are not considered. These reviews are conducted by Centrelink without cost to the client or the JN member. Similarly, a review of a WAT score can be requested. Centrelink will not review SNA results, although jobseekers are permitted to provide new information at a later time, which may lead the SNA personnel to subsequently revise the results. Also, if a JN member considers an IA client to have special needs not identified by Centrelink during the referral process, then that provider may purchase a SNA from Centrelink at a cost of $532. This fee discourages frivolous applications made with an aim of exiting difficult clients.

2. JSCI *performance*

Between August 1998 and June 1999, DEWRSB conducted a post-implementation review of the JSCI in consultation with major stakeholders such as other Commonwealth departments, Centrelink, NESA and JN members. The summary findings were released by DEWRSB in December 1999 [DEWRSB (2000i)]. In addition to feedback from stakeholders, the review provided a statistical assessment of the pool of IA candidates as screened by the JSCI. Overall, the review interpreted the results favourably, stressing that the JSCI was generally successful in identifying the relative disadvantage of jobseekers and in classifying sufficient numbers of jobseekers for IA placement.[102] At the same time, it pointed to problems of misclassification in some cases.

The review found a "significant minority of cases" where there was an incorrect classification of individuals due to incorrect or inadequate information collected during the clients' assessment process.[103] JN members sometimes point out that the JSCI is problematic in this regard, because of its dependence on self-disclosure by clients. Some observers note that the intake procedures at Centrelink are part of a routine operation that may not encourage client openness and disclosure. For example, time pressures may limit the ability of Centrelink staff to draw out clients on issues such as problems of literacy or numeracy. Some clients will say "I've got no barriers", even in cases where serious disadvantage is present. In cases of misclassification, it falls on either the jobseeker or JN member to demonstrate the basis for a reclassification. JN members sometimes remark that while the number of cases of misclassification is fairly small, they require substantial amounts of time to rectify. Moreover, the situation of JN members is complicated because they do not have access to most JSCI screens and cannot directly verify the JSCI information (due partly to privacy considerations with respect to the clients).

Table 3.2 presents the IA selection rates for various groups drawing on information from the post-implementation review. During the period from May to August 1998, the JSCI classified as eligible for IA most very long-term unemployed jobseekers (*i.e.* those unemployed 24 months or longer), but less than one-half of the individuals experiencing long-term unemployment with a duration between 12 and 23 months.[104] Among the special population groups for which data were available, those with IA selection rates of 75% or more included indigenous Australians, individuals with low educational attainment, homeless persons and ex-offenders. The same four groups experienced the highest IA selection rates for early intervention in cases where the individuals' unemployment spells had not yet reached 12 months. Unfortunately, the summary findings did not assess what proportion of those *not selected* for IA eventually became long-term unemployed.

An estimate published by ACOSS suggests that less than 50% of individuals who were, or became, long-term unemployed during the period from June 1998 to September 1999 obtained access to IA [ACOSS (2000b)]. However, the basis for this estimate is not clear.[105] Moreover, ACOSS notes that the proportion of those gaining access to IA appears to have increased in subsequent years as the levels

Table 3.2. Job Seeker Classification Instrument, selection rates for Intensive Assistance, various groups of jobseekers, May to August 1998

Duration of unemployment at time of screening	Percentage selected as candidates for IA	Special groups, all individuals	Percentage selected as candidates for IA	Special groups, individuals unemployed *less than* 12 months	Percentage selected as candidates for IA
Unemployed for 60 months or more	91	Indigenous Australians	92	Indigenous Australians	80
Unemployed for 24 to 59 months	75	Low educational attainment (primary school level or below)	83	Low educational attainment (primary school level or below)	73
Unemployed for 12 to 23 months	47	Homeless	76	Homeless	68
Unemployed less than 12 months	22	Ex-offenders	75	Ex-offenders	61
Memorandum item Long-term unemployed	66	Population aged 45 years or more	64	Non-English speaking background	45
		Non-English speaking background	60	Population aged 45 years or more	43
		People with a disability	57	People with a disability	35
		Sole parents	46	Sole parents	33

Source: DEWRSB, *Performance of the Job Seeker Classification Instrument*, Internet posting (found at http://www.jobnetwork. gov.au/general/services/jsci.htm, on 20 December 2000).

of long-term unemployed fell. (DEWRSB data indicate that currently about four out of five IA participants have been unemployed 12 months or more.) Also, an individual's ultimate failure to obtain access to IA may be due to a variety of factors besides the JSCI score (*e.g.* participation in an alternative measure such as CSP).

Recently, a series of revisions have been implemented with the intention to refine the JSCI instrument and its use. These have included increasing the weights given to the personal factors of clients (and permitting occupational psychologists to override JSCI classification outcomes in exceptional cases), broadening the definition of homelessness (to include those in "accommodation crises"), revising the geographic location factor to more accurately reflect local labour market conditions and expanding the triggers for secondary classification (*e.g.* to include all jobseekers who disclose an intellectual disability). Moreover, following the JSCI review, a reduction in the number of IA categories (from 3 to 2) has apparently helped to reduce the number of misclassifications among candidates referred to IA.

There remain concerns among some JN members that the JSCI score bands for referrals are not sufficiently broad. This arises, for example, among providers that do not receive the contracted capacity of IA referrals from Centrelink and so are

127

left with unfilled IA places at a time when many long-term unemployed are not scored as eligible under the JSCI assessment. Further concerns in this regard are raised by IA providers that are capable of delivering services to the disabled. Some of these IA providers believe that the use of WAT is at the discretion of the Centrelink counsellor. While a secondary classification using WAT may aid the IA provider and client by increasing the level of IA for which the client is eligible, a high WAT score may result in ineligibility for IA and referral to FaCS services. For example, if the client is deaf, then the WAT score will be over the threshold for referral to FaCS. However, some specialist IA providers consider that it would be possible for them to place such an individual into regular employment.

3. Client choice of provider and "exits" from the measures

JN clients can enrol with more than one Job Matching provider, but are only referred to one JST or IA provider. Once commenced with a JST or IA provider, clients count against that provider's contracted client capacity. JST and IA clients remain part of the providers' caseloads until they exit via either an employment, education or training "outcome", via the expiration of their period of service eligibility, or via another "non-payable outcome" (i.e. an exit for which the JN member does not receive a fee).

Given the ceiling on providers' contracted capacity, those who are unable to place a client and obtain an outcome payment have an incentive to "exit" that client (i.e. refer the client back to Centrelink). This enables the provider to acquire a new client with a better potential to successfully attract an outcome payment from DEWRSB. Non-payable outcomes may be initiated by the provider or the client, but depend on Centrelink's agreement. Such non-payable outcomes may occur where a client "breaches" the terms of his or her Preparing for Work Agreement, where the client is working more than 15 hours per week at the time of referral, where a certified medical condition prevents the client from active job search, where a client moves out of the JN member's service area, or where an individual 50 years of age or older takes on a volunteer position and opts to exit IA. (The role of Job Network in job-search monitoring and application of the activity test for allowances is discussed in Chapter 4.)

The issue of *choice of provider* is particularly important for IA clients, where the selection can result in a relatively long commitment. Once the referral is complete and the provider has received an up-front payment, it is difficult for the client to change providers. However, the DEWRSB jobseeker satisfaction survey in 1999 found that only 56% of respondents had made a choice on the basis of provider attributes (e.g. such as convenience of location, reputation or a recommendation) [DEWRSB (2000d)]. A further 11% of respondents had made a choice on the basis of other reasons. About 28% did not choose a provider. As noted in the JN evaluation (stage one), some jobseekers found the process of choosing difficult because of the limited information available. As the system was new in the period covered by the evaluation, some providers had not yet established their reputations or developed an effective approach to marketing. In some remote areas, there was not a choice of provider. In other cases, capacity constraints limited the alternatives (i.e. the preferred provider may have already been at capacity). Moreover, even where clients sought information from providers, the lack of concrete, comparative information about provider performance may have handicapped their decision making.

DEWRSB released an initial report with comparative information on providers operating under the first round of contracts that reflected results for the period from 1 May 1998 through 31 October 1999. Drawing on information from the IES, this comparison used a star rating system (ranging from 1 star for poor performers to 5 stars for the best performers) to characterise each provider by labour market region and type of service.[106] While these results were made available on the JN Internet site, they were not widely publicised or circulated to clients as an aid in making their IA provider choice. This is partly because of concerns that the list became dated: the provider mix changed with the start of the second JN contract period and the performance of some providers may have changed over time. An updated performance report was released in March 2001 with ratings based on data for the period from 28 February 2000 through 31 January 2001 [DEWRSB (2001c)].[107]

E. Job Network information flows and complaints procedures

DEWRSB has organised Job Network such that a substantial share of the stakeholder interaction can be conducted electronically. As indicated above, much of providers' information exchange with DEWRSB and Centrelink occurs via the IES. Administrative sections of this system have in the past been accessed directly by providers via DEWRSB mainframe computers, but this is being shifted increasingly to the Internet which is also used for e-mail correspondence. Employers and jobseekers can find DEWRSB programme, labour market and labour exchange information via the Internet sites for DEWRSB, Job Network and AJS.[108] These can be accessed using any personal computer or the AJS touch-screen units. The AJS site is the public point of access to the IES. In addition, Centrelink and FaCS have their own Internet sites that provide clients with detailed information on options and points of contact.[109]

DEWRSB supplies all JN members with current administrative information (e.g. on payments) and Job Matching providers with limited information concerning jobseekers and vacancies.[110] (Since most vacancies are listed in a semi-open fashion, one Job Matching provider would not learn the employer details from another provider's semi-open vacancy listing.) For JST and IA providers, Centrelink delivers electronic notification of referrals and limited information on client details, education and employment history. With an IA client's consent, the provider may also be informed of more sensitive personal information, but this is not common.

JN members, on the other hand, must provide DEWRSB with the draft activity agreements for each client and administrative information such as that relating to jobseeker contacts and JN member requests to DEWRSB for payment. JN members must also inform Centrelink of information related to possible breaches of the clients' activity agreements and changes in clients' circumstances that may affect their income support payments. Together, these contractual reporting requirements pose a burden on JN members. The DEWRSB tender documentation estimated that communication times alone would amount to two hours per successful Job Matching outcome (including vacancy registration), 20 minutes per JST commencement and roughly ten minutes per month for each IA client. Consequently, JN members were strongly encouraged to cost these communication times and include them in their bid prices.

In cases where either jobseekers or employers have concerns about the service they receive from a JN member, they have recourse to a three-step complaint process that provides supplementary channels for information to flow from the clients back to the providers.[111] First, each JN member is required to have an internal complaints procedure that is notified to clients at the time of initial contact. Second, DEWRSB operates a toll-free Job Network Customer Service Line that can be accessed via telephone. The line is staffed by experts who can provide information and advice or who can investigate complaints. Third, other government authorities such as the Human Rights and Equal Opportunity Commission, the Privacy Commissioner and the Australian Competition and Consumer Commission can address complaints of legal violations. In addition, the Commonwealth Ombudsman, while not able to investigate the actions of contracted agencies, can review actions and decisions taken by DEWRSB to resolve a complaint.

F. AJS and vacancy registration

The JN rules for paid employment outcomes require that the job vacancies be first posted in the National Vacancy Database (except in the case of self-employment placements). Acquisition of *open* vacancies for the National Vacancy Database (*i.e.* those displaying employer contact details) depends largely on listings entered directly by employers via the AJS Internet site. Any employer can log on to the site and post a vacancy. As of late 2000, roughly 7% of all vacancy listings in the database were lodged directly by employers. However, DEWRSB has not sought to market this service aggressively to employers [DEWRSB (2000*g*)]. Employers can also list vacancies via a toll-free employer hotline operated by DEWRSB. In the year ending June 2000, a monthly average of

48 150 vacancies were accessible via AJS. In July of that year, the AJS Internet site had a daily average of 1.4 million hits, with 625 000 pages accessed and 170 000 jobs viewed. The AJS touch screen kiosks receive an even greater number of daily visits, with some 1.8 million pages accessed and up to 400 000 jobs viewed.

Most vacancies listed in the National Vacancy Database are acquired from employers by JN members.[112] These members tend to post the listings for display on AJS in a *semi-open* fashion.[113] Members have every incentive to post such semi-open vacancies because Job Matching fees are awarded to the organisation that handles the placement for the jobseeker (not the organisation that acquires the vacancy). By posting semi-open vacancies, a JN member can prod an interested jobseeker to contact it in order to obtain employers' contact information; if an eligible placement results, the JN member can then log a claim for a Job Matching fee. The use of semi-open vacancies also appeals to some employers who benefit from free screening services available through JN members or who prefer to work with a single Job Matching provider.

In the case of semi-open vacancies, it is not possible for the system to control against multiple listings made by employers through various JN members. Multiple listings can lead to outdated or invalid vacancy listings, for example, in cases where one JN member makes a placement that the other is not aware of or where an employer changes the listing with some, but not all, of the JN members who have posted the vacancy. While the extent of this phenomenon is not known, there is some evidence of a problem with outdated or invalid vacancy listings. DEWRSB job satisfaction surveys in 1999 found 18.5% of jobseekers reported that jobs listed in the National Vacancy Database were no longer available when they contracted employers or JN members about them [DEWRSB (2000g)].

Competition among Job Matching providers gives them an incentive to attempt to hoard information on vacancies, while the needs of an efficient labour market would call for this information to be widely shared [ACOSS (2000b)]. Although providers may generally disseminate semi-open vacancy information to improve their chances of finding the most suitable applicants (a factor in securing future vacancy listings from employers), it may also happen that some Job Matching providers on occasion inappropriately delay listings or post only inadequate information. This might occur, for example, in the event a provider attempts to ensure that its own JST and IA clients have first chance at a referral and placement. Delayed listings violate the JN requirement that Job Matching providers lodge vacancies on the National Vacancy Database as soon as they are acquired from employers. DEWRSB has taken multiple steps to warn JN members against it and to monitor members' behaviour in this regard (*e.g.* through audits and tracking the length of time between vacancy listings and jobseeker referrals). In addition, the IES system will not accept a claim where the placement date precedes the vacancy creation data. Where questions arise, DEWRSB contract managers can request that providers submit supporting documentation to substantiate claims.

AJS offers jobseekers the opportunity to list a basic resume in a resume bank that can be searched by employers (as of December 2000, there were about 47 600 active resumes listed). Employers do not have access to jobseekers' addresses or telephone numbers. Where they wish to contact a jobseeker, they may do so via e-mail or via AJS.[114] In the latter case, the jobseeker is notified and asked to contact the employer. While there is no requirement for active matching of vacancies by JN members, AJS does offer such an option to jobseekers who use AJS to post a resume. The system will conduct overnight matching of new vacancies to resumes and sends e-mail notification to jobseekers where matches are found. Registered employers can also request automatic job matching for vacancies, with e-mail notification of results. The pool of vacancies is kept current by an automatic screening process: those not viewed or updated for 90 days are automatically deleted.

There is no requirement for employers to list vacancies on the National Vacancy Database or notify Job Network. However, the Commonwealth Public Service must notify vacancies for permanent positions to the *Commonwealth Public Service Gazette* and positions in this gazette are listed on AJS [DEWRSB (2000g)]. The DEWRSB employers survey in 1999 found that over one-half of all employers in manufacturing, communications, accommodations and cafes had lodged a vacancy with Job Network in the 12 months preceding the survey, whereas less than one-quarter of all employers in government/administration, agriculture or education had done so [DEWRSB (2000e)]. In terms of occupational composition, the National Vacancy Database listings available through AJS are primarily blue-collar and lower-level white collar.

G. Job Network outcomes

1. The unemployed and job search issues

Table 3.3, Panel A, highlights difficulties unemployed jobseekers report facing in finding work. The share reporting an absolute lack of vacancies declined substantially as the period of economic expansion during the 1990s advanced. The proportion reporting no difficulties at all also increased. However, among those who were unemployed at the end of the decade, there was a somewhat larger proportion reporting difficulties linked to personal characteristics or situation. These problems sometimes indicated special needs and related to issues such as employer perceptions of the jobseeker's age (too young or old) or the jobseeker's lack of skills and work experience, health and transportation problems, and difficulties related to childcare and family responsibilities.

Table 3.3.   **Job search experience of unemployed persons**
Percentages

Panel A - Main difficulty in finding work			
	July 1992	July 1997[a]	July 1999[a]
No vacancies at all	31.9	12.7	10.0
No vacancies in line of work	17.1	9.1	7.9
Too many applicants for available job	..	14.5	12.1
Considered too young or too old by employers	13.8	14.5	15.4
Lacked necessary skills/education	9.5	12.1	11.2
Insufficient work experience	8.0	10.4	10.1
Own ill health or disability	4.2	6.0	6.9
Too far to travel/transport problems	3.9	5.3	5.8
Language difficulties	2.6	2.6	2.4
Unsuitable hours	1.9	2.3	3.7
Difficulties with childcare/other family responsibilities	1.2	2.4	2.5
Other difficulties[b]	2.6	3.0	3.7
No difficulties reported	3.2	5.3	8.4

Panel B - Active steps taken to find work			
	July 1992	July 1997[a]	July 1999[a]
Registered with the CES / Centrelink (in 1999) and —	**82.4**	**76.6**	**64.6**
Took no other active steps	0.7	0.4	0.4
Contacted prospective employers	77.9	74.1	62.8
Took other active steps	3.8	2.1	1.5
Not registered with the CES / Centrelink (in 1999) and —	**17.6**	**23.4**	**35.4**
Contacted prospective employers	15.5	21.9	32.2
Took other active steps	2.1	1.5	3.2
Memorandum item			
Total unemployed (000s)	**900.1**	**717.5**	**591.0**

.. Data not available.
a) Excludes persons who have been laid off.
b) Includes persons who reported difficulties with ethnic background.
Source: ABS, *Job Search Experience of Unemployed Persons, Australia*, Catalogue No. 6222.0, various issues.

Table 3.3, Panel B, highlights the job-search methods of unemployed jobseekers. (The data presented here are based on an ABS survey providing a representative sample of the full population of unemployed jobseekers.) The table shows a much smaller share of unemployed jobseekers registered with Centrelink as of July 1999 than were registered with CES in July 1997 or July 1992. In the recent period, about one-third of all unemployed jobseekers failed to register with Centrelink, indicating a declining rate of usage of the "public" employment service by this group. The number of unemployed jobseekers who did not register but instead contacted employers through other channels doubled. Those looking for part-time work were more likely to fail to register than

133

those looking for full-time work. Still, some 22% of those looking for full-time employment also failed to register. The survey did not provide information on the reasons for failing to register.

Among the jobseekers who register with Centrelink and who subsequently receive Job Matching, JST or IA services, DEWRSB surveys indicate that most appear to be satisfied. However, a variety of problems are also reported by clients in accessing services. Some find the Job Matching services difficult to navigate. One reason they are sometimes frustrated appears to be the fragmentation of the Job Matching service [ACOSS (2000b)]. That is, there is no one-stop shop for jobseekers wanting to compare all the available information including employer details on all potentially-suitable vacancies in the system (via AJS they may only compare the publicly available information). The high proportion of semi-open vacancies means that jobseekers must often contact a number of Job Network providers if they wish to review in detail the full range of vacancies, a process that may be time-consuming, costly and demotivating [DEWRSB (2000g); also Kelly et al. (1999)].

2. Client referral and commencement

A further issue is the failure of many clients referred to JST and IA to actually obtain the corresponding services (i.e. they do not commence). Table 3.4 presents information on the referrals and commencements for JST and IA based on data from DEWRSB's Job Network evaluation (stage one) [DEWRSB (2000d)].[115] The table highlights the large share of clients referred to these measures, but failing to commence; roughly 60% of JST referrals and 30% of IA referrals do not result in a commencement.

There are a variety of reasons for failures to commence, some of them fully acceptable under the JN provisions. Research from the JSCI post-implementation review indicates that many of the most disadvantaged jobseekers who failed to commence IA were either exempted from participation (e.g. due to ill health),

Table 3.4. **Job Network referrals and commencements**[a]

	Referrals (number)	Commencements (number)	Commencement rate (percentage)
Job Search Training			
Total of which:	181 800	73 500	40.4
Long-term unemployed	53 813	22 271	41.4
Intensive Assistance			
Total of which:	631 500	438 500	69.4
Long-term unemployed	378 900	277 571	73.3

a) Referrals and commencements for the period 1 May 1998 to 30 September 1999.
Source: DEWRSB, Job Network evaluation, Stage one: Implementation and Market Development, Canberra, February 2000.

134

referred to the CSP or no longer in need of assistance from the system [DEWRSB (2000d)]. A similar situation exists for JST. Providers interview newly referred jobseekers and can refer them back to Centrelink if they determine that the individual is unable to participate fully in the 15 working days of training (e.g. for study or health reasons) or to benefit from training at that time. Jobseekers not in receipt of an activity-tested allowance (e.g. youth with no allowance) participate on a voluntary basis. Others may find employment during the interval between referral and commencement. On the other hand, those in receipt of an activity-tested allowance may face a breach in their allowance if they are referred and fail to attend the initial interview or fail to participate in the activity once they are accepted by the provider. (See Chapter 4 for a more detailed discussion of breaching.)

In consultation with NESA and Centrelink, DEWRSB has introduced a range of measures intended to increase commencement rates. As this basic approach was being implemented, a report issued by the Australian National Audit Office (ANAO) noted the low commencement rate for JST and recommended actions similar to those already under way [ANAO (2000)]. ANAO found that no single option would resolve the problem and recommended that DEWRSB "should examine a wide range of possible solutions and do this in an open and consultative manner…". In addition, ANAO suggested that DEWRSB "should also consider improving its understanding of the perceptions and needs of jobseekers through commissioning of independent research of jobseekers to help determine underlying deficiencies in JST from their point of view."

While ANAO found the referral system works well with respect to IA, with JN members operating on average at roughly 95% of their contracted capacity, it did note some local problems with client flow. These arose where, due to imbalances in the geographic distribution of contracted IA places, variation in local labour market conditions, and the exercise of choice by clients, some providers operated at less than 85% of their contracted capacity. However, ANAO did not issue a specific recommendation as it considered that DEWRSB had "taken steps to meet particular difficulties in a timely manner".

Table 3.5 presents the characteristics of those who actually commenced JST and IA during the period from 1 May 1998 to 30 September 1999. For both measures, participants were mostly prime-age men. JST participants were mostly short-term unemployed, whereas IA participants were mostly long-term unemployed. IA participants included substantially greater shares of individuals who were older, indigenous, of non-English speaking status or with disabilities. The relatively high proportions of individuals entering IA who face particular labour market disadvantages provide an indication that where the client referral and induction process is successfully carried through, it tends to channel those with greater needs to the measure that offers the greatest amount of assistance. 135

Table 3.5. **Job Network: characteristics of those commencing measures**[a]
Percentages of the total[b]

	Job Search Training	Intensive Assistance
Gender		
Male	65.9	70.0
Female	34.1	30.0
Duration of unemployment		
Less than 12 months	69.1	36.7
12 months and over	30.3	63.3
Age		
Less than 25 years old	36.2	22.8
25 to 49 years old	57.5	58.6
50 years old or more	6.3	18.7
Allowance Recipients		
Newstart	..	86.7
Youth	..	7.1
Disability support pension	..	0.6
Non-partnered parenting	..	2.5
Other	..	2.0
Youth not on allowance	..	1.2
Special groups[c]		
Indigenous	0.6	5.0
Non-English speaking background	11.9	21.5
Persons with disabilities	7.3	16.7
Sole parents	0.5	0.7

.. Data not available.
a) Referrals and commencements for the period 1 May 1998 to 30 September 1999.
b) Some columns do not add to 100% because unknowns were excluded.
c) Special group characteristics are not mutually exclusive.
Source: DEWRSB, *Job Network evaluation, Stage one: Implementation and Market Development*, Canberra, February 2000.

3. Outcomes monitoring

The first stage of the official DEWRSB Job Network evaluation found that among those who had entered IA between May and July 1998, more than 90% had exited by the late 1999.[116] However, among those exiting IA, only 20% had employment, education or training outcomes qualifying for JN member outcome payments. The remaining 80% exited IA without a paid outcome. Nearly one-half of all IA exits occurred when the clients reached the end of their period of IA eligibility without a result. Others exited prior to the end of their referral, including some who may have found a job on their own.

Additional information on the destinations of JN participants is available from subsequent DEWRSB analysis using post-programme monitoring survey data collected three months after clients cease to receive assistance under the main JN services [DEWRSB (2000*f*)]. These data are presented in Table 3.6 and cover a

Table 3.6. **Observed post-assistance outcomes for Job Network and Working Nation participants**[a]

Percentages of participants three months after exiting each measure
(except numbers as noted)

Labour market measure	Number of exits enumerated	Labour market status					Other outcome indicators		
		Employed			Unemployed	Not in the labour force	Further assistance[b]	Education and training	Positive outcomes[c]
		Total	Full-time	Part-time					
Job Network									
Job Matching[d]	(95 504)[e]	69.7	42.6	27.1	26.8	3.5	..	10.0	72.9
Job Search Training[f]	54 785	40.5	21.3	19.3	49.2	4.8	5.3	12.7	49.0
Intensive Assistance[f]	317 929	34.2	15.5	18.7	47.5	15.2	3.1	8.6	41.1
Level A	220 957	38.8	17.9	20.8	44.0	14.0	3.2	9.0	45.8
Level B	96 972	24.1	10.1	14.0	55.2	17.7	3.0	7.7	30.7
NEIS[f]	6 474	82.6	52.6	30.0	11.1	6.5	..	8.4	84.7
Working Nation[g]									
Job Clubs	45 309	24.9	11.6	13.3	40.5	2.9	31.7	7.4	29.9
Various intensive measures	497 758	27.4	14.2	13.2	44.5	6.2	22.0	9.7	34.6
JobSkills	24 458	28.1	14.4	13.8	56.0	4.1	11.7	7.8	33.4
JobTrain	102 858	23.6	9.6	14.0	41.7	4.7	30.0	8.6	29.9
JobStart	83 258	48.3	34.4	13.8	39.8	3.5	8.5	5.9	51.5
LEAP	16 278	22.4	13.1	9.3	59.3	5.1	13.1	8.9	29.3
New Work Opportunities	27 290	17.9	8.0	9.9	62.5	4.9	14.8	4.4	21.1
SkillShare	151 204	30.3	13.9	16.4	44.5	7.4	17.8	11.5	38.6
Special Intervention	92 412	13.1	5.4	7.7	39.5	8.6	38.7	12.7	24.2

.. Data not available.

a) DEWRSB uses a number of data sources including Post Programme Monitoring surveys and DEWRSB administrative data to assess labour market outcomes and further assistance statuses of jobseekers 3 months after they exit assistance.

b) Further assistance includes commencements in IA, JST, NEIS, Work for the Dole, Indigenous Employment Programme and several DETYA programmes including New Apprenticeships, Literacy and Numeracy, and Advanced English for Migrants.

c) The positive outcomes indicator reflects the share of *individuals* who achieved either employment or education and training outcomes. It is less than the sum of the outcomes in those categories because some individuals achieved outcomes in both.

d) Post assistance outcomes for Job Matching relate to individuals placed between 1 March 2000 and 30 June 2000 and outcomes achieved by September 2000.

e) For job matching, only a 10% sample of exits were enumerated. For the other Job Network measures shown, an attempt was made to fully enumerate exits for the periods concerned.

f) Post assistance outcomes for IA, JST and NEIS relate to individuals who ended their participation in these measures between 1 July 1999 and 30 June 2000 and whose outcomes were achieved by 30 September 2000.

g) The Working Nation outcomes refer to the year ending 30 June 1996. Job Clubs are considered by DEWRSB to be similar to JST. The line "various intensive measures" refer to the combined results for JobSkills, JobTrain, JobStart, LEAP, New Work Opportunities, SkillShare and Special Intervention.

Sources: DEWRSB, *Labour Market Assistance Outcomes*, Canberra, September 2000, and correspondence with the Australian authorities.

more recent period than the evaluation, including the first months of the second JN contract period.[117] They provide more detailed information on the situation of those who exited, reflecting the labour market status of individuals at the time of follow-up regardless of the outcome payments to JN members and regardless of the durations of placements.

As shown in the table, the main measures targeting individuals with moderate or severe labour market disadvantage (*i.e.* JST and IA levels A and B) had employment success rates of between roughly 25% and 40%. Part-time employment accounted for nearly half of the JST employment outcomes and more than half of those for IA. These flows indicate that the majority of participants in JST or IA remained unemployed or moved out of the labour force following their participation in these measures. Even where DEWRSB defined a positive outcome to include enrolment in educational and training measures or employment, only about half of JST participants and about two-fifths of IA participants were found to have a positive outcome at the time of the post-programme monitoring. At the same time, very few of those who exited JST or IA were in receipt of further assistance through an alternative labour market programme. Only the Job Matching and NEIS measures had a majority of positive outcomes using the DEWRSB definition.

Table 3.6 also presents outcomes data on the status of participants three months after they exited Working Nation measures.[118] This comparison indicates that average employment rates were somewhat higher for participants who exited JST and IA-level A than for those who exited most of the intensive measures under Working Nation. Larger shares of Working Nation participants went on to further assistance than was the case with Job Network. At the same time, a greater share of former IA participants left the labour force than was the case for the Working Nation measures.

It should be noted that all such outcome comparisons must be treated with caution as they do not control for changes in labour market conditions, the characteristics of participants, or a variety of other factors. Moreover, the outcomes comparisons are to a certain extent influenced by the conditions for exiting the various measures. For example, Job Matching can be open-ended and exit is generally by placement into a job, whereas JST participation is for a short period of time and exits may be due to the end of the programme. Another example concerns Jobstart subsidies under Working Nation, which entailed placements into jobs where the employers undertook to retain the employees for at least three months after the end of the subsidy in some cases.

Chart 3.2 presents data on the monthly placement flows for the CES and Job Network, adjusted for comparability. Except during the initial transition period, Job Network has delivered results similar to those of the CES. This is an important observation in view of the substantial reduction in labour market programme expenditures pointed out in Chapter 1. It points to a fairly strong improvement in the gross productivity of Job Network in comparison to CES: the Job Network delivered about the same gross placement results at a lower cost. However, this

Chart 3.2. **Monthly vacancies and placements**
Percentages of dependent employment

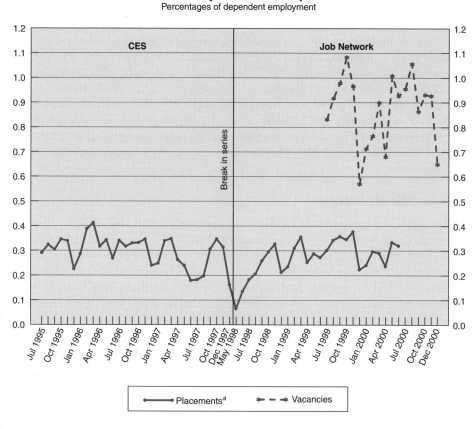

a) Very short-term casual jobs, labour market programme places and other placements that would not qualify for payments under Job Matching contract guidelines have been excluded by DEWRSB for comparison of CES placements with similar Job Network Job Matching placements.
Sources: Direct submissions by national authorities for placements and vacancies; and ABS, *Wage and Salary Earners, Australia,* Catalogue No. 6248.0, Table 1, various issues, for trends data on dependent employment.

comparison does not control for the types of clients placed and, therefore, the results could be biased.

Working Nation targeted an especially difficult-to-place client group in focusing on individuals unemployed 18 months or longer [ACOSS (2000*b*)]. Under Job Network, less than two-thirds of IA clients are long-term unemployed, as are less than one-third of JST clients (Table 3.5). This difference in approach may have contributed to the relatively high share of CES placements accounted for by those unemployed between 12 and 24 months (18%).[119] Job Network had a lower

139|

proportion of such placements (13%, excluding Job Matching-only clients). CES also had somewhat higher shares of placements among those with educational attainment of less than completed secondary school, indigenous Australians and persons with disabilities. On the other hand, Job Network had a higher proportion of placements comprised of those unemployed 24 months or more (17% for Job Network as compared to 13% for CES). However, as noted in stage one of DEWRSB's Job Network evaluation, in the absence of a counterfactual (*i.e.* a comparison or control group *not* participating in IA), it is difficult to interpret these results and to rigorously evaluate the effect of IA on client outcomes. Stage two of the evaluation moves to address this issue, using comparison groups to assess the effectiveness of JST and IA (see Chapter 5, Section E, for a discussion of the stage two results).

4. International comparisons

International comparisons can be used to make a rough assessment of certain aspects of employment service performance. Table 3.7 presents OECD indicators of the basic flows, stocks and market share for the employment service in Australia and other countries which the OECD has reviewed in recent years. Comparisons of placements must be treated with some caution as countries vary in their exact definition of a placement.[120] Based on the available data, it appears that with respect to placements as a share of hirings Job Network's market share is in the mid-range of countries, placing sixth among the 12 countries for which data are available. Its score for placements as a share of dependent employment is similar.

Public employment services vary widely in their ability to acquire vacancies, as shown by the indicator for registered job vacancies as a percentage of hirings. The performance of Job Network is somewhat above the median with respect to this indicator for the countries shown in the table. In terms of registered vacancies as a share of dependent employment, Job Network is in the mid-range of countries.[121] The rate of filling registered vacancies with placements is an important indicator concerning the delivery of results for employer clients. By this indicator, the Job Network performance is also in the mid-range, ranking seventh among the 14 countries for which data are available. One factor that may influence vacancy results is the practice of some employers of listing a given vacancy with multiple JN members. For example, this would contribute to lower the apparent rate of vacancy filling (since only one potential placement would potentially result from the multiple listings of a single vacancy by a given employer).

H. Enhancement of Job Network placement activity

The preceding discussion of placement activity under Job Network points to results that are not dramatically different from those under Working Nation and that are about average with respect to market share indicators for other OECD

Table 3.7. **Basic employment service flows, stocks and market share indicators**

	Australia[a] 2000	Austria 1999	Denmark 1999	Finland 1999	France[b] 1999	Germany 1999	Greece 1996	Ireland 1996	Japan 1999	Korea[c] 1998	Netherlands 1999	Portugal[d] 1996	Switzerland 1999	United Kingdom 1999	United States 1998
Employment service administrative data (000s)															
Annual vacancy registrations	742[e]	299	227	251	1 790	4 043	..	45	5 862	335	247	73	143	2 724	7 372
Annual placements[f]	397[g]	232	74	129	1 560	2 928	8	17	1 730	138	204	43	145	1 430	1 886
Labour market data															
Dependent employment (000s)	7 701	3 238	2 468	1 966	14 200	34 002	2 068	1 034	53 305	12 191	5 581	3 183	3 020	24 172	127 842
Monthly hiring rate (%) (approximate)[h]	2.2	3.0	..	3.1	2.8	2.3	2.3	1.6	..	1.7	1.4	1.4	1.3	2.2	..
Derived indicators (%)															
Registered job vacancies/hirings	37	29	..	33	37	45	..	22	..	13	25	13	24	45	..
Registered job vacancies/dependent employment	10	9	9	13	13	12	..	4	11	3	4	2	5	11	6
Placements/hirings	20	22	..	17	33	33	2	8	..	6	21	8	24	24	..
Placements/dependent employment	5	7	3	7	11	9	0.4	2	3	1	4	1	5	6	1
Placements/registered job vacancies	53	78	33	51	87	72	..	38	30	41	83	59	101	52	26

.. Data not available.

a) 1999/2000 financial year.

b) Private non-agricultural sector only.

c) Placement and vacancy data refer to the chain of public employment service offices administered by the Ministry of Labour.

d) Data for Portugal refer to the continent only, except for the stock of registered vacancies and ratios involving this stock which include the islands.

e) About 9% of these vacancies were lodged directly on AJS by employers and were not managed by Job Network. As in a number of other countries, placements into such vacancies are generally not recorded.

f) For Australia, this refers to unsubsidised placements into vacancies notified to the National Vacancy Database and filled with the assistance of the Job Network including unpaid outcomes. Definitions for the other countries vary.

g) Placements of Job Network-eligible clients amounted to 263 000 in the same period. In general, a provider can claim an outcome payment for such placements.

h) Monthly new hirings as a percentage of dependent employment. Estimates for each country are based on a combination of data from labour force surveys, employer surveys or administrative records of hirings kept by the employment service.

Sources: **Australia**: Direct submissions by national authorities for vacancies and placements; OECD *Economic Outlook*, No. 69, June 2001, for dependent employment; and ABS, *Successful and Unsuccessful Job Search Experience*, Catalogue No. 6245.0, *Labour Force Survey*, Catalogue No. 6303.0, various issues, for hirings; **other countries**: OECD PES database.

countries for which data are available. While jobseeker and employer perceptions of the Job Network are generally quite positive, a non-negligible minority also reports some dissatisfaction with services. Although the results to-date have been achieved in the face of significantly reduced labour market programme expenditure, it remains to be seen whether adjustments to the system can be implemented that substantially improve placement performance, particularly for the most disadvantaged jobseekers.

The need to diffuse information on best practices is receiving increasing attention within DEWRSB. With the conversion of employment service delivery to a competitive market, DEWRSB faces a particular challenge in identifying and promoting ways to improve services to jobseeker clients. Beyond their tender materials and contractual reporting requirements, many JN members regard their operational information as proprietary and to some extent business-confidential. In the face of competitive pressures, many are reluctant to share information that would undermine their position vis-à-vis other JN members. At the same time, while the ability of clients to choose providers was intended to help encourage performance improvements, the initial lack of readily-available provider performance information meant that some clients' may not have had access to all the information they needed in this regard. It may be that the release and dissemination of updated performance information in March 2001 has helped to close this gap.

DEWRSB collects best-practice information via its contract managers, in discussion with NESA and through its on-going evaluation process. It supports exchanges of ideas via meetings with providers and a periodical (the *Job Network Bulletin*); providers are encouraged to share information. DEWRSB has also planned a small study to identify best practices and it intends to disseminate the findings in order to help JN members boost their performance. Beyond these on-going efforts, however, it may be possible to boost the systematic and detailed collection of information of client treatments through a modest expansion of the administrative data system (*e.g.* to include information concerning the *types* of contacts that providers have with clients).

A further source of insight for potential programme enhancements may be found in evaluation work by independent researchers using standard social scientific methods. While there have already been a few completed assessment efforts by researchers co-operating with individual JN providers (*e.g.* Eardley *et al.*, 2001), there may be possibilities to bolster such efforts. In particular, independent evaluation work on Job Network appears to be constrained somewhat by difficulties in arranging access to providers. Such access depends on direct contacts and negotiation with individual JN members. In practice, many providers may not regularly collect the full range of requisite data or may be reluctant to share data or provide access for researchers due to privacy or business confidentiality concerns. Given that JN contracts allow for collection of data by DEWRSB for evaluation purposes, DEWRSB might be in a position to facilitate improved access and special data collection for researchers.

The available qualitative information and outcomes data point to a number of areas where adjustments are required in order to improve results. In some cases, such adjustments might best be developed on the basis of future field trials, research or evaluation work. Examples include:

- Adjustments to encourage more unemployed jobseekers not in receipt of an unemployment allowance to register and profit from Job Matching services (*e.g.* based on an assessment of the reasons that an increasing number of unemployed jobseekers fail to register with Centrelink, which makes it difficult even to assess or address their needs). This may have economic implications in that Job Network may ease their placements into employment or assist them to prepare for work in areas where there are vacancies, thereby helping to boost effective labour supply.

- Adjustments to the payments system to encourage inter-provider job referrals in cases where a jobseeker might best be served through placement into another provider's closed vacancy (*e.g.* through a system whereby both the vacancy-listing and client-placing Job Network providers receive a fee for a successful job match). This may simplify referrals for clients and improve Job Matching results.

- Adjustments to expand the eligibility for access to Job Network services for jobseekers not in receipt of activity-tested benefits or others not receiving income support payments [Abello and Eardley (2000)]). Access to Job Network services may facilitate the entry into employment among those who would like to work in these groups.[122]

- Adjustments to ensure delivery of an improved mix of JST services in line with the needs of jobseekers and the relative effectiveness of the various options under JST. This may work to improve not only the rate of commencement but also outcomes.

While the flow of selected IA clients and available IA places are generally in balance and providers are operating near capacity, it may be that some of those not selected for IA could benefit from participation if additional places were made available. For those long-term unemployed not currently assisted via IA, for example, further research may help to shed light on the most effective way to address their needs whether via IA, CSP, disability programmes or other measures. While the failure to stream many long-term unemployed into IA may be appropriate given their needs, it is not clear that all of this group are getting the assistance they need to facilitate re-entry into employment.

143

Finally, there are questions about the impact of the exemption from Mutual Obligation and job-search requirements during the period of participation in IA and the restoration of these requirements once clients exhaust their IA entitlements. These points are discussed in more detail in Chapters 4 and 5.

Table 3.A.1. **Selected employment assistance measures: Job Network, CSP and DES**

Type of service	Principal Centrelink assessment tools	Client eligibility	Brief summary of main provider services to clients	Client referrals	Participant inflows (year ending 30 June 2000)
Job Matching (Job Network, DEWRSB-funded)		Job Matching providers confirm the eligibility of clients via IES at time of registration. Eligible clients include all Job-Network eligible jobseekers[a] and other registered jobseekers who are: – not in full-time education or training; or – not working in paid employment for 15 hours a week or more; or – not in receipt of Mature Age Allowance; or – not an overseas visitor on a working holiday visa; or – not prohibited by law from working in Australia.	Providers acquire job vacancies from employers (to qualify for a Job Matching fee vacancies must provide *at least* 15 hours of paid employment within 5 days from the start of work). Providers match and refer eligible jobseekers to suitable vacancies. They record placements on the IES and confirming with employers that the placement has met the minimum duration requirements.	Eligible clients may self-refer to Job Matching providers based on information provided by Centrelink, which includes a listing of contact information for all local Job Matching providers (those in other areas are available upon request) or may be enrolled with their choice of providers by Centrelink. All eligible clients are encouraged to enrol with all local Job Matching providers. Newstart and Youth Allowance recipients must enrol with *at least* one provider within 14 days of registration with Centrelink.	295 535 (of which, 75 327 were Job Matching-only clients).
Job Search Training (Job Network, DEWRSB-funded)	JSCI	Centrelink determines client eligibility. Providers must conduct an assessment interview with all clients referred to them. Where barriers are identified that would result in a jobseeker not benefiting from participation, the provider may notify Centrelink who may then remove the jobseeker from the provider's caseload. Potentially eligible clients should have current skills and/or experience and no major barriers to employment and include Job-Network eligible jobseekers[a] and certain unemployed persons returning to the workforce after *at least* two years of unpaid care-giving.	Providers assess client barriers to employment. They negotiate an individually-tailored Job Search Skills Plan with the client that includes practical job-search activity and aims to reduce barriers by improving client motivation, job-search skills and search network. Providers must deliver 15 full, consecutive working days of assistance to the client (which may include course-based assistance).	Centrelink will refer JST-eligible clients to providers of their choice subject to available capacity. If a valid choice is not made, Centrelink may automatically refer Newstart or Youth Allowance clients to a local provider with available capacity.	56 108

145

Table 3.A.1. **Selected employment assistance measures: Job Network, CSP and DES** (*cont.*)

Type of service	Principal Centrelink assessment tools	Client eligibility	Brief summary of main provider services to clients	Client referrals	Participant inflows (year ending 30 June 2000)
		Eligible clients generally: – are registered as unemployed for 3 months or more; – have JSCI scores below the threshold for IA or CSP participation (currently, this means *less than* 24 points); and – are not in NEIS or a similar labour market programme.	Providers must offer Job Matching services.		
Intensive Assistance (IA) (Job Network, DEWRSB-funded)	JSCI *plus* in some cases further classification[b] involving: 1) a Special Needs Assessment (SNA) triggered by JSCI question responses or other contact, or 2) secondary classification such as a disability review using the Work Ability Tables (WAT) and triggered by a client request or a disclosed or observed disability	Centrelink determines eligibility and classifies clients as either Level A or Level B funding based on their JSCI score. Potential eligibility applies to those Job Network-eligible jobseekers[a] unemployed for *at least* 52 weeks or classified as being at high risk of long-term unemployment. Jobseekers are excluded if they are: 1) currently in an external labour market activity, such as Mutual Obligation; 2) registered with a specialist provider; or 3) evaluated as having a moderate or severe disability level according to the WAT (*i.e.* a WAT score of 50 or more). A SNA may lead to a voluntary referral to CSP. A WAT score of 50 or more makes client eligible for a voluntary referral to DES.	All providers (general or specialist): – provide Job Matching service; – negotiate a Preparing for Work Agreement with the clients (including *at least* one activity as required for Newstart or Youth Allowance recipients, *e.g.* job search or training); and, if a job is not found within 13 weeks, an IA Support Plan that provides for tailored, needs-based support (*e.g.* training); – other services as laid out in the provider's tender (in the Declaration of Intent) including such elements as job-search assistance, training, work experience or post-placement support.	Centrelink refers eligible clients based on their choice of provider(s) where places are available. Clients in the client group for local specialist providers (*e.g.* for disabled, migrant or indigenous jobseekers) may choose that specialist or a generalist provider. Clients receiving Newstart or Youth Allowances who fail to choose a provider are auto-referred to a generalist provider, who is notified of the referral *via* IES and must follow it up.	324 490.

146

Table 3.A.1. **Selected employment assistance measures: Job Network, CSP and DES** (*cont.*)

Type of service	Principal Centrelink assessment tools	Client eligibility	Brief summary of main provider services to clients	Client referrals	Participant inflows (year ending 30 June 2000)
IA Level A[c]		These IA-eligible jobseekers have a JSCI score in band A (currently 24 to 32 points, which signals the presence of significant disadvantages for entry into employment).	12 months of IA service with the possibility of extending the period for a further 6 months by mutual agreement between the client and the provider (*i.e.* for a total of 18 months).	As indicated above.	Level A was introduced as a category from 28 February 2000 and budgeted as 75% of IA commencements.
IA Level B[c]		These IA-eligible jobseekers have a JSCI score in band B (currently 33 or more points, which signals the presence of very significant disadvantages for entry into employment).	15 months of IA service with the possibility of extending the period for a further 6 months by mutual agreement between the client and the provider (*i.e.* for a total of 21 months).	As indicated above.	Level B was introduced as a category from 28 February 2000 and budgeted as 25% of IA commencements.
Project Contracting (Job Network, DEWRSB-funded)	Jobseekers are screened by the criteria for legal entitlement to work in Australia.	Eligibility is verified by the Job Network provider. Participation is open to all jobseekers legally entitled to work in Australia, with preference going to those on income support.	Providers deliver labour exchange services and information for employers and jobseekers.	There is no formal referral process. Providers seek jobseekers using Australia Job Search database listings or other appropriate channels.	19 500 (year ending 30 June 1999).

Table 3.A.1. **Selected employment assistance measures: Job Network, CSP and DES** (*cont.*)

Type of service	Principal Centrelink assessment tools	Client eligibility	Brief summary of main provider services to clients	Client referrals	Participant inflows (year ending 30 June 2000)
New Enterprise Incentive Scheme (NEIS) / Self-Employment Development[d] (Job Network, DEWRSB-funded)	At time of possible referral: NEIS provider assesses jobseeker application. At time of approval for NEIS Allowance: NEIS Advisory Committee assesses business plan.	Eligibility is verified by the Job Network provider. Unemployed who are registered with Centrelink and: – *at least* 18 years old; – available to participate in NEIS training and work full-time in business; – receiving Newstart or Youth Allowance (or certain other forms of government income support) or an Aboriginal or Torres Strait Islander participating in a CDEP scheme; and – not an undischarged bankrupt.	NEIS provider: – screens potential NEIS participants, – provides accredited NEIS training; – convenes NEIS Advisory Committees; – provides mentoring and on-going support to NEIS participants; – monitors NEIS businesses and provides quarterly reports to DEWRSB.	There is no formal referral to NEIS providers. Eligible jobseekers can self-nominate for participation in Self-Employment Development and can select potential NEIS provider. NEIS provider screens candidates; Centrelink approves candidate's activity based on NEIS provider recommendation; NEIS Advisory Committee assesses commercial viability of business plan; DEWRSB approves start of business and pays NEIS allowance.	6 642.
Community Support Programme (CSP)[d] (Outside of Job Network, but funded by DEWRSB)	JSCI and SNA	Centrelink determines client eligibility. These jobseekers must be either: 1) in receipt of an unemployment allowance and identified under a SNA as having special needs, or 2) 15 to 20 years of age and not on income support, but registered with Centrelink as unemployed and identified as having special needs addressed within the CSP framework. A SNA is undertaken to assess the particular employment barriers faced by the individual, with a view to recommending the best referral channel: IA or CSP. Clients in receipt of a Disability Support Pension are not eligible to participate in CSP.	Depending on client needs, may include: – counselling; – assistance to secure stable accommodation; – assistance to secure drug or alcohol rehabilitation; – other tailored assistance, as needed to ready the individual for referral to IA.	Referral to the CSP is voluntary.	7 249.

Table 3.A.1. **Selected employment assistance measures: Job Network, CSP and DES** (*cont.*)

Type of service	Principal Centrelink assessment tools	Client eligibility	Brief summary of main provider services to clients	Client referrals	Participant inflows (year ending 30 June 2000)
Disability Employment Services (DES)[d] (Outside of Job Network, FaCS-funded)	JSCI and WAT	Centrelink determines potential client eligibility with respect to Job Network clients. These jobseekers must be moderately or severely disabled (*i.e.* with a WAT score of over 50). Eligibility is not related to receipt of unemployment allowances.	Providers tailor assistance which may include open employment services (training, placement and post-placement assistance), supported employment services (provider directly employs and supports jobseeker), or rehabilitation services.	Referral to DES is voluntary.[e] Clients may also directly approach DES service providers.	27 000 (approximate inflows from all channels).

a) In order to be eligible for Job Network services, jobseekers must be registered as unemployed with Centrelink and either: 1) a recipient of a Newstart or Youth Allowance (or certain other types of government-paid income support), 2) a youth aged 15 to 20 years and not in full-time education or training, or 3) an Aboriginal or Torres Strait Islander participating in the CDEP scheme). Job Network eligibility excludes those in receipt of an Age Pension (from services other than Job Matching) or Mature Age Allowance.

b) Job Network providers can request a Centrelink review of classification if additional information comes to light concerning the client. Additionally, if the provider feels that a client has a special barrier to employment that prevents the client from being able to benefit from IA, but which is not captured by the JSCI or WAT, then the provider may request and pay for a Special Needs Assessment. This may result in the client being removed from the provider's books and offered assistance through CSP or other specialised channels.

c) The minimum fee to providers for a level A client who finds employment and sustains it through 26 weeks is $9 219. Thus, in principle the providers have more financial resources available to provide additional services for a level B client. Also, note that prior to 28 February 2000, IA inflows were split into three sub-categories based on degree of labour market disadvantage: 3.1 (67% of commencements), 3.2 (26% of commencements), 3.3 (7% of commencements). A higher number indicated higher level of labour market disadvantage.

d) NEIS, CSP and DES are discussed in more detail in Chapter 5. CSP and DES are not operated under the Job Network.

e) Participation in DES is voluntary. However, a disabled client scoring above the WAT threshold for DES eligibility (*i.e.* 50 points or more) cannot enter IA. If an IA review results in a client's WAT score being adjusted over the threshold for DES, then that client will be "exited" from IA (unless both the IA provider and the client agree that the client should continue in IA).

Sources: DEWRSB, *General Information and Service Requirements for the Employment Services Request for Tender 1999*, Canberra, June 1999; DEWRSB, *The Members Information Guide, Section 11, Intensive Assistance*, Canberra, May 1999; and various agency Internet sites accessed during 20-21 December 2000, including: DEWRSB (http://www.dwrsb.gov.au/), Centrelink (http://www.centrelink.gov.au/), Job Network (http://www.jobnetwork.gov.au/) and FaCS (http://www.facs.gov.au/); and OECD Active Labour Market Policy database.

Chapter 4

Unemployment and Related Benefits

A. Overview

Most OECD countries provide social insurance benefits as the first line of social protection. Social insurance benefits are financed through social security contributions and, thus, are conditional upon an earnings history, with the benefit level being related to previous earnings but independent of current unearned income and assets. Australia, however, has, except for industrial injury insurance and compulsory superannuation,[123] only assistance benefits. Assistance benefits are financed through general taxation and paid at a flat rate, subject to means-testing against current income (including unearned income) and assets. For prime-age people in Australia, the main assistance benefits for basic income support are those for the sick, the disabled, the unemployed, partners of these groups and parents.

Assistance benefit levels in Australia are fairly generous in comparison with assistance benefit levels in other countries. Payments for a couple with two children as a percentage of net disposable income at average earnings levels were estimated to be, in 1992, below levels in the Netherlands, Switzerland and several Nordic countries, but above levels elsewhere, including Ireland and the United Kingdom which have relatively similar benefit systems [Eardley *et al.* (1996a), Table 7.6].[124] Net replacement rates in 1997 for long-term benefit recipients after tax and including family and housing benefits (with the main benefit income usually from social assistance) confirm this pattern. However the long-term replacement rate for a single person in Australia is only at a median level in comparative terms, being lower than in Austria, Belgium, France, Germany and the United Kingdom [OECD (1999b), Table 3.5]. The means test for assistance benefits in Australia is relatively generous: as compared with assistance benefits elsewhere, assistance can be paid to people who have significant amounts of other income and assets. The relatively generous means test may partly compensate for the lack of insurance benefits where such a test would not apply.

The basic income support benefits fall into two main categories: pensions, which include disability benefit as well as old-age pensions; and allowances,

151

© OECD 2001

which originally covered short-term contingencies (sickness and unemployment) but now also cover some longer-term situations (*e.g.* the unemployed aged over 60, widows). As shown in Table 4.1, pensions are slightly more generous than the allowances in terms of the basic payment level and considerably more generous

Table 4.1. **Selected income support and related payments and programmes, September to December 1998**
Payment, free area or income **per fortnight**

PENSIONS

Age Pension: Males 65 years or over, females 61 years or over
Disability Support Pension: Unable to work full-time for *at least* the next 2 years due to disability with a rating of *at least* 20 points on impairment scales
Parenting Payment Single: Sole parent with dependent child under 16 years

Payment/programme	Level of benefit	Free Area/Disregard	Withdrawal rate	Cut-Out Point
Single	$357.30	$100.00*	50%	$825.40*
Couple	$298.10 each	$176.00 combined*	25% each	$1 379.20* combined

ALLOWANCES

Widow Allowance: Women 50 years or over with no recent workforce experience
Sickness Allowance: Temporary incapacity for work or study, and medical certificate
Youth Allowance: Unemployed aged up to 20 years and students below 25 years
Newstart Allowance: Adult unemployed actively looking for work
Mature Age Allowance: 60 years or over, receiving income support for *at least* 9 months and no recent workforce experience
Partner Allowance: Partners of income support recipients with barriers to employment related to previous limited participation: restricted to people born before July 1955
Parenting Payment Partnered: Partnered parent caring for dependent child under 16 years
Special benefit: People ineligible for another payment and unable to earn or obtain livelihood

Payment/programme	Level of benefit	Free Area/Disregard	Withdrawal rate	Cut-Out Point
Below 18 years, at home	$145.40**	Unemployed: $60.00	Unemployed: 50% on $140.00, 70% thereafter	
18-20 years, at home	$174.80**	Students: $230.00	Students: 50% on $310.00, 70% thereafter	
Up to 20 years, away from home	$265.50**			
Single 21 years or more	$323.40**			Single 21 years or more: $582.71
Mature age, 60 years or more	$349.90			
Each member of a couple; partner; widow	$291.80			Each member of a couple: $499.71
Special benefit	Discretionary	100%		

Table 4.1.　**Selected income support and related payments and programmes,
September to December 1998** (*cont.*)
Payment, free area or income **per fortnight**

FAMILY PAYMENTS

More than the Minimum Rate: Children under 16 years
Student rate: Full-time dependent students 16-18 years
Guardian Allowance: Additional payment for sole parents receiving More than the Minimum Rate,
　including students

Payment/programme	Level of benefit	Free Area/Disregard	Withdrawal rate	Cut-Out Point
More than Minimum Rate for child under 16	$96.40 per child under 13 years, *plus* $125.40 per child 13-15 years	$23 400.00 per year for one child *plus* $624.00 for each extra child	50%	Minimum rate only payable from $27 191.00 per year (child under 13 years) *plus* $4 415.00 per extra child: $28 699.00 (child 13-15 years) *plus* $5 923.00 per extra child
Student 16-18	$23.50 per student			
Minimum Rate (both categories above)	$23.50 per child	$65 941.00 per year for one child *plus* $3 298.00 for each extra child	"Sudden death"	
Guardian Allowance	$37.70	Reduced after More than Minimum Rate	50%	

*　*Plus* $24 per fortnight for each child.
**　Benefits of unemployed aged up to 20 and students aged up to 25 are reduced by 25% of parents' income in the
　previous financial year over a certain threshold (unless a parent is currently on income support).
Source:　Whiteford (2000).

in terms of the means test. Sole parents receive a payment which resembles pensions in terms of the generosity of the income test. Above a certain threshold level of assets ($215 750 for a single non-home-owner) allowances are not payable at all but pension payments are only reduced by $3 per fortnight for every $1 000 of assets. There are also benefits which provide additional income. Parents, including many not on basic income support, receive additional family payments for each child and there is a small additional guardian payment for sole parents, and people in private rented accommodation may be entitled to assistance with housing costs.

Table 4.2 shows the number of beneficiaries of basic income support in various categories from 1965 to 1998. In 1998, after old-age pensioners, the largest categories of beneficiary were unemployment (790 000), followed by disability (633 000), parenting payment single (370 000) and parenting payment partnered (237 000), with much smaller numbers on all the other allowances and pensions, except for Student Assistance and Veterans Pensions.[125]

153

Table 4.2. **Number of recipients of basic income support payments, 1965 to 1998**[a]
Thousands

Pension or Allowance	1965	1970	1980	1990	1995	1997	1998
Age (including Wife) Pension	631.6	785.6	1 352.7	1 364.3	1 618.3	1 716.8	1 718.8
Disability Support (including Wife) Pension[b]	120.3	150.7	297.0	419.9	586.2	618.8	633.2
Carer Pension	–	–	–	8.8	20.1	29.6	34.0
Parent Payment Single[c]	29.7	44.1	161.6	248.9	324.9	358.9	372.3
Widows[d]	–	–	–	–	63.7	36.4	38.3
Sickness Allowance	10.2	8.8	36.8	79.2	46.1	15.8	16.3
Dependent Partners of above[e]	4.2[f]	3.9[f]	13.1	26.3	–	–	–
Unemployment Allowances[g]	12.7	13.0	311.2	419.8	795.5	801.8	790.3
Dependent Partners of above[e]	3.5[e]	4.4	66.3	126.0	–	–	–
Mature Age Allowance	–	–	–	–	39.0	53.4	50.7
Partner and Mature Age Partner Allowances	–	–	–	–	231.8	79.4	82.1
Parenting Payment Partnered[h]	–	–	–	–	–	239.3	236.6
Special Benefit	2.4	3.8	20.9	27.9	20.5	14.6	10.2
Total social security pensions and beneficiaries (not including Student Assistance and Veteran Pensions)	851.0	1 058.5	2 338.0	2 808.4	3 746.2	3 964.8	3 982.9

– Not applicable or not available.
a) Including in their own right the dependent partners of direct recipient of cash payments.
b) Includes Sheltered Employment and Rehabilitation allowees in relevant years.
c) Includes Class A Widows Pension, Supporting Mothers/Parents' Benefit and Sole Parent Pension.
d) Includes Class C Widows Pension, Widowed Persons and Bereavement Allowances.
e) Partners of unemployment, sickness or special benefits received partner Allowance from September 1994 and Parenting Allowance from July 1995.
f) Estimates.
g) Includes Job Search, Newstart and Youth Training allowances.
h) Originally Parenting Allowance – excludes those receiving only Basic Parenting Payment.
Source: Whiteford (2000).

Total social security expenditure in Australia in 1997 was 18.5% of GDP, lower than in all EU countries except for Ireland and Portugal but marginally higher than in Canada (statistics from the OECD database on public expenditure). There is a degree of statistical illusion in the available figures because relatively little tax is paid on income support payments[126] in Australia. Nevertheless, the low spending is mainly due to the flat-rate and means-tested nature of the benefits. OECD (1998c) estimated that the lowest three deciles of the population by household income receive 58% of social security transfer payments, a higher share than in any of the other 12 countries in the sample. Although some other countries rely quite heavily on means-testing of benefits for the working-age population, it has a declining role for old-age pensions. Owing to this pronounced degree of targeting, the degree of net redistribution to the poorest 30% is significantly higher than in many other countries, despite the relatively low level of spending. The flat-rate nature of unemployment benefits has probably tended to put a floor on the bottom of the earnings distribution and thus helped to sustain a relatively compressed earnings distribution, although the benefit system is unlikely to be the only factor involved and some increase in dispersion occurred during the 1980s [Whiteford (2000); Chapter 6 of this review].

The proportion of the working-age population that is jobless (not in paid employment) has been close to 32% since 1965, rising a few points above it in the early 1980s recession and falling slightly below it by the year 2000. However the proportion of the working-age population receiving income support payments increased from about 4% in 1965 to 22% in 1998 [RGWR (2000a), Figure 2.1]. The proportion of the working-age population that was neither in paid employment nor receiving income support has therefore fallen from about 30% in 1965 to 20% in the early 1980s and 10% by 1996.[127]

Unemployment fell considerably towards the end of the 1990s. The ratio of unemployment beneficiaries to labour force survey unemployed increased rapidly between 1990 and 1995, peaking at over 110%, but quite recently it has declined, falling below 100% early in 2001 (see Chart 4.1). The incidence of long-term unemployment according to the labour force survey (defined by ABS prior to April 2001 as the proportion of all unemployed people who state that they have not had two weeks of full-time work for at least a year) has fallen from a peak of 37% in 1993 to 24% in 2000 and 2001, and a recent definitional change has reduced this to about 20%. By contrast the proportion of beneficiaries who have an official long-term beneficiary status rose sharply after 1996, reaching 61% towards the end of 1999. In August 2000, just over half of all people with an official long-term beneficiary status were not paid benefit for at least one fortnight in the previous year and on this basis the 61% incidence of long-term benefit receipt in 1999 might be reinterpreted as 30% [advice from DEWRSB]. The long-term beneficiary unemployment share still seems high by most standards, so that although some fall has occurred, there is a need for further progress. Section E further discusses trends in beneficiary unemployment and its duration, in terms of the impact of both definitional factors and activation measures.

B. Benefit entitlement structures: withdrawal rates, individualisation and other features to facilitate taking up work

The exceptional degree of reliance on universal and reasonably generous assistance benefits has led Australia to face potential disincentive problems arising from the means-testing of benefits at an early stage. A number of innovations in entitlement structures which reduce these disincentives are discussed in this section. Eligibility requirements, often referred to in Australia as the activity test, also affect incentives but these will be discussed separately in Sections C and D.

155

Chart 4.1. **Unemployment beneficiaries and labour force survey unemployment, relative number and long-term shares**

Ratios

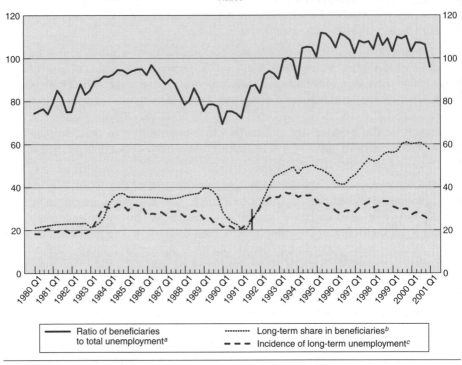

Ratio of beneficiaries to total unemployment[a]	Long-term share in beneficiaries[b]
	Incidence of long-term unemployment[c]

| Break in long-term share in beneficiaries series after 1991 Q2.

a) Beneficiaries refer to recipients of Unemployment Benefit, Job Search Allowance, Newstart Allowance, Youth Training Allowance and Youth Allowance, other than full-time students. The series shown is the number of beneficiaries divided by total labour force survey unemployment in percentage.

b) Long-term unemployment beneficiaries divided by total unemployment beneficiaries in percentage. Table 10 from Whiteford (2000) gives an annual series for the long-term share in beneficiary unemployment from 1980 to 1997. This is shown here for years 1980 to 1990 inclusive (annual data were interpolated to give quarterly estimates). From 1991 onwards a second series supplied by the Australian authorities is shown. The series coincide in 1992 and 1997 (for the other years of overlap, the share is lower in the series given by Whiteford).

c) Long-term unemployment divided by total unemployment in percentage, on a labour force survey basis.

Sources: Space-Time Research Website: www.str.com.au, Table 1: Unemployed persons by State (Aust), age and duration, from February 1978, (for total and long-term unemployment), accessed on May 09, 2001; Whiteford (2000), Table 10, from Department of Social Security, *Annual Report*, various years (for long-term beneficiaries from 1980 to 1991); and direct submissions from national authorities (for total and long-term beneficiaries from 1991 to 2001).

1. *Withdrawal rates*

For old-age pensions, the dollar-for-dollar reduction of benefit against income was first modified with the introduction of a free area (the amount of earnings allowed without any reduction in benefit) and a tapered means test in

1969. For unemployment benefits, a free area of $6 per week and a tapered reduction in benefit at a 50% rate up to a certain threshold (followed by a reduction at a 100% rate until the right to benefit was exhausted) was introduced in 1980. The free area was subsequently increased reaching $30 per week in 1986 [Vroman (2000); Warburton, Vuong and Evert (1999)]. As from 1987, this type of benefit income test was applied on a fortnightly rather than a weekly basis, a change which improved the return from irregular patterns of work (*e.g.* three days all within one week of a fortnight). At the start of 1995, for a single person, the free area was $90 per fortnight, the next $80 of earnings led to withdrawal of benefit at 50% rate, but over a wide range of earnings, from $170 to $432, benefit was still reduced dollar for dollar leaving no incentive to increase earnings within this range. In the Working Nation reform of July 1995, the free area was reduced to $60 per fortnight, with still a 50% taper on the next $80 but then a 70% taper applied to earnings of $140 to $514 per fortnight, at which point the right to benefit was exhausted. This structure, after some uprating of the limits, continues to apply.

Until recently families with children affected by reductions in the "More than the Minimum" rate of family payment (described in Table 4.1), could face particularly high effective marginal tax rates on earnings. For example, in 1998 a couple with two teenage children and a single earner gained a net $42 from the first $100 per week of earnings, but only gained a net $81 for the next $500 per week of earnings implying an effective marginal tax rate of nearly 85% over this range (the gain was reduced to $63 if rent assistance was received). A comparison of the scheduled benefits and taxes for a family with two children found that the effective marginal tax rate (taking into account regular taxes and contributions as well as benefits) for earnings in the range of 50% to 150% of Average Production Worker (APW) earnings, in 1992 was 55%, the highest for 18 OECD countries in the study [Whiteford (2000), Tables 4 and 5].

The 2000 New Tax System (NTS) package, in addition to raising various benefit rates, introduced changes to reduce effective marginal tax rates in many situations. For low-income families, Family Payment was replaced by Family Tax Benefit Part A which can be claimed in respect of young people up to age 21 (if they are not receiving Youth Allowance); the income test threshold for couples with dependent children was increased (disregards for dependent children themselves were abolished) and the withdrawal rate for the family benefit was reduced from 50% to 40%; and tax thresholds were increased and the lowest marginal tax rates were reduced. As a result of these changes, since July 2000 a family with a single earner and two teenage children in the age group 13-15 gains $46 from the first $100 per week of earnings and a net $141 for the next $500 per week of earnings, considerably more than in 1998. The NTS package also reduced withdrawal rates for the pension forms of benefit from 50% to 40%.

157

2.   Individualisation of benefits

A particular consequence of means testing is that, within couples, a partner who is unemployed is disqualified, or partly disqualified, from benefit when the other partner has significant earnings. With high benefit withdrawal rates, an unemployed couple gains little when one partner enters low-paid work. The resulting disincentive to work when a partner is unemployed clearly could influence the concentration of unemployment in households where no other person is employed.[128] The particular problems which arise from means testing of benefits for a couple on their joint income were initially tackled in 1990, by introducing an "earnings disregard" of $30 per fortnight for each member of a couple in addition to the pre-existing $60 per fortnight "free area" which applied to the couple's combined earnings.[129] In July 1995 benefit entitlements were individualised further. The higher rate of benefit for an unemployed person with a dependent spouse was abolished, and Parenting Allowance (now Parenting Payment-Partnered) and Partner Allowance were introduced. Parenting Payment-Partnered can be claimed by the spouse of an unemployed claimant who has care of a child under the age of 16. Partner Allowance can be claimed by a spouse born before July 1955 (thus, over 40 years old in 1995, but this limit rises each year) without recent labour market experience. Spouses who are unable to claim these benefits can generally claim only unemployment benefit, which requires them to seek and be available for full-time work.

It is still the case that one partner's entitlement to benefit can be exhausted if earnings of the other partner are sufficiently high. One partner's income adds to the other's for benefit entitlement purposes insofar as it exceeds the amount necessary to preclude payment of their own allowance. In the case of unemployment benefits, in 1998, the system parameters implied that income in excess of $499.71 per fortnight would be counted as income for the partner (see Table 4.1). Hence, a disincentive for an earner to declare cohabitation with a non-earner remains. Even when neither partner has income or assets, basic payment rates – as shown in Table 4.1 – are about 10% lower for members of a legally-recognised partnership than they are for two single people living together.

3.   Part-time work and benefit

Trends in the number of beneficiaries with income from part-time work are shown in Chart 4.2. The individualisation of benefit in 1995 created a discontinuity in these statistics: on the old basis, the proportion of beneficiaries with earnings rose from 5% in the mid-1980s to about 18.5% in May 1995. On the new basis, the proportion has fluctuated at around 14% for some years: it has increased to about 16% recently.

Chart 4.2. **Proportion of unemployment beneficiaries with earnings**[a]
Percentages

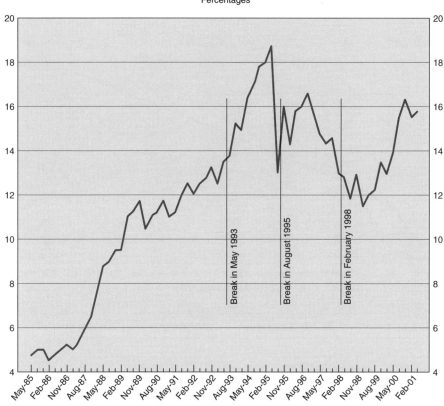

a) Before May 1993, income was classified either "continuing income "or" casual in come". This chart uses "casual income" because income from employment was most likely to be classified as casual. Since May 1993, income has been classified as either "earned income" or "unearned income". Prior to the July 1995 changes, a married recipient was counted as having earned income if either partner had earned income. Following the July 1995 changes, a person is only counted as having earned income if he/she is in receipt of Job Search Allowance/Newstart Allowance and earning from part-time or casual work. The 1998 break results from a change in the source of data. Data were produced using quarterly statistics.

Sources: Until February 1998, data come from *FaCS Annual Report 1998/99* (Section 3.1 on Labour Market Assistance, Figure 1) from http://www.facs.gov.au/annreport99/html/part2/Out3/02_03_01.htm). From May 1998 onwards, direct submissions from national authorities, Labour Market Analysis Section, Parenting and Employment Programs Branch.

Warburton, Vuong and Evert (1999) analysed the behavioural effects of the 1995 change to the income test using administrative data for May 1995 and August 1996. Changes to the income test in 1995 resulted in a small drop in the return to part-time work at low level of earnings, and relatively large increases in

159

Chart 4.3. **Schedules for net income at different levels of gross earnings before and after July 1995 changes to the income test**
Case of a couple with one earner

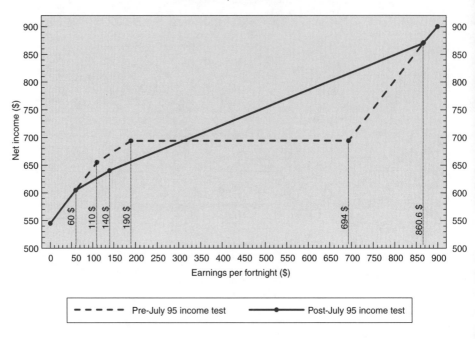

Source: Warburton, Vuong and Evert (1999).

the return to part-time work at the earnings level of the old cut-out point (see Chart 4.3 for the case of a couple with one earner). The expected change was, therefore, a decrease in part-time working at low earnings (below about $240 per fortnight) and an increase above that. In order to isolate behavioural effects, "comparable data sets" containing only unemployed people whose financial circumstances at each date were such that they would have been paid benefit at the other date (the total number of recipients would have increased through an entitlement effect of the higher cut-out point), were used. The results, summarised in Table 4.3, indicate that there was a significant shift from low to higher levels of part-time earnings, but also that many individuals with earnings initially around $150 reduced their earnings to zero when the size of the free area was reduced.

Overall take-up of part-time work only increased significantly for married females. This is likely to partly reflect the individualisation of benefits, as well as

Table 4.3. **Change in the number of unemployed with earnings in certain ranges between the May 1995 and August 1996 comparable data sets**

	All categories	All categories	Single female	Single male	Married female	Married male
Earnings range ($ per fortnight)	Percentage distribution in 1995	Percentage point changes in the number of people in each earnings range from 1995 to 1996				
Up to $60.00	16.6	−2.2	−4.1	−1.8	1.2	−0.6
$60.01 to $140.00	34.0	−6.7	−12.2	−3.6	24.7	−9.2
$140.01 to $240.00	25.8	−3.6	−7.8	−6.3	53.3	−3.7
Over $240.00	23.7	10.3	8.5	2.3	64.6	10.1
All earnings levels	100.0	−1.1	−4.8	−2.8	36.4	−1.3
Memorandum item						
Total number of earners in 1995	120 265	120 265	42 500	40 702	6 131	30 932

Source: Warburton, Vuong and Evert (1999).

the changed income taper. In many cases, couples with a husband working part-time would, prior to the reform, have been subject to a 100% withdrawal rate on the wife's earnings above the "disregard" of $30 per fortnight. The improvement in incentives for married females in such cases would have been much larger than for other groups. Moreover, prior to the reform a husband could claim an addition to benefit for a dependent wife without a requirement on her to be available for work. Increased employment in part-time as well as full-time jobs could reflect the application of an availability requirement with associated delivery of labour market assistance to married females, independently of the impact of financial incentives.

Warburton, Vuong and Evert (1999) show that beneficiaries who have earnings are considerably more likely to leave unemployment benefit and that the proportion leaving increases with the amount of earnings.[130] They suggest on this basis that encouraging unemployed people to undertake part-time work (by making its benefit treatment more favourable) is an effective strategy for moving them off payment, and comment that "The dichotomous world of unemployment and full time employment is long gone. It is time this received greater public recognition". While this is a reasonable consideration, there are still several arguments for caution:

- The fact the part-time workers have relatively high off-benefit transition rates does not directly prove that a more favourable benefit treatment of part-time work will increase the total volume of transitions to full-time work.[131]

- Few people will disagree, in the abstract, with the proposition that effective marginal tax rates (EMTRs) of 70% or more are too high. However, for a given

161

level of full unemployment benefit, it is mathematically only possible to reduce benefit reduction rates at a low levels of earnings by increasing them, by the same amount, at higher levels of earnings. Depending on earnings distribution, for a given policy change the increase might affect more people than the decrease. This explains why detailed OECD analysis has held back from recommending a strategy of general lowering of benefit reduction rates, instead making recommendations concerning the spouses of the unemployed, targeted groups for whom full-time work may not be a realistic option, and in-work benefits (which are usually subject to a minimum hours requirement) [OECD (1994c, 1997f)].

- Canada's recent Self-Sufficiency Project (SSP) experiment, which was designed with a view to maximising "work" effects and minimising "windfall" and "entry" effects, paid an earnings supplement to assistance beneficiaries only when they entered full-time work (30 or more hours per week). The idea was to prevent most people from reducing their work effort in response to the programme. This design was successful, in that full-time employment rates and earnings, for the group offered the supplement increased so sharply that benefit savings more than paid for the costs of the earnings supplement [Greenwood and Voyer (2000)].

- The process of transition from unemployment first into part-time work and later from there into full-time work is too complex to be easily assisted or made effectively obligatory by employment services, which focus their efforts on proposing placements. For example placement resources are not effectively used if jobseekers commonly take up part-time work just when a full-time placement has been organised for them, a well-known phenomenon in relation to referrals to JST and Work for Dole.

The Australian government continues to actively monitor and research the effects of the EMTR approach, so as to improve incentives and their operation.

Across a number of labour market assistance benefits (including Parenting Payment – Single) the percentage of customers with earnings in 1999/2000 was 12.6% [FaCS (2000a), Table 30]. Probably 10% to 15% of part-time workers in Australia are (at any one point in time) combining earnings with a part-payment of one of the benefits designed primarily to provide basic income support (the percentage is uncertain notably because some part-payments relate to people in full-time work). However the proportion would probably be considerably higher if the calculations included only those part-time workers who are potentially eligible for working-age income support payments (e.g. those without a full-time working spouse disqualifying them from payment). Cutout points for unemployed workers are still considerably below average earnings[132] and this suggests that most full-time workers would not have much incentive to qualify for benefits by reducing their working hours.[133] Nevertheless, for workers earning the federal minimum wage ($10.50 per hour as of Spring 2001), a job with half-time hours (17.5 hours per week) attracts $80 per week of benefit, as well as $183.75 of earnings. While many minimum-wage workers will still prefer full-time work, this benefit treatment could significantly increase the proportion that prefer part-time work.

4. *Return to work benefits*

Income support recipients cite the costs of employment, including the start-up costs of employment or education, as a major barrier to participation. RGWR (2000*b*, pp. 26-28) recommended that more attention should be given to informing people about the assistance that is available in this area, mentioning a provision allowing the retention of concession cards upon entry to employment. Centrelink automatically issues Health Care Cards to Newstart recipients. A Health Care Card provides pharmaceuticals at reduced or zero cost ($3.30 per prescription, up to a limit of $171.60 in a calendar year) everywhere in Australia, and a varying range of health, household, educational, recreational and transport concessions which are granted by state, territory, and local governments and private organisations. During the first nine months' receipt of Newstart Allowance, successive cards with a 12-week validity are issued automatically.

Currently, after 12 months of continuous benefit receipt the person becomes eligible for a Health Care Card or Cards whose validity extends for six months after any entry to work that leads to cancellation of the benefit payment. Despite this provision, the loss of the card in the long term is still a disincentive for a permanent return to work and the relatively automatic coverage of high or unpredictable health care and related costs that arises within an uninterrupted benefit claim may be a factor in the persistence of long-term unemployment in the 1990s in Australia.[134]

As another incentive for return to work, long-term unemployed people who take up a full-time job qualify for an Employment Entry Payment of $104. An Education Entry Payment of $208 is also available. These payments, limited to one in any 12-month period, are usually automatic once the person informs Centrelink of his or her return to work.

C. Eligibility conditions for unemployment benefits

1. *An historical overview*

Suitable work

Labour market behavioural criteria for receiving unemployment benefits have changed repeatedly during the past 30 years. In 1974, the general requirement that beneficiaries should be available for work and willing to take it

163

became more precise: moving to a location where no suitable work was available was defined as failing to meet the work test, a provision which is present in few other countries.[135] Work was considered "suitable" if it corresponded to former experience, qualifications, training or occupation. As from 1976, the definition of suitable work was broadened after a reasonable period. In 1989, the definition of suitable work was broadened further to include part-time, temporary and casual work. Under Newstart Allowance, which has applied to the long-term unemployed since 1991 and from the start of an unemployment spell since 1996, acceptance of work without occupational or related restrictions can be required.

Claim continuation and registration for placement

Until 1981, the CES registered claimants, issued benefit claim forms and administered the "work test", in effect acting as an agent for the Department of Social Security (DSS). In 1976, personal lodgement of an income statement with the CES every two weeks was required. However in 1977 a review of the CES was highly critical of what it saw as a confusion of roles, considering that involvement in the administration of unemployment benefits meant a continuing image that the CES was an "unemployment office". In response to these criticisms, during the 1980s the task of registering claimants and income statements and later the administration of fortnightly evidence of job search were transferred to the DSS [O'Donnell (2000), citing the 1977 review of the CES by J.D. Norgard].

In 1985, the government set up a Social Security Review chaired by Professor Bettina Cass. Cass (1988, p. 142) reported that, although registration with the CES remained a legal precondition for receiving benefits, benefits were being paid in situations where registration with the CES had lapsed. She considered that during the decade to 1985 "work testing had become a relatively low administrative priority, although it was tightened in principle" and "resources were not made available for work testing". The report also stated that there was official concern that lack of attention to verifying job search was leading to non-detection of over-payments, *e.g.* where beneficiaries were already in work or had ceased job search. In 1986 the CES was required to report lapses of registration and the unemployed were required to list two job-search contacts per fortnight, paralleling developments in the United Kingdom where Restart reforms had begun.

Activity tests, action plans and job-search reporting

In July 1991, Unemployment Benefit was abolished and replaced with Job Search Allowance for people unemployed for less than a year and all unemployed people under 18, and Newstart Allowance for those 18 and over who were unemployed for more than a year. In 1995, Job Search Allowance for people under 18 was replaced by the Youth Training Allowance. In September 1996, all other Job Search Allowance beneficiaries were transferred to Newstart Allowance. An effect of these changes has been that the legal conditions for Newstart Allowance, *e.g.* the requirement to enter into a Newstart Activity Agreement at administrative discretion, were introduced first for the long-term unemployed and later for all new entrants. Currently, both the Preparing for Work Agreement (introduced in July 2000) prepared at the time of application for benefit and the Preparing for Work Agreement prepared on participation in Intensive Assistance or Job Search Training are legal Newstart Activity Agreements.

The job-search reporting requirements introduced in 1986 were strengthened in 1996 with the requirement that more detailed employer contact information (the employers' name, phone number and type of job applied for) should be listed for job applications reported on the SU19 (claim continuation) form, the issuance of a Jobseeker Diary (JSD) as a standard procedure, and the more frequent issuance of Employer Contact Certificates (ECCs) which have to be signed by an employer as proof of job application at administrative discretion. In addition to these mechanisms for regular contact and job-search verification, Table 4.4 describes administrative campaigns of interviews with the unemployed in 1987, 1989, 1990 and 1991, and the 1987 introduction of a requirement for new applicants to provide an employment separation certificate (signed by the previous employer) and answer a work intentions questionnaire.

Although specific changes were introduced in the 1986 to 1996 period, it is not clear that these made benefit eligibility conditions particularly strict. The interview campaigns in 1987-1991 only involved interviews with the long-term unemployed every one or two years, which is by any standards a low frequency of contact. Also, according to some commentators [Baldock (1994); Eardley *et al.* (1996*b*)], with the introduction of the Newstart "activity test" in 1991 the "old work test" was dropped. In legal terms this is not correct. Under the activity test, job search requirements were generally strengthened while allowing certain groups to undertake activities other than, or in addition to, job search, but accepting offers of suitable work is still required – as is shown by the fact that benefit sanctions for refusing a specific offer of suitable work have continued. However, a perception that the "work test" had been dropped did arise, and may have encouraged, or reflected, a change in practical emphasis on it.

Labour market programmes

A requirement for unemployed jobseekers to accept referrals to a labour market programme does not appear to have been widely applied in the 1980s, although some politicians did suggest then that young people should be required to participate in a "work for unemployment benefits" programme [Yeend (2000)]. From the early 1990s, the long-term unemployed were commonly required to participate in training under the Skillshare programme. Under Working Nation, people who had been on unemployment allowances for more than 18 months were required to accept a place on a job creation programme although, in the short life of the initiative, this requirement was not systematically implemented (see Chapter 5.B). Under the Mutual Obligation Initiative of 1998 (see below) participation in Work for the Dole could be made obligatory for youth unemployed for more than six months, and since then such requirements have been extended.

Relaxation of requirements for certain workers

Table 4.4 illustrates a trend in the 1980s and 1990s towards relaxation of eligibility requirements in specific circumstances. In addition to the reduction in income tapers (documented above), reporting requirements for those in part-time work were relaxed and the long-term unemployed were allowed to do more voluntary work. In 1986, relaxed reporting was permitted for long-term unemployed

Table 4.4. **Selected changes to labour market behavioural criteria for benefit eligibility to 1997**

1974	Suitable work defined as work in the person's usual occupation **or** work in which the person's experience, qualifications and training could be used. Situations of failure to meet the work test are defined: moving to a location where no suitable work is available; deliberately making themselves unacceptable to employers; seeking only occupations for which they are not qualified or for which vacancies are rarely available; adopting a style of presentation (*e.g.* dress) clearly inappropriate for the employment sought.
1976	Definition of "suitable work" is broadened after a reasonable period. Personal lodgement of an income statement is required each fortnight. Six-week sanction for voluntary unemployment.
1986	Enforcement of the requirement for registration with the CES. Requirement for listing of job search efforts on the form (SU19) lodged fortnightly. Long-term unemployed aged over 55 given the option of lodging this form only every 12 weeks.
1987	Automatic reviews established for people in receipt of benefit for more than 2 years, and additional Unemployment Benefit review teams established. Sanction for voluntary unemployment revised to 2 weeks in first instance but increased up to 12 weeks for repeated infractions. New applicants are required to provide an employment separation certificate (signed by the previous employer) and answer a work intention questionnaire.
1988	Unemployment Benefit for young unemployed (aged 16 and 17) replaced by Job Search Allowance (JSA), with reporting to the CES every fortnight and Job Search Training or other ALMP participation after 6 months.
1989	Intensive interviews of all long-term unemployed aged 21 to 54 (Newstart, joint DSS and CES activity). Procedures for CES to report work test infractions to DSS are clarified. List of allowable activities for the long-term unemployed widened to include full-time training and full-time voluntary work for 4 weeks, and part-time English courses. Definition of suitable work broadened, to include part-time, temporary and casual work (previously only full-time work).

Table 4.4.   **Selected changes to labour market behavioural criteria for benefit eligibility to 1997** (*cont.*)

1990	Intensive interviews of all long-term unemployed. Long-term unemployed who take part-time employment earning *at least* 35% of average male full-time earnings, are no longer required to seek full-time work. Sanctions for failing to reply to correspondence or attend interviews are increased.
1991	Unemployment Benefit replaced by JSA for short-term unemployed, with a detailed mail questionnaire after 3 months and a CES interview after 6 months. Long-term unemployed have to make a separate claim for Newstart Allowance (NSA) involving an intensive interview and a Newstart Activity Agreement (contractual obligation to undertake an agreed course of action). Newstart allows full-time training and voluntary work 8 weeks per year.
1993	Unemployed for over 6 months allowed to do 6 weeks full-time voluntary work per year. Lower age limit for relaxed reporting (every 12 weeks rather than 2 weeks), and for removal of the requirement to search for full-time work if in part-time work, reduced to 50 years.
1994	The current distinction between "activity test" sanctions (relating to voluntary unemployment, refusal of work, etc.) and "administrative" sanctions is introduced. Mature Age Allowance (MAA), not subject to the activity test, was introduced for the long-term unemployed aged over 60. Arrangements allowing temporary retention of secondary benefits and partial retention of earnings, during casual work, are extended. Sanctions depend *inter alia* on time unemployed (a feature abolished in 1997).
1995	Youth Training Allowance (YTA), paid only to those in approved training, job search, or employment preparation activities, replaces JSA for customers under 18 years. Exemptions from the activity test in various cases (development of self-employment or co-operative ventures, participation in a broader range of study, training and voluntary work) introduced. Benefit entitlements (previously a payment to the head of household depending on family size and family income) are individualised so that both partners in a couple are required to look to work in return for the payment (subject to transition arrangements).
1996	JSA abolished and NSA paid from the start of an unemployment spell. Procedures for lodgement of fortnightly continuation forms (SU19) eased in remote areas. Job Search Diary (JSD) introduced, use of Employment Contact Certificates (ECCs) increased, and jobseekers required to provide full contact information about employers they have applied to (on SU19 forms).
1997	Sanctions take the form of a reduction in benefit rather than a non-payment period (except for repeat cases). Activity test infractions now include failure to attend a job interview, failure to declare earnings, and failure to complete a labour market programme. Work for Dole scheme (targeted on 18 to 24 years old) introduced. Unemployed for over 3 months allowed to do 12 weeks full-time voluntary work. New benefit agency, Centrelink, established.

Sources: Advice from the Australian authorities and OECD Secretariat.

workers aged over 55 and this limit was lowered to 50 in 1993. The Mature Age Allowance (MAA), not subject to an activity test, was introduced in 1994 for long-term unemployed aged over 60. In May 1999, 47 000 people were on MAA and 111 000 people out of a total 745 000 on Newstart Allowance were aged over 50.

Another significant relaxation of requirements occurred recently with the decision to make participation in the CDEP scheme by indigenous workers voluntary. Until 1997, for places in a CDEP scheme for indigenous workers had been treated as "suitable work" so that participation was, if places were available, in principle compulsory (see Annex C for further details).

Benefit sanctions

From 1947 to 1979, benefit could be stopped for between two and twelve weeks, at administrative discretion, following a voluntary quit, refusal of suitable work, cessation of registration with the CES and failure to take reasonable steps to obtain employment. Between 1984 and 1986 the lower limit was raised to six weeks. The current distinction between "activity test" and "administrative" breaches (this is the term used for benefit sanctions in Australia) was introduced in 1994, and since 1997 sanctions have taken the form of a temporary reduction in the level of benefit rather than a non-payment period (except in the case of third time offenders).

2. Current eligibility conditions

Benefit eligibility is still governed, for most unemployed people, by 1991 legislation on Newstart Allowance, as amended. In general, Newstart Allowance is payable if a person (a) is unemployed; (b) satisfies the activity test, or is exempted from it; and (c) is prepared to enter a Newstart Activity Agreement or is exempted. The "activity test" is a complex construct. It covers, for example, voluntary quit of a previous job and failure to declare earnings as well as the current activities of the jobseeker, and the terms of the activity test allow clients to undertake a limited range of activities such as voluntary work while other requirements are reduced.

Availability for work and suitable work

Unemployed people who temporarily travel within Australia or who undertake charitable work are still considered to be available for work, provided they remain contactable and otherwise satisfy the activity test. People with constraints on job search and possible work (e.g. with child-care responsibilities) are considered available if they satisfy the activity test (but they will often qualify for a separate benefit such as Carers Allowance, or Parenting Payment partnered or non-partnered, if any child is aged under 16 years).

In general, all kinds of work are considered "suitable". Pay must conform to minimum award standards and there are some other safeguards, e.g. the unemployed may not be required to accept work replacing other workers who are on strike, and cannot be required to take a job where union membership is a precondition, nor work to which they have genuine moral, cultural or religious objections. Employer-paid training for an apprenticeship wage may also be suitable. Work involving a commute of more than 90 minutes (with some exceptions in locations where longer commutes are habitual) or travel costs greater than 10% of the gross wage is not considered suitable.

Prior to Job Network, refusal or failure to attend a job interview as instructed by the CES was a failure of the activity test, and deliberate behaviour to discourage a potential employer was judged to be a refusal of work. Under Job Network, JN members are required to advise Centrelink when they consider that a jobseeker has failed to meet their Activity Agreement, and this includes not attending interviews when requested or declining an offer of suitable employment. Employers can also report possible breaches of the Activity Agreement through the Employer Hotline. Centrelink then investigates the breach recommendation or employer report. These procedures differ from those which commonly generate sanctions for refusal of suitable work in other countries. For example, in many countries there is a standardised form which employers are often asked to return to report the outcome of referrals. In the United Kingdom sanctions cannot be imposed on the basis of a report by a private employer unless the refusal of work relates to a vacancy which was notified to the jobseeker by the Employment Service [Chatrik *et al.* (1999)]. Thus it is not clear *a priori* whether the Australian procedures will generate enough reports of adequate quality to maintain the suitable work requirements effectively.

Independent job search

Jobseekers are required to demonstrate independent efforts of job search as an activity test requirement. In 2000 the requirement for reporting job-search acts on SU19 forms was increased to three contacts with employers and one contact, which however may be only *via* a touch screen, with a JN member. For jobseekers who have been issued a JSD, the minimum number of applications was increased from 2 to 4 per fortnight and the maximum from 8 to 10 per fortnight [DEWRSB (2000c); O'Loughlin (2000)]. The actual number is "calculated" in light of education, age, local labour market, transport, etc. Job search is also monitored using Employer Contact Certificates (see Section D below). At the same time, job-search requirements for workers with part-time work between 30 and 50 hours per fortnight were halved.

Mutual Obligation

When the notion of "reciprocal obligation" was introduced by Cass (1988), it referred largely to measures such as including part-time work in the definition of suitable work (while reducing income tapers) and expanding the job-search reporting requirement. The current Australian government interprets Mutual

169

Obligation, as introduced in 1998, as follows: "that it is fair and reasonable to ask unemployed people to participate in an activity which both helps to improve employability and makes a contribution to the community in return for payments of unemployment benefits" [John Howard, cited in Curtain (2000)]. Currently jobseekers are required to undertake a Mutual Obligation activity over a six-month period after six months on payment (for 18-24 year olds) or twelve months on payment (for 25-34 year olds). The requirement then applies to eligible jobseekers for at least 6 months in every 12 months thereafter. Some groups (jobseekers living in isolated areas, those with part-time caring responsibilities and those eligible for Community Support Program) are exempt [Kemp (2000a)].

Participation in Intensive Assistance satisfies Mutual Obligation requirements automatically. In other cases, Mutual Obligation requires participation in one of a list of activities shown in Table 4.5. The options listed at the bottom of the table, CDEP (for indigenous people), Literacy and Numeracy Training, New Apprenticeships Access, Advanced English for Migrants and JPET (for youth at risk of homelessness) are only open to specific target groups [Kemp (2000a)]. Therefore for most unemployed the main "optional" options, although still subject to the availability of appropriate opportunities, appear to be part-time work, education and training, voluntary work, defence force reserves, Green Corps, relocation and Work for the Dole. If none of these options are commenced on the jobseeker's own initiative, Centrelink makes a direct referral normally to Work for the Dole or in some exceptional cases, to JST.[136] All the labour market programmes on the Mutual Obligation menu of activities exist as separate programmes such that places can be filled by referral process outside the Mutual Obligation interview process. Except in the case of Work for the Dole and CDEP, participants do not receive an additional payment to offset participation costs.

The concept of Mutual Obligation seems likely to remain important in Australian labour market policy, notably because all political parties gave a sympathetic reception to the McClure Report which proposed extensions of it to MAA, Disability Support Pension, and Parenting Payment recipients. Eardley *et al.* (2000) cite several earlier surveys, including one showing substantial support for Work for the Dole among participants themselves, and cite new findings from a general opinion survey conducted between April and June 1999: between 72% to 84% of respondents support requirements on young unemployed and long-term unemployed to "take part in a 'work for the dole' scheme", "undergo a training or retraining program", "undertake useful work in the community" and "improve reading and writing skills". Support falls to between 36% and 63% when older unemployed (aged 50 and more) and unemployed with young children are considered and is lower again when people affected by a disability are considered.[137]

Table 4.5. **Mutual Obligation Options in 2000/01**

Activity	Broad estimate of distribution of jobseekers in activities in 2000/01[a]	Participation requirement[b]
General programmes mainly accessed through Centrelink referrals		
Intensive Assistance	156 000	Up to two years of individualised job preparation and support.
Job Search Training	6 000	The length of the course (usually 3 weeks) followed by 14 weeks of more intensive job search.
Work for the Dole	50 000	The length of the project (generally 6 months) involving on average 12-15 hours of activity a week.
Activities mainly chosen by jobseeker initiative		
Part-time work	23 000	A minimum of 8 hours a week for *at least* 4 months out of 6 months.
Voluntary work	12 000	A minimum of 12-15 hours a week for *at least* 4 out of 6 months.
Education or training	12 000	A minimum of 6 hours contact a week in an accredited course. Completion of a course of *at least* 4 months or a full semester for longer courses is required or supplementation with another activity for shorter courses.
Relocation	2 000	Movement to another area which has a higher demand for the young person's skills or significantly higher employment prospects followed by 14 weeks of more intensive job search.
Green Corps[c]	400	Green Corps participants will not have to satisfy mutual obligation requirements while receiving a training allowance.
Programmes for special groups		
Literacy and numeracy training	10 000	Up to two semesters involving 6-15 hours of activity a week.
Job Placement, Employment and Training (JPET) Programme	500	The length of the programme with contact hours per week varying depending on individual need. Young people who cease to participate in JPET before the end of 26 weeks will need to undertake another mutual obligation activity.
Community Development Employment Programme	18 500	CDEP participants will not have to satisfy mutual obligation requirements whilst participating.
Jobs Pathway Programme	10 000	The length of the programme. Young people who cease to participate in JPP before the end of 26 weeks will need to undertake another mutual obligation activity.
New Apprenticeship Access Programme	5 000	Completion of the course which is generally 6 months. Jobseekers who cease to participate in training before the end of 26 weeks will need to undertake another mutual obligation activity. Clients must be otherwise eligible.
Advanced English for Migrants Programme	1 700	Completion of the course which is generally 6 months. Jobseekers who cease to participate in training before the end of 26 weeks will need to undertake another mutual obligation activity. Clients must be otherwise eligible.
Total jobseekers in activities	**307 100**	

a) This table contains a combination of the number of programme places that have been funded and the expected number of jobseekers in particular activities, for example, part-time work.
b) Chapter 5 describes many of the programmes listed in this table.
c) A further voluntary service option, participation in Defence Force Reserves, was added in July 2000 (no estimate for participant numbers is yet available).
Source: Advice from the Australian authorities.

D. Centrelink processes

1. Initial claim procedures and agreements with jobseekers

At the beginning of an unemployment spell, reasons for separation from a previous job are reported on an Employment Separation Certificate. Centrelink officers contact the employer, and interview the customer in cases of conflicting statements. A doubt that remains after full investigation acts in the customer's favour. Initial entitlement to benefit also depends on some other conditions. People who have liquid assets or have received a redundancy or severance package over certain thresholds may have to wait for a period of time before payments can start. There is now no prior assessment of whether suitable work is available for the claimant, in contrast to previous arrangements where a claimant had to obtain a statement from the CES that no suitable work was available in order to support an application for benefit to DSS. After a claim has been accepted registration with a JN member, who may attempt placement and report any refusal of work, is usually required.

The activity-focused Preparing for Work Plan was introduced in late 1999, originally for jobseekers who had been unsuccessful in their job search for three months or longer. The Preparing for Work Agreement (PfWA) was introduced in July 2000. It includes an agreement to fill in a JSD and return it upon request, to register with a JN member (for Job Matching) and, for the relevant age groups, to enter Mutual Obligation when the time comes. The PfWA is negotiated with all jobseekers at the first detailed registration interview. As from July 2000, people in the relevant age groups are asked to choose a Mutual Obligation option in their initial Preparing for Work Agreement, although the option may be varied later on.

2. Claim continuation and job-search reporting procedures

At the first detailed registration interview, jobseekers are generally issued with a fortnightly Application for Payment (claim continuation) form (SU19) and a JSD. The income record asks for earnings to be listed for each day of the fortnight. If the JSD is not issued, a variant form of SU19 which requires listing of contacts as described in Section C can be issued. The SU19 must be lodged at the Centrelink office in person, except in areas without a Centrelink office where other arrangements are allowed. FaCS is attempting to ensure that unemployed people hand in the forms at reception where a Centrelink officer checks the form is filled out corrected, signed and dated. However in practice Centrelink premises sometimes have a letter box so that no personal contact with the jobseeker occurs when forms are lodged.

The JSD provides for listing up to ten employers contacted each fortnight with name, address, telephone, job description, the person contacted and the type of vacancy (advertised, word of mouth, JN vacancy or other). Listed contacts do not necessarily have to be interviews, only approaches to employers. Each JSD covers seven fortnights and must be returned in person after 12 weeks. Although failure to return the Diary can be sanctioned as an administrative breach (see Table 4.6), Centrelink in practice blocks payment of benefit when a fortnightly Application for Payment form is posted without the Diary when it is due. This makes it possible to enforce JSD requirements without breach action in most cases (a breach might still be imposed if, for example, the Diary has been lost for unacceptable reasons). The JSDs, introduced in 1996, are reported to be fairly well accepted by jobseekers now. The number of JSDs issued increased from 402 000 in 1998/99 to 616 000 in 1999/2000. Given that there were 709 000 unemployment beneficiaries on average, this indicates that even in 1999/2000 less than a quarter of unemployment beneficiaries at any point in time were maintaining a JSD. In 1999/2000, 73% of JSDs were rated as satisfactory, 13% as marginal and less than 2% as unsatisfactory [FaCS (2000a)].

People judged to be "at risk" of failing to meet their activity test obligations can also be required to return Employer Contact Certificates (ECCs). "At risk" groups include those with questionable reasons for ceasing work; who incurred previous activity breaches; and who have various risk factors for job search, e.g. past or spousal self-employment, work as an actor. Applications must be for advertised vacancies or to employers who have work, according to word of mouth. If a cold-canvassed employer has no work, the jobseeker should approach another employer to get the ECC completed. The administration of ECCs reportedly encounters some resistance, e.g. when the jobseekers say they do not want the employer to know they are on benefits or that employers have refused to sign/stamp, and from employers close to Centrelink offices, who may get too many callers asking them to fill ECCs. Recently a new procedure has been introduced, with seven ECCs (one per fortnight, each requiring two employer contacts) being issued to jobseekers who are engaging in 14 weeks of intensive job search following participation in JST or relocation to meet Mutual Obligation requirements [Kemp (2000a)]. This probably accounts for the increase in the number of ECCs issued from 63 000 in 1998/99 to 232 000 in 1999/2000. This remains a low figure, being equivalent to less than one ECC for every three person-years of unemployment.

3. Three-month and nine-month review process

A jobseeker's first JSD has to be returned with a review form which is sent to clients after 10 weeks of unemployment. Centrelink staff in the light of both the JSD and the review form, and on the basis of additional risk factors, select 40% of cases for a face-to-face interview. A similar procedure, not usually involving JSDs, is repeated after nine months of unemployment.

4.   Administration of Mutual Obligation and referrals to Work for the Dole

When jobseekers in the eligible age groups first become eligible for Mutual Obligation after 6 or 12 months in unemployment, they have a Mutual Obligation Initiative interview with Centrelink which informs them of the requirements. Jobseekers, except for those referred to Intensive Assistance (see above), are issued with Mutual Obligation Diary which is a JSD with additional pages where Mutual Obligation activities can be listed. For each activity listed, attendance dates and hours must be filled in and signed or stamped by the part-time employer or the contact person for the activity, allowing the Centrelink office to tally total hours spent in Mutual Obligation activities. Referrals to Work for the Dole are made when a person has been subject to Mutual Obligation requirements for six weeks, but has not been referred to Intensive Assistance or JST or begun any other Mutual Obligation option. Mutual Obligation periods later in the spell do not involve a formal Centerlink interview, and people whose Mutual Obligation diary does not list participation in another approved Mutual Obligation Activity are therefore "auto-referred" to Work for the Dole.

5.   Referrals to the Community Support Program, Job Network and JST

The referral procedures are mainly described in Chapter 3. It may be noted that jobseekers are not required to comply with referrals to JST or Work for the Dole if they they take up another Mutual Obligation option such as part-time work. By contrast, following an initial referral to Intensive Assistance jobseekers are generally required to stay in the programme, until they have done enough work to justify a payment to the provider for a successful IA outcome.

6.   The application of eligibility conditions within Intensive Assistance

When a jobseeker is referred to Intensive Assistance, Centrelink drops the requirement for fortnightly lodgement of SU19 forms and instead requires only the return of an income statement every four weeks. Until January 2001, the requirement was only for return of an income statement every 13 weeks. Centrelink also drops requirements for reporting job search contacts, in a JSD or by another method.

Intensive Assistance providers negotiate an Activity Agreement with the unemployed person: forwarding of the Activity Agreement to DEWRSB and its approval by DEWRSB triggers a payment to the provider for a commencement. The Activity Agreement could in principle require reporting of job-search actions (to the IA provider) but in practice such provisions do not appear to be used. In the first JN contract period, many Activity Agreements also appear not to have not specified any minimum frequency of in-person (or indeed any) contact with the provider. However, in the second JN contract period, many IA providers have undertaken in their Declaration of Intent to DEWRSB to interview clients with a minimum frequency (this may be once every two weeks or once every month) and this is now written into Activity Agreements. Since JN members must now register each contact with an IA client on the IES computer screen, DEWRSB contract managers can monitor provider compliance with their commitment to interview clients with a minimum frequency, and advise providers if they are falling short. This in turn pressures IA providers to submit participation reports to Centrelink about clients who fail to attend interviews. Any breaches that result are activity test breaches (see below), because non-compliance with the Activity Agreement is the legal basis for them. As of September 2000, there was evidence of increased breaching of clients for non-attendance (see below).

Centrelink does not refer unemployed people to vacant jobs, but it has been taking some steps to oblige the unemployed to apply for known vacancies, again *via* Activity Agreements. In the Sydney area, when labour demand was buoyant in the run-up to the September 2000 Olympics, Centrelink agreed with DEWRSB on a policy of requiring attendance at job fairs. DEWRSB contract managers indicated to JN providers that they should include this requirement in variations of jobseekers' Activity Agreements. As these examples illustrate, DEWRSB and Centrelink in co-operation – using the powers of DEWRSB contract managers to monitor JN providers and the powers of Centrelink to impose breaches – are able to apply selected activity requirements with a degree of area-wide or even nationwide consistency.

7. Long-term case management

Participation in most labour market programmes lasts six months or less, and unless some other event leading to exit occurs, participation in Intensive Assistance lasts for between 12 months (level A, without extension) and 21 months (level B, with maximum permitted extension). However, over 60% of unemployment benefit recipients have been on benefit for more than 12 months and about 40% have durations of over two years [FaCS (1999c)]. So there are many unemployed people for whom participation in Intensive Assistance is just one episode within a long spell of unemployment. Policies for handling such situations, in terms for example of whether people exiting Intensive Assistance are issued with Job Search Diaries or Mutual Obligation Diaries, or can be referred directly to Work for the Dole, etc. were initially not very clear, with a risk that many jobseekers might fall through the gaps or that practices would vary by location for no particular reason.

By default, responsibility for longer-term case management in such cases might appear to lie with Centrelink. However, there is no fixed schedule for Centrelink reviews after the 12-week and 9-month reviews (which apply to only a proportion of clients), other than the re-application of JSCI at least every

175

12 months, and no mechanism for Centrelink to maintain individual case management records which might, for example, include the outcomes of a psychological assessment, remedial training undertaken and jobs applied for during Intensive Assistance. The lack of arrangements for transferring records is believed to be actually required by the Privacy Act 1988.[138] The general principle of moving the long-term unemployed from one "activation" system to another – avoiding inertia, and when one thing has not worked, trying something else – is probably sound from the point of view of its impact on unemployed people. However it creates additional issues of continuity, co-ordination and coherence which merit careful consideration. Simpler and better coordination and sequencing of programmes and assistance will be an aim of the government's Welfare Reform initiative.

8. Breach activity

Background

Table 4.6 shows the schedule of benefit sanctions introduced in 1997 [Moses and Sharples (2000)]. Except in repeated cases, sanctions take the form of a temporary reduction in benefit rather than a stop. The distinction between "activity test" and "administrative" breaches is somewhat arbitrary with, for example, failure to report to an Intensive Assistance provider and failure to return ECCs counted as "activity test" breaches but failure to return the JSD is counted as an "administrative" breach.

In the second half of 1997, as shown in Table 4.7, the incidence of benefit sanctions in relation to labour market behavioural conditions during the benefit period (not including breaches for voluntary quit) was 3.3% per year per person in the stock of unemployed, 7th out of 13 countries for which statistics were available [Grubb (2001)]. Australia, however, had the lowest incidence of sanctions among countries that apply a regular job-search reporting requirement. By contrast,

Table 4.6. **Schedule of unemployment benefit reductions and non-payment periods**

	First breach in a 2-year period	Second breach in a 2-year period	Third and subsequent breaches in a 2-year period
Activity test breach	18% reduction for 26 weeks	26% reduction for 26 weeks	Benefit stops for 8 weeks
Administrative breach	16% reduction for 13 weeks (with option of a 2 week non-payment period)		
Employment-related exclusion period for moves to areas of lower employment prospects	26-week non-payment period		

Source: Advice from the Australian authorities.

Table 4.7. **Unemployment benefit refusals and sanctions,
10 July 1997 to 30 November 1997**[a, b]

	Persons	Incidence (%)[c]
Initial conditions	**10 743**	**2.21**
Move to area of lower employment prospects	19	0.00
Quit	7 730	1.59
Misconduct	2 994	0.62
Labour market behaviour	**10 283**	**3.30**
Refusal of suitable work	**1 028**	**0.33**
Failure of activity test – CES	355	0.11
Other DSS and CES activity test	673	0.22
ALMP or related action plan	**5 668**	**1.82**
a. Refusal or quit of ALMP	7	0.00
Work for Dole	7	0.00
b. Failed to agree or carry out action plan	5 661	1.82
Failure to agree Newstart plan	2 952	0.95
Failure to carry out Newstart plan	2 709	0.87
Insufficient evidence of independent job search	**3 587**	**1.15**
Employer Contact Certificate	579	0.19
Jobseeker Diary	2 560	0.82
SU19	448	0.14
Administrative infractions[d]	**35 509**	**11.41**
a. Non-declaration of income or family circumstances	8 407	2.70
b. Other contact with PES	27 102	8.71
Non-attendance at interview	5 122	1.65
Non-response to correspondence	7 670	2.47
Non-attendance 12 weeks/9 months review	2 168	0.70
Failure to contact CES	9 160	2.94
Failure to keep appointment with CES field staff	732	0.24
Failure to notify changed circumstances	623	0.20
Non-return of Jobseeker Diary	1 572	0.51
Other	54	0.02
Total	**56 535**	
***Memorandum items*: Benefit claims**		
Annual new claims (1997, estimate)[e]	**1 250 000**	
Average stock of claims (1997, estimate)	**800 000**	

a) Refusals and sanctions relating to labour market criteria and administrative requirements related to placement work, not including refusals due to failure to complete an initial application in full or an initial determination of lack of entitlement or availability for work. Grubb (2001) gives statistics for benefit refusals and sanctions classified to the same main headings for 13 other countries.
b) Cancellations of claims at the time of intensive reviews (32 000) are not included.
c) Incidences are calculated as percentages of the flow of new benefit claims in the case of "initial conditions", and as percentages of the stock of claims at an equivalent annual rate otherwise.
d) Administrative infractions according to an OECD classification, which does not correspond to the Australian category of "administrative" breaches.
e) New claims estimated from Jobseeker Diaries issued and exempted, at an annual rate.
Source: Report by national authorities.

sanctions for non-compliance with administrative requirements, such as attendance at interviews with the employment service, at over 10% per year per person unemployed, were the highest recorded. This is largely because many countries only apply sanctions of defined duration for a narrower range of more substantive offences (refusal of work or to enter labour market programmes and failure to seek work).

Non-application of breaches after the initiation of a procedure

In 1999/2000, 302 000 breach penalties were imposed but a further 188 000 (38% of the total) were either recommended but not imposed, or imposed but overturned. About two-thirds of participation reports from Community Work Coordinators (in relation to Work for the Dole) and other Mutual Obligation providers, but less than half of the participation reports from JN members, result in a breach being imposed [Moses and Sharples (2000)]. Among the reasons for JN reports not leading to breaches are: the jobseeker may have been eligible for referral in the first place, but had a change of circumstances such as returning to work before starting Job Network; "[i]nterface problems between the Centrelink and DEWRSB computer systems" which can result in Job Network letters being sent to the wrong address (about 9% of cases in 1999) and jobseekers being referred to programmes when they are ineligible for participation (these interface problems have to a large extent been resolved); Job Network did not provide sufficient documentation for the report (about 12% of cases in 1999); and the JN report was for a Centrelink-only breach category such as "customer voluntarily unemployed" (about 9% of cases in 1999). However, the most common reason for not imposing breaches (about 30% of cases in 1999) was the "customer provided Centrelink with sufficient evidence to support their claim" [Moses and Sharples (2000); DEWRSB (2000d)]. Because of privacy requirements, JN members do not usually get feedback from Centrelink on the nature of this evidence. In some cases the evidence appears to have been, in the early period of Job Network, only a client's statement that he or she slept in or didn't receive the letter. A joint project between DEWRSB, Centrelink and FaCS reported that the issue of "reasonable excuse" was frequently raised by JN providers, and in August 1999 as an outcome of the Activity Test Quality Assurance Project, Centrelink issued new guidelines indicating that a "reasonable excuse" must be a matter outside the control of the jobseeker and must be accompanied by action to notify the JN provider of the circumstances and arrange a subsequent appointment [DEWRSB (1999d)].

Frequent breaches for non-commencement and non-attendance

Most participation reports from JN members relate to failure to start JST or Intensive Assistance (Table 4.8). Failure to start on the programme is reported in relation to about 12% of JST referrals and 15-20% of IA referrals [DEWRSB (2000d),

Table 4.8.   **Breaches resulting from reports by Job Network members, 1999/2000**

Job Network service	Reason for breach	Number
Intensive Assistance (approximately 300 000 commencements and 240 000 average stock in 1999/2000)		
	Did not attend interview-with Service Provider	35 275
	Fail to enter into activity agreement	11 449
	Fail to carry out an activity agreement	10 353
Job Search Training (approximately 60 000 commencements in 1999/2000)		
	Did not contact Service Provider within 7 to 14 days of referral	10 003
	Delay/fail to enter Job Search Skills Plan	498
	Fail to enter/comply Job Search Skills Plan	929
Job Matching (approximately 600 000 Job Matching only enrolments and 600 000 stock in 1999/2000[a])		
	Failed to enrol with Job Network member	140
	Fail to attend job course or interview	2 266
	Fail to start job/course as planned	1 382
	Unwilling to undertake suitable work	714
Total Breaches		**73 009**

a) Job Matching only enrolments are estimated as NSA claims and Youth Allowance (other than full-time student) claims granted in the previous year (about 900 000), *less* IA commencements. Several non-beneficiary categories may enrol, but some new claims may not lead to enrolment in either service. Job Matching achieved about 300 000 placements in 1999/2000: an individual could be placed more than once within a benefit spell.

Sources: Advice from the Australian authorities and OECD Secretariat estimates.

p. 118], but only about half of these reports result in a breach being imposed. As noted in Chapter 3, actual rates of non-commencement following referral were about 60% for JST and 30% for IA, it appears that non-commencements of IA result in a participation report in about one-half the cases and an actual breach in about one-quarter, while non-commencements of JST result in a report in only a fifth of cases and an actual breach only one time in ten. It should be kept in mind that there are legitimate reasons for non-commencement, such as starting work and temporary sickness.

In 1999/2000, rates of breaching had roughly doubled as compared to the latter half of 1997 (the period covered by Table 4.7). This appears to be due to several factors [Moses and Sharples (2000)]. The substitution of non-payment periods for rate reduction periods (in most cases involving a lesser total loss of benefit) made Centrelink staff more willing to impose breaches. New activity test requirements were created with the introduction of Job Network, Work for the Dole and other Mutual Obligation initiatives: in 1999/2000, over a third of all breaches were classified under these headings. Procedures for detecting failure to declare earnings appear to have become more effective through a programme of matching Employment Declaration Forms (lodged with the Australian Tax Office by employers) against unemployment benefit claims. Breaches in some longstanding categories such as failure to return the JSD, unsatisfactory completion of the JSD and failure to attend interviews scheduled after 12 weeks and 9 months also increased significantly. However breaches in the categories of voluntary quit, dismissal for misconduct and failure to reply to letters decreased.

The increase in breach rates in the latter 1990s may also reflect the economic upturn. Moses and Sharples (2000) comment that according to one view "as the labour market strengthens, those still reliant upon income support are more likely to be non-genuine jobseekers". Among the evidence they see for this is that the proportion of breaches for non-declaration of income is significant and "on a very conservative estimate, 27% of people who are breached do not reclaim within six weeks… a significant proportion must have an alternative source of income".

In practice, and following the new guidelines issued at the end of 1999, there are many breaches relating to failure to attend Intensive Assistance, and non-attendance is not a long-term option for clients who have been referred. However the rigorous process of evidence-based decisions assuring natural justice remains time-consuming and costly. IA providers consider it difficult to get a breach, even in simple cases of non-attendance. This is partly because many participation reports do not lead to breaches but also because three breaches (the third resulting in temporary cessation of benefit) have to be applied before a person referred is taken off their books. In this environment, the conversion of referrals from Centrelink into paid commencements is a major focus of operational effort for Intensive Assistance providers. Some organisations employ full-time staff just to handle breaching procedures. One provider in the Sydney area has tight procedures, telephoning the person a few days ahead to remind them to attend (as already notified by letter), maintaining full documentation of all such steps, investing time in relations with the relevant Centrelink offices and visiting them so as to personally hand dossiers over to the responsible person.

The rate of breaching for failure to enrol for Job Matching is only about 1/500 of the rate of breaching for failure to commence in IA. This could be because the enrolment process is simple, not requiring any direct contact with providers whereas IA participation requires substantial activity from the jobseeker. Also breaches for non-enrolment in Job Matching would require a Centrelink initiative to breach, whereas JN providers have an incentive to recommend breaches because their income depends upon enrolments.

DEWRSB (2000d, p. 118) reports the rate of "compliance breach" recommendations under Intensive Assistance (*i.e.* breaches for non-compliance with an Activity Agreement) as 1% of the stock per month in the first quarter of 1999/2000. The 1% figure may include failures to enter into an agreement: breaches for failure to comply with the terms of an agreement already signed averaged only about 0.4% of the stock per month in 1999/2000 (Table 4.8). The contrast between the 15% to 20% breach rate for failure to start, and a subsequent monthly breach rate about 40 times lower, suggests providers may have devoted much more effort to starting jobseekers in IA than to ensuring their continued attendance after starting. However this may have changed since the evaluation comments that "In the second tender, there has been a stronger emphasis on JN members undertaking more structured activities with the jobseeker in Intensive Assistance, which may affect the future level of compliance breaches".

Infrequent breaches for behaviour in the labour market

Sanctions for refusal of suitable work initiated by JN members, which appear in the Job Matching categories "fail to attend/fail to start job, course or interview" categories, total about 0.6% of the stock of beneficiaries per year. This exceeds the zero or near-zero rates reported from Belgium, Japan and New Zealand, but it remains low as compared to many other countries [Grubb (2001)]. Low sanction rates can arise either because direct referrals are not made or because evidence of refusal is not acted upon. Job Matching providers appear to directly refer jobseekers to vacancies fairly frequently. However they could be reluctant to act for various reasons, *e.g.* reputation with jobseekers, a fear that their employers will regard formal reporting and breach procedures as an unnecessary burden, or their own pressure of work and the lack of any clear return to business results from breach action. Nevertheless, many Job Matching providers are also IA providers, and IA providers appear to have an incentive to clarify the principle that suitable job offers should be accepted.

Breaching and hardship as issues for case management

Individual case management of the long-term unemployed can require many decisions about benefit sanctions. In Australia under the Skillshare programme "seminars titled 'Management of the Difficult Client' produced a litany of misery and frustration from managers and trainers struggling with clients who seem reluctant to genuinely commit themselves to complete, or even begin, preparation for work. They described clients as angry, disinterested, resistant, uncooperative, unmotivated, explosive, intoxicated, not knowing what they wanted, having psychiatric disorders, disrupting classes, using poor relationship skills, and many other exasperating attributes" [List (1996)]. This is in line with experience elsewhere that the long-term unemployed are often not much interested in the assistance that is offered [Finn (2001)]. Intensive interviews with the long-term unemployed, for example, are usually made compulsory [OECD (2001*b*)], probably for this reason. So it seems likely that the compulsory nature of participation in Intensive Assistance case management is important in ensuring its impact.

At the same time, with recent increases in breach rates attention has been drawn to cases where unnecessary hardship arises from breaches. Hanover Welfare Services claims that about one breach penalty in eight is imposed on a

181

homeless person, and considers that such breaches often leave people more dependent on crisis services [Heinrichs (2000)]. ACOSS (2000b) cites several cases where breaches were imposed when there were specific extenuating circumstances, and on people suffering from extreme shyness, substance dependency, or a history of homelessness.

Against this background, it is clear that case managers need to be involved in breach decisions. They need to recommend breaches to get people who are capable of working or preparing for work to participate and co-operate, but they also need to be considerate of the circumstances of individuals when recommending breaches. This raises the question of whether it is appropriate for case managers in private or community organisations, which have extensive freedom to decide on their operational strategies, to play such a role. Many countries may feel that case managers should be government employees, because guaranteeing a fair and uniform application of benefit eligibility criteria is government's responsibility. However, in Australia Centrelink retains the ultimate authority about whether to proceed with a breach recommended by a third party, while in other countries with wholly public systems, extreme variations in sanctions rates, between regions and through time, arise [Grubb (2001)]. Within the current system Australia should continue with efforts to establish clear guidelines and to ensure that appropriate and correctly documented breach recommendations will normally be applied by Centrelink. At the same time, when a person's non-compliance was unintentional and a breach would be counterproductive, case managers should be encouraged to note the particular circumstances which would make breach action inappropriate, and notify new information when relevant since Centrelink officers can revoke a previous breach decision on the basis of new information. Some specific issues concerning sanctions for failure to commence with a JN provider could only be resolved by introducing more continuity in case management, since when case managers have been unable to contact a person they cannot consider individual circumstances, and Centrelink has little track record to go on when considering a breach decision.

Alternative procedures for non-attendance

OECD reviews of the Public Employment Service conducted since 1991, which have covered many Member countries, have in some cases described procedures for handling non-attendance, or commented upon situations where the benefit and placement services do not communicate adequately. But in many countries issues of attendance and participation in employment counselling or case management seem to be handled satisfactorily with both less administrative effort and fewer and less severe sanctions than is the case in Australia at the moment.[139] This is partly because most other countries do not require jobseekers to start in counselling at a different address from the one they habitually attend after a year or more of unemployment, as is the often case for Intensive Assistance. But also, when the issue is only non-attendance at a regularly-available service such as counselling, the device of stopping benefit until the person attends is often used in the place of a sanction. As noted above, Centrelink currently stops benefit without imposing a sanction following failure to return the JSD and this may apply to failure to return some other documents (e.g. 12-week review forms), but this type of procedure is not used in relation to non-attendance at the placement service.

Under Job Network unemployed people could be required to lodge fortnightly Application for Payment forms with their IA provider, or Centrelink could require that Applications for Payment be accompanied by a certificate from the IA provider. Retrospective payments would be possible for the same reasons that currently justify making them after a missed Application for Payment. Most current participation reports and breach decisions in relation to IA would then no longer be needed. Some common standards (in particular, the frequency of contacts with the IA providers which trigger payment should be uniform, e.g. once every two or four weeks for all providers) would be desirable to ensure a degree of horizontal equity, but these need not impinge greatly upon the ability of IA providers to adopt differing case management strategies. For Job Search Training, such a procedure might be applicable but difficulties with it could arise if, in some remote localities, a month or more passes between the starting dates of one course and the next.

Appeals

As discussed above, in 1999/2000, in 38% of cases either a participation report did not lead to a breach determination, or an initial breach determination was overturned. About 3% of breaches initially imposed are appealed to an Authorised Review Officer. Further levels of appeal, to the Social Security Appeals Tribunal and the Administrative Appeals Tribunal, are possible. As shown in Table 4.9, at each

Table 4.9. **Reviews and appeals of decisions concerning eligibility for Newstart Allowance, 1999-2000**[a]

Memorandum item: Newstart breaches finally imposed	302 435	
Level of appeal	Review requests	Changed decisions (%)
Authorised Review Officers	10 569	28.7
Social Security Appeals Tribunal	1 544	26.5
Administrative Appeals Tribunal	216	30.1

a) In the case of Newstart Allowance the majority of eligibility decisions reviewed probably relate to breaches, but some will relate to issues such initial refusal to grant benefit and benefit reduction related to income and assets.
Source: FaCS Annual Report 1999-2000, p.145, Table 33.

stage of appeal about 30% of requests for a review result in a changed decision. ACOSS (2000c) considers this to be evidence that many of the original decisions are wrong. However, this rate of variation on appeal needs to be seen in the light of the fact that only a small minority of decisions at each level are appealed. ACOSS (2000c) considers that the low appeal rate reflects lack of knowledge about appeal rights, the complexity of the process, and incorrect information provided by Centrelink: however, it could also be because in most cases there are no good grounds for appealing. In relation to one important reason for breaching, the non-declaration of income, ACOSS points out that breaches arise due to the requirement that earnings from a new job should be declared to Centrelink immediately even though they may not actually be paid for up to a month.

E. The labour market impact of administration, entitlement and eligibility conditions

1. Comparisons of beneficiary unemployment with survey-based measures

Cross-tabulations of regular labour force survey data against administrative data for benefit status are not available for Australia. However such cross-tabulations have been made for the Survey of Employment and Unemployment Patterns (see Chapter 5 for a more detailed description of this survey). In the matched SEUP Population Reference Group samples for September 1995 and September 1996, only 34% of the individuals who were classified as unemployed were receiving unemployment benefit, and 48% were receiving no benefit (18% had another benefit, *e.g.* sole parent or partner). At the same time, 31% of unemployment beneficiaries were classified in the survey as employed (18% part-time, 7% full-time and 6% self-employed) and another 5% as out of the labour force [ABS (2000h), average of Tables 3.7 and 3.8]. People in receipt of unemployment benefit appears to have been heavily under-represented among survey respondents,[140] and the status of non-respondents may differ from that of respondents. The findings do suggest that the population receiving unemployment benefits differs greatly from the population unemployed according to surveys, in line with experience elsewhere.[141] Much of the difference is related to differences in the ways FaCS and the ABS measure unemployment numbers as mentioned further below.

As shown in Chart 4.1, the ratio of unemployment benefit recipients to total labour force survey unemployed reached about 95% in 1986, fell below 75% in 1990 and 1991 and then rose to reach 110% in 1995 and stayed around this level until quite recently. This ratio is fairly high in comparative terms [for ratios in other countries, see OECD (1998f), Table 1.7]. At the same time the long-term share among benefit recipients, which was 60% in the year 2000, is unusually high. It is much higher than in the 1980s, and much higher than in current labour force survey figures, and contrasts with the general experience of OECD countries during the recovery phases of the cycle when the long-term share in unemployment usually falls.[142] Australia still had early in 2000 over 400 000 long-term benefit recipients, and the total had fallen less than 20% from its historical peak. This suggests, even if a large adjustment is made for definitional peculiarities of the statistics, that much remains to be done in terms of tackling long-term unemployment. In the United Kingdom the number of long-term benefit recipients is now about 250 000, a quarter of the peak 1990s level and a fifth of the peak 1980s level, for a labour force three times larger than Australia's.

2. The influence of definitional factors on beneficiary unemployment

The individualisation of benefits in 1995 could have increased the ratio of beneficiaries to unemployed, since part of the basic payments to an unemployed couple became conditional on both partners claiming benefit. However its impact appears to have been limited, because most partners formerly treated as dependants claimed parenting payments rather than unemployment benefit. In the latter 1990s, about 14% of unemployment benefit recipients in the latter 1990s had some earnings and 5% were counted in the population receiving unemployment payments but had nil payment for the fortnight because of casual income: however the overall proportion with earnings has increased by only a few percentage points during the 1990s. Between 1994 and 1997, about 50 000 unemployment beneficiaries transferred to Mature Age Allowance (see below) but there was a roughly offsetting increase in the number of temporarily incapacitated (i.e. sick) workers receiving unemployment benefit, following a change in the rules which allowed this.[143] An adjustment of the beneficiary total to exclude those who are temporarily incapacitated or in part-time work or casual work (but not adding in Mature Age Allowance beneficiaries) would give a ratio of beneficiaries to unemployed of about 85% rather than about 110% in 1999.

Within the total of beneficiaries, definitional factors have strongly affected the incidence of long-term beneficiary status. Since July 1991, an "allowable breaks" rule has been in place, which permits cancelled recipients to maintain their existing income support status if they reapply for benefit within the 6 or 13 weeks allowable for the short-term unemployed and the long-term unemployed respectively. Since March 1995, a person with earnings which preclude payment (i.e. who is nil paid for the fortnight) remains "current on payment" for a period up to twelve weeks (a restorable cancellation occurs at 10 weeks and a non-restorable cancellation occurs at 12 weeks: before March 1995, these periods were four and six weeks respectively). As a result, a jobseeker with long-term beneficiary status who re-enters unemployment will retain long-term status after a period of up to 25 weeks in full-time work with no benefit.[144] The impact of these provisions on the incidence of long-term beneficiary status could have taken several years to

185

fully work through into the figures shown in Chart 4.1, since they only affected reclassifications of status (i.e. the existing stock of beneficiaries was not reclassified when these rules were changed).

Earlier research has reported that as many as 30% of individuals who have received income support continuously for a year are employed at some point during the year [Warburton, Opoku and Vuong (1999); Landt and Pech (2000)], so that the number of long-term benefit recipients would be this much lower if the "clock" were set back to zero even after a small amount of part-time work. FaCS (1999a, Figure 2) reports that among those classified as long-term beneficiaries in March 1998, 13% had both some earnings and at least one fortnight in the last 26 without payment; a further 28% had had some earnings, but without a break in payment; and 16% had had at least one break in payment, but without earnings. Only the 13% figure appears to correspond to the definition of a break in the unemployment spell used in ABS data prior to April 2001 in terms of two weeks in full-time work. On the other hand, the sum of the first two or even all three figures might be considered to correspond to the ABS definition of a break after April 2001.[145] So definitional adjustments appear to go some way towards explaining the apparently high incidence of long-term benefit receipt, but it is not clear that they can provide a full explanation. Analysis of labour market policy is further complicated by the fact that another administrative concept of duration – duration of registration on the IES system, rather than duration on benefit – is used as input to the JSCI and for referrals to JST and participation in Mutual Obligation.

3. The influence of policy on beneficiary unemployment

Possible explanations for the changes shown in Chart 4.1 include:

- **The link between benefit administration and placement services:** as noted in Section C.1, following a period of breakdown in this link, in 1986 Australia introduced measures to ensure that jobseekers were in contact with the CES and that job search was monitored. This might account for the fall in the ratio of beneficiaries to labour force survey unemployed over the following years.

- **Eligibility conditions:** as noted previously, the introduction of the "activity test" in 1991 seems initially to have been interpreted as meaning that the "old work test" no longer applied, and in 1994 the labour market conditions for benefit were removed for many older workers with the creation of Mature Age Allowance: reduced emphasis on eligibility conditions might be responsible for the relatively rapid increase in beneficiary unemployment in the early 1990s.

- **Measures to increase the incentive for people on unemployment payments to take up casual and/or part-time work**. These include the

Working Nation changes introduced on 1 July 1995 lowered the 100% withdrawal rate to 70% and removal of earnings disregards. Connolly (1999) estimated that the numbers of males and females on unemployment payments responded not only to the numbers of unemployed people of each gender (as estimated by the ABS), but increasingly after 1991 to the incentive for and availability of part-time work. However, Connolly put qualifications on his finding about the latter effect.[146] One reason for thinking that this factor may be of limited importance is that the recorded incidence of part-time work by unemployment beneficiaries has not increased very much in the 1990s (Chart 4.2): also, the recent fall in the beneficiary/unemployed ratio in 2000 and early 2001 coincides with an increase in the incidence of part-time work.

- **Working Nation:** entries to Working Nation labour market programmes, which took the long-term unemployed off the register, peaked around the end of 1994. Since the duration of participation was between 6 and 12 months, participants were typically short-term unemployed during much of 1996 but could become long-term unemployed again by 1997 [Warburton, Opoku and Vuong (1999)]. This is likely to account for the fall in the incidence of long-term unemployment in 1996.

- **Impact of job-search monitoring, Job Search Training and Mutual Obligation and other measures as compared to the impact of Intensive Assistance:** Job search monitoring by Centrelink and its predecessor has intensified since 1996. There is direct evidence (see below) that the more recent version of Reciprocal Obligation, *i.e.* Mutual Obligation, increases rates of exit from short-term unemployment. Referrals to JST have a large "compliance" effect. which also affects short-term unemployment [DEWRSB (2001*a*)]. Yet for the long-term unemployed in ongoing Intensive Assistance these measures did not apply, and contact with IA clients may at first have been too infrequent to have had a comparable impact on exit rates from long-term unemployment. These patterns could explain why the beneficiary total (ratio to unemployed), and the long-term share within it (which may have been still drifting upwards due to the 1995 definitional change), did not fall in 1998 and 1999.

- **Lagged impacts and tighter management of Intensive Assistance.** Centrelink's activation measures, mentioned above, affect long-term beneficiary unemployment only with a lag, given that about 40% of people on Newstart and Youth Allowance have been unemployed for more than two years. By 2000, these measures were probably having an impact on long-term unemployment, yet the impact on short-term unemployment also increased, as the measures were intensified during the year. The second tender round results, with the average performance of surviving IA

187

providers being nearly 25% above the average for the first Job Network [Riggs (2001)], as well as steps to increase the frequency of contact with clients, improved IA performance quite sharply. More than 54 500 IA participants were placed into jobs lasting at least 13 weeks in the year to February 2001 [DEWRSB media release, 14 March 2001]. This seems to be an increase of at least 15 000 per year on comparable placements in the year to September 1999 [estimated from DEWRSB (2000d, Figure 6.2)], which is enough to reduce the incidence of long-term unemployment by one percentage point after a year. Such factors could explain a fall in the relative beneficiary total and long-term share from the second quarter of 2000, and more sharply in early 2001.

Along the above lines, Australian experience may be consistent with the principle that when "activation" measures are effective, they can have a large impact on unemployment levels and may affect the beneficiary measure of unemployment more immediately than the labour force survey measure.[147]

4. The impact of Mutual Obligation

Richardson (2000), using data from the FaCS Longitudinal Data Set through to July 1999, has examined the impact of the Mutual Obligation requirements introduced on 1 July 1998. Applying a natural experiment methodology, she compared the exit rates of a "treatment group" of people aged 23 and 24 years who entered unemployment in the first six months of 1998, who would face Mutual Obligation requirements later in the year if their spell duration reached six months, with those of a "control group" of people aged 25 and 26 who were not (at that time) in the target group for Mutual Obligation. Exit was defined in terms of cessation of income support payments for four consecutive fortnights (employment outcomes are not recorded in the data set).

Similar groups who had entered unemployment a year earlier, before the introduction of Mutual Obligation, were used as further controls. In 1997, the 23 and 24 year-old and the 25 and 26 year-old groups behaved similarly, with exit rates increasing up to fortnights four or five of the unemployment spell, then peaking and subsequently steadily declining. However in 1998 the exit rates of the 23 and 24 year-old group had a marked second peak, mainly within fortnights 12 to 17 inclusive. This is interpreted by Richardson as a response to the Mutual Obligation requirements. According to regression analysis, exit rates increased by 50% to 60% in these fortnights (when they averaged about 5% per fortnight for the control groups), and by smaller proportions (averaging about 20%) in subsequent fortnights, up to the 38th. For any given inflow to unemployment, these changes imply a reduction of 15% to 20% reduction in the number of people remaining unemployed after 17 fortnights and a reduction of 30% to 35% in the number remaining unemployed after 38 fortnights. The continuing positive impact of

Mutual Obligation suggests that the "retention" effect of participation in Work for the Dole and other options may be small or negative, and this could well be an improvement on the performance of earlier programmes (see Chapter 5 for an explanation and discussion of "retention" effects).[148] Additional regressions detected no increase in the subsequent rate of re-entry to unemployment of the 23 and 24 year-olds in 1998 who had exited in fortnights 12 to 17.

The data for the 25 and 26 year-old group of 1998 show a less marked peak in exit rates, also around fortnights 12 to 17. This might be due to an "announcement" effect[149] with media reports about Mutual Obligation and friends' experiences, etc., having some impact on the behaviour of individuals who were not actually subject to its requirements. Referrals of people in the 25 and 26 year-old group to JST at about the same unemployment duration that Mutual Obligation options came in could be another factor.[150] Whatever the reason, the use of 25 and 26 years-olds in 1998 as a control group may have led to some understatement of the impact of Mutual Obligation. The average survival rate into long-term unemployment of 23 and 24 year-olds was about 14% lower than for the 25 and 26 year-olds, but the survival rate for the latter group itself seems to have been reduced nearly 10% by an increase in the hazard rate over fortnights 12 to 17. On this basis the impact of Mutual Obligation – when components such as JST referrals which also apply to individuals not in Mutual Obligation are included – appears to have been to reduced the rate of survival into long-term unemployment by about 20 to 25%. "Announcement" effects may be short-lived and the impact of Mutual Obligation might have fallen as unemployed people become more familiar with its real content. On the other hand the programme may also be contributing to attitudinal changes whose impact could keep increasing and extend beyond the specific target groups, in line with government objectives. It may be noted that governments usually pay continuous attention to inflows and outflows from the benefit register, and the impact Mutual Obligation was having was probably clear to policy-makers by the end of 1998: it could thus have influenced decisions to extend the programme.

This evidence indicates a substantial early impact of Mutual Obligation on a particular group of the unemployed: its total impact could potentially be increased by steps such as researching and adjusting the different components of the programme, providing more case management assistance to participants, and extending some of its principles into Intensive Assistance.

F. Related benefits

1. *Mature Age Allowance*

Mature Age Allowance can be paid to people who are aged over 60 years but less than Age Pension age and who have received income support for at least nine

189

months and are on Newstart Allowance at the time of the claim. Benefit rates are the same as for Newstart Allowance. People on Mature Age Allowance receive a Pensioner Concession Card, which is often more favourable in terms of travel concessions, and are exempt from the Newstart activity test. At the same time they may remain registered as unemployed and qualify for an Employment Entry Payment of $104 if they find work. Centrelink automatically sends out letters to eligible people inviting them to claim.

In 1993, just before the introduction of Mature Age Allowance, about 10% of men aged 60 to 64 years were receiving an unemployment payment. By 1999, the proportion receiving an unemployment payment, including Mature Age Allowance (which had become the main form of unemployment payment for this age group), had risen to nearly 15%.[151] By contrast, the proportion of the working-age population in general that was in receipt of an unemployment payment fell from about 7.7% in 1993 to 6.2% in 1999. Thus, the incidence of unemployment payments increased by about 85% for the male 60 to 64-year age group relative to the working-age population in general over these years. This may plausibly indicate the impact of, in effect, ceasing to apply labour market behavioural eligibility conditions to a means-tested unemployment benefit. The Government, in its *Statement on Welfare Reform* [FaCS (2000b)] announced its disposition to improve services, opportunities and financial incentives for older unemployed people, but there is an issue of whether an impact at all comparable to that of eligibility conditions applied to unemployed benefits can be expected from such measures.

Some eligibility conditions for Newstart are significantly relaxed for workers aged over 50. Workers in part-time employment paying 35% of average male full-time weekly earnings, and workers engaged in voluntary work of 32 hours per fortnight, satisfy the activity test and thus are not required to look for any other work.

2. Parenting payments

In Australia, parents can receive income support until their youngest child is aged 16 without being available for work (Table 4.1). Many other countries apply lower limits.[152] The number of sole-parent beneficiaries has increased dramatically, from about 30 000 in 1965 to 162 000 in 1980 and to 397 000 in 2000. Since the individualisation of benefits in 1995, nearly 220 000 Parenting Payment-partnered (PPP) beneficiaries also qualify for a benefit without a work requirement [FaCS (2000b)]: the total number of parenting payments is approaching the number of unemployment payments or disability payments. One parent in a couple can elect for PPP and there is, for example, no eligibility restriction on a wife giving up part-time work when the husband becomes unemployed, in contrast to some social assistance systems where either parent in an unemployed couple can be required to work.

Parenting Payment – single (PPS), as a pension, is paid at a higher level than PPP. There can therefore be some incentive not to declare living arrangements. The larger free area and lower rate of taper of PPS gives more incentive to work and a higher cut-out point with respect to earnings (up to $1 130 with one child, rather than $566, in 2001). In 1999/2000, 24% of PPS beneficiaries were in work with average earnings of $415 per fortnight, compared to 5.8% of PPP beneficiaries in work with average earnings of $155 per fortnight [FaCS (2000a), p. 135]. However, in the general population, the overall rate of part-time employment for married/cohabiting mothers (36%) is considerably higher than for lone mothers (26%) [2000 data from ABS, supplied by DEWRSB].

3. Disability benefits

The number of Disability Support Pension (DSP) beneficiaries has grown from 108 000 in 1965 to 272 000 in 1985 and to 602 000 in 2000 (June figures), reaching almost 5% of the working-age population. DSP, like PPS, is paid at a higher basic rate and with a lower rate of taper with respect to part-time earnings than Newstart and other Allowances. Although 8% of beneficiaries have income from work, the benefit savings from this remain very small as compared to the benefit cost of inflows to the DSP eligible population over recent decades.

In 1999, 20% of DSP beneficiaries had psychological/psychiatric conditions and 31% musculo-skeletal conditions. These Australian figures are in between those for the Netherlands in 1970 (when 2.6% of the population had a disability benefit) and 1988 (when the share had grown to 6.0%). In the latter case, entries to disability benefit on grounds of psychological conditions rose from 13% to 31% of the total, and entries on the grounds of motor disorders (back pains, repetitive strain injuries, etc.) rose from 25% to 33%, suggesting that most of the growth was concentrated in categories which are less open to objective medical verification [Aarts and de Jong (1992), Tables 2.13 and 2.15; OECD (1993)]. Reductions in the Dutch disability benefit rates in 1987 had little effect in reducing the number of recipients, but 1990 legislation introducing tougher criteria, with medical re-examination of beneficiaries aged under 50 after 1993, had a large impact [Madigan (1999)].

The 1991 Disability Reform Package (DRP) aimed to introduce a more active system of income support. It brought in rehabilitation, training and labour market programs, intended to bring people with disabilities into employment rather than leaving them with a long-term dependency on income support, and replaced the Invalid Pension with DSP, under which recipients are allowed to work part-time and retain a large proportion of their earnings. However whereas qualification for the Invalid Pension depended upon 'permanent incapacity to work',[153] qualification for DSP requires only moderate levels of incapacity, expected to last for two years, and which prevent work of 30 hours a week or more at full wage rates.

191

For the potentially large group of people with a partial loss or temporary loss of work capacity who had to claim unemployment benefits prior to 1991, but can now claim DSP, the reform had the effect of removing the availability-for-work condition for benefit eligibility. There is a risk that this move in the direction of a more passive system has had an impact outweighing that of the active reform measures.

According to some observers the government has in the past directed specialist employment agencies to put clients onto DSP and provided financial incentives for this [PWDWA website; Horin (1999)]. This may refer to the payment system for Contracted Case Management under Working Nation (see Chapter 5.B): under present Job Network arrangements, transfer of an unemployed person to disability benefit does not result in a paid outcome. Along similar lines to earlier debate in the Netherlands, Argyrous and Neale (2000) argue – referring to experience in the early 1980s, when references to economic and social factors in determining eligibility for DSP (then, the invalid pension) were briefly removed and annual new grants were almost halved – that slightly over half of all DSP recipients in 1999 can be classified as "imputed labour market disabled" as opposed to "imputed medically disabled". The DSP entry criterion of 20 points on impairment tables, equivalent to about a 20% to 25% level of disability, seems relatively low, potentially including people who can be quite productive at work. MacDonald and Jope (2000) describe occupational psychologists deciding whether to refer clients to DSP on essentially social grounds (concerns about whether DSP status would be more socially isolating than NSA status). Thus, there are a variety of indications that, in the 1990s, decisions to allow or encourage entry to DSP were not strictly restricted as would seem appropriate given the potentially immense long-term cost – transfer to a non-activity-tested benefit may significantly influence employment prospects for up to 40 years ahead – of each entry to DSP.

At the same time, some factors suggest scope for further growth in beneficiary numbers. People with Disabilities Western Australia (PWDWA) emphasises that while 5% of Western Australians report a disability caused mainly by musculo-skeletal problems,[154] less than a quarter of them are receiving DSP (however, some of the others may be on worker's compensation or other benefits). In general there may be many people with disabilities who are in full-time work, or able to re-enter it, who are not claiming disability benefit or officially identified as disabled. Take-up of benefit could be increased by the growing incidence of self-reported disability, which rose from 13.3% of the adult population in 1981 to 18% in 1993. This growth is thought to reflect increasing awareness of disability conditions and changing social attitudes to people with a disability [Lindsay (1996)]. Overall, any attempt to secure a significant cut in the number of beneficiaries would appear to require quite major changes in medical assessment and labour market criteria. The government's recent statements on welfare reform (see below) may foreshadow decisive moves in this direction. Labour market programmes for the disabled are discussed in Annex D.

G. Welfare reform

In September 1999, the Minister for Family and Community Services announced the government's intention to review the Australian Welfare system. Patrick McClure, Chief Executive of Mission Australia, was appointed to chair a Welfare Reference Group to advise on options for change to income support arrangements aimed at preventing and reducing welfare dependency and for the provision of related employment, education and training services. The Welfare Reference Group received 366 submissions from interested individuals and organisations (many of these are available via www.facs.gov.au), and issued an Interim Report in March 2000 and a Final Report in July 2000.

The Minister's Discussion Paper entitled "The Challenge of Welfare Dependency in the 21st Century" [Newman (1999)] identified the main dimensions of this problem as:

- The proportion of working-age people receiving income support payments had risen from 3% in 1965 to 10% in 1978 and 18% in 1998.

- Increased inequality in the distribution of employment: as well as more two-income families there are now more no-income families, and 850 000 children living in families without a parent in work.

- By 1997/98, most working-age people on income support were not unemployed, but receiving other benefits.

- Over the previous ten years, the number of people on unemployment payments who have been paid for 12 months or more had tripled, while the number of short-term unemployed in these payments had changed little.

- More than one half of lone parents and more than one half of single people aged 55 to 64 received most of their income from social security pensions and allowances.

- Young people from families in receipt of income support are much more likely than other young people to leave school early, become unemployed, become teenage parents and themselves be highly dependent on income support.

The issues for consideration were listed under four main headings of unemployed people, older unemployed people, people with disabilities and parenting payment, with a general emphasis on improving incentives for work and employment assistance, but also encouraging other forms of community activity and participation. The terms of reference called for particular consideration to be

193

given to the broader application of Mutual Obligation, the incentive effects of the design of social security payments for people of working age, and international best practice.

The final report [RGWR (2000*b*)], entitled "Participation Support for a More Equitable Society", identified four particular shortcomings with the current system:

- Fragmented service delivery arrangements, not adequately focussed on participation goals.
- An overly complex and rigid categorical array of pensions and allowances.
- Inadequate incentives for some forms of participation and work.
- A lack of awareness that actors need to fulfil social obligations in order to prevent a decline in "social capital".

The main recommendations addressed the first three points above and called for a broad application of the mutual obligations concept and for social partnerships:

- **Individualised service delivery** was described in terms of a "central gateway and assessment process" to determine entitlement to a participation support payment, assess a person's risk of long-term joblessness and refer people to brokers and service provides. This recommendation was in line with Centrelink's existing role. References to a more complex assessment process with more sophisticated profiling tools, and the need for brokers to understand the history of individuals, their changing circumstances and what has been offered to them in the past, allowing them to move more easily between programmes, implied that increased resources would be needed.
- **A simpler support structure** was described in terms of a possible integrated payment for all adult people of working age (including, in principle, employed and self-employed persons), subject only to a minimum participation requirement and tests on income and assets, and supplemented by various additional needs payments (related to the costs of children, costs of living as the only adult in a household, housing costs, and the costs of searching for or preparing for paid work). The report claimed that the distinction between unemployment payments under which people are generally expected to seek full-time work, and pension payments, where at most part-time work is expected, "has become increasingly difficult to maintain".
- Proposed **incentives and financial assistance to encourage and support participation** included in-work benefits and a "transition bank" (see below), with a call for further consideration of return-to-work benefits and reductions in taper rates on Newstart and other allowances.

- A **broad application of the mutual obligations concept** would include social obligations that extend beyond individuals to business and trade unions and across the whole community. Mutual obligations would be extended to all people of working age. The most specific recommendation in the report was that parents on income support should have an annual compulsory interview when children are aged 6 to 13 years, and be required to enter into a Participation Plan including job readiness and needs assessment, part-time job search and part-time employment, when children are aged 13 and over.

- Under the heading of **social partnerships**, the report called for enhanced community capacity-building (particularly in socially disadvantaged areas), implying that businesses, local government and not-for-profit organisations should work together more efficiently to maximise opportunities for economic and social participation by individuals. Recommendations concerned promotion, support services, research and pilot projects.

The final report does not refer to the concept of welfare dependency as used in the government's terms of reference. Several of its suggestions would facilitate access to benefits[155] and the specific recommendations do not seem to be of a nature to greatly reduce the reliance on income support. However, the report's language did leave the door open to some other, more restrictive, measures, in particular a wider application of Mutual Obligation requirements and tighter assessment procedures for DSP. The government in its official response [FaCS (2000b)] welcomed the report and announced a number of changes which it was disposed to develop further in the context of the 2001/02 Budget:

- Jobseekers will typically undertake JST after three months of unemployment and face a more intensive participation requirement after six months.

- Mutual Obligation requirements similar to those already applying to unemployed workers aged under 35 years will be phased in for unemployed workers aged 35 to 64 years. However minimum hours of participation will be lower and there will be no requirement to participate in Work for the Dole for those aged 40 and above.

- Parents with children aged 6 and over will face participation requirements as recommended.

- Older people of working age currently on non-activity tested payments will be encouraged, but not required, to attend an interview to develop participation plans. The proposal to allow recipients to build up a "transition bank" of their unused income test free areas, up to a certain limit, such that subsequent earnings do not affect benefit payments until the balance in the bank is reduced to nil, will be developed.

195 |

- In assessing eligibility for DSP, information provided by an applicant's doctor will be supplemented with increased reliance on the use of independent government-contracted medical experts.

- Over the medium to long term and subject to further research and consultations, the general recommendation for a unified income support structure, with a single base rate and add-ons to recognise special needs and support participation where appropriate, will be implemented.

(Many of these measures were implemented in the May 2001 budget, as described in the box which appears after the summary and conclusions section of this review.)

Chapter 5

Labour Market Programmes

A. Introduction

This chapter considers active labour market programmes (except for the employment counselling and job-search training provided within Job Network). Section B begins with a review of the history of labour market programmes in the 1990s, comparing programme provision in the Working Nation period, 1994 to 1996, with what preceded it and the current pattern. With some partial exceptions (Work for the Dole, self-employment assistance and programmes financed by JN providers), training and subsidised employment programmes are now open only to special target groups among unemployed people: individuals who are not in any of the target groups do not necessarily qualify for such programmes however long they are unemployed.

Section C considers programme provision within Job Network and Section D considers Work for the Dole (WfD). Section E reviews formal statistical evaluations of Working Nation programmes and evaluations of more recent programmes (including JST and Intensive Assistance, which have been evaluated by the same methods as WfD). Section F comments briefly on several other large programme areas which are described in more detail in Annexes: youth and training programmes including New Apprenticeships (Annex B), Community Development Employment Projects and other programmes for indigenous people (Annex C), and disability programmes (Annex D). Section G describes some specialised programmes that are not covered elsewhere. A notable common thread is the use of tender and contracting arrangements for the delivery of most of the smaller programmes, with payments to providers being related to various indicators of service provision and outcomes, as they are for JN services.

B. Labour market programmes in the 1990s

1. *The early 1990s and Working Nation*

Active labour market programmes were expanded substantially in 1992 and were expanded further under the Working Nation initiative, which was announced in 1994 and was in near full operation for only one financial year, 1995/96. Total spending on active labour market programmes in current dollar terms quadrupled between 1990/91 and 1995/96, according to figures in the OECD data base on labour market programme expenditure.[156] By contrast, spending on unemployment benefits increased by less than 40% over the period.[157] The active share in total (active plus passive) labour market programme spending was a relatively low 18% in 1990/91, and increased to near 40%, which is at or perhaps above the median or the average for European OECD countries,[158] by 1995/96.

The five main employment, education and training measures in Working Nation were [Finn (1997)]:

- Comprehensive case management for long-term unemployed jobseekers and those at risk of becoming long-term unemployed.

- A Job Compact, centred on the offer of a six to twelve month job placement (with placements intended to be primarily in the private sector) to all those who had been receiving unemployment benefits for more than 18 months. The Job Compact incorporated a principle of "Reciprocal Obligation" between the government and the unemployed, whereby the government accepts an obligation to offer case management and training or a job to the unemployed, and the unemployed must then take up the offer or lose their benefits.

- A Youth Training Initiative (YTI) to provide intensive help for young people under the age of 18 in their search for suitable work, training or education.

- An expanded entry-level training system with greater employer involvement in decision-making than existed previously.

- A National Training Wage (NTW), which was to be supplemented by subsidies to entice employers to provide training to young people, adults and the long-term unemployed.

Between 1993/94 and 1995/96 there was substantial new spending on the Employment Services Regulatory Authority (created in 1994), Employment Assistance Australia (which took on case management services from the CES), and private (Contracted Case Manager) services, whose market share however never reached very high levels in the Working Nation period (see Chapter 2). This was not a net increase in spending on employment service administration, because it was financed mainly by transfers from the CES, whose funding fell by more than half as its role became concentrated on initial assessment and referral and basic job matching.

Increased spending on labour market programmes in the early 1990s concerned training, particularly industry and regional assistance schemes, the SkillShare Program (vocational training, provided by community-based, non-government and non-profit organisations) which started in 1988/89, and the

Special Intervention Program (remedial assessment and training in English as a second language, literacy, employment-related skills and personal development needs) which started in 1991/92. From 1993/4 to 1995/96, arguably the entry-level training and Training Wage initiatives laid the foundation of the current New Apprenticeship system, and spending on the Special Intervention Program increased further but overall spending on training increased relatively little.[159]

Thus, the Job Compact, new case management arrangements and increased spending on job creation can be regarded as the main elements in Working Nation that affected the adult unemployed. By 1995/96, spending on direct job creation was approaching total spending on employment services and benefit administration, whereas it had been only about one-third as high in 1993/94, and zero in 1990/91. The main direct job creation schemes were, for adults, Jobskills (a programme which provided work experience combined with formal on-the-job and off-the-job training), New Work Opportunities (NWO) (which provided work with some training, typically in the environmental, age care and community sectors), and for youth the Landcare and Environmental Action Program (LEAP).

Under Working Nation, three sets of eligibility and targeting criteria influenced the services which could be offered to a particular jobseeker:

- Eligibility for the Job Compact arose automatically for all whose unemployment duration exceeded 18 months.

- In making referrals to case management, priority was given to those who had been unemployed for over five years, those who had recently passed the 18-month duration threshold, and a "high risk" group (identified by the Jobseeker Screening Instrument or by staff judgement[160]). Thus the case management target group did not coincide with the Job Compact target group.

- Eligibility for most labour market programmes (with the exception of NWO) extended beyond the Job Compact or case management groups.

According to Chapman [see ESC (1999)] very little money appears to have been set aside for the case management function. The Case Management Activity Agreement which was negotiated with clients typically included a commitment to engage in job search, but also a commitment to accept any position offered as part of the Job Compact. Fee payments to case managers were based on the drawing up of Activity Agreements and securing "outcomes", which were weighted according to the degree of difficulty the unemployed person faced as measured by the Client Classification Level.[161] Outcomes were defined as placement into unsubsidised and subsidised jobs or training and education, so long as the participant was removed from the benefit system for at least 13 weeks. Given the use of this criterion, payable outcomes also included people finding their own job, being transferred to another benefit, or being breached for a sufficiently long period (at this time, a third activity test breach within three years led to a benefit stop for 14 to 18 weeks).

Case manager caseloads were high (the majority of EAA case managers had caseloads of between 100 and 200) and managers appear to have focussed on achieving referral to labour market programmes. A few clients could be referred to self-employment preparation under the New Enterprise Incentive Scheme (described below). Two other possible assignments were to a job with a private or public sector employer, who received a JobStart subsidy for up to nine months, and to approved traineeships generally running for 12 months, with pay at NTW rates and a wage subsidy as an incentive to employers. But in practice there was a rapid increase in expenditure on job creation programmes, driven by a combination of factors:

- Several factors limited the availability of the alternative JobStart and traineeship options, which depended upon finding an employer willing to hire the person. Employer take-up was limited by the weighting of the Job-Compact-eligible and case management priority groups towards the most disadvantaged jobseekers.[162]

- Under Reciprocal Obligation arrangements, the government was obliged to fund additional job creation programme places, despite any misgivings about their cost or effectiveness, because restrictions on funding would have led to a lack of any option for some Job Compact clients (those not accepted by any private employer).

- Case managers received the same payment for placements in an expensive and temporary job creation programme as for placements in a cheaper programme, or even in an unsubsidised job.

The proportion of Job Compact clients (defined as persons unemployed for 18 months or more) placed into "brokered" (job creation) programmes rather than wage subsidy programmes rose from one-eighth in 1993/94 to two-thirds in 1995/96 [DEETYA (1996), p. 47].

The priority given to the Job Compact group had some visible impact on the incidence of long-term unemployment among beneficiaries (see Chart 4.1). However, this fall was small (from about 49% in 1994 to 42% in 1996) as compared to what would occur if unemployment durations of over 18 months had been eliminated.[163] The initial forecast was that the Job Compact group (*i.e.* those unemployed for more than 18 months) would have been reduced by 47% by December 1995, but the actual fall was less than 20%. Inflows to the Job Compact group were higher than expected, possibly related to the withdrawal of labour market programme assistance from those unemployed for 12 to 18 months. In this context, targets for the total number of placements under Job Compact could be met while the proportion of Job-Compact-eligible jobseekers benefiting from the job guarantee remained relatively low. At an operational level, reasons for incomplete implementation of the intended job guarantee appear to be:

- The available resources could to a large extent be spent without implementing the Job Compact guarantee, because eligibility for job creation programmes (except NWO) and case manager outcome payments extended to many unemployed people not in the Job Compact group.

- Some unemployed people in the Job Compact group (particularly those with durations over 18 months but below five years at the start of the Working Nation period) may never have been referred to case management.

- A significant proportion of the Job Compact group may have been referred to case management, but not then have commenced.[164] A third of the CES staff contacted in a survey reported that some clients were left on the waiting list for case management indefinitely [DEETYA (1996), p. 21].

- Case managers considered that about 15% of the eligible population would not benefit from case management, and some case managers were unwilling to place jobseekers with severe barriers to employment in programmes as they believed the resources could be more effectively used to assist other jobseekers [DEETYA (1996), pp. 31, 37].

Even the falls in long-term unemployment that occurred could simply reflect changes in formal status during programme participation (and later, the resetting of the unemployment "counter" to zero after programme participation), rather than increased entries to unsubsidised employment. The government gave considerable attention to evaluating the net impact of Working Nation programmes and the results continue to receive attention in current debate. Evaluations of Working Nation programmes are discussed in Section 5.E below.

2. *Patterns of labour market programme provision after* Working Nation

Following the election of the coalition government in March 1996, in June the government announced a sharp restriction of new activity in job creation programmes and some training programmes. A statement by the employment minister in August announced that, while reducing expenditure markedly, the government would concentrate its efforts on those programmes which had proven most cost-effective in securing real job outcomes [Vanstone (1996a)]. Among the programmes retained were employer incentives and general promotion of apprenticeships and traineeships; regional assistance programmes (subject to some rearrangement); the New Enterprise Incentive Scheme; the Workplace English Language and Literacy and Advanced English for Migrants programmes; and open employment strategies for indigenous people. The large CDEP scheme (although growth in its funding was frozen) and disability programmes (although

201

significant innovations were progressively introduced) were retained, as well as some smaller programmes (JET, JPP and JPET: see Section G below and Annex B). But the existing training and job creation programmes targeted on the long-term unemployed in general were abolished. Plans for the JobStart wage subsidy programme took some time to settle: a budget release actually announced that support for "successful employment programmes such as JobStart" would be increased,[165] but Vanstone (1996a) discussed the disadvantages as well as advantages of wage subsidy programmes and went on to say that "in the early period of operation of the new arrangements wage subsidy funding will be separately identified within the funds made available to EPEs". (EPEs, employment placement enterprises, were the planning title for what later became JN providers: the JN model as finally adopted broke more completely with the former CCM model where the referral of jobseekers to separately-funded labour market programmes was an important option, even attracting an outcome payment.) Subsequently, JobStart was continued into 1997/98 as a programme for the disabled and abolished in 1998/99. The main new programmes created since 1996, which partly substitute for earlier programmes but differ significantly from them, are WfD, CSP and LANT, and aspects of the new Indigenous Employment Strategy (see Sections D and G below and Annexes B and C).

A comparison for each main OECD category of spending (Table 5.1) helps in seeing how the general distribution of spending has changed. First, there has been little overall change in spending within the broad category of public employment services and benefit administration. If spending on benefit administration is excluded, it appears that spending on employment services has risen, but not greatly so. This is because savings from abolishing the CES, the Employment Service Regulatory Authority, Employment Assistance Australia, and Mobility Assistance and Employment Access job search training, and cutting "other administration" costs by 90% (savings totalling $677 million in 1995/96) were enough to cover most of the cost of services now provided by Centrelink for DEWRSB, DEWRSB's JN administration costs, and the direct costs of CSP and Job Network (excluding NEIS) ($843 million in 1998/99). Thus only a small proportion of the savings from "cashing out" the other labour market programmes were diverted to Job Network. Under Intensive Assistance, JN members may finance training (internal or purchased outside) or pay a hiring subsidy, but most IA spending is probably devoted to services (e.g. case management interviews, short courses in job search skills, referral to jobs and free external training and related resources, and general administration) that would be correctly classified under the OECD heading of "employment services and administration", rather than vocational training and employment subsidies.

With the abolition of dedicated labour market training programmes for adult unemployed (except for the special equity – affirmative action for women and

Table 5.1. **Public labour market programme expenditure and participant inflows, 1995/96 and 1998/99**

	Expenditure, million $	
	1995/96	1998/99
1. Public employment services and administration	**1 188.3**	**1 209.0**
Placement and information services	x	x
CES administration	202.0	–
DSS JSA/NSA/MAA administration	438.7	269.1
Systems Division	39.8	x
Administration of DEYTA programmes	x	2.2
Labour market and education analysis	10.5	11.5
Other administration	235.0	21.9
Mobility assistance	20.1	x
Employment Access: job search training	48.9	x
Employment Services Regulatory Authority	52.3	–
Employment Assistance Australia	141.0	–
Community Support Program	–	7.0
Job Network Administration costs:		
Departmental Administration	–	32.4
Services provide by Centrelink on behalf of DEWRSB	–	125.3
Job Network support	–	28.2
Job Network Programme costs:[a]		
Job Matching	–	75.7
Job Search Training	–	22.5
Intensive Assistance	–	550.5
Project contracting/Fee for service	–	2.7
State/territory expenditure[b]	..	60.0
2. Labour market training	**733.4**	**146.3**
a) Training for unemployed adults and those at risk	**690.7**	**134.5**
Employment Access: formal training	168.4	–
Industry and Regional Assistance	53.1	x
Regional initiatives	x	x
Labour adjustment packages	x	40.3
Special equity programmes	–	0.2
Skillshare	162.5	–
Measures for indigenous Australians	4.9	–
Special Intervention	201.2	–
Adult migrant education program (tuition costs)	75.1	84.1
State/territory expenditure	25.5	..
Advanced English for migrants	–	4.4
Literacy and Numeracy Programme	–	3.9
Jobs, Education and Training pre-vocational training	–	1.6
b) Training for employed adults	**42.7**	**11.8**
Skills training	19.9	–
Enterprise training	9.2	–
Workplace literacy	11.6	11.8
State/territory expenditure[b]	2.0	..

Table 5.1. **Public labour market programme expenditure and participant inflows, 1995/96 and 1998/99** (*cont.*)

	Expenditure, million $	
	1995/96	1998/99
3. Youth measures	**304.7**	**338.0**
a) **Measures for unemployed and disadvantaged youth**	**155.7**	**45.3**
Special Trade Training	55.2	–
Jobs Pathway Guarantee	0.5	–
Jobs Pathway Programme	–	5.2
Landcare and Environmental Action (LEAP)	88.8	–
Skillshare Disadvantaged Youth	2.0	–
Accredited training for youth	9.2	–
Job placement employment and training	–	13.3
Work for the Dole[c]	–	26.4
Mentoring pilot for young unemployed people	–	0.4
b) **Support of apprenticeship and related forms of general youth training**	**149.0**	**292.7**
Support for apprentices	75.0	271.4
New apprenticeships access programme	–	6.5
Support for traineeships	74.0	–
Group training scheme	–	9.3
Group training expansion	–	5.5
4. Subsidised employment	**1 530.9**	**528.0**
a) **Subsidies to regular employment in the private sector**	**296.5**	**37.7**
Employment Access: job subsidies	236.4	–
Measures for indigenous Australians (TAP/IEP)	48.1	36.3
State/territory expenditure	12.0	1.4
b) **Support of unemployed persons starting enterprises**	**139.5**	**111.5**
New Enterprise Incentive Scheme	103.9	80.4
Measures for indigenous Australians	33.6	30.7
State/territory expenditure	2.0	0.4
c) **Direct job creation (public or non-profit)**	**1 094.9**	**378.8**
JobSkills	273.1	–
Measures for indigenous Australians	310.5	378.8
New Work Opportunities (NWO)	498.3	–
State/territory expenditure[b]	13.0	..
5. Measures for the disabled	**321.9**	**335.5**
a) **Vocational rehabilitation**	**128.9**	**100.5**
Rehabilitation	122.3	100.5
Skillshare Disability Support Units	3.4	–
Disabled apprentice wage subsidy	3.2	–
b) **Work for the disabled**	**193.0**	**235.0**
Disability Services Program[d]	186.5	232.3
Work Experience Schemes	6.5	–
Intensive and flexible assistance for people with severe disabilities	–	1.6
Payments to voluntary work agencies	–	1.1

Table 5.1. **Public labour market programme expenditure and participant inflows, 1995/96 and 1998/99** (*cont.*)

	Expenditure, million $	
	1995/96	1998/99
6. Unemployment compensation	**6 279.7**	**6 276.1**
Job Search Allowance	3 141.4	–
Newstart Allowance	2 571.1	5 370.7
Mature Age Allowance	436.6	401.7
Youth Training Allowance	130.6	3.7
Youth Allowance	–	500.0
7. Early retirement for labour market reasons	–	–
Total	**10 358.9**	**8 832.9**
Active measures (1-5)	4 079.2	2 556.8
Passive measures (6-7)	6 279.7	6 276.1

Fiscal years from 1st July.
– Nil or less than half of the last digit used.
.. Data not available.
x Data included in another category.
a) Some labour market training and employment subsidies may be provided by Job Network members, but these cannot be disaggregated within the total of Job Network programme costs.
b) Data on state/territory spending is not available for certain programme categories and certain years but this does not mean that such spending was zero.
c) By 1999/2000, Work for the Dole had been reclassifed by OECD as a job creation rather than a youth programme and spending on it had tripled.
d) Disability spending data include only spending by the Commonwealth.
Source: OECD database on Active Labour Market Programmes.

minorities – programme, migrant and literacy/numeracy programmes) and subsidies to regular employment in the private sector and direct job creation for adult unemployed (except WfD and CDEP), total spending on training and subsidised employment fell from $1 560 million in 1995/96 to $562 million (two-thirds of this being job creation for indigenous workers) by 1998/99.

Work for the Dole was a small programme in 1998/99. After expansion to include 25 to 34 year-olds it was expected to cost about $105 million in 2000/01, which is comparable to 1995/96 spending on the former LEAP job creation measure for youth.[166] Further increases are likely with the intended expansion of the target group to include 35 to 39 year-olds. WfD nevertheless, seems set to remain a fairly modest programme since $105 million is only about one-fifth of the current budget for Intensive Assistance and one-tenth of the spending on job creation measures in 1995/96.

Spending on measures for the disabled has been maintained at 1995/96 levels. The New Apprenticeships programme, which corresponds to former apprenticeship and traineeship arrangements, is the only large area of spending where funding has increased since 1995/96.

C. Programme provision within Job Network

1. *New Enterprise Incentive Scheme* (NEIS)[167]

The New Enterprise Incentive Scheme (NEIS) of assistance with self-employment start-up started in 1985/86. The annual inflow of participants reached 1 500 in 1989/90 and nearly 6 000 in 1993/94. It is currently about 6 800. All persons over 18 years old and less than pensionable age, registered for full-time work, in receipt of a pension or allowance, and with a suitable business proposal are potentially eligible. Proposed businesses must be new and not compete directly with existing businesses, unless there is an unsatisfied demand for the product or service or they are to be provided in a new way. They must be legal and reputable and must be assessed as being commercially viable.

After an initial assessment of eligibility, NEIS participants enter six weeks of training, which follows a national curriculum developed for NEIS[168] in line with small business competency standards. In the course of this training, participants produce a business plan based on market research, which needs to demonstrate that the business will generate income at least equal to the basic rate of NEIS Allowance. Commercial viability of the plans is assessed by an NEIS Advisory Committee, which recommends to DEWRSB which clients should be offered the NEIS Allowance. This allowance, broadly equivalent to the basic adult rate of Newstart Allowance, is paid for up to a year. During this year mentoring support is provided. Clients must make business returns every 13 weeks and viability of the business is assessed at 26 and 39 weeks.

NEIS is currently offered from about 350 sites. The NEIS providers' contracts with DEWRSB include both a fee per place determined through competitive tender (but which must cover the full cost of providing NEIS services) and a preferred number of places. At the start of each year providers receive an advance payment of 10% of total contract value, then 90% of the fee per place for each commencement. A further 10% is paid if a participant is not receiving income support three months after the NEIS allowance ceases. Providers are responsible for attracting eligible jobseekers up to contracted capacity, assessing business plans, establishing NEIS Advisory Committees and convening their meetings, and providing mentoring and monitoring business performance. The training element of NEIS is delivered by training providers approved by DEWRSB. NEIS providers can subcontract for provision of mentor support to participants during their first year of business operation, or provide this support directly themselves.

The National NEIS Association (www.nna.asn.au/neis.htm) states that NEIS is DEWRSB's most successful labour market programme. "Around 75% of all small businesses fail in their first year simply because their principals haven't done their homework – failing to plan, research or properly cost their products and services. By contrast, only 25% of NEIS projects meet a similar fate, thanks to their intensive grounding in business management issues… Post Program Monitoring figures show that three months after completing NEIS (*i.e.* generally 15 months after starting the business), 84% of participants are in unsubsidised employment". However, it would probably not be possible to maintain such high success rates if the programme were expanded greatly.

2. Intensive Assistance

Spending by IA providers on behalf of their clients may include payment of fees for training, subsidies to employers who hire clients, payments for specialist assessment, and assistance with travel to interview or travel to work costs (reimbursement of taxi fares, etc.). However providers are paid on the basis of outcomes, and are not obliged to report their spending patterns in detail. According to Raper (1999) "anecdotal evidence suggests that there is rarely more than $200 – $300 spent on a long-term unemployed person by providers in the new Job Network". This appears to refer only to external spending. Providers may offer some vocational training (*e.g.* in computer skills) delivered by their own staff, but on the other hand some of their external spending (*e.g.* on mobility assistance and specialist assessment) falls into the OECD category of employment services and administration.

Abbott (1999*b*) described a variety of training arranged by providers and reported that IA providers who used training were achieving relatively high outcomes. Eardley *et al.* (2001) found that Job Futures providers were helping jobseekers to access a wide variety of free training and training with employers or in other government programmes, and also were purchasing targeted training for clients in short-duration courses (occasionally up to 12 weeks in duration). Many other IA providers reportedly never paid for jobseeker training, but this concerned in particular two large providers (Employment National and Drake) who lost their IA business soon afterwards. Perhaps a large minority of IA providers currently do pay for some training, although it would still generally be short-term in nature.

Because evaluations tend to find that placement and job search assistance are more cost-effective than most longer-term labour market programmes, lack of long-term training under Intensive Assistance might be favourable to performance and cost-effectiveness. The effectiveness of Intensive Assistance depends mainly on the effectiveness of case management. However, effective case management may require regular and fairly frequent contact with clients (an issue already mentioned in Chapters 3 and 4). At the same time, case managers must have something substantive to discuss during contact. The main "tools" available to an IA case manager at the moment appear to be discussions about job search, referrals to vacancies, and referrals to free external services and to in-house programmes. The most successful IA providers appear to be those which are

207

providing in-house some specialist assessment, light training, counselling in job-search, self-confidence and life directions, etc. Nevertheless, IA case managers probably could make good use of further additions to their relatively light "tool kit".[169] In general the objective need not be to place the jobseeker in a long-term programme, but to achieve what is possible in short programmes, maintaining pressure for some activity and presenting opportunities over a period of many months so that when a suitable open employment opportunity arises it is more likely to be taken up.

In other countries which have greatly reduced unemployment such as Denmark, Switzerland or the United Kingdom, discussions around potential referrals to official labour market programmes are an important element in the "tool kit". After one year, Denmark "activates" the long-term unemployed by referral not to a single long labour market programme, but to a variety of shorter and longer-term labour market programmes such that participation occurs 75% of the time. In this arrangement, almost as soon as one placement is finished discussions about the next one need to start. The United Kingdom, particularly before the New Deal, did not spend heavily on labour market programmes, but it nevertheless had in 1996/97 eight or nine programmes (many of them short and cheap to operate, involving job search and counselling) that were offered at particular stages of an unemployment spell or throughout a large part of the spell [see Finn and Blackmore (2001) for a list or programmes and a description of how they are promoted to the jobseeker in fortnightly interviews]. In such arrangements, although individual options are mainly voluntary as a general principle, if no voluntary options are taken up some kind of participation does eventually become compulsory. Most jobseekers choose the "lighter" programmes, and this ensures the continuing availability of places on the longer-term programmes at reasonable cost. Mutual Obligation creates such a framework, but it seems odd to have such a structure of programme provision and obligations yet not use it as "tool" in employment counselling; and conversely it appears that up-front counselling – with a focus on placing individuals into regular job vacancies, in preference to any of the other options – could usefully be provided prior to entry to Mutual Obligation. With Job Network mainly responsible for the function of placement and counselling and Centrelink mainly responsible for referral to labour market programmes, insufficient integration of these functions may be a significant problem.[170]

One way to increase the supply of short programmes for use by IA case managers might be for government to organise a standardised set or programmes with a recognised identity to which IA case managers (rather than Centrelink) can refer jobseekers. This might achieve economies of scale given the fixed costs of mounting a programme (in terms of management time, model testing and evaluation, preparing manuals and support material, training staff, etc.). However,

Australia already has an active training market, and it is not clear that there are large unexploited economies of scale or economies available from standardisation. Financial incentives may be important. As discussed below, JST appears to have a programme net impact which continues undiminished for at least 12 months at an average cost of $13 800, and a much greater impact when "compliance" effects are taken into account so payments to providers based on cost-benefit principles, as outlined in Annex A, might induce IA providers to use programmes of this kind.

D. Work for the Dole

1. *History and administration*[171]

Work for the Dole legislation was introduced in Parliament in May 1997 and pilot projects started late that year. The government has subsequently announced several increases in funding and extensions of participation requirements, and regularly announces new projects. The first Mutual Obligation requirements, with referral to WfD if participants have not taken up any other option within six weeks [three months until July 1999: see Eardley *et al.* (2000), p. 4], were introduced for 18 to 24 year-olds unemployed for more than six months in July 1998. Such requirements were extended to 25 to 34 year-olds unemployed for more than 12 months in 1999/2000.

Participation in WfD is for 24 hours per fortnight for 18 to 20 year-olds and 30 hours per fortnight for those aged 21 and over, for up to 26 weeks in total. Participants receive a supplement of $20.80 per fortnight to their benefit. Jobseekers aged 35 and over can volunteer to participate: upon doing so they become subject to some Mutual Obligation requirements (this may mainly concern matters such as notifying and justifying absences from work due to illness). For participants, the WfD format can have some advantages over voluntary work in terms of the $20.80 supplement to benefit and official monitoring of working conditions on the project.

The stated objectives of WfD are to:

• Develop work habits.

• Involve the local community in quality projects that cater for and assist the unemployed.

• Provide communities with WfD activities that are of value to those communities.

Training is not an objective, although sponsor organisations should provide any training necessary for the work. This absence of training from the list of objectives is probably related to the fact that WfD participants are expected to continue with job search during WfD participation and may be referred to vacancies or take up work at any time.

DEWRSB funds WfD, including bodies known as Community Work Co-ordinators (CWCs) which organise the activities. CWCs may be for-profit organisations and some are also JN members. CWCs place participants with sponsor organisations, which must be not-for-profit publicly funded organisations including charities, church and religious groups, local community associations and service organisations, and local or central government organisations and agencies. Activities may be in areas such as heritage or history, environment, restoration and maintenance of community facilities, tourism and sport, elderly care, childcare and disabled care, natural resources preservation, education, parks, gardens and landscaping, and community radio. In general, sponsors are expected to demonstrate that the local community supports the project (as evidenced by financial or in-kind support provided by the local community), and that the work is additional and does not displace existing work. Sponsors must arrange supervision (with preferably at least one supervisor for each ten participants), submit documentation concerning commencements and participants who leave, inform the CWC of any unacceptable absences or unauthorised absences of three days or more, provide evidence to support participation reports (which may lead to a breach decisions) from the CWC to Centrelink, provide DEWRSB with access to their premises and to accounts and other documents for monitoring purposes, and undertake to clear publicity material and media contacts with DEWRSB via the CWC. Sponsors are expected to provide participants with some post-participation support (*e.g.* referrals to employers, providing references and certificates and possibly maintaining contact with them), although they can subcontract some of these activities to the CWCs.

Sponsor organisations are reimbursed for participant costs (which might include, for example, tools and necessary training for participants) and general project costs (such as rent, salaries and additional insurance). The general requirement for some community co-funding is, therefore, not necessarily a barrier to reimbursement of supervisor salaries. The CWC handles the day-to-day management of sponsor organisations and participants, and may directly assist sponsors with training, management, health and safety legislation issues, etc., in which case it is reimbursed for the relevant costs. Rather than submitting proposals directly to the government, local sponsor organisations can approach CWCs with their ideas and proposals for projects and get help in developing the proposal. The CWC role in promoting and implementing projects, and acting as broker and middleman, can extend to proposing projects to local sponsor organisations. Not-for-profit CWCs can also act as sponsors themselves, *i.e.* directly manage a WfD project. In some areas, successful CWCs provide a variety of possible activities so as to attract and retain greater numbers of participants.

Many CWCs worked as training providers in the early and mid-1990s and, in practice, some options with a significant training element are available.

Community Work Coordinators are contracted through a competitive tendering process. DEWRSB contracts with CWCs tie their funding to the number of potential participants interviewed, referred and placed, with a target that placements at any point in time should be at least 75% of contracted capacity [DEWRSB (2000k), p. 26].[172] Payments to CWCs comprise management fees and work experience fees. Management fees are paid for developing and making available suitable WfD activities, with a payment on a sliding scale, such that payment is reduced if less than 50% of target commencements for the area are achieved and increased if targets are met or exceeded, up to a limit of 150% of the target. Work experience fees are paid for project management, with a payment for each project based on the number of placements contracted, the number of commencements, and actual project expenditure.

2. Referrals, commencements and exits

The referral and commencement process is one of the main concerns of Community Work Coordinators (as it is for JST and IA providers). During 2000, very low ratios of commencements to referrals, typically a third, a quarter or a fifth, were reported by providers. Among the reasons for this are that people often declare temporary illness or a small income from part-time work in response to the referral to WfD, or fail to make any contact, which has increasingly been penalised by a benefit sanction. Minister Abbott has described a WfD project in Sydney where 74 referrals resulted in numerous failures to contact and drop-outs at a later stage due to finding work, illness, etc., so that in the end there were only seven participants; WfD seminars in Sydney in May and June 2000, where only a quarter of the Newstart recipients referred turned up and many of the "no shows" were subsequently penalised by Centrelink; and an analysis of 346 referrals to a large charity having a variety of projects, which resulted in only 110 commencements in the month after referral.[173] From July 2000 referrals to CWCs for participation in WfD have been automated, with Centrelink being responsible for checking eligibility of those whose circumstances change after referrals have taken place. Later in 2000, when the commencement rate on referrals was averaging probably below a quarter,[174] DEWRSB varied the system of payments to CWCs to compensate them for low participation rates (which affect their fees) and increased the "autoreferral rate" to 400%. This means that four people are automatically referred for each vacancy that arises on a project.

CWCs also report that, even after commencement, eligibility for WfD frequently changes. Attendance at a WfD project is not required on any day that the participant has other work, and in this case there is no requirement to make up the lost hours. If enough is earned to reduce benefit payment (even slightly)

211

for two consecutive fortnights, participants may permanently withdraw from the WfD project [DEWRSB (2000k), p. 19].

Although referrals to WfD are triggered automatically for individuals subject to Mutual Obligation, Centrelink also makes "manual" referrals, e.g. for unemployed people who have not yet entered Mutual Obligation[175] and the very long-term unemployed who have already participated in a programme such as Intensive Assistance. Most of the intake to WfD has continued to be long-term unemployed people, rather than short-term unemployed people who are subject to Mutual Obligation for the first time.[176]

3. Assessments of Work for the Dole

Work for the Dole has evoked several types of comment and reaction. It has been criticised as a form of workfare, punitive in character and providing forced or compulsory labour. Although Working Nation had already generalised the principle of compulsory participation in job creation programmes, those programmes paid a wage via the employer, at award wage rates. Burgess et al. (1999, pp. 4,7), noting that prior legislative provisions which prevented recipients from being required to work for their unemployment benefits were removed in March 1997 to enable the introduction of legislation for WfD, suggest that it is a form of compulsory labour which fails on principles of human rights. In Denmark, where programme participants also retain beneficiary status and similar criticisms have been made,[177] participation in job creation programmes has been kept part-time partly to ensure that benefit recipients are not obliged to work at less than the equivalent of a minimum wage. In WfD an adult level of unemployment benefit ($291.80 per fortnight, or higher for a single person, at end 1998), plus the $20 payment for participation in WfD, divided by hours worked (30 per fortnight), corresponds to hourly earnings slightly above the federal minimum wage ($373.40 per week for 38 hours in 1998).

The programme has also been criticised for its lack of explicit employment aims (see the discussion of Mutual Obligation in Chapter 4) and training content. A relatively detailed comparison of WfD with the New Deal in the United Kingdom identified as important differences the lack of any counterpart in Australia to the four month "Gateway" period of one-to-one counselling prior to assignment to a programme in the United Kingdom; and the restriction of WfD to community sector work, which contrasts with private sector involvement in creating places for the New Deal [Curtain (2000)].[178]

Another evaluation approach involves documenting attitudes. Surveys have found support for the scheme among participants and the general public. A survey by the Social Policy Research Centre (University of New South Wales) showed that 82.5% of people support a requirement on young unemployed people to take part in "a work for the dole scheme", and indicated that support for mutual obligation

212

principles is almost as strong among young people themselves and among people who have experienced unemployment in their family as among other groups [see Eardley *et al.* (2000) and the discussion of Mutual Obligation in Chapter 4]. The evaluation of WfD pilot programmes [DEWRSB (1999*b*)] also reported that 75% of participants when surveyed three months after leaving considered that it had improved their self-esteem, and 85% reported it had increased their desire to find a job. A small-scale survey of participants conducted for the evaluation found a statistically significant increase in psychological well-being following participation in WfD, but did not find a significant effect on self-esteem [DEWRSB (1999*b*)]. Another approach to evaluation, estimating the net impact of programmes on outcomes, is discussed below.

E.   Evaluations of the net impact of labour market programmes

1.   Background

This section considers recent statistical evaluations of the net impact of labour market programmes. Such statistical evaluations merit close examination because they are widely cited and have tended to define a certain concept of success in labour market policy, which goes on to influence policy debate and decision. They should not be confused with general programme evaluations such as the evaluation of the employment, education and training elements of Working Nation [DEETYA (1996)] or the Stage one and Stage two evaluations of Job Network [DEWRSB (2000*d*, 2001*b*)], which have provided a wealth of information on, for example, the practical content of the programmes and the services they deliver, procedures for referral to the programmes and profile of participants, incentives influencing programme providers and participants, the history of programme growth and policy adjustments, and the general institutional background.

2.   Evaluations of Working Nation programmes[179]

An important tool for evaluating the micro-economic effect of labour market programmes in Australia has been the post-program monitoring (PPM) surveys undertaken by the responsible Commonwealth department. Questionnaires are mailed to programme participants approximately three months after they complete a programme, asking them to indicate their current labour market activity. PPM surveys have been conducted since the mid-1980s, and although this is not the only method of evaluation that has been used or is possible, the findings have had a large influence on the form and scope of labour market intervention. Although the PPM method has some advantages, especially in terms of providing basic programme monitoring information with little delay and on a continuous basis, the data can be unreliable due to incomplete or unreturned questionnaires. The response rates of those who have and who have not left benefits can be compared, and on this basis DEWRSB has estimated that lower response rates by the employed lead to a 2 to 3 percentage point underestimate of the percentage with positive outcomes.

In some cases, the PPM questionnaire is also addressed to a control group of persons, drawn from social security records and selected to match the programme participants with respect to certain characteristics. Comparison of the PPM outcomes for participants with those of the control group give an estimate of net impact. This is referred to as the matched control group method. Table 5.2 summarises official estimates for the net impact of Working Nation programmes on this basis. The control group in this case consists of unemployed individuals who had not received programme assistance for at least six months, who were matched to the PPM group on the basis of age (in five-year groupings), sex and duration of unemployment (in two-month groupings) at the time of commencement in the programme. Since the questionnaire was sent to the control group three months after this selection process, reported employment statuses in both cases represent a rate of entry to work over a three-month period. Table 5.2 indicates that the JobStart wage subsidy programme had the largest net impact, and the New Work Opportunities job creation programme the least.

Stromback and Dockery (2000) conducted a further detailed analysis of net impact of the programmes in Table 5.2 using data from another source, the Survey of Employment and Unemployment Patterns (SEUP). This survey followed a panel

Table 5.2. **Employment rates for participants in labour market programmes and control groups, 1996**

Programme type	Programme	Net unit cost[a]	Controls	Participants	Net impact
			Percentage in unassisted employment 3 months after exit from programme or selection as a control[b]		
Wage Subsidy (average duration 22 weeks)	JobStart	$1 263	22	50	+28
Brokered and other employment (average duration 23 weeks)	JobSkills	$7 105	19	30	+11
	New Work Opportunities	$10 009	17	21	+4
Training (average duration 9 weeks)	SkillShare	$970	23	30	+7
	JobTrain	$1 173	24	31	+7
Job Clubs (average duration 2 weeks)	Job Clubs	$625	24	36	+12

a) Net cost calculated as gross cost *less* the reduction in income support payments that result from programme participation.
b) Based on outcomes for completions in the month of February 1996, excluding cases where the outcome was participation in another programme.
Sources: Stromback and Dockery (2000), Tables 4.3 and 8.2; and Dockery and Stromback (2000b), Table 2.

Table 5.3. **Comparison of three-month employment status for the SEUP sample**

	PPM outcomes from data matching exercise		Labour market activity reported for SEUP	
	In unsubsidised employment[a]	Episodes with known outcomes	In unsubsidised work	Total number of episodes
Wage Subsidy				
JobStart	38.4%	318	51.0%	787
Brokered and other employment				
JobSkills	26.2%	210	34.3%	289
NOW	20.1%	194	24.1%	249
LEAP	20.7%	58	26.4%	87
Training				
SkillShare	20.7%	1 000	23.3%	1 294
JobTrain	15.5%	575	23.7%	717
Special intervention	9.4%	663	16.7%	844
Job Search Assistance				
Job Clubs	15.9%	377	24.7%	469

a) Calculated as a percentage of spells with known outcomes.
Source: Stromback and Dockery (2000), Table 8.3.

of persons aged 15 to 59 years over a period of three years from September 1994 to September 1997, and collected data on personal characteristics and labour market history on the basis of three interviews in which survey respondents were asked to recall their labour market status for each month of the past year. The main labour market statuses coded are referred to as "working", "looking for work" (which could be combined with work, for example during programme participation) and "absence from the labour market". For consenting persons these survey data were matched to administrative records from the Departments of Employment and Department of Social Security (DSS), which include information on dates of participation in programmes, completion status of the programme and, in many cases, the education and employment outcomes as reported in the PPM questionnaires. After eliminating incomplete records, Stromback and Dockery compared the employment rates of programme participants three months after participation, as recorded in the matched SEUP data, with outcomes as reported in the PPM questionnaires. As shown in Table 5.3, the matched SEUP data show higher employment rates than the PPM questionnaires.[180] This difference probably reflects, in addition to the response bias of the PPM data, respondent errors in recalling dates in the SEUP data.[181]

In a next stage of analysis, Stromback and Dockery (2000) divided the SEUP sample into five periods corresponding to three-month outcomes dates in the first and second halves of 1995, first and second halves of 1996, and last three quarters of 1997 respectively. They compared employment rates three months after leaving

215

Table 5.4.   **The net impact of programme participation in SEUP programme participation and control groups**

		Percentage in unassisted employment 3 months after exit from programme or selection as a control				
		Period 1 1995/1	Period 2 1995/2	Period 3 1996/1	Period 4 1996/2	Period 5 1997
Wage Subsidy	Participants	19.3	18.0	52.3	56.6	60.1
	Control group	7.5	18.2	14.0	13.8	15.8
	Net impact	**11.8**	**–0.3**	**38.3**	**42.8**	**44.3**
Brokered	Participants	17.4	29.5	29.7	26.0	30.8
	Control group	8.9	15.9	14.4	12.3	11.8
	Net impact	**8.5**	**13.6**	**15.3**	**13.7**	**19.0**
Training	Participants	10.1	18.3	18.6	17.3	17.5
	Control group	6.4	17.0	15.7	13.7	16.1
	Net impact	**3.7**	**1.3**	**2.9**	**3.6**	**1.4**
Job Search	Participants	15.5	21.2	19.5	22.1	24.5
	Control group	6.7	19.8	15.1	14.3	16.6
	Net impact	**8.7**	**1.4**	**4.5**	**7.7**	**8.0**

Source: Stromback and Dockery (2000), Table 8.4.

a programme with the employment rates, three months later, of individuals who had been unemployed at the midpoint of each period. These control group data were weighted to match the participant group by gender, age (four groups) and duration of looking for work (eight groups). Estimated net impacts, shown in Table 5.4, were more positive for the wage subsidy and job creation programmes and less positive for the training programmes than had been the case in PPM analysis. Recall problems, as noted above, would be one influence in these results. Regression analysis confirmed the general pattern of results that was obtained using the matched control group method. When this regression-based analysis was extended by including a range of further explanatory variables (including birthplace, marital status, English proficiency, disability, local labour market disadvantage, education, union status, working status of the spouse and willingness to move interstate, all variables that have a highly significant impact on the general hazard rate out of job search), the estimates of net impact were essentially unchanged. This is important because it indicates that net impact estimates based on PPM matched control group methodology are not seriously influenced by omission of these additional control variables.[182] Official reports have also found that a regression method yields similar results to the matched control group method [DEWRSB (2000l, 2001a)].

In contesting the current government's decision to reduce labour market programme spending, commentators and advocacy organisations have frequently cited the official PPM findings for the JobStart wage subsidy programme as evidence that such a programme can be relatively effective [Harding (1998); Freeland (1999); ACOSS (2000b); Eardley et al. (2001)]. Net impacts for JobStart are also still being cited as a point for comparison with current programmes in official analysis [DEWRSB (2000l, 2001a)]. In this respect, it should be noted that gross three-month employment rates for JobStart, in the matched SEUP data, rose from below 20% in Periods 1 and 2 to over 50% in Periods 3 to 5. The timing of this increase corresponds with the introduction of new programme requirements and conditions in July 1994 [see, for example, Baume and Kay (1995), Appendix 12.4].[183] Employers were required to retain the employee for at least three months after the end of the subsidy period, and a $500 lump sum bonus was offered to employers who retained Job-Compact-eligible jobseekers a year after their JobStart commencement. The matched SEUP data set treated only the period of continuous subsidy payment as the period of programme participation, with the result that cases where the employer retained the JobStart participant for three further months were coded as entries to unsubsidised employment. PPM questionnaires were sent out three months after the end of the continuous subsidy period in the case of non-Job Compact participants (who were about two-thirds of the total in 1995/96), and three months after the point at which the 12-month bonus payment could be made (i.e. 15 months after commencement in the programme), in the case of Job Compact participants.[184] Citation of these employment rates as outcomes "three months after assistance" and in "unassisted" or "unsubsidised" work (various terms which successive commentators have copied one from another) seem questionable. In the SEUP data, for example, only the employment outcome rates for the first one or two periods, which were below 20%, should be described in these terms. For the later periods, many non-Job Compact participants may have been kept on for three months after the subsidy period ended because of the programme requirements. In Job Compact cases, employment rates recorded by the PPM survey will reflect entries to unsubsidised jobs between the end of the ongoing subsidy and the 15-month point, which would have been a period of much more than three months.

In general, entries to a wage subsidy programme are motivated partly by the subsidy but also partly by the match between immediate employee and employer needs that motivates unsubsidised hires. A programme under which employers are paid $1 during the first week of a new hire would have a negligible true impact. However, since employers are hiring all this time, there still would be substantial take-up of such a programme. A positive net impact on the employment prospects of participants would be estimated using either PPM questionnaire or econometric methodologies because – even after controlling statistically for other observable factors – employment prospects remain sharply better for people who have recently been hired than for those who have not. To avoid this type of selection bias, which is related to occurrence of the hiring event

217

itself, the control group should consist of comparable unemployed who have recently been hired without a subsidy.[185] This requires data on eligible and non-eligible groups of jobseekers, which could arise for example from random assignment to the subsidy-eligible group at the individual level, or the introduction of the programme in some local areas but not others.[186]

Dockery and Stromback (2000b) discuss another conceptual issue with evaluation findings based on the matched control group method, as applied to PPM data and matched SEUP data. Control groups were selected from persons on the register (or recorded as seeking work) at a date that corresponds to the time when participants leave programmes. However the JobStart and job creation programmes had an average duration of 22 and 23 weeks respectively. Dockery and Stromback argue that a more relevant measure of impact would be obtained by identifying a control group that is comparable to participants just before their entry to a programme, and then following the subsequent status of both groups.[187] But employment rates for the control group three months after the end of programme participation, reflecting flows into employment over an eight-month rather than a three-month period, would be approximately three times higher than those in Table 5.4.[188] Assuming that programme participants do not often enter unsubsidised employment during their participation in the programme, employment rates for participants would be little changed. Thus "the inevitable conclusion would then be that brokered and other employment programs [job creation programmes] have a negative effect, as opposed to the previous conclusion of no positive effect". Further along these lines, Dockery and Stromback (2000a) note that the standard method for estimating the effect of treatment in clinical studies is to match the treatment and control group at the start of the treatment, and that measuring the survival rate from the end of the treatment would involve, for example, eliminating from the comparison any deaths that actually occurred during the treatment period. This is not a new point, even in Australia. The Bureau of Labour Market Research's evaluation of a job creation program which was in place until 1983, the Wage Pause Program [BLMR (1984)] adopted an appropriate methodology in this respect, following participants from their date of entry to the programme, and comparing them with CES registrants who were referred to projects but not hired under the programme.[189]

Some official labour market policy evaluations in Europe increasingly give attention to the negative impact of programme participation on rates of entry to a market job, which is called the "dead-weight", "retention" or "in-lock" effect of programme participation, i.e. they consider rates of entry to market work starting from the time of entry to the programme, as Dockery and Stromback propose [Raïsanen (2001)]. In some cases, evaluations also give attention to increases (or falls) in the rates of exit to a market job prior to compulsory participation in programmes, which may be called "entry", "motivation", "deterrent" or "compliance" effects. In Denmark, an ability to track the programme, employment and benefit (including non-unemployment benefit) status of the entire population from administrative records allows official analysts to see each of these effects as directly as possible, and facilitates a focus on exits from all benefits or entry to unsubsidised employment, rather than other indicators of success [Mærkedahl (2001)]. Such developments have clearly been a major influence permitting the rational development of labour market policy. Random assignment experiments in the United States and systematic pilot testing of new measures in selected employment service offices in the United Kingdom have for many years played a similar role, allowing comparative tracking of outcomes for groups that are and are not eligible for a treatment – rather than only tracking outcomes from the start or the end of participation in the programme.

3. Recent evaluations of Work for the Dole, Job Search Training and Intensive Assistance

Programme net impact estimates

Evaluations of programme net impact in terms of off-benefit outcomes have been published for WfD [DEWRSB (2000*l*)], JST and Intensive Assistance [DEWRSB (2001*a*; 2001*b*)]. Off-benefit outcomes refer to having left unemployment benefit entirely three months after exit from the programme or after selection into the control group: outcomes do not include cases where people took up part-time work with low hours so as to avoid, or to exit from, the programme.[190] In other respects, a standard matched control group methodology (described above) was used for these studies. Off-benefit rates for WfD participants who left assistance in August 1999 averaged 30% three months after leaving the programme, compared with 17% for a matched comparison group three months after selection into the comparison group; off-benefit rates for IA participants who left assistance in August 1999 averaged 31% three months after leaving the programme, compared with 21% for the comparison group; and off-benefit rates for JST participants who left in March 1999 averaged 27% three months after leaving the programme, compared with 24% for the comparison group. The DEWRSB reports call the difference between these figures, *i.e.* 13% for WfD, 10% for Intensive Assistance and 3% for JST, programme net impacts. This leads to an estimated cost per net impact outcome of $22 010 for Intensive Assistance, $13 800 for JST and $11 500 for WfD. On the same basis, cost per net impact outcome for JobStart and Job Clubs (indexed to 1999-2000 prices) were $9 700 and $16 500 respectively,[191] but much higher for all other Working Nation programmes.

The problems in using off-benefit outcomes measured three months after leaving assistance to assess impact are the same as those in using PPM outcomes.

219

When the duration of participation in a programme is fixed, a positive net impact does at least indicate that – for the three months after the programme has ended – ex-participants had a relatively high rate of leaving benefits (albeit that non-participants may still have left more rapidly overall because many entered work while participants were "locked into" the programme.) But when the methodology is applied to programmes from which exit can occur at any time (as is encouraged by design in WfD and Intensive Assistance), a positive "net impact" is liable to be reported for a programme that does not positively influence outcomes at all. For example, suppose that four newly-unemployed people enter employment (in a job which lasts for at least three months) after 2, 5, 8 and 11 months of unemployment respectively: the three month off-benefit outcome rate for a newly-unemployed "control" group is then 25%. If newly-unemployed people are instead put into a "programme" which lasts a maximum of 6 months and which is exited upon finding work – but has no impact on how fast work is found – the first two people will exit after two and five months respectively (i.e. when they enter employment), and the second two people will exit into unemployment after six months, one of them finding work within three months of leaving the programme. Thus the average off-benefit outcome rate, as measured three months after exit from assistance, is 75%. Any suggestion that this 75% rate, compared with the 25% rate achieved by the control group, represents an impact of the programme seems misleading.[192] Yet this is, in effect, what DEWRSB's published net impact studies propose. The size of the statistical bias is attenuated in the "net impact" estimates for WfD and Intensive Assistance (the rules and procedures allow some participants to exit the programme without entering employment or leaving benefit, and this lowers the outcome rate as measured three months after leaving assistance) but it is still present.

A notable feature of the off-benefit outcome rates for ex-participants of WfD and Intensive Assistance is that they are initially (in the first month after leaving assistance) much higher than for the control group, but subsequently converge towards those of the control group.[193] This is because, other things being equal, the employment rate of individuals who are initially employed tends to decline through time as some of them return to unemployment. For JST, a programme of only short duration, this phenomenon does not appear to arise: off-benefit outcomes for ex-participants remain 3% higher than for comparable non-participants even many months after participation, and participants achieve a 45% off-benefit rate after 9 months, whereas comparable non-participants reach this level only after 11 months or more. In this case the estimates of programme net impact appear to be free from any obvious source of bias.[194]

In the case of Intensive Assistance, PPM figures for post-assistance outcomes over May 1998 to September 1999 (i.e. in the first contract period) indicate that only 13% of participants left with a positive outcome within the first three months after commencement, and 20% within five months after commencement.[195] A positive outcome in this case means that the person was in employment (not necessarily full-time) or study three months after leaving Intensive Assistance (not necessarily a paid outcome). This rate of positive outcomes seems relatively low, because in the matched comparison group of individuals who had not been referred to or entered Intensive Assistance, 21% of individuals were off benefits after three months and 27% after five months. However the two sets of statistics refer to different definitions of "outcomes".[196] Data for both participants and the comparison group, using the same definition or definitions of "outcomes" in each case,[197] are needed. But such data might still indicate that IA participants in 1999 left benefits no more rapidly than individuals in the comparison group did.[198]

In terms of measurable impact, the aim and purpose of labour market programmes should be to reduce unemployment and increase employment. This implies a focus on whether programmes achieve high rates of entry to employment or leaving benefit – and not something else, such as a high proportion of positive outcomes among individuals who have recently left the programme. "Survival rates" (i.e. the proportion of participants who are still unemployed at various times after entry to or referral to a programme) and rates of exit from unemployment should be reported, with comparisons between participants and control groups, as basic tracking information.[199] Analytical energies can then be focused on the more substantive and often quite difficult issues which arise in interpreting such statistics. General evaluations (providing information on the practical content of the programmes and the services they deliver, etc., as described at the start of this section) are essential input to this task of interpretation.

Referral and compliance net impact estimates

The recent net impact evaluation for JST and Intensive Assistance compared off-benefit outcomes for a sample individuals referred to the programmes in August 1999 with those of matched comparison groups that had not been referred to or participated in the programmes in the previous six months. Comparable off-benefit outcome rates for the referral samples and their matched comparison groups appear to have been generated, insofar as neither group includes individuals who have already found work at the outset and the same measure of outcomes was used in both cases. However very little information about the results was published. The only information provided is an estimate of "compliance" net impact, which is defined as the "referral" net impact (the estimated impact on off-benefit status three months after referral[200]), less the "programme net impact" (a separate estimate of programme net impact that occurred within three months of referral may be involved here). In 1999, of all individuals referred to JST, 9.9% are reported to have gone off benefit within three months due to a "compliance" effect, *i.e.* as a result of the referral to the programme, but without commencing in the programme. The corresponding figure for IA is 2.3%. In the case of JST, the inclusion of impacts associated with compliance effects reduces the programme's estimated cost per additional off-benefit outcome to just $1 400, making it by some distance the most cost-effective of all current and past programmes that have been formally evaluated.

Indications that these labour market programmes may achieve most of their impact through "motivation" or "compliance" effects are in line with, for example, other evidence that many jobseekers leave unemployment to avoid Mutual Obligation requirements (see Chapter 4), and similar results from Denmark [see Maerkedahl (2001)]. Such findings strongly confirm the importance of incentive factors, and specifically of requirements which may tend to counterbalance the disincentives which arise from payment of unemployment benefits. However "programme" impacts can also be important, as illustrated by findings that some JN service strategies are more effective than others.

Service strategies

The Job Network Stage two evaluation reports results of a comparative evaluation of service strategies for JST and Intensive Assistance. Top-performing and bottom-performing providers were identified, with performance assessed in terms of a range of outcome indicators with controls for local labour market conditions and the characteristics of jobseekers. For JST, 52% of the jobseekers with the top-performing providers reported being sent to a job interview, compared with only 21% of jobseekers with bottom-performing providers. There were no differences reported in terms of some other dimensions of assistance, such as writing resumes and job applications. For Intensive Assistance, 35% of jobseekers with the top-performing providers reported being sent to a job interview, compared with 19% of the jobseekers with the bottom-performing providers. Referrals resulting in a paid full-time job were reported by 25% and 9% of jobseekers respectively. The jobseekers with top-performing IA providers reported receiving job-search-skills training or job-specific-skills training (*e.g.* a computer course or special certificate course) relatively less often, although they had a more positive opinion of the training that they did receive and of the encouragement and support provided. This finding suggests that the case for more training, even job-search training, in general is not clear-cut. A traditional employment service strategy, focusing on direct referrals of jobseekers to vacant jobs, seems to be the key to success. As regards general service quality, it is not clear whether their clients obtained work because they received better service, or clients reported greater satisfaction merely because they had achieved better

222

outcomes, and more detailed research and more precise documentation of the services provided by the top-performing providers would be helpful.

These Australian findings may be consistent with findings from an evaluation of Swiss PES offices, which concluded that measurable variables (among them, referrals to jobs) could explain only 15% to 25% of variations in performance, the rest being related to non-measurable factors such as organisational structure, enterprise culture and the quality of various services [OECD (2001*b*)].

F. Three large programme areas: youth and training, indigenous and disability programmes

Currently, youth and training programmes are managed by DETYA, indigenous programmes are managed by ATSIC and DEWRSB, and disability programmes are managed by FACS. For many of the individual programmes, Centrelink manages related income support issues and assesses client eligibility for the programmes, and/or refers clients to the programmes.

Programmes in the youth and training area (Annex B) include the Enterprise and Career Education Foundation (ECEF), Jobs Pathway Programme (JPP) and Jobs, Placement, Employment and Training (JPET), which promote transitions from school to work with particular attention to groups at risk. With the expansion of New Apprenticeships, direct funding of vocational training has been increasingly delivered in an employment rather than an unemployment setting. Rather than school-leavers and the unemployed people being offered a programme of training for the unemployed, New Apprenticeship options may be promoted to them. Specialised language, literacy and numeracy training is still provided directly during the unemployment spell.

A large proportion of non-Job Network spending is on a few relatively large programmes – the Community Development Employment Projects (CDEP) scheme for indigenous people (Annex C) and the Commonwealth Rehabilitation Program (CRS Australia), open employment and supported employment services (now called Business Services) for the disabled (Annex D). In these areas, policy changes take on the character of reform to long-established institutions. Social and employment services for the disabled have been provided by a community sector, with funding from government, long before such ideas were applied to mainstream employment services. This experience indicates a risk with a strategy of community and private sector provision of services: the provider sector may itself become a political force, resisting certain types of change, so that policy flexibility is not necessarily increased. Infrastructure costs can make rapid changes of policy inherent costly, regardless of institutional arrangements.[201] Another major issue, for supported employment for the disabled as well as CDEPs, is that participants often remain for many years, financed by near-indefinite subsides, so that even with a fairly limited intake the programmes can become expensive.

223

Recent policy changes have attempted to increase the focus of these programmes on achieving private employment outcomes, but the providers are naturally reluctant to lose their best workers. Also, for disability employment services, principles of funding providers according to the assessed needs of individuals and the services delivered to them are being introduced.

G. Specialist programmes for severely disadvantaged jobseekers, labour market re-entrants and regional initiatives

Australia has several relatively small labour market programmes, apart from those described in this chapter and Annexes B, C and D, which address the needs of particular target groups. CSP provides specialised assistance for the unemployed who are unlikely to benefit from regular employment services. JET and Return to Work are targeted on re-entrants to the labour force. The Regional Assistance Program provides some federal funding for projects, proposed by Area Consultative Committees, that promote small business, human capital development and infrastructure at a local level.

1. Community Support Program (CSP)[202]

The Community Support Program was introduced in May 1998. About 15% of those eligible for case management under Working Nation were found to have disadvantages so severe that they were not in a position to benefit from employment-related assistance. During preparations for Job Network, CSP was developed to respond to these needs [DEETYA (1996); Vanstone (1996a)]. Specialised assistance helps these clients more effectively, while exclusion from Intensive Assistance may be considered necessary, given the principle of paying IA providers on the basis of employment outcomes. CSP tries to assist jobseekers who are not ready to participate in Intensive Assistance due to serious and/or numerous personal barriers to gaining employment such as drug or alcohol addiction, very poor literacy and numeracy, psychological problems and homelessness. Eligibility for CSP is restricted to jobseekers in receipt of Newstart or Youth Allowance, or aged 15-20 and not on income support, who would be better served by assistance other than that available in Job Network.

Centrelink occupational psychologists make referrals to CSP (see Chapter 3) and, with the jobseeker's permission, pass their detailed written report on the jobseeker on to the CSP provider. This is considered important to ensure that participants do not have to retell their story and are referred on to appropriate assistance. CSP organisations help participants access counselling, stable accommodation, drug or alcohol rehabilitation programmes and other activities addressing significant or debilitating personal development needs. They may refer people to another organisation, or provide services directly. Referrals are for up to two years, during which the assistance provided should allow the person to access Intensive Assistance, transfer to a more appropriate form of income support or secure employment.

The programme is delivered by community, private and public sector organisations (75% are community organisations), selected and contracted through a competitive tender process. DEWRSB sets the policy and provides the funding for the programme: Centrelink conducted the tenders, managed contracts and administered CSP on behalf of DEWRSB until July 2000 when this role was transferred to DEWRSB. The recognised CSP outcomes are achievement of an employment outcome, overcoming special needs and becoming eligible for Job Network Intensive Assistance, and commencing receipt of a more appropriate type of income support (such as Disability Support Pension). In the first contract period, running to February 2000, the fees paid were $700 on commencement, $300 after six months and $500 after 12 and 18 months. Placement in employment could attract a further $1 000 after 13 weeks and $1 000 after 26 weeks. In 1999, funding for the programme was increased from $15 million to $30 million per year. Under second round contracts which started in July 2000 the services are being provided from 330 sites, up from 218 in the first tender round.

In April 2000 an official review of the programme was announced, but its appearance was delayed. The terms of reference expressed some concern about the voluntary nature of the programme, and outcomes for those who are assessed as eligible for it but do not enter. It also noted that many providers were providing the services directly, rather than acting primarily as a broker towards other services as had been intended. Four agencies which deliver the programme have collaborated to produce their own evaluation [MacDonald with Jope (2000)]. This found that the programme was very effective in that it has a high retention rate, and helps participants to overcome employment barriers and improves their confidence and motivation: but it called for the continuation of assistance beyond two years if necessary, and for increased overall funding, given that it was often difficult to refer clients on to other suitable programmes.

2. Jobs, Education and Training (JET)[203]

JET is a voluntary programme introduced in 1989 with the aim of helping sole parent pensioners to enter or re-enter the workforce and hence reducing programme outlays. JET has since been expanded to cover recipients of partnered parent, widow and carers allowances, and partners of people on other income support payments. Centrelink is responsible for service delivery though specialist JET Advisors who are located in selected Centrelink offices. In 1999/2000, Centrelink had about 120 JET Advisors, about 61 000 new clients were interviewed and 15 000 training courses were funded for clients for a programme cost of about $17 million.

Participation in JET is voluntary. JET eligible customers are invited to participate through mail contacts with letters being sent out by an automatic system to target groups. These include all teenagers on qualifying payments and Parenting Payment clients whose youngest child has recently entered primary school (at 6 years) and secondary school (at 12 years) who have no or low earnings: additional groups may be targeted. Other ways of contacting potential customers are through community outreach to, for example, housing commissions, child care centres, even hospitals/maternity wards with a range of nationally produced publicity products; and by maintaining awareness of JET among those who are in a position to refer potential participants.

The main services provided to participants are preparation of a return to work plan; information, advice and referrals to further services including help with finding child care; and financial assistance with training. Up to $600 of training fees can be financed, with six-week computer courses being a popular option. Training for retailing and to improve general self-confidence after many years out of the labour market are also common. When there is a need to do longer courses, a supplement to regular benefit of $62.40 per fortnight can be paid if the person is doing at least a 50% study load.

JET clients can volunteer to be scored for Intensive Assistance. One difficulty with JN service is that JET clients often want only part-time work with low hours, which does not attract a payment, and job close to home. JET clients are also eligible for small business courses, which are run as part of NEIS.

3. Return to Work Program[204]

Return to Work is a programme introduced in 2000 to assess skills, identify training needs and build the confidence of people seeking to re-enter the labour force after an absence of two or more years due to their roles as carers of children under the age of 16 or of the aged, chronically ill or disabled. The programme is open to those not on income support. Those on income support must be registered as unemployed. When the youngest child turns 16, a person who has been on Parenting Payment and eligible for JET has to transfer to Newstart Allowance and if a referral is not made to JST or Intensive Assistance a referral to Return to Work may be made.

Among the main services provided are skills, training and career planning. According to the request for tender, an individual return to work programme would be developed during an introductory interview lasting one to two hours, and where services such as referral to other career counselling or training are provided, an exit interview would take place three to six weeks after the introductory interview, or when the training is completed. The programme lends itself primarily to facilitating access to training rather than fully funding training.

One programme Managing Agent has been contracted by DEWRSB for each state/territory following tenders in October 1999. The current contracts are expected to provide 16 000 places over two years at a cost of $9.6 million.

4. *Regional Assistance Program* (RAP)[205]

State initiatives to promote employment have been briefly described in Chapter 2 and will not be described further here. The Commonwealth's Regional Assistance Program (RAP) provides about $30 million annually to fund specific projects which promote small business development, general regional economic development and infrastructure, tackle skill gaps, improve links between industry and schooling and training, and address the employment needs of disadvantaged groups (excluding projects measures which would duplicate existing school-industry programmes). Financing for Area Consultative Committees (see Chapter 2), whose remit includes the identification and facilitation of RAP projects, is also budgeted under RAP. In many cases RAP co-finances projects with state and local governments or local industry [Abbott *et al.* (2000)].

Labour Adjustment Packages (LAPs) have in the past been provided in a number of industries, including steel (1983-89), textiles, clothing and footwear (1988-96), automotive (1991-96), rail (1993-96) and forestry (1995-2000). They were managed by DETYA to help companies shedding labour and individuals made redundant from particular industries to gain employment in other industries, through on-site counselling, skills training, wage subsidies and relocation assistance. In a background paper to the 1996/97 budget, the incoming government described these as small, compartmentalised programmes and announced their abolition. The forestry package was, exceptionally, maintained through to 1999/2000 as a measure within the Regional Assistance Program.

Chapter 6

Workplace Relations and Wage Determination

A. Introduction

Labour market performance also depends on the efficient functioning of labour relations and wage determination systems. In most industrialised countries, these systems have been evolving for over a century and now constitute a set of complex social arrangements relating workers, employers and their collective representatives. In addition, a regulatory structure of more or less "interventionist" character is usually set by national, and sometimes regional, governments. The capacity of these actors to define a framework that allows for workplace co-operation and conflict resolution, and that encourages adaptation rather than resistance to change has an obvious bearing on the capacity of economies to allocate human resources efficiently, secure good jobs and minimise joblessness.

Australia's labour relations system has evolved in a manner different from that of all other OECD Member countries (with the partial exception of New Zealand) to the extent that the term "antipodean exceptionalism" has been coined for it. The main feature of this exceptionalism is the long-established quasi-judicial system of conciliation and arbitration by means of federal and state tribunals. In fact, conciliation and arbitration have historically played a larger role in shaping employer-employee relations, and in setting the actual terms and conditions under which Australian workers offer their labour, than has independent collective bargaining.

Only in recent years, under the impact of several major pieces of legislation, has strong decentralised bargaining evolved and the role and impact of the arbitration system been considerably diminished. The latest milestone in this process was the 1996 Workplace Relations Act (WRA) of the current Liberal/National coalition. This Act, as well as further workplace relations reform measures undertaken since 1996, aim to encourage co-operative labour-management relations and determine wages and working conditions, as far as possible, at enterprise or workplace level, with a view to improving labour market efficiency, and increasing employment, productivity and real wages. The government has stressed the linkages it sees between workplace relations and employment, by combining these previously separate portfolios in one single government Department. This chapter outlines the important shift in emphasis from arbitration to decentralised bargaining, analyses the major features of current labour-management relations and indicates some preliminary effects of the Australian industrial relations reform process.

B. The evolution of the regulatory environment

Australia's unique arbitration system dates back to the turn of the century and to the very founding of the country itself [Castles (1985); McIntyre and Mitchell (1989); Curtain (1992)]. When the Australian Federation was created in 1901, its Constitution empowered the federal government to settle interstate disputes by means of conciliation and arbitration, while giving it only limited power to directly enact labour legislation.[206] A federal Court of Conciliation and Arbitration was subsequently established (its successors have been the "Conciliation and Arbitration Commission" and, since 1988, the "Australian Industrial Relations Commission" – AIRC), which was to first conciliate by achieving amicable agreement between the parties and, if this was not possible, to unilaterally determine terms and conditions of employment "by equitable award".[207]

To an extent, the compulsory arbitration setting reflected politicians' concerns about the high level of strikes before the turn of the century, as well as their intention to have the "two sides of industry" implicated in a tight, quasi-judicial, framework of joint regulation. Throughout most of the 20th century, arbitration tribunals provided the principal institutional framework for determining employment conditions. Consistent with the federal character of the country, the arbitration system was based on both federal and state tribunals. The federal system governs employment in fields where employer/employee relations or disputation have been classified as "interstate" in character, and therefore covers varying proportions of employees in various states. Employment in the federal government, in federal territories and in the state of Victoria, which has referred its corresponding powers to the Commonwealth, is also covered. Historically, the federal level has encompassed between one-third and one-half of all employees.

Taken together, federal and state awards have tended to cover around 80 to 90% of Australian wage and salary earners. To some extent, awards have tended to set only minimum rates of pay or basic conditions of employment, with the opportunity to set "over-award" pay rates and conditions through bargaining, dependent on sectoral or regional labour market conditions (such agreements would then normally be ratified by the arbitration commission as "consent awards" and, in the past, occasionally be incorporated into subsequent "paid rate" awards). Thus, the award system was more flexible *de facto* than it appeared to be in a formal sense. However, large groups of employees were not covered by any "over-award" settlements or other bargained agreements, and awards determined their actual salary. Importantly, up to the most recent period, agreements could only override award provisions when they brought improvements in wages or working conditions for employees.

In cases of "inter-state" industrial conflict or any demands on the adverse party, either side can refer a case to the federal Commission, which was in the past also able to intervene on its own accord "in the public interest". Where the matter cannot be settled by conciliation, the Commission proceeds to arbitration which usually takes a quasi-judicial form: participants serve claims upon each other, witnesses are called and evidence examined. Arbitration decisions are legally enforceable. Up until the 1990s, National Wage Cases heard by the federal Commission (and the flow-on of these to state jurisdictions) were the principal means through which wage increases were provided to wage and salary earners. Accordingly, they constituted important annual events in the national economy: after public hearings, the Commission laid down general principles, including wage adjustments, which were then applied throughout the award system by means of supplementary hearings for particular occupations and industries [Mitchell and Scherer (1993)]. By contrast, over the last decade the number of Australian employees whose wages and conditions are governed by (individual or collective) bargaining has greatly increased (see Sections D and E below).

The arbitration system has allowed for widespread "extension" of awards to all firms in an industry, beyond the employer or employer association that was initially party to the dispute. In the individual states this is usually done through the state commission declaring a "common rule", while in the federal system, which in principle covers only employers that are signatory to the award, the same effect is reached in a more roundabout way, by "roping in" additional employers through identical demands (so-called logs of claims) served by the union.

Up to the recent past, this Australian industrial relations system, although "exceptional" through its arbitration focus, thus belonged to the group of OECD countries with "highly centralised, highly co-ordinated" wage determination systems [OECD (1994a, 1997c)]. It offered benefits for both workers and employers. Businesses accepted arbitration in exchange for tariff walls and industrial stability. Unions gained legitimacy as respondents to awards and profited from increased membership through explicit or implicit preference clauses contained in many arbitration rulings; and the "conveniently belong" rule regulated inter-union rivalry by allocating members to existing union organisations on the basis of established occupational or sectoral boundaries.[208]

Several advantages of the Australian arbitration system have been noted [OECD (1988)]. In comparison with rather fragmented bargaining systems such as in Italy or the United Kingdom, it layed down procedures for the orderly settlement of disputes of right and disputes of interest, limiting (at least in theory) recourse to industrial action. Also, arbitration has been a mechanism by which broader economic concerns could be brought to bear on industrial relations outcomes. Other observers have identified a number of dimensions of inefficiency or "irresponsibility" of these institutional arrangements which have in the past negatively affected workplace relations, among which:

- A ready recourse to the centralised settlement of disputes by outside actors – at some distance from their point of origin – which has served to undermine direct negotiation and bargaining, which is the main method of conflict resolution in most other OECD Member countries.

- The fragmentation of union bargaining authority through multi-unionism in the workplace (craft, industrial and general unions) and the ensuing demarcations between areas of union activity.

- The "lowest-common-denominator" basis of awards which, like industrial bargaining in some other OECD countries, lack a mechanism for taking into account the particular needs of a workplace and company productivity [Niland (1978); Strauss (1988); Curtain (1992)].

- The failure of the award system to deliver the industrial peace which it had originally set out to guarantee.

Another issue is the continuing existence of separate federal and state industrial relations jurisdictions. The fact that a large number of worksites have some employees covered by the federal arbitration system and some by the relevant state system forces employers to deal with two distinct systems of labour law (even though the actual terms and conditions of employment awarded by the tribunals may not be all that different). Some efforts are underway to harmonise regulations through complementary legislation and co-operative arrangements between the federal and some state tribunals (*e.g.* dual membership), but much is dependent on the political constellation at federal and state levels at any given time. A most significant event in this context was the 1997 transfer by the government in Victoria (the second most populous state) of a large part of its industrial relations powers to the Commonwealth government. However, other state governments have not followed suit, so that there are currently still six different workplace relations systems in place in Australia, and significant numbers of employers continue to be bound by two separate jurisdictions.[209]

C. The employment relations parties

1. *Trade unions*

Trade unions grew comfortable with the conciliation and arbitration system, as it provided them with protected legal status, avoided problems of union recognition characteristic of many other industrial relations systems, ensured their representational monopoly within a given occupation or industry (through the "conveniently belong" rule) and offered broad guarantees of social equity.[210] Membership grew to the extent that, by the mid-20th century, Australia had the highest trade union density among all market economies. Based on union records, density reached over 60% in the 1950s and stayed at 50 to 55% through to the 1980s, before declining sharply[211] [Peetz (1998)]. The absolute number of union members peaked in 1990 at 2.6 million members; it fell to about 1.9 million by 2000. Despite the high membership, most unions established only a weak presence at the workplace level, as they concentrated their resources on the centralised wage-fixing system. There is no legal backing for works councils or shop stewards, and although certain awards have guaranteed shop stewards rights to carry out union business during working hours, their activities have remained relatively limited.[212]

As in Britain, Australian unionism originally developed on a craft basis. Up to the most recent period, the trade union structure was characterised by a large number of small and medium-sized organisations, and a mixture of craft unions, industrial unions, and general conglomerate organisations. After it merged with several federations of white-collar unions in the 1970s and 1980s, there is now only one national peak body, the Australian Council of Trade Unions (ACTU), covering over 95% of all union membership. The bigger member unions are usually organised in branches, often covering a particular state (where they are registered with state tribunals). Trades and labour councils are the state-level counterparts to the ACTU. Table 6.1 illustrates the extent of trade union fragmentation at the end of the 1980s, and the subsequent trend towards concentration. Of around 300 unions in 1989, about half had less than 1 000 members. Further, half of total membership was in comparatively small unions with less than 50 000 members.

Since the mid-1980s, the ACTU has promoted the organisational restructuring of the trade union movement through amalgamations of branch and craft unions. At the time, employer groups were also complaining that work organisation and company productivity were hampered by the existence of too many separate unions within the same enterprise. The federal Labor government supported amalgamation by increasing the minimum membership requirement for unions from 1 000 to 10 000 workers.[213] As a result, by 1996 the number of unions had fallen by more than half to 132, of which only 49 were active at federal level. Currently, almost all members in federally registered trade unions belong to 17 large organisations. This transformation was considered necessary to better service union members and assist local chapters in enterprise and workplace bargaining, the main target of workplace relations reforms undertaken since the late 1980s. To further overcome union fragmentation, the ACTU has actively

233|

Table 6.1. **Number of unions and union members by trade union size**

Size of union	Unions				Members			
	Number		Per cent of total unions		Average number per union		Per cent of total number	
	1989	1996	1989	1996	1989	1996	1989	1996
Under 100	38	21	12.7	15.9	45	39	0.1	–
100-249	31	12	10.4	9.0	170	175	0.2	0.1
250-499	26	18	8.7	13.6	341	378	0.3	0.2
500-999	41	11	13.7	8.3	703	782	0.8	0.3
1 000-1 999	42	14	14.0	10.6	1 417	1 407	1.7	0.7
2 000-2 999	12	10	4.0	7.6	2 466	2 510	0.9	0.9
3 000-4 999	25	6	8.4	4.5	3 950	4 183	2.9	0.9
5 000-9 999	19	6	6.4	4.5	7 309	7 667	4.1	1.6
10 000-19 999	19	10	6.4	7.6	13 755	14 310	7.7	5.1
20 000-29 999	12	2	4.0	1.5	26 620	24 700	8.7	1.8
30 000-39 999	10	5	3.3	3.8	35 017	35 360	10.3	6.3
40 000-49 999	6	2	2.0	1.5	45 177	44 100	7.9	3.2
50 000-79 999	7	3	2.3	2.3	64 723	71 467	13.3	7.0
80 000 and over	11	12	3.7	9.0	127 983	166 175	41.3	71.9
Total	**299**	**132**	**100.0**	**100.0**	**11 406**	**21 216**	**100.0**	**100.0**
Memorandum item	1990				1996			
Trade union density	**40.5**				**31.1**			

– Nil or less than half of the last digit used.
Sources: ABS, *Trade Union Statistics, Australia*, Catalogue No. 6323.0, 30 June 1989 and 30 June 1996; and *Employee Earnings, Benefits and Trade Union Membership, Australia*, Catalogue No. 6310.0, various issues.

promoted negotiations within "single bargaining units" [Peetz (1998); Davis and Lansbury (1998)].[214]

The ACTU has been a driving force – up to a certain limit – behind workplace relations reform, and the shift in emphasis towards enterprise bargaining, over the past two decades. It now considers collective bargaining as the "key method for achieving improvements in wages and employment conditions"; importantly, it sees a continuing role for bargaining at industry level, which is anathema to the current government position, and claims that many employers are willing, or would even prefer to, engage in more traditional branch negotiations or pattern bargaining.[215] However, the union also remains strongly committed to the "maintenance of comprehensive and relevant awards"; its wage claims and related demands continue to set the stage for the annual proceedings at the AIRC around the "National Wage Case", or what is currently called the "Safety-Net Review" [ACTU (1997, 2000); see DEWRSB (2000j), for an account of the safety-net review for 1999/2000].

2. Employer associations

After some initial resistance to the system of compulsory arbitration, Australian employers accepted the setting of awards at industry level, and the quasi-automatic union recognition, in exchange for tariff protection, labour relations stability and guarantees of managerial prerogatives in the workplace, which arbitration rulings tended to provide.[216]

Australian employer bodies have historically been fragmented, constituting more or less temporary alliances in response to union claims. A broad-based national employers' association, the Confederation of Australian Industry (CAI), was only formed in the 1970s, and merged in 1992 with the Australian Chamber of Commerce to create the Australian Chamber of Commerce and Industry (ACCI). The ACCI represents employer interests by lobbying the federal government on a wide range of economic and social policy issues and by providing submissions to the AIRC in annual wage cases. It has a federated structure with state, regional and local chambers, and integrates most of the key industry associations. State chambers represent members' interests before the state industrial relations commissions; they also consult companies on enterprise bargaining, participate in educational institutions, such as apprenticeship centres, and support business start-ups and international trade. The chambers, therefore, combine the classic tasks of trade associations with those as a representative of employers of labour.[217]

Other associations compete with the ACCI to speak on behalf of business interests. Of particular importance are the Australian Industry Group and the Business Council of Australia (BCA). The Australian Industry Group is the result of a merger of MTIA (Metal Trades Industry Association) and the Australian Chamber of Manufactures. These associations, which had split from the CAI in the 1980s, failed to join the newly established ACCI in 1992 and attempt to rival the latter as representatives of manufacturing interests.

The BCA was created in 1983 as an organisation comprised of the chief executives of major (currently about 100) Australian companies. It has had some influence as a pressure group arguing for decentralisation of labour-management relations, and has made independent submissions to National Wage Cases and Safety-net Reviews. CEOs and research staff are organised in Task Forces that focus on policy priorities, including the reform of workplace relations and dismissal legislation. It is not the least due to BCA influence that the business community has taken its distance from the compulsory arbitration system, and is shifting preferences towards non-union and non-award types of labour relations.

All of the above business organisations agree that the process of decentralising industrial relations and of emphasising enterprise negotiations over industrial bargaining and award-setting should continue. They also

235|

emphasise the need for relaxing unfair dismissal legislation, in an attempt to tailor workplace relations to the needs of the enterprise. The BCA and ACCI, in particular, have submitted briefs to the Australian Parliament outlining their support for recent Government bills which support these aims [ACCI/BCA (2000); BCA (2000a, b); ACCI (2000)]. The BCA is also vigorously calling for an end to the duplication, inconsistencies and demarcation disputes resulting from the co-existence of state and federal jurisdictions, and for the establishment of a unitary system as "the best model for enabling Australian enterprises to develop efficient and effective workplace relations" [BCA (2000c); Thatcher (2000)].

3. Federal and state industrial relations commissions

The first federal tribunal – the Commonwealth Court of Conciliation and Arbitration – was established under the Conciliation and Arbitration Act passed by the Federal Parliament in 1904. The Court had both arbitral and judicial powers: it could make awards specifying terms and conditions of employment, and could interpret and enforce awards, if necessary by imposing fines and penalties.

The Act underwent several revisions which, *inter alia*, separated the arbitration and judicial powers. It was overhauled by the 1988 Industrial Relations Act, which established the Australian Industrial Relations Commission (in place of the Australian Conciliation and Arbitration Commission), and for the first time provided for persons to hold dual appointments on the national Commission and a state industrial tribunal, in an effort to reduce the aforementioned regulatory inconsistencies between federal and state levels. Its competencies were further modified by the 1996 Workplace Relations Act, which requires it to take into account the needs of the low paid, as well as economic factors such as productivity and high levels of employment. Currently, work of the Commission includes, above all:

- Establishing and maintaining a system of enforceable awards that determine minimum wages and working conditions for employees.
- Assisting employers and employees in agreement making, and validating ("certifying") agreements entered into by the bargaining parties.
- Preventing and settling industrial disputes, if possible by conciliation but, as a last resort, through "cease-and-desist" orders and compulsory arbitration.
- Handling unfair dismissal claims, against the provision that termination may not be "harsh, unjust or unreasonable".
- Dealing with organisational matters concerning unions and employer associations, such as registration, amalgamation or representation rights.

As of mid-1999, there were 43 "primary" members of the Commission, and 27 "dual appointees" whose primary appointment was to a state industrial

Table 6.2. **Selected AIRC caseload categories**

	July 1994 to June 1995	July 1995 to June 1996	July 1996 to June 1997	July 1997 to June 1998	July 1998 to June 1999	July 1999 to June 2000
Dispute notifications	3 588	4 103	3 696	3 273	2 841	2 679
Award variations	3 860	2 198	2 544	3 195	3 171	1 970
Agreements (conciliation, variation, etc.)	2 859	3 946	4 772	6 587	9 001	6 885
Suspension or termination of bargaining periods	21	37	31	102	75	87
Orders in relation to industrial action	39	12	114	293	335	425
Termination of employment	7 514	13 643	10 621	8 092	8 146	7 498
Full Bench matters (including appeals)	477	285	355	411	400	434

Source: AIRC (2000).

tribunal. AIRC staff consists of about 200 civil servants. Cases are heard and decided through a panel system, where some applications are handled by one commissioner only, and others by benches of three, five, or seven commissioners. Table 6.2 gives an indication of the types of cases handled by the AIRC in recent years. It shows, *inter alia*, that assistance in agreement-making, which includes conciliation during bargaining and certification of final outcomes, has significantly increased in importance since 1994/95.[218] By contrast, there has been a decline in the number of dispute notifications, reflecting the fact that industrial conflict is at historically low levels. The relatively large number of award variation cases is due to the requirement under the Workplace Relations Act for the AIRC to systematically review, set aside or simplify existing awards (see Section D below). The most important AIRC ruling[219] is still the annual wage case, which usually implies a week or more of hearings and extensive written submissions by interested parties, after which the Commission determines minimum wage rates for a large spectrum of occupations, not only at the bottom of the wage scale, but also for higher-skilled, middle-income employees.

As is evident from Table 6.2, one of the main functions of the AIRC consists of interpreting and implementing Australia's unfair dismissal legislation (see Box 6.1 for comparative information on Australia's employment protection legislation). Employee claims relating to "unfair dismissal" or "unlawful termination" matters are lodged directly in the AIRC or state tribunals for conciliation. In recent years, about 8 000 such claims are made annually in the federal system, while several thousand additional claims are made to state tribunals.[220] The commission will first attempt to settle the matter by means of a conciliation conference – a private, confidential meeting, chaired by a member of the commission; there is usually no transcript or record taken of the conciliation proceedings other than of the eventual settlement.

Box 6.1. EPL in Australia

The OECD has assessed on several occasions how Australia's employment protection legislation (EPL) compares with that of other OECD countries. EPL is defined as covering a number of areas, including dismissal procedures, severance pay and notice requirements, remedies for unfair dismissal, as well as restrictions pertaining to the use of temporary labour contracts. Australia has consistently come out as one of the countries with the least strict EPL in the OECD area. An initial ranking in the OECD *Jobs Study* placed Australia in the bottom quintile of countries in terms of EPL strictness [OECD (1994b)]. An update of the available information undertaken for the late 1990s, showed the country still in the bottom quintile; the only countries with less strict EPL were the United States, United Kingdom, Canada and Ireland [OECD (1999d)].

Australia was ranked particularly low on procedural requirements in case of individual dismissal[1] and on the criteria used and compensation given for unfair dismissal.. Employee conduct and economic redundancy (retrenchment) are legitimate grounds for dismissal, although subject to whether it is "harsh, unjust or unreasonable". There are also relatively low legal requirements for notice periods and no requirements for tenure-related severance pay in case of individual dismissal (although there is tenure-related pay in lieu of notice requirements).

However, consistent with Australia's workplace relations system, the majority of employees are also covered by notice periods and tenure-related severance pay through awards and industrial agreements. Often award standards may exceed the legally required notice periods, while severance pay entitlements are usually more generous than the notice periods for dismissal. In turn, notice periods and tenure-related severance pay entitlements in bargaining agreements are generally higher than those set by award.

Employer discretion is enhanced through provisions which exclude certain employees from seeking relief for unfair dismissal in the federal jurisdiction. These include workers on probation or engaged for a specific task, and all workers under employment contracts for a specified period. The 1996 Act also allows the exclusion of employees when their particular conditions of employment or the size or nature of the enterprise would cause substantial problems to the firm's viability (Section 170c). In addition, proceedings for unjust dismissal are restricted to persons earning less than $71 200 a year (adjusted annually by indexation), and compensation is limited to a maximum of six months salary. The Act also aimed to deter frivolous applications through the introduction of filing fees, and set a maximum time of 21 days for filing unfair dismissal claims [Waring and de Ruyter (1999); MacDermott (1997)].

Australian regulations of temporary employment are also comparatively lax. There are no restrictions on the type of work or areas of economic activity where temporary work agencies can become active. In contrast to many other OECD countries, which specify "objective" or "material" reasons for the granting of fixed-term contracts, these can be used at will. Current legislation neither specifies a maximum number of successive contracts or contract renewals, nor their maximum duration or cumulated duration. Upon continuous renewal, the

---

Box 6.1.   **EPL in Australia** (*cont.*)

employer nevertheless runs the risk of a tribunal, or industrial court, invalidating the contract after determining that its primary purpose was to avoid termination laws [see Chapter 1, Box 1.1, and Murtough and Waite (2000*b*), for a discussion of "temporary" and "casual" forms of employment in Australia].

Notwithstanding this comparatively low strictness of overall EPL requirements, debate continues in Australia as to whether current provisions constitute serious disincentives to hiring. Particularly for small businesses, the Commonwealth government has repeatedly contended that "unfair dismissal laws are still holding back job creation and deterring employers from taking on new employees" [DEWRSB (1998)]. The main Australian employer associations are supporting the exclusion of small businesses from employment protection provisions [ACCI/BCA (2000); BCA (2000*a* and *b*)]. In consequence, the government introduced the Workplace Relations Amendment (Unfair Dismissals) Bill 1998, proposing to exclude new employees of small businesses (those employing 15 or fewer employees) from unfair dismissal proceedings, and to require six months continuous service before any new employee can make an unfair dismissal application to the AIRC.[2] The Bill passed the House of Representatives, but was rejected twice by the Senate (where the government coalition does not have a majority).

This political impasse needs to be seen against the background that small business employment has indeed picked up considerably since the mid-1990s, as well as against some contradictory evidence from employer surveys. The government bases its analysis on several surveys, such as the Yellow Pages Small Business Index Survey, according to which about a third of small employers have indicated that they would have been more likely to recruit new employees if they had been exempted from unfair dismissal laws. By contrast, the 1995 Australian Workplace Industrial Relations Survey (AWIRS) found that, among the small businesses surveyed, less than one in ten identified changing unfair dismissal laws as a significant desired efficiency change [Morehead *et al.* (1997), p. 312].

---

1. Nevertheless, in case of legal proceedings, the tribunals will usually consider whether there were warnings, provision of an opportunity to the employee to answer allegations and, particularly in the case of redundancy, whether employee or trade union representatives were notified.

2. Tenure length before eligibility for unfair dismissal compensation arises ranges from 1 to 24 months in OECD countries. Some countries also exempt small companies from unfair dismissal regulation. In Germany, for example, the employment threshold for unfair dismissal protection is five full-time employees per establishment [see OECD (1999*d*)].

Over one-half of the caseload is settled by conciliation, and another one-fifth is either dismissed, withdrawn or settled by other means prior to or during conciliation. If no agreement is reached, the commission issues a certificate setting out that conciliation has failed, after which the applicant must choose whether to proceed to arbitration by the commission or to bring court proceedings

---

in respect of unlawful termination. Most applicants decide to continue the AIRC process, but a large majority of cases are withdrawn, settled or otherwise discontinued before final arbitration. Thus, only about 5% of initial claims lead up to an arbitration ruling, based on the Commission's determination as to whether the particular termination was "harsh, unjust or unreasonable". About half of all arbitration rulings are in favour of the applicant, whereupon the Commission will issue an order for compensation and/or reinstatement [AIRC (2000)].

4. *Federal and state governments*

Finally, federal and state governments play a comparatively larger role in industrial relations than is the case in most other OECD Member countries. For example, for many years Australia has had a special ministry for Industrial Relations. In the current setting of the Department of Employment, Workplace Relations and Small Business (DEWRSB), a large number of staff continue to work on labour relations issues, keeping track of bargaining settlements, preparing submissions for tribunals, etc. In recent years, various federal governments prepared, and were successful in passing, at least three major pieces of legislation which aimed at decentralising the Australian system of wage determination: the 1988 Industrial Relations Act under the Hawke government; the 1993 Industrial Relations Reform Act under the Keating government; and the 1996 Workplace Relations Act under the Liberal/Conservative coalition of Prime Minister Howard (see Section D below).

In addition, state governments (as well as state tribunals) continue to issue labour regulations that may differ from those at federal level. The states are not faced with the constraints regarding labour regulation which were imposed on the federal level by the Constitution. Therefore, they have often tended to set the pace in such matters as hours of work, job security or workers compensation [Brooks (1994)].

D. Main features of industrial relations reform

Industrial relations reform has been a key component on the agenda of all major Australian political parties over the past two decades. Starting in the mid-1980s, it was increasingly felt that the rigidities of the award system had led to a number of shortcomings: it was hampering the organisational flexibility of workplaces and business adjustment to a changing economic environment; it had failed to guarantee industrial peace; and it had failed to deliver, or contribute to, sustained employment growth. Reform was initially set in motion through a series of *Accords* made between the ACTU and the Labor Government after 1983,. Under these Accords – a type of "corporatist" arrangement tackling economic modernisation, financial deregulation, and social policy – the government undertook liberal economic reforms, while the ACTU committed to wage restraint in exchange for a greater influence on social and labour policies.[221]

Initially, the Accords continued the highly centralised wage-setting framework, with a reliance on wage increases set by the AIRC through National Wage Case decisions, and a commitment by trade unions to refrain from overaward bargaining ("no extra claims"). However, from the end of the 1980s, the emphasis shifted towards decentralisation of wage setting and the encouragement of productivity-related enterprise bargaining emphasising working-time and functional flexibility. The main stepping stones of this shift in focus are outlined in Table 6.3 which includes policy initiatives both under the Accord, and under the more recent Liberal/National coalition government.

Table 6.3. **Stepping stones in Australian workplace reform**

Year	Key developments at federal level
1987	The AIRC introduced a two-tiered wage system, with the second tier offering percentage increases in exchange for productivity improvements, which met certain efficiency requirements set by the AIRC. Matters typically addressed included greater working time and functional flexibility, changed overtime rates, and removal of some restrictive work practices.
1988	The AIRC's "Structural Efficiency" principle provided for wage increases based on the joint review of existing awards, focusing in particular on skills-related career paths, multi-skilling and flexible forms of personnel utilisation.
1989-1992	The *Industrial Relations Act 1988* created a formal stream of enterprise bargaining through "Certified Agreements", *i.e.* collective agreements to be filed with and vetted by the AIRC. Later amendments facilitated the certification process and required the Commission to determine whether agreements satisfied statutory tests, including a "no-disadvantage" test (*i.e.* an agreement should not include provisions that are inferior to relevant existing awards).
1994	The *Industrial Relations Reform Act 1993*, which came into force in March 1994, extended the scope for enterprise bargaining by allowing for workplace agreements to be negotiated in non-union workplaces, subject to the "no-disadvantage" test as above (Enterprise Flexibility Agreements – EFAs). EFA procedures permitted union objection at the stage of certification. The Act also included provisions based on ILO Conventions (equal pay, anti-discrimination, unfair dismissal) on the basis of the External Affairs power of the federal constitution.
1997	The *Workplace Relations Act 1996* (WRA), which came into effect in January 1997, effectively ends "paid rates" awards and restricts them to a safety net of minimum wages and other core conditions of employment. It also guarantees the choice of bargaining agent and allows to conclude bargaining agreements with individual employees (AWAs). The Act makes Certified Agreements and AWAs subject to a new type of "global no-disadvantage" test, where individual conditions are allowed to fall below award level.
1998-2000	Further reform bills submitted by the Commonwealth Government on unfair dismissal, award simplification, agreement making, and secret ballots prior to industrial action met resistance in the Senate. However, amendments to make separate wage rates for youths more widely available, and to exempt them from the age discrimination provisions of the WRA, were adopted.

Sources: DEWRSB (1997); OECD (1998*a*); and Chapman (2000).

241

The most recent wave of workplace reform began with the election of the Liberal/National government in 1996 and the subsequent adoption of the WRA. One of the top priorities of the new government was to reinforce and accelerate the move towards agreement making at the level of the enterprise and to further scale back the compulsory arbitration and award system.[222] Trade unions had already become disenchanted with the introduction of non-union bargaining under the previous Labor government; now they were confronted with a much more radical decentralisation and fragmentation of the industrial relations system, including a focus on individual forms of negotiations, which could completely bypass trade union representatives.

Nonetheless, the 1996 WRA did not go as far as New Zealand's 1991 Employment Contracts Act, which abolished that country's arbitration system altogether.[223] Instead, a mixed system remains characteristic for Australia, with most employees covered by awards setting their minimum terms and conditions *and* by bargaining agreements containing the actual pay arrangements. The AIRC retains arbitral powers over "allowable matters", *i.e.* enumerated issues that can be addressed in awards. The government had originally intended a more radical break with past arrangements, but some of the more far-reaching provisions of its draft bill were softened by the opposition parties in the Australian Senate (in particular the Australian Democrats who held the balance of power in the upper house), which also vetoed proposals by the government to further amend the Act in 1999 and 2000. The main elements of the 1996 reform are outlined below.

1. A focus on agreement making

The WRA has further increased the emphasis on bargaining and made enterprise agreements the principal focus of the federal workplace relations system. It has also strengthened the element of "contestability" of employee representation for bargaining purposes, first introduced by the previous Labor government. The Act provides, *inter alia*, for two types of agreements: Certified Agreements (CAs); and Australian Workplace Agreements (AWAs). CAs are collective agreements made between employers and either trade unions or directly with employees, which are then filed for certification with the AIRC to benefit from certain legal protections; importantly, they can now completely replace awards. Trade unions are to be involved only when workers request it (except in the case of so-called "greenfield agreements"), and the share of non-union certified agreements has slowly risen to around 13% in 2000, with the share of employees covered by such agreements at about 11%.

The aim of the legislation is to emphasise single-employer agreements, while multi-employer bargaining is tightly circumscribed and certification of such agreements is subject to testing against the "public interest" by a Full Bench of the AIRC. Before certifying an agreement, the AIRC needs to be satisfied that a valid majority of employees have approved the agreement and that it meets the "no-disadvantage" test, *i.e.* that, when considered as a whole, the agreement is no less favourable to the employee concerned than the relevant award and any relevant laws. This new global no-disadvantage test allows flexibility for trade-offs in wages and working conditions, and contrasts with the previous legislation which required the test to be applied "line-by-line" for any single provision. For example, wage increases and modifications in overtime rates can now be assessed as part of a package. The AIRC can also approve CAs when they do *not* meet the no-disadvantage test, provided that to do so would not be "contrary to the public interest", *e.g.* in the case of an acute business crisis. This provision can be considered the equivalent of contractual "opening clauses" in other OECD countries (*e.g.* Germany and Austria), which tend to apply to businesses in economic difficulty.

In an important break with Australia's collectivist legacy, the 1996 Act introduced a new category of formalised individual contracts, the Australian Workplace Agreements (AWAs). AWAs are made directly between employers and employees and must be signed individually. Employees can appoint a bargaining agent of their choice, but uninvited union involvement is prohibited.

An AWA completely displaces any federal or state award that covers an employee, although it may often contain provisions from existing awards. AWAs are lodged with the newly created Office of the Employment Advocate, which needs to check whether the employee genuinely consented to this type of agreement and whether the AWA meets the no-disadvantage test, in the same more flexible, comprehensive form as described above for CAs. When there are doubts as to whether the AWA meets the test, the Employment Advocate can refer the agreement back to the parties for amendment or, as a last resort, refer it for decision to the AIRC.

The introduction of both non-union CAs and AWAs are evidence of the overall intention of the WRA to provide more "choice" in the process of agreement making,[224] and to increase the scope for direct employee participation in bargaining. AWAs in particular, while unlikely to ever represent a major share of bargaining agreements (currently less than 2% of employees are covered by them), have become an important political symbol both for the government's workplace strategy, and for the ACTU and the opposition Labor Party, who would like to see them completely abolished.[225] ILO Committees have also been critical of what they perceive as an undue focus in the WRA on individual forms of bargaining (see Box 6.2).

2. Simplifying the federal award system

The move to decentralised agreement making has been underpinned by changes to the award system. The new role of awards was set as providing a safety-

Box 6.2.   ILO Comments on workplace relations regulation in Australia

Both the Committee of Experts on the Application of Conventions and Recommendations (CEACR), and the Committee on Freedom of Association (CFA) of the International Labour Office have made a number of critical observations on the conformity of Australia's workplace relations regulations with ILO Conventions 87 and 98.[1] The CEACR's main comments are briefly summarised below [ILO (1998a, 2000)], followed by the response of the Australian Government:

Convention 98 on the Right to Organise and Collective Bargaining

The Committee considers that:

- The WRA fails to promote collective bargaining, as required by the Convention. It gives primacy to individual over collective arrangements and to enterprise bargaining over sectoral bargaining. Instead, bargaining levels should be freely determined by the bargaining parties. "By merely allowing collective agreements, rather than promoting and encouraging them, the requirements of the Convention are not met".

- The WRA does not appear to sufficiently protect workers against discrimination (e.g. dismissal) for union membership, when negotiating a *multiple business* agreement, as such legal protection applies mainly to single-enterprise bargaining.

- Back pay for time not worked during industrial action (strike pay) is illegal in Australia, which violates the principle that the parties should be free to determine the scope of negotiable issues.

- An employer of a new business appears to be able to choose which organisation to negotiate with ("greenfield agreements").

Convention 87 on Freedom of Association and the Right to Organise

- The WRA protects strikes only during negotiations for a certified agreement, i.e. an agreement concerning a single business or part thereof. Therefore, it unduly restricts the right to strike for negotiations above enterprise level. When a strike is "unprotected", it may give rise to civil liabilities and dismissals of striking workers.

- The prohibition of industrial action in support for a claim for strike pay is not held to be in conformity with the right to strike guaranteed by the Convention.

- Sympathy action and secondary boycotts are unlawful. The Committee believes that workers should be able to take such action, provided the initial strike they are supporting is lawful.

- The AIRC can terminate or suspend bargaining when potential industrial action is threatening to cause significant damage to the Australian economy or a significant part of it: this is beyond what the ILO considers justified restrictions for "essential services".

244

Box 6.2.   ILO Comments on workplace relations regulation
in Australia (cont.)

The Australian Government has submitted comments and clarifications to
the CEACR and stated that it is committed to an ongoing dialogue with the ILO on
this matter in order to lead the ILO to understand that Australian law is not in
breach of the Conventions:

- The provisions of the WRA concerning certified agreements, and the
  availability of collective' agreements outside the formal system,
  sufficiently promote the principle of collective bargaining. Individual
  AWAs are always underpinned by an award and are meant to add choice
  for employers and employees; they do not detract from the promotion of
  collective bargaining in the sense required by Convention 98.

- Employees have sufficient access to remedies in respect of dismissal or
  other prejudicial conduct on account of union membership or union
  activities. Any exclusion of employees from a remedy was made in
  accordance with ILO Convention 158 on Termination of Employment.

- It is reasonable to prevent improper demands for strike pay, as unions, it
  is argued, would otherwise force employers to concede strike pay – if
  necessary through further strikes – and this kind of pressure is
  inconsistent with the norms of the Australian workplace relations system.

- Greenfield agreements only operate for a maximum period of three years;
  upon expiry, nothing prevents other unions from challenging the initial
  bargaining agent's representational status.

---

1. These two Conventions have been adopted by a large majority of OECD countries and
   were ratified by Australia in 1973. ILO Committees have also been critical of certain
   labour relations practices in other OECD countries relating to C. 87 and 98 (e.g. the legal
   possibilities for replacing striking workers in the United States, or the denial of the right
   to collective bargaining for civil servants in Germany).

---

net of minimum wages and conditions of employment, rather than, as previously,
detailed prescriptions of actual wages and conditions. Thus, while there are few
remaining "paid rates" awards, employees who are not covered by collective or
individual bargains, retain access to minimum rates of pay and employment
conditions via the award system. The AIRC arbitrates claims to adjust the
minimum safety net, but has little scope to set terms and conditions above the
minimum.

Since 1997, a process of award simplification has been under way in order to
confine award-regulated employment conditions to twenty "allowable matters", as
required in the WRA, with all other terms being settled at enterprise or workplace
level.[226] Award simplification goes together with a reduction in their overall

number, by providing a convenient opportunity for the industrial parties to amalgamate or consolidate multiple federal awards applying in a particular industrial sector or a particular enterprise. As of March 2001, almost 700 awards had been simplified, and another 870 were undergoing simplification. In addition, since 1997 almost 1 500 have been set aside by the AIRC or deemed to be no longer current (for example, due to award amalgamations or because they were replaced by agreements). Thus, by March 2001 the total number of federal awards had decreased to about 2 300, down from 3 200 in 1997, and most of these had undergone, or were undergoing, some kind of simplification process.[227]

Nevertheless, due to the enormous complexity of the old arbitration system, and to some uncertainty as to what constitutes an "allowable matter", progress in award simplification has proved slower than initially expected. The 20 matters still constitute quite an extensive list, but proposals by the government to advance simplification and speed up agreement making by further reducing the number of allowable matters, have not met with success in the Australian Senate. Also, many employers have remained passive participants of the award system. Other employers and their unions do not necessarily wish to bargain about *all* allowable matters, and decide to leave certain award specifications intact, with which they have grown comfortable over the years. Many agreements, therefore, take up only a portion of the allowable matters and are "add-on" agreements to existing awards, while comprehensive agreements that regulate the whole range of matters have remained relatively scarce.

In sum, although the importance of the award system has been downgraded, it remains a crucial element of employment regulation in several respects. First, it provides the basis for the "no-disadvantage" test by the AIRC, which thereby retains its authority to annul bargaining agreements that, on balance, fall short of terms and conditions of employment set under relevant awards. Next, it provides legal minimum entitlements for most Australian workers and determines real wage increases for many low-paid workers in industries such as wholesale and retail trade, restaurants and accommodation services. Awards remain mostly occupational or industrial-based and continue to provide a framework for workplace negotiations which restricts employer discretion at the bottom of the wage scale.

3. Freedom of association and industrial action

The new Act propagates the principle of freedom of choice and freedom of association, focussing equally on the right to join or *not* to join an existing (union or employer) organisation. Thus, Australia has replaced an important part of its "union security" arrangements (*i.e.* legislated or arbitrated provisions ensuring a union foothold in the enterprise), following the prominent examples of the United Kingdom and New Zealand during the 1980s and 1990s.[228] Membership of all organisations now needs to be voluntary, which rules out closed shops and preference clauses for union members. The AIRC is no longer permitted to grant such preferences, and existing provisions ceased to have effect with the passing of the WRA. The Act facilitated the establishment of new unions by relaxing (but not entirely abolishing) the "more conveniently belong" restriction on registration, by reducing the minimum number of members for a union to be registered to 50, and by allowing the formation of enterprise unions to which relaxed registration criteria apply.[229]

In addition, the Act facilitated union disamalgamations (based on the rationale that some of the amalgamations of the 1990s had occurred under pressured circumstances, and that smaller-scale unions provide better services to their members), and restricted trade union officials' right of entry into enterprises under the 1988 Industrial Relations Act, by introducing complex arrangements where such officials need to obtain a permit from the Australian Industrial Registry to enter a workplace subject to awards.

As in the United Kingdom, there was in the past no legal framework specifying the right to industrial action. The Industrial Relations Reform Act 1993, for the first time, protected the right to such action, and the right to lock out, during a bargaining period. Under the current WRA, certain conditions need to be fulfilled for such action to be "protected", i.e. exempt from civil liability. Most importantly, bargaining has to be in relation to a single-business CA or an AWA, which implies that negotiations for branch or sectoral agreements do not enjoy protection. The AIRC needs to be notified of pending disputes and is required in most cases to conciliate; the Commission's centrality to dispute resolution thus continues, albeit with a shift of focus from compulsory arbitration to conciliation.

The WRA has made it unlawful for employers to pay employees for time not worked during strikes and for employees even to accept such strike pay. This is in contrast to other OECD Member countries (with the exception of Korea), where the determination of any back pay is left to the autonomous decision of the bargaining parties; particularly in European countries such as France, Italy or Spain, where union strike funds are weak or non-existent, such back pay is often an element of dispute settlement, and the need for any government intervention to outlaw such practices is not immediately evident. Further, provisions banning secondary boycotts (i.e. sympathy or solidarity action by employees not party to an original dispute), which had been removed from the Trade Practices Act by the previous Labor government, have been restored to the Act, and contraventions are subject to court injunctions, damages and fines. Finally, the federal government has introduced an amendment bill in Parliament that would withdraw legal protection to strike action that had not been authorised by secret ballot.

247

E. Outcome indicators

This section looks at some statistical indicators accompanying the paradigm shift in industrial relations in Australia. In particular, it focuses on the economic and labour market outcomes which might be associated with the trend away from centralised arbitration towards decentralised enterprise bargaining. There has been considerable international debate on the relative merits of centralised and decentralised bargaining. Despite the remaining relevance of the (mainly occupational and industry-based) award system, comparative analyses of bargaining systems have started to classify Australia alongside those OECD Member countries whose predominant bargaining level is at the enterprise (i.e. Canada, Japan, Korea, New Zealand, the United States and the United Kingdom). The OECD Jobs Study had outlined the option of diminishing the importance of upper-level bargaining, to leave enterprises free to respond flexibly to market trends. The empirical evidence on the issue remains mixed: some research has confirmed the original Calmfors/Driffill hypothesis of a statistical relationship between countries' predominant bargaining levels and indicators of performance relating to employment and unemployment, while further OECD research did not find any significant relationship with the exception of earnings inequality, which is more pronounced in decentralised systems [OECD (1994b, 1997c); Calmfors and Driffill (1988); Elmeskov, Martin and Scarpetta (1998)].[230] The text below considers the evolution of five outcome indicators: bargaining and award coverage; trade union membership; strike frequency; earnings dispersion; and labour productivity.

1. Bargaining and award coverage

Although a number of surveys have been carried out over the years by the Australian Bureau of Statistics concerning award and agreement coverage of Australian employees, the data do not always clearly distinguish workers paid through awards and workers whose pay is set by collective bargaining or other employer/employee negotiations. This is due to the Australian history and practice of "over-award" bargaining. Still today, only a minority of bargaining agreements with wages provisions – 9% of those valid at 30 September 2000, but covering as much as 18% of employees – can be considered as comprehensive agreements that address all matters normally contained in awards and thus totally replace them.

A large number of employees are covered at the same time by an award (for minimum safety-net conditions), by a registered collective (now also individual) bargaining agreement, and by individual, informal "top-ups" agreed with their employer. In addition, while most collective agreements are formalised under the WRA and certified by the AIRC, a minority of agreements are not registered with

248

Table 6.4. **Methods of pay determination**

	Awards only	Registered collective agreements	Unregistered collective agreements	Registered individual agreements	Unregistered individual agreements	Total
Males						
Private	18.8	23.6	1.7	1.8	54.2	100.0
Public	8.7	81.4	2.5	4.4	3.1	100.0
All sectors	16.8	34.9	1.8	2.3	44.2	100.0
Females						
Private	35.5	21.0	1.3	1.2	40.9	100.0
Public	10.8	84.7	0.8	1.7	1.9	100.0
All sectors	29.9	35.5	1.2	1.3	32.0	100.0
Persons						
Private	26.8	22.3	1.5	1.5	47.8	100.0
Public	9.8	83.2	1.6	3.0	2.5	100.0
Full-time	15.3	37.8		47.0		100.0
Part-time	39.9	34.6		25.5		100.0
All	23.2	35.2	1.5	1.8	38.2	100.0
Selected industries						
Mining	5.9	39.7		54.3		100.0
Manufacturing	11.4	37.0		51.6		100.0
Construction	15.0	23.8		61.2		100.0
Retail trade	34.9	28.7		36.5		100.0
Hotels and restaurants	64.7	6.7		28.6		100.0
Transport and storage	18.4	40.1		41.5		100.0
Government administration and defence	15.3	77.9		6.8		100.0

Average weekly total earnings ($)[a]

	Awards only	Registered collective agreements	Unregistered collective agreements	Registered individual agreements	Unregistered individual agreements	Total
Males	480.90	850.40	709.80	914.40	834.40	780.20
	62	**109**	**91**	**117**	**107**	**100**
Females	378.30	591.80	442.90	562.60	575.80	520.60
	73	**114**	**85**	**108**	**111**	**100**
Persons	416.10	722.30	605.50	787.70	728.10	652.80
	64	**111**	**93**	**121**	**112**	**100**

a) Figures in bold refer to the proportion of wages in each category to total wages.
Source: ABS, Employee Earnings and Hours, Australia, Catalogue No. 6306.0, 27 March 2001.

the Commission or state tribunals and remain "informal". All this illustrates the difficulties involved in classifying employees according to their type of coverage. The latest available results on types of coverage with respect to pay determination are available from the ABS Employee Earnings and Hours (EEH) survey conducted in May 2000. Table 6.4 presents some results from the survey, based on data from approximately 7 000 businesses.

It is evident, first, that at 23%, employees totally reliant on awards are now a declining minority; by comparison, the 1990 EEH survey had shown a share of two-thirds of employees reliant on award pay rates (with the rest paid above award rates or outside the award system). The category of workers paid at the award rate represents those who are eligible to receive the annual safety-net adjustment, but would not receive any pay increase without that adjustment. Gender and sectoral differences are important. Over one-third of women in the private sector did not have any over-award payments. At the other end of the spectrum, less than 9% of men in the public sector were still paid at the award rate. Information available on average weekly earnings by type of coverage indicates that persons paid at the award rate earned less than 60% of those covered by registered collective agreements, and 64% of all persons surveyed. For full-time adult workers, these rates were 67% and 73%, respectively [ABS (2001a)].

Data in the table referring to collective agreements represent mainly enterprise agreements, as sectoral bargaining has all but ceased to exist in Australia. According to DEWRSB's workplace agreements database, only 1% of employees covered by agreements that have been certified under the WRA are covered by a multi-employer agreement. A further 3% of employees under agreements certified in 1998-99 are covered by "pattern agreements" where similar or identical outcomes in wages, conditions, expiry dates, or a combination of these, can be identified. Such pattern agreements are mainly concentrated in the construction industry [DEWRSB (2000a)].

According to the May 2000 EEH survey, collective agreements, most of which are registered with federal or state commissions, determined the pay of 37% of total employees and 24% of those working in the private sector. These figures are not particularly high in an international comparison. The largest category of employees is covered by "unregistered individual agreements" (38%). This category includes the currently 12 to 15% of Australian employees – mainly at the higher end of the pay scale – who have their pay determined by individual agreement only, without reference to existing awards or collective agreements.[231] Judging from the parameters of the survey, the majority of employees in this category are both covered by minimum safety-net awards and receive over-award payments by informal individual agreements.[232] Finally, Table 6.4 shows the proportion of employees covered by registered individual agreements to be 1.8%, which corresponds to the number of about 150 000 AWAs that have been registered with the Employment Advocate since 1997.[233]

Part-time employees are considerably more likely to be paid at the award rate than full-time employees (40% compared to 15%). They are less likely to be covered by collective or individual agreements. A breakdown by industrial sector shows that hotels and restaurants are the branch with the highest share of employees with award coverage only (65%), while government administration and defence is the branch with the highest proportion of employees paid at wage rates set by collective agreement (78%). There are also significant differences in pay-setting arrangements between large and small enterprises (not shown in the table). Almost one-third of employees in firms with up to 99 staff, but only 8% of employees in firms with over 1 000 staff were directly reliant on the award rate. By contrast, less than one fifth in the smaller-size companies, but over 80% in the larger size, were paid at the collective agreement rate. These differences in collective agreement coverage by firm size conform to results from other OECD countries relying on enterprise bargaining, such as Canada, the United States, Japan and Korea.

A limited comparison is possible of the May 2000 ABS data with previous surveys. DEWRSB's own *Award and Agreement Coverage Survey* (1999*a*) found similar results for the categories of employees paid at the award rate, and paid through registered collective agreements (22% and 42%, respectively), with most of the variance to be explained through the different survey populations (firms with five or more employees in the DEWRSB survey). By contrast, at the time of the 1995 Australian Workplace Industrial Relations Survey (AWIRS), which covered over 2 000 workplaces with 20 or more employees, the proportion of employees paid at the award rate was still at 33% [Morehead *et al.* (1997)]. Although caution is required due to some non-congruent classifications, in addition to the varying survey populations, the data seem to support the hypothesis of diminishing reliance on awards and increasing reach of bargaining over the last decade. Without a doubt, government policy has been an important driving force behind this shift in focus, although it is likely that other factors, such as structural changes in the labour market, technological change, and increased competition in product markets, have also been important.[234]

2. *Trade union membership*

National unionisation rates tend to differ by wide margins in the OECD area, with high levels associated more often than not with more centralised/coordinated bargaining systems. In four member countries (France, Korea, Spain and the United States), density is currently below 20%, while in most of the Nordic countries, it is stable at above 70%. Outside the Nordic region, density rates have trended downward, sometimes precipitously, since the end of the 1970s. As shown in Chart 6.1, Australia is no exception.

Total membership was still stable in Australia, or even increased somewhat, during the 1980s, reaching over 2.6 million members in 1990, before declining to 1.9 million today. However, in view of the relatively strong Australian employment growth during the two decades, the union density rate declined steadily from about 50% in the mid-1970s to less than 25% in 2000. In the OECD area, declines of a similar magnitude occurred only in France, New Zealand and Portugal [OECD (1997*c*); Ebbinghaus and Visser (2000)].

Chart 6.1. **Trade union membership and density, Australia**

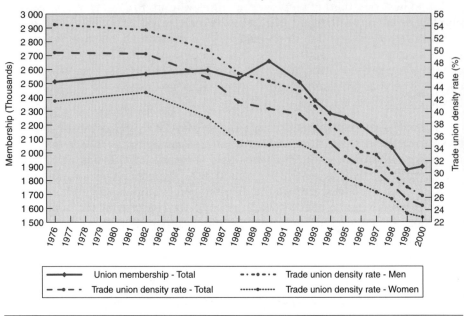

Union membership - Total
Trade union density rate - Total
Trade union density rate - Men
Trade union density rate - Women

Sources: ABS, *Employee Earnings, Benefits and Trade Union Membership*, Catalogue No. 6310.0, various issues ; and *Trade Union Members*, Catalogue No. 6325.0, August 1988.

Table 6.5 throws more light on detailed trends in density rates. Density declined for both men and women, but less so for the latter, so that women have increased their proportion in total membership. Density is lower for part-time employees, mainly because these are often "casual" workers whose membership rate, at 9%, is extremely low. Membership decreased at a lower rate among older employees than among the 15 to 34 age groups.

By 2000, union members represented less than half of employees in all industries except electricity, gas and water. By contrast, in the mid-1970s, they still represented around two-thirds or above in at least four industrial sectors (mining; electricity, gas and water; communications; and government administration). As in other OECD countries, service-sector growth industries tend to have below-average density rates. Industries with the lowest membership (agriculture, trade, business services, restaurants and hotels) are also those that tend to employ the highest shares of casual workers. Finally, as in many other OECD countries, density is higher (and declines have been slower) in the public than the private sector; and in large enterprises.

Table 6.5.   **Trade union density by selected indicators**

	1976	1986	1992	1998	1999	2000	Percentage change 1976-2000ª	1992-2000ᵇ
Total	51	46	40	28	26	25	−49	−35
Males	56	50	43	30	28	26	−50	−35
Females	43	39	35	26	23	23	−47	−34
Full-time employees	..	..	44	31	29	28	..	−34
Part-time employees	..	..	25	20	18	17	..	−28
Permanent employees	..	51	46	34	31	31	..	−33
Casual employees	..	21	17	12	11	9	..	−35
Age group								
15-19	} 43	28	23	17	14	..	..	−39
20-24		42	32	20	17	..	..	−47
25-34	52	48	41	25	23	..	−56	−44
35-44	52	48	43	33	30	..	−42	−30
45-54	58	53	47	34	32	..	−45	−32
55-59	62	55	46	32	31	..	−50	−33
60-64	60	53	45	31	29	..	−52	−36
65+	24	13	13	13	17	..	−29	+31
Selected industries								
High density								
Mining	63	72	58	33	35	32	−49	−40
Electricity, gas and water	83	51	77	55	50	53	−36	−35
Communications services	88	80	76	57	48	38	−57	−37
Government administration	72	60	61	45	41	38	−47	−33
Education	..	..	60	48	46	44	..	−23
Low density								
Agriculture	20	15	13	8	5	5	−73	−62
Wholesale trade	} 27	} 25	17	13	10	10	..	−41
Retail trade			26	21	17	18	..	−35
Property and business services	..	..	20	11	10	8	..	−50
Hotels and restaurants	..	..	23	13	10	10	..	−57
Sector								
Public	..	71	67	53	50	47	..	−25
Private	..	35	29	21	20	19	..	−31
Firm size								
Less than 10 employees	..	..	..	9	9	..	..	..
10-19	..	..	..	18	16	..	..	..
20-99	..	..	..	32	29	..	..	..
100 or more	..	..	..	44	41	..	..	..

..   Data not available.
a)   Figures in bold refer to percentage changes from 1976-1999.
b)   Figures in bold refer to percentage changes from 1992-1999.
Sources: ABS, *Employee Earnings, Benefits and Trade Union Membership*, Catalogue No. 6310.0, various issues; and ABS, *Trade Union Members*, Catalogue No. 6325.0, various issues.

253

Among possible explanations for the decline of union membership in industrialised countries, the literature tends to cite structural economic and labour market characteristics (workforce composition, growth of services sector, etc.); institutional and political factors (union recognition provisions in labour law; deregulation policies; union access to political parties and governments, etc.); employer policies; and union organising skills [OECD (1991)]. The available literature on this topic shows that compositional factors have indeed been significant. For the period 1982-92, a shift-share analysis by Peetz (1998) found that between 16 and 37% of the decline in union density (depending on whether industries at one-digit or at two-digit level are chosen) can be explained by between-industry employment changes. Further analysis by Wooden (2000) found that, for the same period, 25% of the decline was explained by shifts in the industrial structure of employment (on the basis of 25 industries), 16% by the decline in public sector employment and 14% by the relative growth in casual employment arrangements.

However, these (and other) factors are non-additive, and it seems that over the past two decades, the rapidity of the decline in Australia cannot be fully explained by structural change. By contrast, there are some indications that institutional factors, in particular the changes in the legislative framework and the resulting trend towards decentralised bargaining have played an important role. Against the background that the Industrial Relations Reform Act of 1993 (which came into force in March 1994) is usually considered to have accelerated the trend towards decentralisation, it is important to note the decline of union density between 1994 and 2000. During this time period, membership and density declined by 17% and 29%, respectively, while the same indicators declined by 10% and 16% in the six preceding years from 1988 to 1994.

The main features of the 1993 and 1996 legislation that are likely to have had a negative bearing on union membership have been outlined above. They are, in particular:

- The introduction of mechanisms for employers to bypass unions and deal directly with employees, in particular individual contracts (AWAs) and non-union certified agreements.
- The prohibition of closed shops and union preference clauses set by the AIRC.
- Increased sanctions for industrial action.
- Restrictions to union rights of entry to workplaces.

While other institutional factors, such as the poor workplace organisation of unions, the lack of a works council tradition, and a growing hostility of some employers who are ready to use the "anti-collectivist" elements in the new legal framework, may also have been important, the legislative framework seems to go some way in explaining the severity of union decline. As noted by the Australian Bureau of Statistics, the legislative changes may have contributed to a perception among workers that the role of trade unions has become less relevant and less effective and, as a result, to a decreasing propensity to acquire or maintain membership [ABS (2000a)].

3. Industrial disputes

Another measure for the functioning of industrial relations systems is the frequency of strikes and lockouts. Chart 6.2 shows workdays lost through strikes and lockouts per 1 000 employees in Australia compared with a range of other OECD countries from different geographical zones, as well as the (weighted) OECD average. With between 60 and 90 lost workdays per 1 000 workers over 1997 to 2000, the Australian strike rate is much lower than a decade earlier, and almost 10 times lower than around 1980. The number of disputes and the number of workers involved also declined between the early 1980s and late 1990s, by a factor of four and three, respectively.[235]

Nevertheless, as strike rates in other OECD countries also trended downwards sharply, the Australian rate remains well above the OECD average. In the 12-year period between 1988 and 1999, Australia was tenth out of 26 OECD countries in terms of strike rates; in 1998 it was seventh and in 1999 fifth. However, Panel B illustrates further that when comparing five-year averages since 1980, the Australian rate of reduction in strike activity turns out to have fallen by a slightly higher degree than the OECD average (although less than Italy, New Zealand or the United Kingdom).

As in many other OECD countries, over half of all strikes tend to occur in only two industries: manufacturing (particularly metal products and machinery) and construction. However, lost work-time per employee is particularly high in mining and stevedoring [see OECD (1999c), for an analysis of strike activity in the waterfront industries]. Among the causes of disputes, "managerial policy" and "physical working conditions" tend to account for over two-thirds. Australian industrial disputes are also known for their short duration, with strikes of two days or less often accounting for half of all working days lost during a year [ABS (2000i, 2001c)].

It is difficult to isolate the cause of changes in strike activity in a given country. Commentators of declining strike rates in the OECD area tend to cite factors such as mass unemployment, diminishing trade union organisation or new dispute settlement procedures [Aligsakis (1997)].[236] The strike rate in Australia declined during the transition from centralised arbitration and award-setting to decentralised enterprise bargaining. This is interesting to note, as a compulsory arbitration system would normally be considered as providing binding settlements and making strikes unnecessary or even illegal: quite clearly this has

255

Chart 6.2. **Strike rates**
Number of working days lost through strikes per 1000 employees

Panel A - **Annual data (1980-1999)**

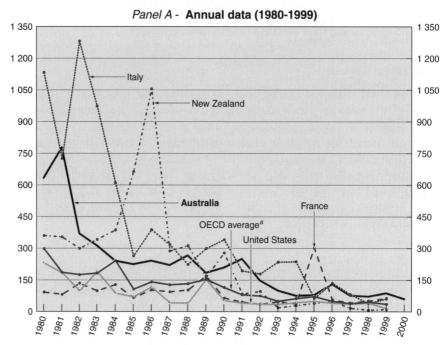

Panel B - **Index of five-year averages**[b]

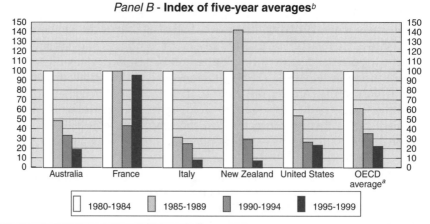

a) Weighted average of OECD Member countries, with the exception of the Czech Republic, Hungary, Mexico and the Slovak Republic.
b) The period 1980-1984 is indexed at 100.
Sources: ABS, *Industrial Disputes*, Catalogue No.6321.0, various issues; ILO, *Yearbook of Labour Statistics*, 2000; and OECD, *Labour Force Statistics, 1980-2000*, Part II, 2001, forthcoming.

not been a feature of the Australian arbitration model, as tribunals were unable to contain disputes arising during over-award bargaining, or about managerial control. To a certain extent, the arbitration system even encouraged industrial action by employees, as this served to ensure the involvement of the federal and/or state commissions.

As Chart 6.2 shows, the major part of the decline in strike activity occurred before the enactment of the 1996 Workplace Relations Act (with the largest declines between 1981 and 1984, and again 1991 and 1994).[237] Strike rates have been relatively stable since 1997, but are still, as noted above, among the highest in OECD countries. The relationship between the new legal compliance framework with its distinction between "protected" and unprotected (i.e. unlawful) industrial action and its prohibition of strike pay and secondary boycotts on the one hand, and the decline in industrial disputes on the other, should therefore not be exaggerated, although it seems that the latter provision played a role particularly during the 1998 waterfront dispute.

4. *Wages and earnings dispersion*

Any analysis of the effects of Australian workplace relations change would obviously need to consider quantitative indicators of wage adjustment, such as any increase in earnings differentials, against the background of declining union representation and increased enterprise-level bargaining. An analysis of possible linkages between bargaining structures and economic performance in the OECD Employment Outlook [OECD (1997c)] found a robust relation between the degree of bargaining centralisation/co-ordination and cross-country differences in earnings dispersion. Further, in the public debate in Australia, workplace reform has been criticised for the adverse effects it is assumed to have had on earnings inequality.

Charts 6.3 to 6.5 give some indications of aggregate and relative wage movements in Australia over the past two decades. The evolution of real wages up through the early 1990s shows the restraining influence of the various Accords between the Labor Government and the Australian trade union movement. In fact, as Chart 6.3 shows, the real wage level in 1991 was about the same as in 1980. However, since then, related to strong growth in labour demand, real wages have grown by about 2% annually, which is one of the strongest growth rates in the OECD, and real compensation per employee (an indicator that includes employers' non-wage labour costs) increased at similar rates.

There has been an increase in wage dispersion in Australia from 1975 to the late 1990s, as suggested by labour force survey data on differentials between the first and ninth earnings decile presented in Chart 6.5. However, this increase has been modest in comparison, *inter alia*, with the trend in the more decentralised labour markets of the United States, the United Kingdom and New Zealand. By

Chart 6.3. **Real wages per employee**[a] **in selected OECD countries**
Index 1980 = 100

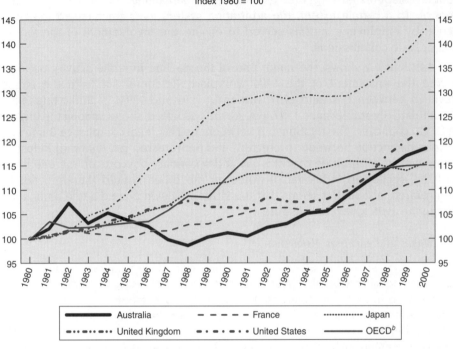

———— Australia	– – – – France	·············· Japan
•··•··•··•· United Kingdom	•·•··•··•· United States	———— OECD[b]

a) Real wages per employee are calculated as nominal wages divided by the private consumption deflator.
b) Unweighted average of 18 OECD countries: *Austria, Belgium, Canada, Denmark, Finland, France, Germany, Ireland, Italy, Japan, the Netherlands, Norway, Spain, Sweden, Switzerland, Turkey, the United Kingdom and the United States.*
Source: OECD Economic Outlook, No. 69, June 2001.

contrast, dispersion is more pronounced, and has increased at a faster rate than in most of continental Europe, including the Nordic countries, Germany, or the Netherlands.

The recent strong real wage growth accounts for an important difference in trends in wage dispersion between the 1980s and 1990s. While in the 1980s increased earnings dispersion was accompanied by falls in real wages particularly for low-wage workers, real wages have increased across the earnings distribution during the 1990s, although at a lower rate for workers at the bottom decile. A breakdown by gender shows that the increase in dispersion has been greater for men than for women, particularly in the 1990s. The gender pay ratio (the ratio of the female to male average hourly wage for full-time workers) has remained stable

Chart 6.4. **Real compensation per employee and labour productivity, Australia**
Index 1980 = 100

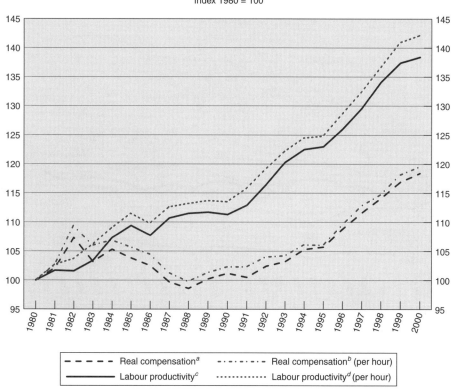

a) Real compensation per employee is calculated as nominal compensation per employee, divided by the private consumption deflator.
b) Real compensation per hour is calculated as nominal compensation per employee working hour, divided by the private consumption deflator.
c) Labour productivity is the ratio of output to total employment.
d) Hourly labour productivity is the ratio of output to the number of total annual hours worked.
Sources: OECD Economic Outlook, No.69, June 2001, except for employment and average annual hours worked which are Secretariat estimates.

since the mid-1970s, at about 85% [see Norris and McLean (1999) and Borland (1999) for more detailed discussion].

It is difficult to disentangle the various potential factors behind the increase in earnings dispersion in Australia. For example, the extent to which increased dispersion reflects the pattern of strong employment growth, technological change, as well as employer demand for employees in relatively high-wage occupations – *i.e.* compositional factors – is difficult to determine. True, the trend increase in dispersion began during a period of more centralised wage-fixing and

259

Chart 6.5. **Trends in earnings dispersion D9/D1,[a] selected OECD countries**
1976 - 2000

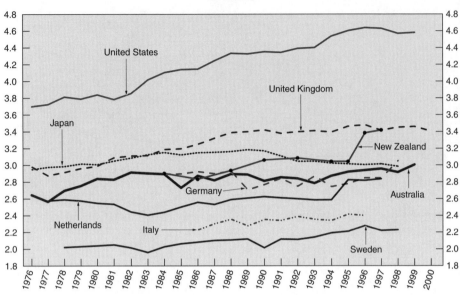

a) D1 and D9 refer to the upper earnings limits of, respectively, the first and ninth deciles of employees ranked in order of their earnings from lowest to highest, *i.e.* 10 per cent of employees earn less than the D1 earnings limit and 90 per cent earn less than the D9 earnings limit.
Source: OECD Structural Earnings database.

has not been more rapid in the 1990s than in the previous decade. It is nevertheless likely that the introduction of enterprise bargaining has had some limited impact. One indication is the growing dispersion in rates of wage increase agreed through wage bargains certified by the AIRC, which seems to reflect a stronger link of remuneration with enterprise performance [OECD (2000*b*), Charts 26 and 27)]. Using AWIRS 1995 data, Wooden (2000) also argues that changes in bargaining structure have been associated with rising wage differentials, particularly *within* occupations.

The minimum wage rates set by the AIRC during the annual safety-net reviews could, in theory, try to offset the trend towards rising wage dispersion. The ACTU, in particular, has been pursuing this approach with its "living wage case" submissions to the Commission. Throughout the 1990s, the AIRC has tended to opt for flat-rate increases of minimum award rates to push up the purchasing power of those paid at the very bottom of the pay scale. In 1997, the Commission also established a federal minimum wage across industries and occupations, which was set at the lowest level of the Metal Industries Award (then at $9.50 per hour or $359.40 weekly for full-time adult employees). However, flat-rate increases have been moderate, to the extent that minima have fallen further behind mean weekly earnings. In 2000, the basic federal minimum weekly rate for adult male full-time workers was at 46% of average weekly earnings while the ratio for adult females stood at 58% [O'Neill and Shepherd (2000); ABS (2001b)].[238] Although in decline, these ratios are higher than in other OECD countries with minimum wage legislation, with the possible exception of France [OECD (1998b); OECD minimum wage database].

5. *The rise in productivity*

As noted above, the push for decentralised agreement making since the late 1980s has been justified mainly with the prospects of improved business performance – against the background of a growing consensus to the effect that the centralised and adversarial industrial relations system had imposed extensive restrictions on firms' ability to adjust to a changing economic environment, had allowed poor management and work practices to develop, and was thus not suited to maximising productivity. By contrast, the WRA aims explicitly for co-operative and decentralised workplace relations as avenues for increased labour market efficiency, employment growth and higher productivity.

Chart 6.4 (in connection with Chart 6.3) shows that labour productivity has improved markedly during the 1990s and has advanced somewhat faster than real wages (by a cumulative 23% in the 1990s), so that unit labour costs have remained relatively stable over the decade. Research by the Australian Productivity Commission (1999) has shown that the country's productivity growth (both labour and capital productivity) has turned around from relatively sluggish during the 1970s and 80s to above-average in the 1990s. From a sectoral perspective, labour productivity growth was particularly strong in mining, electricity, gas & water, finance & insurance and communication services. Importantly, the strong productivity growth was not accompanied by a decline in the employment/population ratio.

As pointed out by Wooden (2000), this shift in productivity performance implies that Australians are working harder, smarter or both. To what extent can it be explained by changes in bargaining structures? Thus far, the evidence is inconclusive. For example, while surveys, in line with international developments, show increasing reliance in Australian companies on more flexible work arrangements such as team-working, and greater participation of staff in decision-making, and while changing award structures are generally credited with having facilitated this trend, it is not clear whether new and innovative work arrangements are more prevalent in workplaces under collective agreements than in others.

261

On the other hand, enterprise surveys tend to show that most managers from workplaces where collective agreements have been concluded rate these agreements as positive for enterprise performance, in particular for labour productivity. Summarising the available evidence from AWIRS 95, Wooden (2000) concludes that the presence of enterprise agreements is indeed associated with productivity improvement, but above all in those companies which report that their labour productivity levels are inferior to those of their competitors.

F. Summary

The institutional arrangements that regulate workplace relations in Australia have changed markedly during the 1990s, with a downward shift in the level of pay determination and the gradual superposition of enterprise bargaining over arbitration. The move towards enterprise bargaining has accelerated the decline of trade union density. A number of observers also give it some credit for the improved productivity performance of the Australian economy over the past decade. By contrast, it has had less of a causal relationship to declines in industrial disputes and increasing wage differentials.

Nevertheless, many important features associated with the compulsory arbitration model remain, keeping Australia's "antipodean exceptionalism" alive. The current workplace relations model remains predominantly based on the conciliation and arbitration power and still involves considerable complexity; if anything, the reforms have added to this complexity by putting another layer of formalised bargaining agreements on top of the existing award system. The "no-disadvantage" test still provides a strong nexus between awards and agreements. Industrial awards continue to play a significant role in wage-setting, in particular at the bottom end of the pay scale, and the process of concluding "comprehensive agreements" which determine all employment conditions and pay requirements, thus completely replacing awards, is comparatively slow. Indeed, a majority of collective agreements are still adjuncts to awards rather than stand-alone documents.

In addition, with the exception of Victoria, state industrial relations systems have not changed as rapidly as at the federal level, and the need for harmonisation is as acute as ever. Reflecting political alignments, state legislation does not necessarily share the federal level's preference for single-enterprise agreements. Recent changes of government at state level are suggesting moves toward more highly regulated industrial arrangements, and it is not even assured that, for example, the state of Victoria will continue to grant its workplace relations powers to the federal level.

Thus, there is scope for further harmonisation and simplification of the workplace relations system. Due to Australia's federal constitutional set-up, and to constellations in party politics, a radical abandonment of the arbitration model (along the lines of New Zealand's Employment Contracts Act) seems unrealistic at least for the medium term. By contrast, Australia will, in all likelihood, continue with the focus on agreement-making at enterprise level and will not return to the previous, highly centralised system of pay determination. After all, the main features of workplace reform between 1988 and 1996 were widely accepted throughout the political spectrum – not the least on the premise that previous arrangements had not been conducive to maximising business performance and productivity.

However, the detailed road map for further reform is far from certain, against the background of competing paradigms followed by the major political parties. The federal coalition government, with its "second wave" proposals (many of which take up previously submitted proposals that were watered down in the Australian Parliament), is committed to pushing ahead with reform that would further enhance the primacy of enterprise bargaining and narrow the role of the AIRC. In addition, the government is canvassing the policy option of basing workplace relations on the Corporations power in the Constitution, in lieu of the conciliation and arbitration power. This would bring the overwhelming majority of employees (up to 85%) under the federal umbrella and remove the dual coverage of firms by federal and state awards. By contrast, judging from the current platform of the Australian Labor Party, Labor would go back on some of the elements of the WRA, in particular those facilitating non-union and individual agreements, would give a more friendly hearing to the complaints by the ILO (as outlined above), and might favour a new balance between enterprise and sectoral forms of collective bargaining.

263

Annex A

Optimal Payment Mechanisms for the Competitive Provision of Employment Services

1. Structure of this annex

In a simple model where the government pays unemployment benefits of limited duration and its objective is to minimise government expenditure, and there are no externalities (this issue is explained below), optimal incentives for employment service providers can be created simply by making them liable for the cost of unemployment benefit payments to their clients. The government could make up-front payments to induce providers to take on clients on this basis, and use competitive bidding procedures to minimise these up-front payments. Any provider which devised a more cost-effective placement strategy would be able to take clients on at a lower price and gain an increasing share of the business.

This annex identifies various factors in the environment of a service such as Intensive Assistance which diverge from or complicate this initially simple model, considering how the payment system can be modified while preserving the property that providers are motivated to choose an optimal level of spending on employment services. Issues are considered under headings of: the optimal fee for employment outcomes; the case for paying the full value of employment outcomes; competitive determination of a threshold for outcome payments; mechanisms for thin markets; cash-flow and risk minimisation; and sharing risk through the taxation of profits.

2. The optimal fee for employment outcomes

In a real world environment, off-benefit outcomes often arise without employment outcomes. Paying a fee for employment outcomes, rather than making providers pay the cost of unemployment benefits, does not in itself change incentives and it facilitates a more sophisticated treatment of non-employment off-benefit outcomes.[239] Examples of off-benefit outcomes that should probably attract no fee are those due to a change in family status or other income in the family unit, transfer to another type of benefit, and exit from the labour force. Education and training outcomes should probably attract a secondary fee, as they do under current IA arrangements.

The fee paid for employment outcomes should reflect their net impact on total social welfare – their social value. Although a model for estimating the full social value of employment outcomes could become very complex, the value attached to each additional week or month in employment can usefully be thought of as the sum of three main components:

265

- The impact on **government finances**. This consists of the benefits saved and taxes paid on earnings.

- The impact on **the worker's utility**. This includes net earnings from employment, less the loss of unemployment benefits, plus a valuation of the utility or disutility of work itself. Extreme discourses are often heard implying that the value of employment is very high (unemployment is described as a human tragedy of great proportions) or in certain circumstances, very low (the obligation to work in a job creation programme may be seen as a violation of human rights). In a more moderate approach, it seems reasonable to assume that entry to employment usually leaves the average unemployed person at least slightly better off, overall.

- The impact on **the employer and the local community**. The employer normally benefits and other externalities from employment (*e.g.* impact on crime and intergenerational welfare dependency) are generally believed to be positive.

The impact of employment outcomes on the worker's utility may become somewhat negative when employment outcomes are achieved through more coercive strategies (*e.g.* workfare requirements and strict enforcement of suitable work rules), and may be more strongly positive when unemployment benefits are low or earnings in work are high.[240] But as a general starting point, the social value of employment outcomes should be taken to be at least equal to their net impact on government finances because the average impact on the other parties involved is unlikely to be negative. It also appears that employment outcomes should be valued below total earnings in work, because earnings are compensation for work effort rather than being a pure (costless) gain to the worker.

The social value to be attached to an additional week or month in employment is not likely to be particularly high for hard-to-place workers. Hard-to-place workers often face constraints (*e.g.* intermittent illness, care for relatives, long travel-to-work distances, a perception that work is difficult or onerous or a personal aversion to authority structures) which make the personal disutility of work relatively high for them. Also their earnings and other conditions in employment may not be particularly advantageous.[241]

One feature of the IA environment is that, whereas the social costs of unemployment cumulate for as long as unemployment continues, participation in case management is limited in duration. In this context, an optimal fee structure appears to involve two main components:

- A fee related to the weeks or months that clients spend in employment during a fixed period of provider responsibility for them (*e.g.* 12 or 18 months).

- A final payment which reflects the impact of the services provided during case management on employment status after exit from case management. In a simple model this might be based only on whether the client is employed or not at the time of exit. If the fee is zero when the client is unemployed on exit, the fee when the client is employed on exit would be the valuation of the difference in the expected future employment rates between this initially-employed-on-exit case and the initially-unemployed case. These employment rates tend to converge through time as unemployed on-exit people find work and employed people return to unemployment, and again it is not clear that paying a higher fee for outcomes in the case of more disadvantaged clients is justified.[242] In more complex models, information on factors such as the training received by clients and the stability of their jobs as observed after exit from case management could be taken into account.[243]

In general, the fee for an employment outcome would reflect its current and expected future social benefits relative to the baseline case (unemployment) for which the fee is zero. This is essentially a parameter to be defined by government, and the rationale for having the IA outcome fee (along with the commencement fee) determined by competitive tender, as was the case in the second JN tender round, is not clear. An early, stable return to work, such that the client is still in an apparently stable job upon exit from case management which has lasted 12 to 18 months, appears to merit a valuation (assuming that a zero fee is paid if the same person remains continuously unemployed and leaves case management with poor future prospects) equivalent to about 30 months' unemployment benefit, *i.e.* about $24 000.[244]

3. The case for paying the full value of employment outcomes

The case that the government should actually pay fees for employment outcomes at the margin (*i.e.* for each additional employment outcome, above some threshold level) which fully reflect their value to society depends upon two important considerations:

- Optimal outcomes are obtained when the government as "principal" pays providers as "agent" 100% of the benefit which is derived from their actions, at the margin. This is a standard result in simple incentive models [McMillan (1992), Chapter 8]. There can be a case for deviating from this simple principle when outcomes are uncertain and agents are risk-averse. However for employment services, merely setting the size of outcome payments well below the social value of employment outcomes is not likely to be the best method of handling risk.

- Any negative externalities are small, *i.e.* the placement of one client in a job does not significantly detract from the employment chances of another client.[245] Negative externalities clearly arise in the short run (over a period of a week, the placement of one person in a vacancy usually prevents another person from getting the job). In the long run – as illustrated by the fact that countries with different-sized labour forces have rather similar employment rates – total employment adjusts to effective labour supply. This suggests that steps to improve jobseeker skills, employability, and the effectiveness of job search do not suffer from long-run negative externalities.[246] The long-run point of view, where an individual employment outcome is valued on the same basis as an increase in total employment, needs to guide short-run action if corresponding results in the labour market are to be obtained.

If these arguments are correct, cost or budgetary objections to high outcome fees carry little weight. If employment outcome fees are correctly defined, increasing them up to the point where they reflect the value of unemployment benefits saved and taxes gained will in the long run actually improve the government's budget balance.

4. Competitive determination of a threshold for outcome payments

Cost-benefit considerations, as outlined above, indicate the appropriate level of employment outcome fees at the *margin*, not on average. In a competitive model of operation, providers would bid or tender for referrals of clients on the basis of available information about their characteristics. Bids might relate to block contracts for referral of a group of clients over a period of time, since this would reduce transaction costs and help to ensure universal service provision. This might imply some limits on the jobseeker's right to choose a provider.[247] The market price for referrals of easy-to-place clients would be relatively high, reflecting a relatively high expected income from outcome fees. Net fee

267

income (income from outcome payments, less spending on purchasing referrals) would correspond to the cost of providing an optimal level of service.[248] If, for a particular client group, service provision has no impact on the placement rate, no service would be provided for that group and competition for referrals would result in the net fee income from it being zero (except for frictional costs). Net fee income per client taken on would be relatively low both for very easy-to-place clients (if any), for whom service provision would on average shorten the unemployment spell by only a few weeks, and for very hard-to-place clients (if any), who rarely find work even with considerable help.[249] Even with a high level of outcome fees, the market would not generally use expensive forms of placement assistance for easy-to-place people.[250] It is not clear whether the total net fee income of the employment services sector, under such arrangements, would be more or less than it is under current IA arrangements.[251]

One objection to this type of competitive mechanism may be that prices should not as a matter of principle be placed on (referrals of) jobseekers. An alternative but mathematically equivalent way of implementing the same incentive structure is to have providers bid for a contracted threshold employment rate (this employment rate could be defined relative to the maximum months of employment outcomes potentially payable, which might, for example, be 30 months per referral if the period of active participation in case management is 15 months) for each group of jobseekers. Jobseekers are assigned to the provider which has committed itself to the highest threshold employment rate, and this provider is then paid only for employment outcomes above the contracted threshold level. Actual employment outcomes would typically exceed contracted threshold levels, resulting in a net payment from government to providers which covers the costs of service provision. (The payment system might penalise providers when employment outcomes fall below the contracted threshold level, but this would rarely occur.) The contracted threshold employment rate would (to a useful approximation[252]) measure the employment rate that, according to the experience of providers themselves, arises when no significant service is provided.

5. Mechanisms for thin markets

In principle the threshold employment rate across all the clients in a particular area could be estimated econometrically (*i.e.* using data on employment outcomes, the characteristics of clients and the local labour market, and expenditure for each employment service office or region) when it is not actually observed in a competitive market. In thinly-populated regions that are unable to support a competitive employment services market, the government could engage just one provider on the basis either of a competitive tender for the threshold level of employment outcomes, or econometric estimates of where the threshold is expected to lie. Because the tendering and the econometric estimation approaches in principle should give the same result, each approach could be used to cross-check the result that is generated by the other, with particular attention to assessing whether results where there is a local monopoly differ from results where there is competition.

6. Cash-flow and risk minimisation

The payment of advances on expected fees would minimise providers' cash-flow problems without distorting the incentives facing long-term survivors in the business. For example, 80% of expected net fee income from each referral of a group of jobseekers could be paid out over the first year, roughly in line with a typical pattern of service provision.

Service provision may tend to precede the corresponding employment outcome fees (which would relate to the months spent in employment, not the date of entry to employment) by a year or more, on average. In order to minimise variations in provider profitability for reasons which lie beyond their control, contracted threshold employment outcome rates could be varied according to formulae which compensate the average provider for changes in general background factors (e.g. the nationwide unemployment rate, or benefit legislation).

7. Sharing risk through the taxation of profits

Even under arrangements which shield providers as far as possible from risk factors which are beyond their control, any system where they are paid the full value of employment outcomes (but only for outcomes which exceed the levels that would arise in the absence of significant service provision) would face providers with considerable financial risk. Localised and unpredictable changes (e.g. layoffs by a large local employer, which lead to a deterioration in the local labour market not anticipated at the time providers bid for referrals of jobseekers) or providers' own early mistakes might generate rather large swings in profitability.[253] For example, an individual case manager may have responsibility for 80 clients over a period of 15 months (some clients being employed during this time). If the maximum fee income per client is $24 000, a windfall change of 5 percentage points in the rate at which such maximum outcomes are achieved will affect total fee income by about $77 000 per year ($24 000 × 80 × 12/15 × 0.05), an amount comparable to the total salary and overhead costs for the case manager. Because such a high level of risk could be borne only by large businesses, it might in itself threaten the effectively competitive or contestable nature of the employment services market.

An appropriate method of further reducing risk, so as to allow a wide range of providers to participate on acceptable terms, is to have a high "marginal tax rate" (albeit implemented through variations in fee payments, rather than the national tax system) on providers' profits (negative as well as positive) above a normal rate of return. This would allow the government to slow down, to a desired degree, the rate at which poorly-performing providers are driven out of the market. The advantage of handling provider risk by taxing profits (as opposed to alternative methods of reducing risk, such as reducing outcome fee levels below the social value of employment outcomes) is that this would not distort providers' decisions about the level of spending on inputs such as training for clients, or more generally the best placement strategy. The strategy which maximises profits after-tax is the same as the strategy which maximises profits before-tax.[254]

This approach, taxing profits, would also ensure that when a third party (for example, a state employment service or the jobseeker himself or herself) generates an employment outcome without receiving a fee, the provider retains only part of the windfall profit, the rest going to central government as usual. This could be desirable for the public acceptability of competitive arrangements. If the whole of the benefit savings that result from a jobseeker taking up work are paid to an employment services business (as is, in effect, required by incentive considerations), it may seem inherently reasonable for the government to have at least a large share in the profits of the business.

Since profits are the difference between income and expenditure, a tax on provider profits is equivalent to a tax on provider income with a subsidy to provider costs at the same rate. Instead of imposing a 75% marginal tax rate on profits, employment outcome fees of $24 000 could be replaced by fees of $6 000 while at the same time providers are paid subsidies covering 75% of the costs of their business inputs. This arrangement would

269

avoid the need for government to define a normal rate of return above or below which a marginal tax on profits would apply (although issues about subsidies for the purchase of capital assets and who owns them would remain).

Although this type of model of competitive provision has not been implemented in the employment services area, contractual arrangements involving similar complications are widely used. For example, defence contracts allow contractors to pass a proportion of cost overruns onto government, and manufacturing subcontractors are often allowed to pass part of any cost increases they face onto the firms which they supply [McMillan (1992)]. Under Working Nation, Contracted Case Managers were able to use government labour market programmes to place their clients at an effective subsidy rate of 100% (i.e. zero cost to the provider), whereas the effective subsidy rate for IA providers who refer clients to labour market programmes is currently zero. Subsidising input costs at a rate between 0% and 100% would be a compromise between more extreme arrangements that have already been used at various times in Australia as well as other countries.[255]

It may be noted that an arrangement where government subsidises 75% of provider input costs is equivalent to one where government pays all input costs (providers might then have the status of employment service offices within the public sector), but calculates the profits generated by the operations of each employment service office in the sense of an economic cost-benefit analysis (attributing a value to employment outcomes and costing inputs, as in the model proposed here), and then pays 25% of the profits (or charges 25% of the losses) so calculated to a body which has managerial control over the provider. Something approximating this is now done in Switzerland, where the federal government pays each canton a bonus based on the relative performance of the employment service offices which it manages.[256] In public employment services, if information systems which allow the relevant cost-benefit calculations to be made have been put in place, contestable or competitive provision could be introduced in cautious, progressive or partial way (e.g. allowing private providers to compete with government-run offices in the same area, or introducing competitive markets in some employment service regions but not others).

Annex B

Training and Youth Programmes

The youth and training programmes described here fall into three main areas. Firstly, there a several programmes which facilitate and assist youth transitions into work and apprenticeships. Second, the New Apprenticeship programme delivers training, in a work environment, to people of all ages: although it is not targeted on unemployed people or those at risk (the usual definition of a labour market programme), it is important as a potential destination for school leavers and the unemployed. And third, there are programmes of language, literacy and numeracy training for the unemployed.

1. *Enterprise and Career Education Foundation (ECEF) and Jobs Pathway Programme (JPP)*[257]

The Australian Student Traineeship Foundation (ASTF) was established in 1994 to support the development of senior-school vocational educational programmes that incorporate workplace learning. "School-industry" programmes, for example, may both encourage schools to offer courses which lead to qualifications in demand by local industry and arrange visits by local industry managers to explain their industry and its career opportunities to school students. The Enterprise and Career Education Foundation (ECEF) replaced the former ASTF in February 2001. The ECEF will build upon the work of the ASTF, engaging business to provide information and learning opportunities to young people about enterprise and career options and developing sponsorship arrangements, and focusing on the integration and coordination of structured workplace learning activities with other programmes and school-to-work transition activities.

The Jobs Pathways Programme (initially called Jobs Pathway Guarantee) was introduced in 1995, and targets young people who risk falling through the cracks and becoming unemployed. Schools, group training companies, public and private training providers and other community based organisations are contracted to provide employment and mentoring support services to eligible young people. Around $22 million was provided for the programme in 2000/01, allowing it to assist up to 70 000 young people from more than 1 600 schools across Australia. Regions with a high "regional descriptor score" (a term used in the JPP Guidelines), which reflects the level of youth unemployment and the rate of school retention, have priority for funding.

JPP specifically targets assistance to people in one or more of the following groups:

- Those who are participating in a school-industry programme without a guarantee of future employment.
- Those that would benefit from a school-based New Apprenticeship.
- Those with poor literacy and numeracy skills, from a non-English speaking background, or whose highest level of secondary studies is or was below year 12.

271

- Indigenous Australians.

As from 1999/2000, following a review commissioned at the time of the 1999/2000 Federal Budget, the programme has been refocused, from assistance aimed solely at achieving employment outcomes for school leavers, to providing assistance for all 15-19 year olds planning on making the transition from school to work. It now can include other types of outcomes and a wider range of assistance. Providers must first make an initial assessment of each eligible young person's needs in terms of making the transition from school to work.[258] Assistance then includes referral to a professional career counselling workshop; literacy/numeracy assessment and subsequent referral to appropriate training; referral to pre-vocational training, advice and information about New Apprenticeships; advice about the local job market and services available through Job Network members; and assistance with applications/resumes and interview preparation. Desired outcomes include, as well as employment, a return to further education or training (including towards the achievement of a recognised Year 12 certificate) at a school or another training institution, commencement of a school-based vocational programme or part-time New Apprenticeship, or other action to improve overall capacity to compete in the labour market. Participation in JPP satisfies Mutual Obligation requirements for young unemployed people aged 18 and 19, and young people who express this preference may be referred by Centrelink. The provider is not obliged to accept these referrals, but must respond within two weeks and advise of the reasons if a referral is declined.

Key performance indicators monitored for the programme are the proportions of eligible participants who are assisted in regions of demonstrable need, and the proportions who remain at school to pursue a school-industry or school-based New Apprenticeship programme, who have left school to pursue further education or training, and who enter employment or a New Apprenticeship. Kellock with Bruce (2000) describe a variety of innovative approaches developed by providers and, considering that competition between JPP providers results in reluctance to collaborate and duplication of services, call for more emphasis on sharing good practice and creating national benchmarks and common core materials in a context of longer-term contracts with providers and additional overall funding. However some of the approaches which they describe as innovative appear to be outside the current contractual remit, which focuses on assisting young people on an individual basis.

2. Job Placement, Employment and Training (JPET)[259]

JPET was established in 1992 as a pilot programme with 44 projects nationally, and found in an unpublished 1995 evaluation to be effective, comparing well with other labour market programmes thanks to a "unique holistic case management approach, coupled with a high level of flexibility". It targets young people aged 15 to 21, with priority to 15 to 19 year olds, who face multiple barriers to participation in education, vocational training, or employment and who are homeless or at risk of homelessness: and/or refugees, ex-offenders or wards of the state. JPET providers:

- Provide professional assessment of barriers.
- Develop an individual programme plan for each client.
- Provide, refer to, or organise remedial training (not necessarily of a vocational nature) or other assistance designed to address the barriers associated with family breakdown and poor life skills.
- Provide appropriate support for clients, educators, employers and trainers.

- Develop links with local employers of young people which result in employment projects and employment of JPET clients.
- Monitor and collect client and service data using the required forms.

Clients may be referred to JPET from a wide range of sources, including self-referral, JPET agency workers, community agencies, school staff, Centrelink and the police. Service providers are expected to maintain appropriate links with other organisations to assist the referral process. Like JPP, JPET is a Mutual Obligation option for 15-21 year-olds. Following a referral to JPET by Centrelink, and conditional on an assessment of eligibility by the JPET provider, youth referred as a Mutual Obligation option must be given a place within six weeks and, if necessary, be given priority over other referrals. Clients must maintain regular contact with the JPET provider, who must exit them with notification to Centrelink if no contact is made for more than a month.

As a general principle, the intention of the programme is that around 90% of clients may be given intensive support for up to six months, and the remaining 10% of clients may be given intensive support for up to nine months. Intermittent contact may be maintained over a longer period. The JPET provider must manage their workload to accommodate this, while also meeting their tender outcomes under the contract. Overall, client contact must not exceed 52 weeks in a two-year period for 90% of clients and 78 weeks for the remaining 10% of clients.

Providers are chosen by tender and financed by DETYA on an annual cycle, with the possibility of renewing contracts without further calls for tender. Until recently payments to providers have been made in relation to completion of various stages of the programme by participants. Currently three equal payments are made and the programme is aiming to shift accountability primarily towards outcomes, rather than inputs and processes. An evaluation of the programme is due to be completed in May 2001.

3. New Apprenticeships

New Apprenticeships is not primarily a labour market programme, but it can be an important destination for unemployed workers. Since 1996, the increase in spending on training within employment relationships has been an important counterpart to reduced spending on training for the unemployed. With increased take-up by prime-age workers in recent years, New Apprenticeships is also no long primarily a youth programme.

The number of starts in traditional four-year apprenticeships – predominantly in areas such as manufacturing, construction and public utilities – has historically been somewhat cyclical. After peak levels were recorded in 1989 and 1990, starts had fallen 20% by 1994/95 and at least a further 10% by 1996. Traineeships were introduced in 1985 to provide a system of structured training, along apprenticeship lines, in non-trade occupations. Initially, traineeships were targeted at 15-19 year-olds, and were largely in service and white-collar areas and at Certificate II level (in contrast to apprenticeships which are at Certificate III level or higher). They subsequently evolved to include Certificate training at any level and in most industries, with a training duration based on competency achieved and access available to people of any working age. For a decade, the take-up of traineeships remained fairly low. However in 1996, following a recent change in government policy, traineeships overtook traditional apprenticeships in terms of annual starts.[260] This was associated with a shift towards commencements by trainees aged 20 and over [Ball and Robinson (1998), Table 7].

The incoming government in 1996 announced a Modern Australian Apprenticeship and Traineeship System (MAATS) which in January 1998 was officially renamed as "New

Apprenticeships". The New Apprenticeships programme set out to create a unified framework for traditional apprenticeships and shorter courses, further blur the boundaries between school and work with school-based and part-time options, encourage expansion of apprenticeship-type training into new industry and occupational areas, and encourage employers to put their existing staff into training. In practice, traditional apprenticeship activity – although benefiting from a cyclical recovery – has not greatly changed in the latter half of the 1990s.[261] Employers and trade unions in these industries resisted, or did not see the need for, the introduction of new and perhaps lower-level qualifications based on shorter-duration training. However the total number in New Apprenticeships has greatly increased. Participation in traineeship-type training, which in stock terms had been a quarter of participation in apprenticeship-type training in 1995, grew to nearly the same level in stock terms, and 2$\frac{1}{2}$ times as great in terms of inflows, by 1999. The total number of trainees in trade and related occupations (electrical, construction, food processing and hairdressing, etc.) where apprenticeships are traditional grew only slightly, while the number of trainees in non-trade occupations (managers and professionals, clerical and sales workers, production and transport workers, and labourers) grew eightfold, reaching 49% of all trainees in 1999. The proportion of people in training who are aged 25 and more, which was probably below 10% in 1995, grew to 15% in 1997 and to 30% in 1999 [NCVER (2000a)], and this share exceeded 50% in 2000. The total number of apprentices and trainees in training as at 30 June 1999 represented around 2% of the Australian resident 15-64 year-old population. This compares with 1.1% in 1995.

New Apprenticeships involve off-the-job training typically for one day a week in the case of apprenticeship-type programmes of three to four years' duration and two days a week in the case of traineeship-type programmes of one to two years' duration. Traditionally, the employer might hire the young person, e.g. recommended by word of mouth, send the necessary forms to the State Training Authority and send the apprenticeship/trainee to a local TAFE college which delivers a standardised package based upon the national curriculum for the trade. However, a proportion of the training would often take place on the job. According to the New Apprenticeship model,[262] an employer wishing to hire a trainee or train an existing employee can contact a New Apprenticeships Centre (NAC) which will advise and assist with all stages of the process. The NAC can help the employer to identify training that will lead to a nationally recognised qualification, and complete the appropriate Contract of Training and register it with a State/Territory Training Authority (STA). The employer is visited by representative of the STA or in many cases a representative of a NAC, who explains the employer's role, rights and obligations in taking on an apprentice/trainee. The employer must then identify a suitable Registered Training Organisation (RTO) to deliver the "off-the-job" training for the New Apprenticeship. The apprentices/trainees might be recruited through an employment agency, a NAC or a Group Training Company (see below). A feature of the current system which is particularly relevant for existing employees is Recognition of Prior Learning (RPL), whereby skills which a worker has already acquired are recognised permitting accelerated completion of training to a particular standard. This in itself is a structured process, implemented by a RTO for a fee and involving promotion materials, record-keeping systems, assessment instruments and appeal procedures. The RTO works with the employer and the apprentice/trainee to deliver training and assessment appropriate to both the requirements of the business and the training programme, and issues the qualifications on completion [DETE (1999)].[263]

New Apprentices are employed under industrial agreements and federal or state awards where wages reflect the amount of time spent in training. The National Training Wage Award introduced under Working Nation in 1994 has facilitated the take-up of New

Apprenticeships by employers. It provided for a wage reflecting the time that the employee spends in off-the-job training as well as factors such as years of school and training completed in a single national determination (previously provision for training wages was only on an industrial case-by-case basis) applying to adults as well as youth. Additional flexibility, which may for example be used to change the mix of work and training time or create part-time wage arrangements, has become possible through use of Australian Workplace Agreements and Certified Agreements under the 1996 *Workplace Relations Act* (see Chapter 6). Commonwealth incentive payments for employers, in standard cases in 2000, are $1 375 at commencement, $1 375 when the apprentice progresses from Certificate II to Certificate III or IV training, and $1 650 upon completion of the training, so that the total incentive is $4 400 for a standard longer-term apprenticeship. This is about 5% of a full-time minimum wage when averaged across four years (perhaps 6% or 7% of an apprenticeship wage). There is no overall shortfall of applicants but places are usually open in retaining or hospitality and there are marked shortages of applicants for some traditional trades such as automotive trades. Recent national statistics suggest a likely final attrition rate around 23% to 30% (after four years) for apprenticeships commenced between July 1994 and June 1996 [Ray *et al.* (2000)], but around 45% (after one year) for traineeships commenced in 1996 [Grey *et al.* (1999)]. Traineeship non-completion was voluntary in more than half the cases, but it was motivated by factors such as a perception that wages were too low and dissatisfaction with training content or workplace relations. It is not clear whether traineeship non-completion rates have increased since 1996: in some localities completion rates below 50% have been estimated recently but these are subject to under-recording. In 1997, only 40% of New Apprenticeship non-completers were in unsubsidised employment three months after cessation. This proportion rose to 70% by 2000 [NCVER (2001), Table 56]. The improvement might be due to the economic cycle and growing proportion of older workers and existing employees in the total. Overall it appears that high rates of non-completion and low rates of employment following non-completion remain a major problem for traineeships, but it is not clear that it has got worse with the rapid expansion of New Apprenticeships. Employment outcomes for those who complete apprenticeships and traineeships are good: 13% of trainees are unemployed upon completion of their contract, but this declines to 7%, 8-9 months after completion [NCVER (2001), Table 58]. (However, future employment prospects tend to be quite good anyway for employees who already have a year's tenure with an employer.)

New Apprenticeships Centres (NACs) were the fifth arm of Job Network in its first contract period. They were, however, separated from the Job Network for the second contract period and DETYA took over their management. NACs are contracted to provide comprehensive advice to employers and New Apprentices. They market the programme and promote it by helping employers set up the apprenticeships and by administering Commonwealth incentive payments to employers. The fees payable by DETYA to New Apprenticeships Centres are structured in instalments, 50% when a Training Agreement is registered, 20% when continued employment is confirmed after three months and again at the mid-point of the New Apprenticeship, and 10% upon successful completion. Providers are required to provide services against a regional profile which outlines expected activity by industry type, AQF level and the age of New Apprentices. Other key performance indicators include data accuracy, timeliness of processing and satisfaction levels of those assisted. NAC contracts may be just one of the activities of a larger organisation. Among the contractors are Job Network providers and community organisations. The cost of NACs is about one-fifth of the funds provided by DETYA for employer incentive payments.

The policy process in the training area is quite complex, since states have constitutional control over the regulation of apprenticeships but it is generally in their

275

interest to help local employers and workers access Commonwealth financial incentives and related measures. At state and territory levels, the term "new apprenticeships" is not widely used. Victoria, Queensland and Tasmania recently commissioned reviews of the state apprenticeship and traineeship systems [Schofield (2000)]. Following upon this initiative, a Senate committee reported on the quality of vocational education and training in Australia [EWRSBE (2000)]. It reported fears that state training authorities were not adequately monitoring the quality of training particularly in the new areas,[264] that employer freedom in specifying training modules to meet their needs is leading to narrow or non-portable qualifications, and employers were not meeting their obligations to provide adequate and relevant training, for various reasons but at least in some degree because they were claiming incentive payments with no intention of providing proper training. There were also concerns that completion rates should be higher. Among its recommendations were that no Commonwealth incentives should be made available for fully on-the-job apprenticeships or traineeships and that Training Plans should stipulate the proportion of training to be delivered off the job; that flexibility in the selection of training modules should be limited to ensure the portability of the qualifications obtained; and that Commonwealth incentives should be refused to employers who have a persistent pattern or high incidence of events which lead to non-completion of training. In response to some of these concerns, the Commonwealth government tightened eligibility criteria in 1999, restricting incentive payments for longstanding existing workers to training agreements with a duration of more than two years, and the Queensland and Victoria state governments introduced additional restrictions and checks on employers. In 2000 there was no further growth in New Apprenticeship commencements from the previous year, but numbers in training nevertheless grew by over 10% [NCVER (2000b)].

In conclusion, the MAATS/New Apprenticeship model and its promotion have been extremely successful, building on earlier changes, in bringing state-supervised forms of employment-based training into new industries and non-trade occupations where it was previously almost entirely absent and in persuading employers to put their existing workers, including prime-age workers, into training. NCVER (2001) notes that Australia now ranks fourth in the world (behind Switzerland, Germany and Austria) in terms of the relative coverage of the apprenticeship system in the workforce, and is a world leader in terms of coverage of adult apprentices. One counterpart to the latter, however, is that youth (15 to 19 year-olds) participation in appenticeships/traineeships has risen only modestly. A more general objection to such a comparison is that the content of the training differs between countries. Policy now needs to consolidate the major expansion in employer-based training already achieved, continuing with the principles of more flexible occupational categories, employer choice, and incentives and promotion, at the same time taking measures to improve the quality of training. In this perspective, measures could include:

- Incentive payments to employers in the longer term could be related to completions and other positive outcomes, with commencement fees being essentially an advance payment (perhaps restricted to smaller employers who can be disproportionately affected by one or two trainees' decisions to quit).

- Future expansion of the system should be in occupations that have higher or intermediate skill requirements, since labourer occupations do not have skill levels that require intensive apprenticeship-style training arrangements [NCVER (2001)].

- There should be clearer separation of certification from the delivery of training, with stronger enforcement of uniform certification criteria on individual employers and apprenticeships. This could be consistent with sectoral employer representatives having a large role in defining the criteria, as in countries with a strong apprentice tradition, aiming to ensure that the qualifications acquired will be valued.

- More should be done to assess and then promote the net impact of training and of the resulting qualifications. Research has shown that future employment outcomes for those who complete a New Apprenticeship are good, but are they better than for non-apprentices who have acquired a similar tenure with their employer? How strong is the direct evidence that employers value traineeship qualifications in the new areas by taking them into account in hiring decisions or paying a wage premium for them, and what influences success in this regard?

4. Group Training scheme[265]

Group Training schemes developed in Australia in the 1980s as an alternative to apprentices entering into an indentured contract with a single employer. The schemes are normally organised by employer associations or regional development bodies on a not-for-profit basis. Where firms are too small to take on a full-time apprentice, or where the firm's work is too specialised to provide an apprentice with broad experience, the Group Training Company organises their workplace experience by leasing them on a rotating basis among several different firms. The individual firm is spared the risk and cost of taking on a full-time apprentice.

Enterprises hosting New Apprentices pay the Group Training Company a fee based on wage costs and the group training company as the primary employer receives various forms of financial support from state and Commonwealth governments. In 2000, there were around 220 Group Training schemes which employed over 36 000 New Apprentices. Group Training Companies have played an important role in periods of economic downturn by employing "out of trade" apprentices discarded by their original employer. During the period 1990 to 1994, despite a 23% decline in the number of apprentices in Australia, the number of group training apprentices increased by 28%. The schemes appeared to have played a major role in encouraging women to take up apprenticeships in traditionally male domains, and in encouraging structured training in emerging areas such as tourism and retailing [OECD (1997e)].

5. New Apprenticeships Access Programme (NAAP)

The NAAP provides preliminary training, which must lead directly into a New Apprenticeship, to young people who are disadvantaged in the labour market.[266] Except for some special cases, a participant must be registered for employment assistance with Centrelink, and must be an early school leaver still aged under 25, long-term unemployed, assessed as eligible for Intensive Assistance but not yet receiving it, indigenous, disabled or a sole parent.

NAAP is delivered through a network of state based brokers, a national broker and a small number of direct providers servicing niche client markets. The training courses run for a maximum of 26 weeks and must not constitute a full qualification as this would render participants ineligible for subsequent New Apprenticeship employer incentives. The current completion rate for NAAP training is around 75% of commencements. Provider/worker performance is assessed on the basis of the numbers of commencements and completions and placements in New Apprenticeships and full-time general employment achieved within a two-month period after participation.

277

6. Literacy and Numeracy Training (LANT)

Literacy and numeracy factors are important for long-term unemployment. Sushames and Goodwill (2000) describe three groups of unemployed clients in the LANT programme: the "difficult under 20s" who often have had problems at school, and lack self-awareness and knowledge of behaviour appropriate to work situations; those who have "missed out", owing for example to learning difficulties, prolonged sickness or being refugee migrants whose earlier circumstances made schooling impossible; and the "over 30s", women entering or returning to the workforce and people who have been engaged for many years in heavy work, such as labouring that did not require or maintain literacy skills, but now need to make a transition.

There are various estimates for the proportion of the unemployed having literacy and numeracy problems. DEETYA (1996) reported, in respect of data from 1994 to 1996, that about 7% of jobseekers had a literacy/numeracy problem according to administrative records, while according to responses to DEETYA's Longitudinal Cohort Study 21% of the same individuals had such a problem. Shortly afterwards a 1996 ABS survey (conducted for the Australian component of the International Adult Literacy Survey, which is co-ordinated by the OECD and Statistics Canada) led in 1997 to two "Aspects of Literacy" publications (ABS Catalogue nos. 4226.0 and 4228.0). These reported that about half the unemployed had relatively poor literacy and numeracy skills.

The Special Intervention Program (see Chapter 5.B) was closed down in May 1998 [Crowley (2000)]. Following a competitive tender process, 69 organisations were contracted by DETYA to provide LANT for three years [Kemp (1999)]. However this training actually became available only from September 1998 and access to it was at first restricted to the Mutual Obligation client group [Rahmani (2000)]. Although the government had announced that it was setting aside a total of $143 million over four years for the programme, take up at first was so low that actual programme spending in 1998/99 was only $3.9 million, and a number of contracted providers had to be paid out [McKenna (2000)].

In January 1999, Prime Minister Howard announced that young people claiming unemployment benefits would, in cases where Centrelink identified potential literacy and numeracy barriers, be required to participate in professional assessment and, where appropriate, training [Wright (1999)]. According to Minister Kemp [Kemp (1999)], participation would in relevant cases be a requirement (rather than an option) for people subject to Mutual Obligation. This led to claims that a "learn for the dole" programme (a reference to Work for the Dole) had been introduced. From August 1998 to December 1999, Centrelink referred 17 081 jobseekers to assessment and 7 875 to training, of whom 81% commenced LANT. Providers return assessments of a National Reporting System (NRS) level, with those classified to Levels 1 and 2 considered eligible for training. Although Centrelink does require certain jobseekers to attend assessments, providers report quite high drop-out rates from training, yet benefit sanctions do not seem to be a major issue and it may be that the compulsory dimension of the programme has not been much developed in practice. By July 1999 eligibility for LANT had been broadened, and a survey conducted from November 1999 to January 2000 reported that only 12% of participants were undertaking LANT to fulfil their Mutual Obligation requirements. A large proportion of referrals concern those in other age groups, or different phases of the unemployment spell.

Job-search requirements are generally maintained during participation in LANT and the post-implementation review report in July 2000 identified some problems associated with this [Rhamani (2000)]. The message that training is important can be difficult to reconcile with the expectation that it will be dropped if any job becomes available. Also, to facilitate effective job search the training is limited to 6 to 15 hours a week. However there is a contract requirement that the hours of training delivered each week should be adjusted to ensure training is completed in forty weeks, and there is a target of 400 hours of training (for NRS Level 1 clients). The review suggested that LANT could become a full-time programme (more than 20 hours per week) of shorter duration, although it also acknowledged that some clients might not be able to cope with such intensive training. It would seem logical, where structured and reasonably intensive training has been started, to at least exclude short-term and casual jobs from the ongoing requirement that any work available should be taken up.

7. Adult Migrant Education and Advanced English for Migrants Programs[267]

The Adult Migrant English Scheme (now the Adult Migrant English Program, AMEP) was introduced in 1948. Until 1977, English classes were taught on ships carrying migrants to Australia. Full-time courses aiming to equip professional and semi-professional migrants with adequate English for employment were introduced in 1969. In the 1990s, new arrivals were given a legal right to 510 hours of tuition or the hours it takes to achieve "functional English", whichever comes first. Humanitarian entrants with experience of torture and trauma are provided with up to 100 hours of special preparatory classes. AMEP provides tuition to migrants and refugees within five years of their arriving or gaining permanent residence in Australia. Skilled migrants are liable for a charge as part of the visa application process, with an exemption for family and humanitarian entrants. Part-time and full-time courses are offered at a range of times – day, night or weekends – and in a variety of venues, as well as at home through a Distance Learning programme or with the help of a Home Tutor, who is a trained volunteer. Free childcare can be arranged during class times. In addition to teaching English, AMEP courses provide information on the Australian way of life and advice on accessing essential services. As can be seen in Table 5.4, spending on AMEP exceeds that of many of the labour market programmes, but AMEP has a broad focus with tackling labour market barriers being only one of its several aims. In 1997, competitive tendering for the delivery of AMEP was introduced.

The Advanced English for Migrants Program (AEMP) has a narrower labour market focus. It is open only to people registered with Centrelink as unemployed and seeking full-time work who already have a relatively high level of English (a National Reporting System rating of at least Level 3 on a 1-5 scale) and for whom further training will allow entry into employment or further vocational courses, or recognition of their overseas qualifications. Applicants are first referred to an AEMP training provider, who assesses the jobseeker's language proficiency and recommends a suitable course. Courses are block funded to the States and Territories and are generally provided through the training and further education (TAFE) system, although Victoria and the Northern Territory contract other providers to deliver the training.

The 2000/01 budget announced a decision to amalgamate AEMP with LANT, with funding of $138.7 million over four years for the new language, literacy and numeracy programme. It will be available from the beginning of 2002 and is expected to offer four types of training: basic English language; advanced English language; literacy; and numeracy.

Annex C

Indigenous programmes[268]

Spending on training and subsidised employment programmes for indigenous workers increased substantially in the late 1980s and early 1990s. The CDEP scheme, described below, was expanded; training and wage subsidies were provided under the Training for Aboriginal and Torres Strait Islander Program (TAP); and a scheme of assistance for indigenous self-employment was introduced. The CDEP scheme remains the largest. As from July 1999, training, wage subsidy and self-employment programmes managed by DEWRSB and a new incentive for placing CDEP participants into private sector employment have been grouped together in the Indigenous Employment Policy.

1.   *Community Development Employment Projects* (CDEP)

General description

The CDEP scheme, providing income in exchange for work, started in 1977 in 12 communities in the Northern Territory at the initiative of several aboriginal villages. It was motivated by concern that dependence on receipt of benefits was failing to improve the situation in communities. Community leaders proposed to link a work obligation to the payment of benefits. The government agreed to give money which had previously been paid in the form of unemployment benefits to the CDEP, which would then use it to employ local people on work of value to the local community. By the mid-1980s, the scheme was present only in 30 remote communities. It expanded over the next decade to about 250 communities in urban as well as remote locations, after which growth slowed again [Altman *et al.* (2000)]. CDEPs now encompass 262 communities and 31 000 participants.[269] Participants are still mainly (95%) located in rural regions rather than the capital cities, with many living in remote communities which may be hundreds of kilometres from the nearest town.

As shown in Table 5.4, spending on CDEP is greater than current or prospective future spending on Work for the Dole, although it should be kept in mind that the figures for Work for the Dole do not include payments of unemployment benefit to participants. CDEP participation is for 16 hours (two days) of work per week (in some cases, 15 to 18 hours over up to three days). There is no time limit on participation in CDEP, and payments are not reduced when participants have significant additional income.[270] The Aboriginal and Torres Straits Islander Commission (ATSIC), which represents the indigenous population through an elective structure, supervises and administers CDEP.

Analysis of the 1991 Census indicated that dependence of the indigenous labour force on CDEP and unemployment-related benefits ranges from less than 30% in the coastal areas of South Australia, Victoria and New South Wales, to over 50% in Northern Territory and large parts of Western Australia. There was not a strong tendency for CDEP employment to displace unemployment benefits, since a 10 percentage point increase in CDEP employment was found to be associated with only a 3.6 percentage point decrease in the unemployment benefit recipient rate [CAEPR Issue Brief 10, 1996]. A detailed analysis of relatively remote communities in the Northern Territory found that in the CDEP communities 56% of the adult population was employed (32% full-time, 23% part-time), with 87% of the employment classified to community services and public administration, while in the non-CDEP communities 20% were employed (10% full-time, 10% part-time) with 47% of the employment classified to community services and public administration. However reported average adult incomes were actually slightly higher in the non-CDEP communities, mostly because a higher proportion of people were earning over $16 000 a year (roughly equivalent to a low full-time wage) [CAEPR Issue Brief 5, 1996].

Wages and income support payments for participants and non-participants

The creation of CDEPs in a particular location continued in the early years to depend upon the emergence of suitable proposals from the local community. However in the communities with CDEP, even if the community had decided to voluntarily forego their rights to unemployment benefit as is commonly described, this would not necessarily be the case for all individuals within the community. At first the Commonwealth government maintained a strong line, refusing to pay unemployment benefit in locations where CDEP places were available. Thus a split emerged between communities where CDEP existed and was considered to be an income support as well as a work programme such that no other income support was paid, and communities without CDEP where unemployment benefits were provided.

The government's refusal to pay unemployment benefits (in communities where CDEP operates) appears to have weakened over time. Altman (2000) reports that up until the late 1980s the CDEP scheme was only introduced to remote communities on an "all-in" basis. The 1991 social security act excluded CDEP participants from qualifying for Newstart Allowance [Sanders (2000)] but the significance of this provision would depend on whether the administration automatically defined individuals living in CDEP communities to be CDEP participants. Sanders (1997) stated that work within a CDEP was treated by DSS as "suitable employment", such that potential applicants for NSA should be willing to undertake it and would lose eligibility for NSA if CDEP employment remained available, unless CDEP wages are lower than what the participant's allowance would be. According to a review of the programme [Spicer (1997), p. 48], many CDEP participants were being paid as little as $30-40 per week in "sit-down" money or as a consequence of the community's application of no-work-no-pay rules which required participants to work a certain number of hours to qualify for the full wage rate. This suggests that DSS offices were still then refusing to pay unemployment benefit, in cases where the CDEP stated that work was available but the person had done little or no work.

The Spicer review estimated that up to one third of CDEP participants were not working. It recommended that the scheme's character as an income support programme be removed, so that participants who did not wish to work in it would be returned to the social security system "where they would attract the full range of entitlements available to a NSA recipient" [Spicer (1997), pp. 40-44]. The government appears to have accepted this interpretation of the entitlement conditions for NSA. Currently, although an individual's participation in CDEP is defined by appearance of his or her name on a schedule provided by an authorised officer of a CDEP grantee organisation, CDEP participation is clearly stated to be voluntary.[271] Thus many indigenous communities now have both rights to unemployment benefits, and finance for a local CDEP, although the latter was originally granted in return for giving up rights to unemployment benefits. Recently, given the context of welfare reform, Mutual Obligation and measures to make participation in job creation programmes obligatory, some aboriginal community leaders are considering making CDEP participation compulsory again, but there appears to be no Commonwealth initiative of this kind.

In 1997, the Human Rights and Equal Opportunities Commission argued that there was a lack of consistency or uniformity in the way DSS and other government agencies treated CDEP participants, which resulted in them in some situations getting the "worst of all worlds". Following this criticism, CDEP participants instead of being excluded from Newstart were defined to be already qualified for Newstart by virtue of being a CDEP participant, without any requirement to satisfy activity test criteria. They were granted a social security number, Health Care Card and rent subsidies (corresponding to the rights of other Newstart recipients) and a CDEP participant supplement (CPS) of $20.80 per fortnight (corresponding to the community work supplement which is paid to participants in Work for the Dole).

The CDEP grantee organisation still receives block financing on an average per participant (APP) basis and determines the actual payment to each individual participant. However CDEP participants are expected (according to the FaCS social security guide: www.facs.gov.au/guide/ssguide/11c212.htm) to earn and be paid at least the equivalent of the income support payment that they would otherwise be on. Given that APP funding corresponds to income support levels, this condition implies that grantee organisations must pay each participant the equivalent of the income support payment they would otherwise be on. Yet because the payments are made through the CDEP grantee organisation, and they are not significantly means-tested and are commonly referred to as wages, the Australian Bureau of Statistics treats CDEP participants as employed – in contrast to Work for the Dole participants, who are classified as unemployed in its statistics.

Spicer's recommendation that non-working participants should be removed from the scheme implies that they should either have been induced to voluntarily quit or, in the case that CDEP payments have been equalised with income support (so that there is no incentive for quit), expelled. However there is no evidence that an exodus of non-working participants has occurred through either of these routes.[272] Given that government policy now in effect requires grantee organisations to act as a channel for the payment of income support, they can no longer adopt a wages policy that would create incentives for participants to work in return for the APP element of their wages. However there is daily monitoring of participation [Altman (2000)], which would prevent participants from working elsewhere on a full-time basis, and may imply that management problems need be no worse than in many mainstream economy organisations with a set wage structure and barriers to dismissing unproductive employees. Recently. programme conditions have been tightened, to remove from the scheme those who have not participated for a period of at least five consecutive weeks.

Commercial activities

CDEP projects can seek additional revenue by organising additional work, and 40% of the overhead costs for this are paid. Since payments to participants are not means-tested, revenues from such work can be distributed as additional wages. In this context, some split has emerged between CDEP workers on minimum hours who are paid little more than they could get on income support, and who face little pressure for productivity or may not really be working, and those in near full-time work who can make much more than they would get on Newstart Allowance alone thanks to additional earnings from commercial activities. Based on the 1996 Census, about 23% of participants work 35 hours or more per week, and perhaps as many as half earn more than the basic participant rate linked to unemployment payments.[273]

In some communities, CDEP projects have tendered for commercial services such as child care, building contracts and waste collection. Particularly in remote areas the local economy is often dependent on government funding, and the contracts may be for services such as building housing for the indigenous community itself. People working on commercial activities may be paid for up to five days in total, *i.e.* two days for non-commercial work and three further days for commercial work. In principle, to justify the employment of people full-time in CDEP commercial building work, for example, a considerable training element is needed. Although the programme is regularly audited in financial terms, in this area too it is not clear whether the detection of situations where all the work carried out is commercial, or checking that there is some output from the non-commercial work financed by APP block funding, is a recognised objective of this auditing.[274]

Funding restrictions and open employment objectives

Shortly before fully conceding the principle that unemployment benefits could be paid in CDEP communities, the government had already blocked the approval of new CDEP projects and introduced the principle that funding would grow only in line with "natural growth", which reflects increase in population within the communities where CDEP is already located, plus a quota for new projects. In the 2000/01 budget 1 500 new places in new and existing projects in regional and remote areas of Australia were funded (see: www.atsia.gov.au). However such growth falls short of the demand for places, and Taylor and Hunter (1998) remarked that in this context "the emphasis in the search for expanding indigenous employment opportunities has, by default, shifted firmly onto the private sector as well as various options for developing indigenous business and entrepreneurship".

Spicer (1997) stated that a critical challenge for CDEP would be to ensure that it does not become an employment destination for its participants but enables people to move in increasing numbers into unsubsidised full-time employment, and called for a much stronger focus on evaluating the open employment and training outcomes of CDEP participation. At the same time the review proposed an expansion of the commercial activities of CDEP projects, which demonstrate that indigenous people are capable of operating successful businesses and competing with mainstream business, often resulting in a major change in attitudes to racial issues in the wider community.

Although the current government has claimed considerable success for its Indigenous Employment Strategy (IES) promoting entry into the general labour market, with *e.g.* increased indigenous participation in apprenticeships and traineeships, few transitions out of CDEP have been achieved. Peter Shergold, former chief executive officer of ATSIC, recently described CDEP projects as an abysmal failure and the weak link in the IES, with only 180 out of 36 000 participants moving into the workforce over a 12-month period [*The Australian*, 9 November 2000]. AYPAC's analysis of the 1996/97 budget had already predicted that CDEP funding cuts would make participants reluctant to leave CDEP to access training and labour market programmes for fear of losing their place on the scheme (see: www.aypac.org.au). Thus, a situation may be developing where funding for CDEP is seen as an advantage acquired by particular communities and particular individuals within those communities, to which others cannot gain access. To the extent that CDEP participants are

283

now able to combine the equivalent of an unemployment benefit income with the equivalent of earnings from regular commercial activities, this could explain difficulties in getting them to leave for another status where only one of these two sources of income can be received. CDEP organisations have an incentive to retain the most productive workers to ensure the viability of their commercial businesses. It also seems that CDEP commercial operations, backed by effectively permanent wage subsidies, might exploit all the key business opportunities in a particular area and thus tend to undermine the viability of indigenous business activity within other formats.

Popularity of CDEP

There is widespread support for CDEP among communities and people involved in projects. Its flexibility has allowed indigenous communities to achieve community authority building, improved service provision, cultural maintenance, income enhancement, enterprise development and employment. At times, CDEP organisations have met needs that should be addressed by other government agencies. This diversity of objectives and activities can make the success of CDEPs, where evident, difficult to measure and demonstrate [Altman (2000)]. Many people familiar with the scheme would regard the fact that few participants currently wish to leave it for open employment as an indication of its success, rather than its failure.

The success of the original CDEP concept in cases of good management by the grantee organisation, where projects retained extensive community support and achieved more than payment of passive unemployment benefit at no net cost in locations far from any significant open labour market, seems incontestable. Nevertheless, fairly similar claims of success for CDEP may acquire the character of a defence of vested interests when participants enjoy a high net subsidy level that is not available to others with comparable needs. Against such a background, it remains very important to keep track of what is really happening in different types of CDEP and indigenous communities, rather than relying only on an economic theoretical approach or the views of groups that benefit, directly or indirectly, from the high subsidy levels. As regards remote locations where little open employment is available, government should assess the impact of recent reforms on traditional models of CDEP operation and if necessary consider further reform. In locations where open employment can be a real option, it does seem important to achieve a degree of neutrality, in terms of the overall subsidy level for individuals with comparable levels of disadvantage, between CDEP and open employment options. The government could also direct any additional financing for such locations towards projects with a significant link to the open labour market, and indeed there are signs that it has done this in some cases.

2. Indigenous Employment Policy

An Indigenous Employment Policy was announced in May 1999. Against a background where up to 70% of the jobs occupied by indigenous people are publicly funded to some extent, this policy was specifically intended to create employment and training opportunities in the private sector, across all business sizes. Among the initiatives were the Structured Training and Employment programme (STEP), the Wage Assistance Program, the CDEP Placement Initiative and the Indigenous Small Business Fund.

Structured Training and Employment programme (STEP)

This programme provides structured training, usually involving New Apprenticeships for five or more people.

The Wage Assistance programme

Indigenous benefit claimants are given a "Wage Assistance Card" which can be shown to potential employers indicating that an employer hiring the person can be paid up to $4 400 over 26 weeks ($2 200 for part-time work). It is restricted to one-half of the work force up to ten employees, declining to one-quarter for larger workforces. Wage Assistance is not payable in respect of CDEP employees. Opportunities are self-canvassed by jobseekers or through Job Network members. Intensive Assistance outcome payments can be claimed for placements with Wage Assistance, and IA providers in some cases top up the payment to the employer. In late 2000, the approval rate had built to nearly 200 positions a month.

CDEP Placement Incentive

CDEP projects receive a bonus of $2 200 for each of their participants placed in a full-time job and off CDEP. Take-up has been relatively low probably for reasons referred to above.

The Indigenous Small Business Fund

The Indigenous Small Business Fund was launched in October 1999 as a joint initiative between DEWRSB and ATSIC. It is intended to help indigenous people to develop business management and planning skills and access capital and support services through encouraging them to participate in NEIS, or the training element of NEIS.

Job Network services for indigenous people

Most indigenous benefit claimants are eligible for Intensive Assistance. However, for various reasons it appears that indigenous clients often do not get the same level of service as non-indigenous:

- Providers may give less attention to indigenous clients because of a perception that they will be hard to place.
- Indigenous workers are informed of their referral to Job Network by letter even thought they may have literacy problems and be reluctant to attend because they perceive the service is not for them.
- Non-attendance by indigenous workers is often not sanctioned owing to an administrative drive to minimise breaches for indigenous workers (earlier research had found that breach rates for indigenous workers were higher than for non-indigenous).

Some of the changes in the second Job Network tender, establishing a specialist provider category and requiring more providers to include indigenous servicing strategies in their tender documentation, have been targeted at increasing participation by indigenous workers.

Annex D

Disability Programmes

While Australia has increasingly throughout the 1990s provided mainstream employment services via external agencies, it has a much longer history of government funding of external agencies in the area of disability services. This annex looks at this history, with particular attention to employment services for the disabled and the government's efforts to apply uniform standards to agencies and introduce mechanisms for assessing the needs of the individual disabled people receiving services from the agencies, as a basis for its funding of these services. A first section gives an historical overview, a second section describes the three main disability employment services – for rehabilitation, open employment and supported employment – and a third section describes some recent reform initiatives.

1. Historical overview

The early years[275]

In Australia "outdoor" (that is, home-based) care for the disabled has always been dominated by voluntary, non-profit and charitable agencies whose major source of income, although they also received public donations, was government – initially from London and then increasingly from the local administration. These agencies subsequently extended their pre-eminence to the provision of institutional care for the disabled.

At the beginning of the twentieth century, disability was considered a health issue, and under the Australian constitution responsibility for health services lay entirely with state governments. Nevertheless, in 1908 the Commonwealth Government introduced means-tested invalidity and age pensions, thus beginning the process through which it has assumed total responsibility for income support. In 1919, a Repatriation Commission was established to reintegrate returning soldiers into the community, with vocational training for ex-servicemen with disabilities as one of its roles. After the second world war, a Commonwealth Rehabilitation Service (CRS) was created. This ensured for the Commonwealth a central and continuing role in vocational education, training and employment programmes for the disabled. But state and territory governments continued to provide and fund the majority of services in education, health, family welfare, housing and transport.

As early as the late nineteenth century, a series of inquiries investigated evidence of incompetence, neglect and corruption in voluntary sector operations, and from these inquiries emerged two themes which are still current. The first was the problem of making voluntary sector agencies accountable to the governments which were financing them. The second was the notion that voluntary agencies were superior to public authorities because they could be more innovative, because they could provide unstinting personal care on individuals and because of the religious influences they could bring to bear. Over the years up to 1950, voluntary organisations were active in establishing sheltered workshops which, under public pressure, later received Commonwealth support.

The 1980s

Until 1983 [according to Grimes (1992), cited by Bourk (2000)] there was a relative vacuum of policy analysis with "no general papers on the political philosophy or the social policy development in this area". By 1983, it was estimated that total Commonwealth funding to the disabled was approximately $5 600 million, spent mainly on income support and direct service provision through the CRS. Commonwealth funding for non-government agencies was generally provided under the Handicapped Persons Assistance Act, with a budget of under $100 million. State funding, which totalled $800 million, was a more important source of finance for them. The services from these agencies, reflecting the concerns of particular advocacy groups, were characterised by "their great diversity, unevenness of effort, uneven geographical distribution of the effort and unequal availability to different groups".[276] At this time the philosophy of "normalisation", according to which the disabled should get help with establishing patterns of life close to those of wider society, living in their own home rather than in institutions and accessing services developed for the general public, had become increasingly influential.

The report of the Handicapped Programs Review (1985) formed the basis for a complete overhaul of Commonwealth programs, including the establishment of a Home and Community Care programme in 1985 and the Disability Services Act (DSA) in 1986. The latter established "competitive employment, training and placement (CETP) services" to assist disabled people to obtain and retain employment in the mainstream labour market, and "supported employment services" (which were meant to differ from the previous sheltered employment model) for people for whom employment at award rates is not a realistic option. This Act, however, ran into acrimonious opposition from large service providers. Many of these had received subsidies over a very long period and acquired substantial capital assets such as nursing homes, sheltered workshops and activity therapy centres, which the DSA intended to progressively replace with smaller services with more community focus while at the same time better monitoring standards of service. Attempts at moving people with severe disabilities into community-based accommodation and into open supported (as opposed to sheltered) employment created anxiety among them and their families. (Some later reports have stated that the quality of life of people who were moved into community-based services without a commensurate move of financial resources often deteriorated, rather than improving.) In the face of a concerted national campaign led by the Australian Council for Rehabilitation of the Disabled (ACROD, the national peak body for the disability services industry), the DSA remained, to a large extent, unimplemented.

The DSA had set a limit of five years for existing services to conform to the Principles and Objectives of the Act. These included requirements for addressing complaints and providing employees with disabilities with working conditions comparable to those of the general workforce (wages in sheltered workshops were often very low). However by June 1992 the majority of existing services, particularly sheltered workshops and activity therapy centres, had still failed to satisfy the government that their operations conformed. Further legislation extended the deadline for another three years, but the government was forced to modify its position and in 1993 announced that sheltered workshops would remain eligible for Commonwealth funding so long as they could meet the Disability

287

Service Standards and improve their focus on open employment for the majority of workshop participants.

The 1990s

In 1992, the Commonwealth enacted the Disability Discrimination Act (DDA).[277] Between 1991 and 1993 all heads of government signed the first Commonwealth-State Disability Agreement (CSDA), which delineated the roles for State and Commonwealth funded services. Under the five-year agreement, Commonwealth responsibilities were defined as employment support services, while State and Territories became responsible for accommodation support, respite care, day services and other support. Responsibility for advocacy services was shared. The second CSDA, signed in 1997, had two tiers involving both multilateral and bilateral agreements between the Commonwealth and States.[278] Also in 1994 the Government launched the Commonwealth Disability Strategy (CDS) as a 10-year planning framework to assist Commonwealth organisations to meet their obligations under the DDA. The CDS was reviewed in 1999 and a refined CDS was launched in 2000. The revised strategy is based around the core roles of Government as policy adviser, regulator, purchaser, provider and employer. All Commonwealth organisations are required to report on their performance in implementing the CDS in their Annual Reports.

In 1994, following a report that had identified inappropriate wage payments and difficulty in objectively measuring skills and productivity as barriers to the employment of the disabled, a Supported Wages System was introduced. Under this system employees are paid in proportion to productivity, with the pro rata wage determined through an independent nationally-consistent and Commonwealth-funded assessment process. This provided a national industry award system for people with disabilities.[279]

Employment services were examined in the Strategic Review of the Commonwealth Disability Services Program [Baume and Kay (1995)]. This found that there was still enormous variation in the cost of services unrelated to the level of disability or level of support provided, and that links between funding and outcomes had not generally been established. It recommended that the Disability Services Program be clearly defined as a labour market programme with funding for only two programmes, employment and employment preparation (not precluding sheltered employment, provided that employees receive award rates of pay). It also recommended standardised assessment of individual needs, with funding for services then following the consumer. ACROD, however, took exception to the categorisation of Disability Services Program as a labour market programme, insisted on the reality that the main distinction was between open employment and supported employment services, and suggested that the national system of assessment would become a complex and expensive mechanism of questionable benefit to disabled [Lindsay (1996)].

In a separate process,[280] following a 1988 report of the Social Security Review, the 1991 Disability Reform Package (DRP) aimed to introduce a more active system of income support (although as noted in Chapter 4, it relaxed the basic eligibility conditions for disability benefits). It brought in rehabilitation, training and labour market programs, intended to assist people with disabilities into employment rather than leaving them long-term dependent on income support. Other measures to assist workforce transition included an employment entry payment and retention of associated fringe benefits. Specialist disability staff were appointed in DEET and DSS, new labour market programmes were created for the disabled and additional targeted places were provided in existing rehabilitation, training and labour market programmes. People with less severe

288

disabilities, after assessment by a Disability Panel drawn from representatives of Commonwealth agencies, were to be placed in the active category of DSP and given access to rehabilitation services and CES retraining and labour market programmes. Under previous arrangements, invalidity pension beneficiaries – being defined as permanently incapacitated for work – had not been able to register with the CES. In a 1995 evaluation of the DRP, groups such as ACROD were critical of this process, reporting that although some Disability Panels worked well many were bureaucratic and costly, and that the majority of people participating in both open and supported employment found their own jobs and were later endorsed as eligible by the panels rather than being referred by the panels in the first instance [Lindsay (1996)].

In the 1996/97 Budget, the Government announced a broad range of reforms for disability employment assistance and rehabilitation services. In recent years (see below for details), More Intensive and Flexible Services pilots have been conducted and evaluated, Disability Panels have been replaced by Centrelink as the body for eligibility assessment and referral to disability service, and a case-based funding has been introduced on a trial basis. By 1999/2000, FaCS spending on labour market services for the disabled (excluding the Continence Aids Assistance Scheme) totalled approximately $328 million. This spending has remained close to 0.06% of GDP in recent years, which is close to a median value in international comparison. About $5.5 million was spent on the Wage Subsidy Scheme (which offers wage subsidies for up to 13 weeks to employers who employ eligible workers with disabilities, and was transferred to FaCS from DEETYA in 1998). The bulk of spending was divided roughly equally between rehabilitation services, open employment services and supported employment services.

2.   Three main disability employment services

Rehabilitation services[281]

In 1998/99, CRS Australia assisted approximately 12 000 people to gain employment or return to a pre-injury job. This included workers entitled to workers' compensation and rehabilitation, as well as Commonwealth-funded clients. In 1999/2000, CRS Australia assisted a total of 6 108 Commonwealth funded clients achieve a durable employment outcome.

CRS Australia's core services for individuals consist of disability assessment and related services such as literacy assessment, vocational and career counselling and Job Clubs. Its core services for employers and insurers concern occupational health and safety, with a focus on injury management and prevention services more than compliance with legislation. The focus of these services is on early intervention for people assessed as having a "capacity to gain" from a rehabilitation program to assist them to obtain or retain unsupported employment or to live independently. In 2001, a trial of contestable provision of Commonwealth funded rehabilitation services began with a range of alternative rehabilitation providers involved.

Open employment services and incentives[282]

Open employment services provide vocational and pre-vocational training, employment placement and varying levels of ongoing support in the open labour market. The 1999 Disability Services Census recorded 309 open employment service outlets with 22 280 people with a disability assisted, including 9 937 jobseekers "on the books" as at

26 May 1999 (that is, registered and receiving a programme of support) and 1 661 full-time equivalent support staff.

A separate Workplace Modifications Scheme provides assistance with the costs of modifying a workplace or purchasing special or adaptive equipment for workers with disabilities. This Scheme is available to individuals with disabilities in receipt of Commonwealth funded assistance through CRS Australia, open and supported employment services and Job Network.

Supported employment services[283]

The 1999 Disability Services Census recorded 510 supported employment service outlets assisting 15 247 people with a disability. Of these, 58% were working permanent full-time, of which 86% were earning less than $80 per week.[284] Supported employment services had 3 418 full-time equivalent staff. In recent years there has been increasing recognition of the value of work by people with disabilities and their capacity to learn the requisite skills. Supported employment services are funded to provide meaningful paid employment for people who, due to their disability, may find it difficult to obtain or maintain employment in the open labour market.

The recent Business Services Review [Carmody *et al.* (2000)] proceeded as a joint initiative of ACROD and FaCS. Its aim was to identify strategies for Business Services to meet needs and provide a valuable and viable employment option for people with disabilities. It promoted a "Business Services modus operandi" where the success of a Business Service is measured by its ability to balance two effectively competing demands, "the provision of supported employment and the operation of a commercially viable business". This is a second significant change in terminology after the promotion of the "supported employment outlet" model in the 1986 Disability Services Act. (The term "sheltered workshop" is still common in many communities, according to an appendix in the Review.)

The Review identified a number of determinants of successful performance, with size of the business, management tenure, the ratio between staff and disabled employees, and product innovation and management orientation all being associated with better performance. It made the case that such factors, rather than FaCS funding, are instrumental in determining the ability of a Business Service to achieve commercial viability. It nevertheless noted that funding levels varied across Business Services from roughly $1 500 per person to over $30 000 per person per annum, and commented that "The establishment of a purchasing framework for securing employment outcomes for people with disabilities from Business Services appears to provide a practical strategy by which many of the current funding inequities within the industry can be addressed. It moves the focus for performance monitoring to the attainment of outcomes within agreed standards and away from monitoring process...[and] also negates the need to separate business and support costs as it would be at the discretion of the Business Services as to how best to use the funds received to meet the outcomes that were being purchased. The current case based funding trial [see below] is being used as a means of obtaining better data to inform the development of a purchasing framework...". The Review also recommended that ACROD should develop an accreditation model for the Business Services Industry that complements the disability quality assurance system, and should be supported by the government to take a lead role in developing strategies to redress the current funding inequities, prepare for the move towards the introduction of a purchasing framework, and achieve continuous improvement for the Business Services sector.

In the area of wages, the Review commented that "pro-rated productivity/competency based wages are still fairly new for the Business Service industry and remain highly dependent on the financial viability of an organisation". It did, however, recommend that Business Services should be required to provide work conditions comparable to that found in other forms of employment. In regard to the transition of employees to open employment, the Review noted that this occurs very infrequently and that, it can be argued, responsibility for this creates an inherent conflict of interest for organisations whose dual purpose is to provide long-term supported employment and operate a commercially viable business. The report considered that, while cooperative links should be established between open employment services, Business Services, and Centrelink, the latter rather than Business Services should provide the necessary support for transition to open employment.

Overall, the Business Services Review drew strong industry support for improvement in overall performance and the need to embrace good practice. It indicates a mutual agreement to proceed, cautiously and on a consensual basis, towards a model where funding follows the client. This should help to reduce the inefficiency and inequity in provision that is implied by extreme variations in government funding. Specific strategies have already been funded to support continuous improvement (by providing financial analysis and business planning support), and to assist the introduction of fair and transparent wages for employees (Award Based Wages Strategy).

Given the low wages earned, the funding of supported employment costing $6 000 to $7 000 per supported employee per year does very little to reduce outlay on Disability Support Pension. The entry of a disabled person into Business Services thus adds approximately 70% to the cost of a full Disability Support Pension over a very long period.[285] To the extent that – with some exceptions – long-run subsidy levels per client within Business Services appear to remain high as compared with open employment options, it may remain difficult to present clients with a real choice between open and supported employment options.[286] So access to these services may still have to be restricted, on the basis of assessing in each case whether the subsidy costs are justified by the improvements to the quality of life of clients and their families from participation in the work activity.

3.   *Recent reform initiatives*

More Intensive and Flexible Services (MIFS) *Pilot*

The Department of Social Security established the More Intensive and Flexible Services (MIFS) Pilot in July 1996 to test the feasibility of providing customised, intensive and flexible services to address the specific needs of people with chronic or unstable conditions, such as psychiatric conditions, high support needs and multiple disabilities. The pilot operated in two sites until June 2000. The objectives of the MIFS Pilot were to assist people with severe disabilities to maximise their social participation in the community, to prepare for and increase participation in vocational programs and, indirectly, to maximise their work outcomes. Services available through the MIFS Pilot included case management services (such as counselling), secondary rehabilitation services (such as physiotherapy) and pre-vocational training (such as mental health support services). The Pilot also facilitated access to State and community services where appropriate. Participation was voluntary, but restricted to DSP recipients who were unable to access or benefit from existing (vocational) employment services.

The Pilot separated the purchaser/provider roles, with Centrelink contracting service providers to deliver individualised assistance, including case management, to Pilot participants. In contrast to the Job Network/case based funding models, MIFS were not funded on an outcome basis but focused on individually tailored services and assistance delivered to meet the needs and developmental requirements of participants. Preliminary data from the MIFS evaluation show that, on average, participant duration on the Pilot was just under one year at an average program cost of just under $2 800. About 70% of participants completed their programs. Over half of the participants achieved a vocational type outcome (including work, commencement of disability employment assistance, voluntary work or study). The evaluation also found that the Pilot enabled many participants to increase their independence, self-esteem, confidence, social and communication skills and improve their quality of life.

Centrelink eligibility assessment and referral process

From 1999, all jobseekers were assessed by Centrelink for eligibility for assistance and streamed to the provider of their choice. Disability service providers were able to provide assistance to jobseekers approaching them directly, but not access FaCS funding assistance without an eligibility assessment of the jobseeker by Centrelink. A Disability Industry Reference Group was established to monitor the effectiveness of the Centrelink assessment and referral service. Its report [DIRG (1999)] found that there was a need to maintain both pathways (i.e. via Centrelink and specialist disability employment services). This was accepted and a distinction was introduced between approaches to Centrelink which are followed by assessment and referral to up to three FaCS providers if the Work Ability Table (WAT) score is above 50,[287] and approaches via a disability specialist service provider, in which case a Centrelink WAT assessment is still required to endorse funding for this provider.

Case Based Funding Trial

The trial of new funding arrangements for disability employment assistance, announced in 1999/2000 was the next step in the reform process. The Case Based Funding Trial was established in November 1999 to test an alternative funding model for disability employment assistance to better link funding to jobseeker needs and outcomes. The objectives of the trial are to:

- Examine the impact of the case based funding on employment outcomes for the range of jobseekers including disability type, location and level of assistance required.
- Assess the suitability of the classification tool in placing jobseekers into differing funding bands reflecting broad support requirements.
- Determine the appropriateness of the trial funding levels in meeting the costs incurred.
- Assess the impact of case based funding on service viability and responsiveness.
- Identify financial incentives and disincentives for improved performance in different service types, sizes and various locations.

Payments in the first phase of this trial were structured according to the client's JSCI score. In a second phase starting in January 2001, there are five levels of funding for jobseekers, with the level of funding determined 50% by the jobseeker's JSCI score and 50% by a new Disability Pre-employment Instrument (DPI). The latter is completed by the provider after staff have worked with the jobseeker for at least four weeks, and then scored by FaCS. Up to 75% of the total funding available for a jobseeker can be paid over a period of 12 months. After a jobseeker has been in employment for 26 weeks, the balance becomes payable. The provider then completes a Disability Maintenance Instrument which is scored by FaCS. This determines the level of ongoing funding to the provider for maintaining the client in employment over the next 12 months. There are four funding levels for maintenance plus an Independent Worker Payment for jobseekers not requiring on going support. This is to encourage self reliance. The trial will be evaluated with the final report due in November 2001.

Another trial, of a new independent quality assurance system for disability services funded under the Disability Services Act 1986, has recently been completed with a final report due in November 2001. This trial tested performance indicators against each of the quality standards.[288]

Notes

1. The overall increase in the number of employed persons has also been accompanied by a slight increase in the rate of multiple jobholding among employed persons. Between July 1991 and August 1997, this rate increased from 4.3 to 5.2% [ABS (1998b)].

2. Industry is defined here using the International Standard Industrial Classification (Rev. 2) and includes mining and quarrying, manufacturing, electricity, gas and water, and construction.

3. A further indicator of the particularities of the structure of the Australian economy can be found in its structure of trade. Manufactured products accounted for only about 48% of Australian exports of goods (in value terms) in 1998. This relatively small share is due, in part, to the important role played by natural resource based-exports. Among OECD countries, only Iceland, New Zealand and Norway have smaller shares of manufactured products in their exports of goods.

4. There is a strong correlation between part-time working and casual employment. In August 1999, 65% of part-time workers were employed on a casual basis and 70% of casual workers worked part-time [ABS (2000), Employee Earnings, Benefits and Trade Union Membership, Catalogue No. 6310.0, Canberra, February].

5. In this comparison, part-time employment refers to persons who usually work less than 30 hours per week. A number of caveats apply concerning international comparisons of part-time working. For a discussion of these issues, see OECD (1999d); and Van Bastelaer et al. (1997).

6. The countries covered in this comparison were Australia, Canada, Finland, France, Germany, Japan, Netherlands, Spain, the United Kingdom and the United States.

7. The countries covered in this comparison were Australia, Canada, Finland, France, Germany, Japan, Spain, Switzerland and the United States.

8. This assessment covered Australia, Belgium, Canada, Czech Republic, Finland, France, Germany, Hungary, Italy, Japan, Netherlands, New Zealand, Portugal, Spain, Sweden, the United Kingdom and the United States. See OECD (2000e), pp. 52-56, for notes and a discussion of the methods for the comparison.

9. Gross flows refer to the total number of persons who changed region of residence over one year.

10. While there is a relatively low rate of upper secondary completion in Australia, it should also be noted that there is a relatively high rate of adult access to formal education, in part through Training and Further Education (TAFE) courses. The TAFE courses are generally short in duration and feature flexible admission policies and teaching methods. For an international comparison of adult access to formal education see OECD (2001a).

11. Using data from the Australian Longitudinal Survey and the Australian Youth Survey, a recent report by the Australian Council for Educational Research highlights changes in non-completion of secondary school during the 1980s and 1990s [Lamb et al. (2000)]. In discussing the interaction of labour market developments and education, the authors frame the dynamics as being driven by declining full-time employment opportunities for teenagers. This decline meant that those who did not complete year 12 of their schooling experienced a "growing dependence ... on available vocational education and training opportunities." As a result, there was a rise in the proportion of those not completing secondary school who nevertheless undertook further study, particularly among males.

12. An OECD international assessment of regional unemployment disparities found that at the state level, the disparities in Australia were comparatively modest [OECD (2000e)]. For example, the coefficient of variation for Australia in 1999 was the lowest among the 23 OECD countries for which data were available. However, when the basis for the assessment was shifted to the level of the small-area labour market (59 regions), the disparities increased substantially in Australia. The coefficient of variation was the fifth highest among the 23 OECD countries (also assessed at the small-area level).

13. This income support includes age pensions, single-parent payments, disability support pensions and labour market allowances (including unemployment benefit payments prior to 1991, payments under the Job Search Allowance, Newstart Allowance and Youth Training Allowance from 1991 to 1997, and payments under the Newstart Allowance and Youth Allowance schemes from 1998).

14. Data for these indicators were drawn from national sources for use in an OECD study. The cross-country comparisons vary somewhat depending on the selection of indicators. (e.g. the Gini coefficient is comparatively sensitive to income transfers in the middle of the distribution.) For a discussion of the data, concepts and methods, see Förster (2000). Atkinson et al. (1995) provide a useful international comparison of income distribution during the 1980s. Also, see OECD (1999a).

15. Whiteford (1998) argues that standard measures may overstate the extent of comparative inequality in Australia if, for example, employers' contributions to social security schemes are not included as part of wage and salary income. Employer-paid social security contributions do not exist in Australia, while in some other OECD countries such as France and Sweden the contribution rates can be substantial. If these contributions are regarded as deferred earnings and included as income for purposes of measuring inequality, then the gap between those receiving benefits and those in work would be greater in countries where employers make such contributions. For those countries, inclusion of the employer contributions would lead to higher measured inequality, but there would be no effect on the indicators for Australia. The OECD data discussed in the text and shown in Table 1.7 exclude such contributions.

16. This is based on ABS calculations of the Gini coefficient for "all income units". Income units are defined by ABS as "one person, or a group of related persons, within a household, whose command over income is shared." It is thus a narrower concept than "household" (which is "broadly defined as a group of people who usually reside and eat together").

17. The poverty line based on 50% of median equivalent income for a family unit of two adults with two dependent children was $353 weekly for the year ending June 1996.

N.*b*. references throughout this review are to Australian dollars, unless otherwise indicated.

18. The poverty rate was slightly above average for one-person households for women aged 45 to 59 and men aged 45 to 64 (10.5%). The poverty rate was substantially higher for single youths aged less than 25 years (21.3%), but this figure does not take into account parental support of youth who are not full-time students and who are therefore assumed to be independent.

19. The Parliament consists of the Queen (represented by the Governor-General) and two Houses (the Senate and the House of Representatives).

20. One famous exception occurred in 1975 when the Governor-General (John Kerr) intervened controversially to dismiss Prime Minister Gough Whitlam and call elections for both houses of the Australian Parliament in an effort to break a deadlock in the passage of a budget and formation of a government.

21. Parliament of Australia (2001), "The Parliament: An Overview", www.aph.gov.au/parl.htm.

22. Attorney-General's Department (2001), "Australia's Legal System", law.gov.au/auslegalsys/auslegalsys.htm.

23. Australian Department of Foreign Affairs and Trade (2001), "Fact Sheets: Australia's System of Government", www.dfat.gov.au/facts/system_of_government.html.

24. For a brief summary of the context for the white paper and the full employment policy, see Quiggin (1993).

25. DEWRSB was set up under an administrative reorganisation in 1998, acquiring responsibility for employment services operations from a predecessor agency known as the Department of Employment, Education, Training and Youth Affairs (DEETYA). DEETYA had been established in March 1996, as a successor to the Department for Employment, Education and Training (DEET). The 1998 reform also led to the establishment of the Department of Education, Training and Youth Affairs (DETYA) which assumed responsibility for youth training programmes. See Chapter 2 for details of the institutional changes.

26. A further innovation was the use of a multiple targeting approach in conjunction with a job creation measure in the early 1980s. This was the first time such a targeting approach had been utilised in Australian labour market programmes. Its primary target was combating long-term unemployment, but it also assigned secondary targets that required proportional participation by age, gender, ethnicity, indigenous status and region [Freeland (1998)].

27. The formal citation for the report is: Kirby (1985), *Report of the Committee of Inquiry into Labour Market Programs*, AGPS, Canberra.

28. Examples include the 1983 OECD Review of Youth Policy, the 1985 Quality of Education Review Committee, and the 1986 Social Security Review.

29. One example was the Community Employment Program, a temporary job creation scheme that targeted the long-term unemployed. Under this measure provision of support for job search was expanded with Job Search Training Courses (3 to 5 day sessions) and Job Clubs (intensive training over a three-week period) added to its menu of services [Finn (1997)].

30. The Kirby report of 1985 also had recommended the establishment of traineeships as an alternative form of entry-level training for youth. As implemented in the second half of the 1980s, this training was to be of shorter duration and more flexible than

apprenticeships, with participants engaging in unpaid off-the-job training. Traineeship wages were supported by government wage subsidies. However, until the advent of the Working Nation initiative (discussed below) take-up remained well below expectations (under 20 000 annual commencements, whereas the target was 75 000).

31. SkillShare was based on the previous Community Youth Support Scheme that provided counselling, advice, support and activities through community centres. SkillShare, however, included a much stronger training element and focused assistance more on reinserting unemployed youth into employment or formal education.

32. Already under the Fraser government some activation steps were introduced such as periodic mandatory interviews. Also, the CES was engaged to monitor and assess the claimants' job search efforts [Finn (1997)].

33. Also, in 1990, the Disability Reform Package tightened eligibility and encouraged the disabled to work within their capacities.

34. The evolution of long-term unemployment is influenced by a variety of factors in addition to labour market policy. However, as indicated in Chart 1.7, the period of operation of Working Nation (1994-1996) was associated with a fall in long-term unemployment.

35. Other brokered programmes included JobSkills, NEIS and the Landcare and Environmental Action Program, all of which were established under earlier governments, but continued to operate under Working Nation.

36. Also, a formal tendering process was introduced for other measures including the Jobskills, JobTrain, and Landcare and Environment Action Programs.

37. Other services are available to assist client groups with special labour market needs. For example, Aboriginals and Torres Strait Islanders have access to a range of employment assistance options through the Indigenous Employment Policy. Individuals with severe disabilities have access to the Disability Employment Assistance Program (DEAP).

38. Newstart and Youth Allowances are the only allowances related to labour market participation. A one-off Employment Entry Payment is available to assist some income support recipients who are starting work.

39. The discussion here concerns activity-tested allowances. A broader review of "welfare reform" in Australia has also been under study by the government (see Chapter 4).

40. The Youth Allowance provides financial support for full-time students aged 16 to 24; other young people up to 21 who are looking for work full-time, combining part-time job search and part-time study, doing other approved activities (including voluntary work), or who are ill; and certain other youth. Jobseekers and part-time students who are aged 21 or older and seeking income support must claim the Newstart Allowance instead [Centrelink (2000) Youth Allowance: The Guide, www.centrelink.gov.au/internet/internet.nsf/filestores/ya0007/$file/ya0007en.pdf, July].

41. Accepted Mutual Obligation activities include: part-time paid work; Work for the Dole; CDEP work (CDEP was continued under the reforms); recognised voluntary work; Green Corps (a voluntary programme, overseen by the Department for Education, Training and Youth Affairs, offering youth aged 17 to 20 years accredited training and work in environmental and heritage conservation projects); relocation to areas with better job prospects; approved literacy and numeracy training; part-time study; New Apprenticeships Access Program; Job Search Training plus additional job search

requirements over a 14-week period; Advanced English for Migrants Program; Intensive Assistance; Jobs Pathways Program (school to work support); Job Placement, Employment and Training (supporting youth at risk of homelessness); and participation in the Defence Force Reserves.

42. For example, see Kemp (1997), *Government Initiatives for a Competitive Vocational Education and Training Sector*, speech to the Annual Conference of the Australian Council for Private Education and Training, www.detya.gov.au/archive/ministers/kemp/ks20697.htm.

43. Other groups eligible for the Literacy and Numeracy Program include sole parents participating in the Jobs, Education and Training (JET) strategy, all 15–20-year-old jobseekers registered with Centrelink, participants in the Job Placement, Employment and Training (JPET) programme; 16 to 34 year-olds in receipt of disability support pension; participants in the community support programme; and participants in a community development employment project.

44. A further DETYA literacy initiative is the WELL (Workplace English Language and Literacy) Programme that provides workers with English language, literacy and numeracy skills. WELL provides funding for literacy training in association with vocational training. Under WELL, enterprises, representative bodies (*e.g.* employer organisations and trade unions), local governments or Registered Training Organisations can apply for funding in exchange for taking on the co-ordination of training including lining up training delivery with approved providers.

45. The Enterprise and Career Education Foundation replaced the ASTF in February 2001. It builds on the ASTF's local partnership approach, but with a broader mandate in such areas as career advice, innovation and employability skills.

46. The original measure was called the Job Pathway Guarantee Program.

47. JPET also assists individuals who are in care, refugees or ex-offenders who are not at risk of homelessness.

48. However, the PES functions of jobseeker registration, benefit administration, and referral of jobseekers to labour market programmes are still run by government, primarily through the Centrelink agency.

49. A survey of CES employer clients by Wooden and Harding (1998) showed strong dissatisfaction by employers with CES service delivery and the quality of CES referrals to vacancies.

50. As of June 1999, there were about 1 500 private placement agencies, and about the same number of temporary work agencies in operation in Australia [ABS (2000*b*)].

51. During 1995/96, allocation of jobseekers to contracted private case managers (CCMs), rather than to the public provider, was restrained by doubts about the quality of some of the bids received for contract work. The initial performance of CCMs, in terms of positive jobseeker outcomes achieved, was well below that of the public provider and in the first year of operation CCMs had only a quarter of the market. However this performance gap narrowed in 1996/97, and by the end of the Working Nation programme the CCM share increased to almost 50% [DEETYA (1996), p. 33; Eardley *et al.* (2001), p. 8].

52. Other failings concerned the insufficient co-ordination among the various government actors (DEETYA, ESRA, EAA), incomplete supervisory powers of ESRA over the government's own provider and partially perverse outcome fee structures [Fay (1997)].

53. Four Ministers oversee the DEWRSB portfolio. At the time of writing, these were Tony Abbott (Minister for Employment, Workplace Relations and Small Business; Mal

Brough (Minister for Employment Services; Ian Mcfarlane (Minister for Small Business); and David Kemp (Minister Assisting the Prime Minister for the Public Service).

54. The employment department is thus regulator and purchaser in one, after ESRA was dissolved by the Howard government.

55. They may also act upon recommendations arising from enforcement activities of other agencies, such as Job Network providers (in relation to job search or suitable work requirements, for example).

56. The amount of money set aside for performance payment is a very small percentage of the total annual price (2.5%).

57. Information in this section draws, in part, on Riggs (2001).

58. The public dissemination of Job Network member performance collected by DEWRSB can assist jobseekers to make informed choices. See the discussion of JN performance ratings further below.

59. The government-owned provider is, thus, still the largest provider of Job Matching services.

60. By way of comparison, in the period just prior to the introduction of Job Network (*i.e.* as of June 1997) there were under 700 outlets delivering CES and contracted case-management services to jobseekers.

61. The actual spending figures were about $52 million for Job Matching, $24 million for Job Search Training, about $508 million for Intensive Assistance and $83 million for the New Enterprise Incentive Scheme.

62. The negative outcome for Employment National in respect of Intensive Assistance work in the second tender round was subjected to close scrutiny, and the Probity Adviser's defence of the tender was important in this context.

63. During the first contract period, some Job Matching providers ran into financial difficulties indicating that they had underestimated costs or overestimated revenues. As a result, a certain number of changes to service provision and payment mechanisms were introduced which are explained in detail in Box 2.1.

64. Eligibility for Job Matching is outlined in Table 3.A.1.

65. Some placements are excluded, *e.g.* commission-only jobs, when a jobseeker found employment on his own initiative, jobs for less than 15 hours within 5 days after commencement, and placements of a jobseeker more than twice in a month with the same employer.

66. Jobseekers are assigned to Intensive Assistance levels A or B according to their JSCI score (see Chapter 3). In the first tender round, Intensive Assistance was contracted at a set price and there were three levels of assistance called Flex 3.1, 3.2 and 3.3. The up-front payments were $1 500, $2 250 and $3 000 respectively, the primary interim outcome fees were the same and primary final outcome payments were $1 200, $2 200 and $3 000 respectively. Secondary interim outcome fees and secondary final outcome fees were fixed at $500 in all cases.

67. Many Intensive Assistance providers did in fact submit bids at the floor price, in order to maximise their chance of winning a contract.

68. A primary interim outcome payment occurs where a jobseeker commences employment and either ceases receipt of an unemployment allowance for 13 consecutive weeks or, if not in receipt of such an allowance, works 20 hours or more each week for a period of

13 consecutive weeks. Enrolment in education may also be paid as a primary outcome for young people who have not completed their secondary education.

69. Tenders are submitted by organisations, rather than in respect of individual operational sites. This led to some situations where sites with an above-average performance had to close down because they were part of a larger organisation with below-average performance. At the same time, for bids that implied a major expansion of activity, a good performance record at one site was not necessarily taken as a guide to likely performance after scaling the operation up to many times its original size.

70. The requirement for a minimum of five providers in each region had been intended to promote competition, but in practice did not always ensure that services were easily accessible in the more remote and thinly-populated parts of a large geographical tendering block.

71. A related concern was raised in the Job Network evaluation (stage one) with respect to the equity of access for jobseekers such as Indigenous Australians [DEWRSB (2000d)]. While the evaluation discussed this in the context of targeting, it is also partly related to the number, location and availability of appropriate service providers.

72. Extra costs arose, for example, from additional commencement fees payable for jobseekers continuing in Intensive Assistance, but starting again with another provider.

73. Kelly *et al.* (1999), on the basis of a survey which reported almost complete unanimity among Flex 1 only (*i.e.* Job Matching only) providers that their revenue was inadequate, estimated that the Job Matching fee would need to be approximately doubled, to around $500, to generate sufficient revenue from the service. In the second contract the average JM fee was $362, and there are still reports that JM-only providers face financial difficulties.

74. In the first tender round, some providers may have priced the JM service unrealistically because they did not realise that they could be offered JM business only, without JST or Intensive Assistance.

75. Several observers have argued that outcome fees under the first tender were insufficient for most IA clients. ACOSS (2000, p. 31), in particular, criticised the unbalanced fee structure as leading to "creaming" of the intake and "parking" of the hard-to-place unemployed, on the assumption that providing them with the help they would need to secure employment would cost more than their outcome payments are worth.

76. Although the direct fee paid in the case of level A clients and 6-month employment outcomes is $3 586, limits on IA providers' point-in-time capacity create some additional financial incentive for rapid placements, because these increase the flow of commencement fees. A provider who repeatedly places clients M months after commencement earns (from one slot) a total fee of (C+O) (where C is the commencement fee and O is the outcome fee) every M+3 months (given that a client is only exited when an interim outcome fee is claimed 3 months after placement). For level A clients who (if not placed) are exited after 12 months, the net return to the 12/(M+3) placements per year is [12(C+O)/(M+3)–C] per year, *i.e.* the return is C(9–M)/12 + O per placement. With C = $1 077 and O = $3 586 the total net return to a placement achieved one month after commencement is therefore $4 304 rather than $3 586. The additional payment for an earlier placement ($718) is small as compared to the likely saving in unemployment benefit from placing a jobseeker 8 months

sooner. It may still be enough to explain why a large proportion of IA paid outcomes occur in the first month [DEWRSB (2001*b*), Figure 4.3]: when only one suitable vacancy is available providers may, other things being equal, prefer to submit recently-commenced clients as candidates.

77. The maximum IA outcome fee (for 26 weeks in employment) might on average be associated with a year's benefit saving as well as payments of tax with an average value of about $13 000 ($500 per fortnight for 26 fortnights).

78. In the first tender round, interim outcome fees were the same as commencement fees. Some IA outcomes attract more than the interim outcome fee (when a final outcome payment is made) but there are also many cases where only a "secondary" outcome payment is made.

79. Dockery and Stromback (2000*b*) suggest, on the basis of a 1997 DEETYA study of net programme impact, that even if an IA provider offered no assistance at all, placement rates of around 20% could still be expected. Eardley *et al.* (2001, p. 43) report from a survey of providers that "It soon became clear that on average outcomes of around 10% were occurring naturally without any special or expensive intervention". The 15% figure cited in the text is an average of these two estimates.

80. In the first tender round, paid outcome rates for individuals six months and more after they entered IA, in a typical region, varied from about 25% for the highest-performing provider to 9% for the lowest-performing provider [DEWRSB (1999*e*)]. An analysis of the 1999 Job Seeker Satisfaction Survey focusing on differences between the top-performing and bottom-performing providers found a similar range of variation in the proportion of jobseekers reporting that IA referrals had resulted in a paid full-time job [DEWRSB (2001*b*), Table 4.9]. This suggests that within the constraints of the current environment, providers can at best raise the paid outcome rate by about 15 percentage points.

81. Although information about the profitability of providers was not obtained for this review, it is known that, for example, during the first contract period Employment National earned a profit on its IA business. Yet this profitability was consistent with a relatively poor performance which resulted in loss of business in the second tender round decisions.

82. Centrelink staff may also include service officers for indigenous persons; multicultural service counsellors, together with interpreters, for migrants and clients with non-English-speaking backgrounds; social workers dealing particularly with youths (but also with situations of domestic violence, for example); authorised review officers handling appeals regarding any type of benefit payment; financial information officers advising, for example, pensioners on the use or investment of their retirement income; or simple receptionists who accept claim forms or channel clients to counsellors, sometimes separated by functional areas, but sometimes not. This illustrates the difficulties in calculating or estimating the number of staff who in other countries would fulfil employment-related functions within a PES-type framework.

83. For comparison, at 30 June 1996, the then Government's Client Service Delivery Network, comprising the CES, Employment Assistance Australia, Student Assistance Centres and other specialist employment services, was staffed by about 12 000 persons.

84. The annexed table also presents two non-JN measures (the Community Support Program and Disability Employment Services). They are included here because

Centrelink streams certain unemployed from Job Network and refers them to these measures for special services.

85. DEWRSB's approach to tracking services makes it difficult to determine exactly what services individual clients currently receive. Despite increased monitoring of service delivery under the second round of JN contracts, providers retain broad flexibility in determining the specific services to offer to individual clients and are not required to report on all of these services in detail.

86. One way that DEWRSB monitors its employment assistance measures is through client satisfaction surveys. A programme of surveys was implemented during the period 1998 to 2000 using four separate survey instruments: 1) A telephone survey of jobseeker perceptions of, and satisfaction with, Job Network, conducted in 1999 and covering about 15 000 jobseekers who had used Job Network in the previous 12 months; 2) A telephone survey of employers' use of Job Network, carried out in 1999 and covering about 6 500 employers; 3) Annual surveys of jobseeker satisfaction with Centrelink services covering 3 000 jobseekers who had contact with Centrelink during the proceeding six months; and 4) A survey of JN member satisfaction with Centrelink referral services conducted via telephone with staff from around 900 individual JN member sites. These surveys have served as an input to the on-going JN evaluation.

87. The response rate for the Job Seeker Satisfaction Survey was 72%. The Job Network evaluation (stage one) did not report what share of respondents reported getting paid work [DEWRSB (2000d)].

88. If the individual is still unemployed after the end of the JST service period, he or she is then required to provide documentary evidence of two employer contacts per fortnight over the next seven fortnights (see Chapter 4).

89. The Social Security Act of 1991 requires jobseekers to undertake the activities specified in their negotiated activity agreement in order to continue receiving income support. For recipients of Newstart Allowances and Youth Allowances these activities may include one or more of the following: a job search, a vocational training course, training that would help in searching for work, paid work experience, measures designed to eliminate or reduce any disadvantage the person has in the labour market, development of self-employment, development of and/or participation in group enterprises or co-operative enterprises, participation in a labour market programme, participation in a rehabilitation programme, and/or an activity proposed by the person (such as unpaid voluntary work). Job search activity alone is not sufficient to satisfy the requirements of the Act.

90. The AJS seasonal work information can be found on the Internet at the following address: http://www.jobsearch.gov.au/harvesttrail.asp.

91. In correspondence with the OECD Secretariat, DEWRSB indicated that the response rate for the survey was 50%.

92. A similar survey sponsored by DEETYA in July 1997 found that 32% of all employers who had recruited during the previous 12 months had listed one or more vacancies with CES [DEWRSB (2000h)]. However, it should be noted that by 1997 labour market policy was in flux. Working Nation had already been abandoned and it is not clear whether the performance of CES had fallen in the face of on-going policy reforms including planning for its shutdown in the following year. Unfortunately, comparable data are not available for earlier years [DEWRSB (2000g)].

303

93. One important objective is to identify the need for early intervention for short-term unemployed jobseekers who may have particular disadvantages and, consequently, may be at risk of becoming long-term unemployed.

94. The risk factors include age, educational attainment, vocational qualifications, duration of unemployment, recency of work experience, family status, geographic location, Aboriginal and Torres Strait Islander status, geographic location for other Australians (*i.e.* regional disadvantage for Australians not of Aboriginal or Torres Strait Islander status), transport, contactability, proximity to labour market (*i.e.* whether residence is within 90 minutes of a town or city), country of birth, English language and literacy, disability or medical condition, stability of residence, disclosed ex-offender status and disadvantage resulting from personal factors requiring professional or specialist judgement.

95. The disclosure of information by a jobseeker is in accordance with the Privacy Act of 1988, which provides the jobseekers with confidentiality protection against further release of certain information.

96. In a worst-case scenario, a score of 96 would be attributed to the jobseeker who: is male and over 55 years of age, did not go to school, has no vocational qualifications, has been unemployed for more than 520 weeks, has not had any work experience for 15 years, is living alone, is Aboriginal, has inadequate transport, has no telephone, lives more than 90 minutes from a town or city, was born in Australia, speaks little English, has a moderate disability, is living in insecure accommodation, is an ex-offender who served prison time over one month, and who suffers from other significant disadvantage due to personal factors as assessed by a professional.

97. There is some regional variation in the time to referral under JST depending on a variety of factors such as availability of clients and JST places. Generally, referral of clients to JST occurs between two and six months after the individual's registration as unemployed.

98. Under the first Job Network tender, there were originally three levels of IA service (3.1, 3.2, and 3.3), but with the second Job Network tender these were reduced to two levels.

99. The factors are: disability, low educational attainment, unstable residence, personal factors, disclosed ex-offender, poor language and literacy skills, recency of work experience and duration of unemployment.

100. The WAT instrument takes into account a client's work behaviour and ability to: report regularly for work; persist at work tasks; understand and follow instructions; communicate with others in the workplace; travel to and from and move at work; manipulate objects at work; learn and undertake tasks; and lift, carry and move objects at work.

101. Disability Employment Services may also be accessed by directly approaching an appropriate service provider.

102. A report of the Australian National Audit Office also concluded that overall the JSCI "is proving to be a satisfactory tool as part of the task of scoring jobseekers according to the level of difficulty they have in finding employment" [ANAO (2000), para. 6.41].

103. Abello and Eardley (2000) point out that providers and welfare organisations have also expressed concern about inaccurate client assessment through the JSCI.

104. DEETYA research during the development of the JSCI concluded that no one characteristic such as duration of unemployment was a sufficient indicator of relative

labour market disadvantage. Therefore, the JSCI was designed to take into account a range of characteristics [DEETYA (1998a)].

105. If this estimate is based on IES data referring to Newstart and Youth Allowance beneficiaries, then one reason for the low IA access rate may be the participation of a substantial share of these individuals in part-time or short-term work. The fact that an individual had recent job experience is taken into account as part of the JSCI process and may contribute to classification for less intensive forms of assistance. While some 60% of Newstart and Youth Allowance beneficiaries were long-term benefit recipients [DEWRSB (2000f), September issue], the share who were long-term unemployed according to standard international statistical definitions was lower because many had recent work experience.

106. The star ratings used the following indicators: IA, number of interim outcomes against commencements; JST, number of jobseekers placed into job matching against commencements; and Job Matching, placements against contract.

107. Further comparative reports are planned at each subsequent milestone period (i.e. every six months).

108. The addresses for the corresponding DEWRSB-sponsored Internet sites are: DEWRSB (www.dewrsb.gov.au); Job Network (www.jobnetwork.gov.au/aboutjn.asp); and AJS (jobsearch.gov.au).

109. The addresses for the corresponding Internet sites are: Centrelink (www.centrelink.gov.au) and FaCS (www.facs.gov.au). Also, many JN members have their own Internet sites offering information for clients.

110. Centrelink provides Job Matching providers with information on notifications of jobseeker address changes.

111. See Chapter 2 for a discussion of the Job Network Code of Conduct.

112. Vacancies can also be posted by recruiting organisations who are members of the Recruiting and Consulting Services Association.

113. During the period 1 January 2000 to mid-February 2001, about 90% of the vacancies posted on the National Vacancy Database were semi-open.

114. DEWRSB-provided data for the last five months of 2000 indicate that monthly employer e-mail contacts of jobseekers averaged about 3.5% of the stock of vacancies as of the end of each month (about 1 500 contacts per month). There was substantial variation in this from month to month.

115. A referral is the designation by Centrelink of a JN provider to serve an individual client (including cases where the choice is made by the individual). A commencement marks the start of service provision to the individual by the provider, after any required preliminary steps under Job Network (e.g. a required initial interview). The data cited in the table refer to the first JN contract period.

116. Due to the length of the potential IA eligibility period (12 or 15 months, with the possibility for an extension), the evaluation was constrained to focus on clients entering the Job Network in its first quarter of operation. It should be noted that the JN system results may have improved as the stakeholders gained experience. For example, DEETYA (1996) found that under Working Nation, performance of the contracted case managers improved rapidly following the first few months of operation.

305

117. According to DEWRSB, the overall response rate for the Post Program Monitoring Survey, at around 60%, provides outcomes estimates that are generally accurate to within plus or minus one percentage point at the national level [DEWRSB (2000*f*)]. It should be noted that these outcome data do not control for the duration of participation in measures.

118. The Working Nation outcomes data in Table 3.6 were estimated by DEWRSB for the year ending 30 June 1996 and reflected an adjustment to take into account the status of participants in further assistance (as is done for DEWRSB's Job Network outcomes indicators). A detailed assessment of Working Nation and Job Network programme evaluation approaches can be found in Chapter 5 of the present report.

119. The data in this paragraph on the structure of placements are drawn from [DEWRSB (2000*d*), Table 4.2]. For CES they refer to 1996/97. For Job Network, the data refer to May 1998 to September 1999.

120. For example, some countries count as placements those vacancies filled with the active help of the PES. Others count as placements, cases where vacancies are notified to the PES and filled by PES-registered jobseekers. The data for Australia refer to unsubsidised placements into vacancies registered on the National Vacancy Database that are filled by a member of the Job Network, including unpaid outcomes.

121. Chart 3.2 presents monthly vacancy registrations as a percentage of dependent employment (these data are only available from mid-1999). They indicate substantial monthly fluctuation.

122. Similar options are actively under consideration as part of the on-going government review on welfare reform [RGWR (2000*b*)].

123. Industrial injuries are governed by state law. Compulsory superannuation was introduced in 1992, with employers required to make contributions on behalf of employees at a rate rising to 9% in 2002.

124. Since benefits are often uprated in line with other incomes, comparisons in 1992 data are likely to be partly relevant even some years later. In Australia, replacement rates increased considerably between 1982 and 1992 (by 10 percentage points or more for many family and earning situations) but were then broadly unchanged through to 1997 [Redmond (1999)]. Whiteford (2000)] argues that replacement rates do not provide a consistent comparison of benefit generosity across countries because the full net income from work includes, for example, accruals of pension rights financed through employer contributions. At purchasing power parity, Australian assistance benefit levels in 1991 were only significantly exceeded in a few countries which have substantially higher levels of national income (Canada, Luxembourg, Norway and Switzerland).

125. Veteran service pension is payable five years earlier than the regular age pension to people who have served in the armed forces in danger from hostile forces of the enemy. A veteran invalidity service pension may be granted at any age.

126. DSP and family payments are not taxable. Most other basic rates of pension and allowance are taxable but allowances in the tax system are such that when these are the only source of income over a full year, the effective tax rate is zero [Whiteford (2000), pp. 27, 41].

127. The proportion of the population that is neither in paid employment nor receiving income support is greater than the difference between the proportion that is jobless and the proportion that is on income support shown in RGWR (2000*a*). This is because

some people on income support are not jobless. In 1998, about 8% of DSP beneficiaries [www.facs.gov.au/internet/facsinternet.nsf/whatsnew/29_9_99_fs3.htm] and 12% of those receiving other working-age benefits [FaCS (2000*a*), p. 155, Table 30] had earnings from part-time work. In addition, about 5% of those on Newstart Allowees were nil-paid in a given fortnight [Landt and Pech (2000)]. These figures suggest that, although 22% of the working-age population were receiving income support payments in 1998, nearly three percentage points from this total were not jobless. (By 2000, total numbers on income support had fallen but the proportion with earnings within the total had risen.)

128. In 1993, the proportion of the unemployed in Australia who are in a household where no-one else is employed at 49.9% was higher than in 13 other countries except Ireland and the United Kingdom which have similar assistance benefits for unemployment. By 1996, perhaps influenced by recent policy changes, the proportion in Australia had fallen to about 45%, lower than Belgium, Germany and some other countries [OECD (1995*b*), Table 1.13; OECD (1998*b*), Chart 1.3]. Davies *et al.* (1992) for the United Kingdom, and Dex *et al.* (1995) in an international survey using microeconomic data from five countries estimated specifically that the husband's receipt of means-tested benefits (or to lesser extent, a benefit with a dependents' allowance) reduces wives' participation whereas receipt of insurance-only benefits does not. In Australia, as in many other OECD countries, the wives of unemployed men have much lower employment rates and higher unemployment rates than the wives of employed men but some research has concluded that this is mainly because husbands and wives have similar regional and personal characteristics [Miller (1997)]. Bradbury (1995) shows a decline in employment rates through time when the husband has a long unemployment spell.

129. Prior to 1990 the earnings of both members of a couple were simply aggregated for benefit purposes and if one partner had earnings up to the point where a 100% benefit withdrawal rate applied, any earnings by the other partner were subject to the same rate. With the $30 individual disregards, if one member of the couple earned more than $90 (thus using up both the personal disregard of $30 and the couple's free area of $60), further earnings were subject to a 50% or 100% benefit withdrawal rate, yet the first $30 of earnings by the other member of the couple could be retained in full.

130. With exit from unemployment defined in terms of four consecutive quarters without payment between August 1995 and November 1997, the exit rate was close to 54% for those with near-zero earnings in May 1995, rising to 72% for those with $500 earnings per fortnight.

131. It can probably be shown empirically that people who travel a lot domestically also tend to travel internationally, but this does not necessarily mean that reduced domestic fares will cause an increase in international travel. In the same way, evidence that people often move from part-time to full-time work does not necessarily imply that making part-time work more attractive will increase the take-up of full-time work.

132. As can be seen from Table 4.1, in 1998 the federal minimum wage ($373.40 per week) was considerably below the cutout point for a single person on a pension but above the cutout point for a single person on an allowance.

133. In Belgium and Norway in 1990, an individual's unemployment benefit was reduced only in proportion to hours worked (*i.e.* net income was a straight-line function of earnings, as hours increased from zero to full-time). Assuming normal concavity in the utility function, this makes part-time working a utility-maximising strategy for those

307

workers who would in the absence of benefits have worked full-time. At one stage in Belgium, more than half of all part-time workers were receiving an unemployment benefit, and reforms to discourage this had to be introduced [OECD (1994b), p. 200]. In Australia there is still a sharp kink in the net-income/gross-earnings schedule at the cutout point, such that for workers with full-time earnings substantially above the cutout level, part-time working may not very often be a utility-maximising strategy.

134. Retention of various secondary benefits, particularly the medical concession card, is a significant incentive issue in Ireland. As from 1996 the long-term unemployed have been allowed to retain the card for three years after entering regular employment [OECD (1998f), p. 132]. By contrast, in Portugal and the United Kingdom no such issue arises because free or subsidised health care is available to all citizens under relatively uniform conditions.

135. Table 4.7 suggests that few benefit claims are deferred for moving to an area of lower employment prospects.

136. The Mutual Obligation status of referrals to JST is unclear. According to providers, Centrelink regards part-time work as a valid alternative to JST participation. However, under Centrelink automatic procedures referrals to JST may take place after only two months in some regions and the unemployed would not be subject to Mutual Obligation at this point in the unemployment spell..

137. Roy Morgan Research (2000) reports the results of a survey conducted in April and May 2000, with a similar set of questions and similar findings. There were high levels of support (about 80%) for requiring reporting of job search (including employer verification certificates), and for requiring young people to participate in Work for the Dole. By contrast, a balance of respondents were not in favour of longer-standing benefit eligibility provisions which can penalise people who move to an area with fewer job opportunities, and require people to take any job available.

138. "Service providers necessarily conduct their own and ongoing assessments of individual clients and frequently develop very detailed and sometimes different understanding of peoples' needs, circumstances and so on. There are statutory restrictions on information which Centrelink can pass on to the relevant providers and on information which providers may be able to provide to Centrelink." [Jobs Australia (1999), p. 7].

139. Sanction rates can reach high levels in relation to measures such as off-site job-search courses in the United Kingdom [Finn et al. (1998)], US welfare-to-work programmes and job-search monitoring.

140. About 3.9% of the 15-59 year old SEUP Population Reference Group sample in September 1995 and 1996 were receiving an unemployment benefit, yet total unemployment benefit recipients at the time were about 6.8% of the 15-64 year old population. A matching exercise in Ireland found that over 30% of unemployment beneficiaries were not located at the address where they were registered for the same week [OECD (1998f), Box 4.1] so this might be one of the relevant factors in Australia.

141. Data-matching results are not available for very many countries, but matching exercises in the Netherlands in 1991, in Ireland in 1996, and in Finland in 1998 found that less than half the registered unemployed or unemployment beneficiary population was unemployed according to the labour force survey [OECD (1994b), Table 8.5; OECD (1998f), Box 4.1; Sihto and Myskylä (2000)]. The ratio of unemployment benefit recipients to labour force survey unemployed in 2000 was

about 70% in the United Kingdom and 200% in Ireland, two countries with benefit systems fairly similar to Australia's.

142. In general, countries with high labour turnover (low job tenures) have low long-term share in unemployment [OECD (1999d), Chart 2.3]. Ireland is an exception with relatively low job tenure and high long-term share in unemployment, and according to its beneficiary data Australia would also be an exception.

143. The proportion of all unemployed and Sickness Allowance beneficiaries who were sick/incapacitated increased from 6% in 1993 to 10% in 1999. From March 1996, incapacitated unemployed beneficiaries were no longer required to transfer to Sickness Allowance. Over the next two years the number of Sickness Allowance beneficiaries fell from 50 000 to 15 000 while the number of incapacitated unemployed beneficiaries rose from about 10 000 to 55 000. Within the latter group about 47% have a musculo-skeletal condition and 32% psychological/psychiatric condition [Warburton, Martin, Read and Vuong (1999)].

144. DEWRSB (2000f) states that jobseekers are reclassified as short term recipients only if they remain totally off benefits for a continuous period of more than 13 weeks: however within this statement, clients on a nil payment are not considered to be off benefits. In DEWRSB's IES system, the date of unemployment registration is in relevant cases taken to be the most recent start date on a Job-Network-eligible income support payment, but where there is a previous record the earlier registration date is reactivated using the same "allowable breaks" rules as FaCS. This results in the IES duration of registered unemployment (which is used as input to the JSCI) being usually similar to the Centrelink duration on benefits, in income support cases.

145. Until recently, ABS defined the duration of unemployment as the period from the time the person last worked full-time for two weeks or more (the data used in Chart 4.1 are on this basis). From April 2001, it is defined from the time that a person started looking for work, or last worked in any job for two weeks or more. These definitions, especially after the recent change, may be more rigorous than those used by some other OECD countries where the labour force survey simply asks the unemployed person how long they have been looking for work. In other countries, the incidence of long-term unemployment often seems to be similar or lower in registration data than in labour force survey data [data in OECD (1994a), Tables P and S, allow this comparison for six countries in 1992].

146. Connolly (1999) estimated that growth in the difference between the number of unemployment allowees (including MAA and Widow Allowance) and ABS full-time unemployment (a concept that excludes the unemployed who are looking only for part-time work) was positively and significantly influenced by policies which improved the incentives for casual and part-time work by unemployment allowees.

147. Some activation measures (in particular job-search monitoring) result in increased job search and might increase LFS unemployment in the short run. From a policy point of view it is important to decide how much value should be attached to reductions in benefit recipiency obtained through activation strategies. Lax administration of unemployment benefits is not necessarily a barrier to good general labour market performance: for example, in Ireland LFS unemployment has fallen to low levels recently, yet many older workers remain on benefits, apparently not actively seeking work. But most countries with high benefit coverage regard the impact of activation measures, if it is recognised as such, as a desirable outcome particularly for younger workers.

309

148. The FaCS data set appears to lack information on the programme participation status and employment status of individuals, which are urgently needed for comprehensive tracking and evaluation of labour market policies.

149. For example, in Ireland in October 1996 there was extensive press coverage of findings from a data-matching exercise, soon followed by a publicity campaign [OECD (1998f), pp. 135-147], and the number of beneficiaries immediately fell by about 3%.

150. The median unemployment duration for referrals to JST through to September 2000 was a little over six months [DEWRSB (2001b), Table 3.1].

151. The incidence of receipt of DSP among 60 to 64 year-old men increased slightly between 1993 and 1999. See O'Brien (2000) for data on receipt of DSP, Mature Age Allowance and other unemployment payments by this population group.

152. Mothers must seek work to be entitled for social assistance when the youngest child reaches 6 months to 12 years (depending on province) in Canada, 3 years in Austria, Finland and Sweden, 5 years in the Czech Republic and the Netherlands, school age (for part-time work) in Germany, 6 years in Luxembourg and (for part-time work) in New Zealand, and 10 years in Norway [Eardley et al. (1996a); OECD (1998e); Goodger and Larose (1998)].

153. See Daniels (1999) for a summary history of Invalid Pension: the originally strict eligibility conditions were relaxed by the introduction in 1983 of a separate (but in most respects, similar) Rehabilitation Allowance.

154. The 5% incidence of musculo-skeletal problems cited appears to include people over retirement age (www.pwdwa.org/WelfareReform.html).

155. If all payments were subject to only a "minimum participation requirement" as suggested by the Welfare Reference Group, this would imply a radical relaxation of eligibility conditions for unemployment benefit, although this may not have been the intention of the suggestion.

156. Active labour market programme spending data are not exactly comparable because DSS spending on benefit administration was not included in 1990/91 but was included in 1995/96.

157. Comparability of unemployment benefit spending data for 1990/91 and 1995/96 may be limited owing to the replacement of child and dependent spouse components of unemployment benefit payments in 1990/91 by separate family and parenting allowances, not counted in the unemployment benefit total.

158. In many OECD countries social assistance is not counted as a form of unemployment benefit and total "passive" programme spending is understated relative to spending in Australia as a result.

159. The Youth Training Initiative was targeted on jobseekers aged under 18. Under Working Nation, there was a substantial increase in programme participation for this group, but a fairly large decrease in programme participation among 18 to 20 year-old jobseekers [DEETYA (1996), p. 102].

160. The Jobseeker Screening Instrument operated by CES under Working Nation operated on a relatively basic list of variables (age, education, indigenous or foreign-born status, disability, English-speaking ability and geographic location) available on the jobseeker database. About 5% of new registrants were referred to case management on the basis of JSI. However, CES and DSS staff were able to refer in addition jobseekers identified as at risk on the basis of poor motivation or self-esteem, literacy or numeracy skills and time out of the workforce. In practice, identification of

individuals as "high risk" by JSI were only 2.3% of all new registrations and re-registrations whereas identifications by CES staff were 10.2%. Those identified by JSI had substantially higher rates of remaining unemployed, but those identified by CES staff did not. The CES-identified group was on average disadvantaged, but it had a much higher rates of placement into employment (largely subsidised), which may reflect "creaming" (*i.e.* CES identified clients as being in need of assistance when they requested assistance) [DEETYA (1996), pp. 6-11].

161. The Client Classification Level was assessed for those already identified (via JSI or otherwise) for case management, through a questionnaire administered by the CES [DEETYA (1996), p. 24].

162. It had originally been intended that a much higher proportion of Job Compact placements would be into JobStart, and that NWO would be used mainly to deliver Job Compact places in areas of limited employment opportunities. However, take up of JobStart was lower than expected because employers were reluctant to take on the more disadvantaged clients targeted under Working Nation, even with increased subsidies. Other possible factors included "the nine-month placements which employers considered too long, the unfair dismissal laws which made it difficult for employers to dismiss unsuitable employees and a strong push in the department in 1994-95 to deliberately hold back JobStart in preference to the NTW" [DEETYA (1996), p. 46]. Competition between programmes also contributed. Some employers realised that they could use NWO, which offered a higher subsidy rate without the commitment to providing ongoing employment, instead. In practice, areas of low and high unemployment rates had very similar rates of NWO placement, and by 1995/96, 21% of NWO placements were in the private sector [DEETYA (1996), pp. 41-49].

163. If there were no people with unemployment duration of more than 18 months, the incidence of long-term unemployment would be well below a third.

164. In April 1996 there were 333 700 people in case management. Only about one-half may have been in the Job Compact group, since inflow analysis indicates that 43% were unemployed for over 18 months at the time of their commencement and 54% by December 1995 [DEETYA (1996), pp. 15, 30].

165. This statement appeared in a release "Budget initiatives 20 August 1996: employment assistance" (www.deet.gov.au/Archive/publications/budget/budget96/budget_initiatives/initcont.htm).

166. Costings for LEAP include wages, whereas costings for WfD do not include benefit payments.

167. Information on NEIS is drawn mainly from three websites (www.edna.edu.au/neis/ne_pa/pa_2.htm; www.nna.asn.au/NEIS.htm; and www.jobnetwork.au/general/services/neis/neisinfo.htm) which see for further details.

168. The curriculum for Certificate IV in Small Business Management (NEIS 11190) is available on www.jobnetwork.gov.au/general/services/neis/ncurrdoc.htm.

169. The use of referrals of jobseekers to vacant jobs as an instrument in the case management of unmotivated clients has to be very limited because of the well-known problem that employers will cease to notify vacancies if unmotivated clients are frequently referred to them. Thus other "tools" are needed.

170. The first recommendation of the OECD Jobs Study [OECD (1994c)] as regards active labour market policy, was to integrate the three basic PES functions of placement and counselling, payment of unemployment benefits, and management of labour market

programmes. For countries such as Denmark, Switzerland and the United Kingdom, it can be argued that (although the three functions are by no means entirely integrated within a single institution), the other two functions are, where relevant, called in to support the placement and counselling function. This is not so much the case in Australia where, for example, benefits are not automatically suspended when a jobseeker has failed to attend IA employment counselling, and IA employment counsellors are not usually able to refer jobseekers to most of the labour market programmes, Centrelink having this responsibility.

171. The information on WfD history and administration is drawn partly from Yeend (2000), DEWRSB (2000*k*) and a CWC website (www.amawa.com.au/humanres/workfordole.asp).

172. The exact formula for payments to CWCs has been varied to compensate providers for shortfalls in the commencement rate.

173. These examples appear in speeches made on 30 June 1999, 3 August 2000 and 17 November 2000 (available via www.dwrsb.gov.au/ministers/mediacentre/detail.asp).

174. Up to end 1999, only about one-third of jobseekers referred had failed to commence [DEWRSB (2000*l*), p. 12] but commencement rates declined with the introduction of auto-referral procedures in July 2000.

175. In the Sydney area prior to the Olympics, jobseekers aged under 35 who had not participated in JST were referred to WfD after only three months of unemployment (press release of 14 July 2000 on www.dewrsb.gov.au/ministers/mediacentre/default.asp).

176. The vast majority of WfD participants at end 1999 were drawn from the stock of long-term unemployed rather than recruited as part of the mutual obligation process [Colebatch and Saltau (1999), citing Minister Abbott].

177. A magazine, *The Torch*, considers the "activation" of social welfare recipients to be a violation of human rights and has announced that it will take a case against the Danish government through the courts and if necessary to the European Court of Human Rights (www.faklen.dk/en/the_torch/rights.shtml). Similar accusations have arisen in Canada, Ireland, New Zealand and the United States (hammer.prohosting.com/~penz/workfare/slavery.htm).

178. In Denmark, which has many years' experience in creating jobs of last resort for the unemployed, the private sector is involved but – since there is only partial subsidisation of wage costs and some other restrictive conditions to limit displacement and repeat use – it accounts for only about a quarter of the jobs created [Bredgaard (2000)].

179. Most of the information in this section is drawn from Stromback and Dockery (2000) and Dockery and Stromback (2000*b*).

180. PPM percentages in unsubsidised employment are lower in Table 5.2 than in Table 5.1 because in the latter individuals who had entered another labour market programme are excluded from the denominator in calculating percentages and the matched SEUP labour market program sample may have included a higher proportion of disadvantaged jobseekers.

181. In the matched SEUP data, although programme participation was known from administrative records, labour market status was not. A reported spell in work which extended less than two weeks beyond the end of programme participation (which was recorded administratively) was assumed to consist only of work in the programme: otherwise, it was assumed that a transition to unsubsidised work had occurred. However errors of more than three months in recalling when work in an employment

programme had ended would have led to erroneous coding of a three-month unsubsidised employment outcome. This would not often have occurred for training and job search programmes because participants in them did not often report being in work at the time of programme participation [Stromback and Dockery (2000), p. 13]. However recall problems could cause a general tendency for reported employment rates to regress towards the mean.

182. Poor levels of English proficiency were found to greatly reduce the likelihood of participating in a programme, while being willing to move interstate increased it. When re-estimated with a Heckman two step method to correct for sample selection, the estimates of net programme impact became erratic (except for the JobStart programme in the last three periods).

183. Although the employer obligation and the financial incentive for retaining JobStart employees beyond the end of the subsidy period were formally introduced in July 1994, some months may have elapsed before the effective application of these conditions to new starts. Moreover sanctions to enforce the obligation probably only took the form of rejecting further applications for the JobStart subsidy by employers who had already failed to keep employees on. The impact on three-month outcomes (measured up to 15 months after commencements in the programme) could therefore have come through mainly in the latter half of 1995. PPM outcomes for JobStart were regularly collected before Working Nation reforms to the programme. Sloan (1993) reports an early PPM finding that only 25% of JobStart participants had unsubsidised full-time or part-time jobs three months after the subsidy expired.

184. DEWRSB has advised that PPM questionnaires were sent out three months after the point at which eligibility for the 12-month bonus could arise, in the case of Job Compact clients.

185. A fully comparable control group would include individuals who would have been hired if the subsidy had been available, as well as individuals who were actually hired without a subsidy.

186. When a labour market programme is introduced in some local employment offices, but not others, the displacement and substitution effects of the programme (e.g. when increased assistance for one group of unemployed results in reduced employment counsellor or employer interest in other unemployed in the same area) can be observed. This is not possible when there is random assignment at the individual level.

187. DEWRSB's net impact studies identify a control group having the characteristics that participants had at the time of entry to programmes. The percentages of positive (i.e. employment or other) outcomes reported relate to status three months after exit from the programme (as a percentage of all with known status at this point) in the case of participants, and to status three months after selection (as a proportion of all with known status at this point) in the case of the control group. DEWRSB (2001a) remarks "The selection of the comparison group as described is consistent with the time spent participating in programmes being regarded as a time out of the labour force", which is true but makes it hard to justify the use of the methodology.

188. Dockery and Stromback (2000b) argue that, because rates of entry to employment decline with the duration of unemployment, exits over the entire eight-month period would be more than 8/3 times exits during the last three months.

189. The BLMR study of the Wage Pause Program found a small positive impact from participation (although the method of selection of the control group may have

favoured participants). The BLMR's subsequent evaluation of the Community Employment Program (which succeeded the Wage Pause Program, and continued until 1988) also used a methodology that tracked outcomes from the time of entry to the programme, but the BLMR was closed down before it was completed.

190. In 1999, 35% of welfare recipients covered by Mutual Obligation declared part-time earnings compared to 13% in comparable groups not covered [Abbott (1999a)].

191. ACOSS has reanalysed the programme costings given in the WfD net impact evaluation with an adjustment for the benefit savings attributable to participation in Working Nation programmes. On this basis the net cost of JobStart and of WfD were roughly the same. ACOSS considered that since the latter had much weaker employment outcomes, JobStart was more cost-effective [ACOSS (2000a)]. However see Section 5.E.2 for an assessment of the JobStart findings.

192. Unemployment benefit is a practical example of a "programme" which probably has a high rate of employment outcomes as measured three months after leaving assistance, without this necessarily indicating that it actually has a positive impact on employment outcomes.

193. The difference between the employment rates of ex-participant and the comparison groups (described as "net impact" in the DEWRSB studies) declines from 20% in the first month after exit or selection as control to 10% after five months for WfD, and from 18% in the first month to 6% after five months for Intensive Assistance.

194. Programme net impacts reported for JST include off-benefit outcomes by individuals who commenced but left early, and they could still reflect a "compliance" response, as much as an impact of the services provided. Participants who found work partly avoided, in some cases, the initial requirement to participate for 15 days in the training itself and also the requirement to return Employer Contact Certificates for three months after exit from JST.

195. DEWRSB (2001b, p.60, 89 and Figure 4.3) states that exits from Intensive Assistance (the sum of positive and negative outcomes) are evenly spread, with 14% taking place in the first two months and 16% in the next two: assuming this even spread of exits, 22% (i.e. 14% plus half of 16%) of all exits occur in the first three months: Figure 4.3 indicates that about 61% of these exits involved a positive outcome. The report also states that 42% of outcomes from Intensive Assistance are positive and 48% of these positive outcomes occur within the first five months: Figure 4.3 indicates that about 64% of these positive outcomes occurred in the first three months. Either set of figures (i.e. 22% x 61%, or 42% x 48% x 64%) indicates that only 13% of participants experienced a positive outcome within the first three months.

196. To be recorded with a positive PPM outcome three months after leaving Intensive Assistance, clients usually must have been at least partially employed (or in study) for three months (otherwise they would not have been able to leave Intensive Assistance). This is a relatively stringent precondition for a positive "outcome", as compared to outcomes that are recorded when a person is employed or off benefit at just one point in time.

197. Using administrative data, a "positive outcome" might be defined in several ways: being off-benefit on a monthly basis (the criterion used in recent DEWRSB studies of net impact), being off-benefit for four consecutive fortnights [the criterion used by Richardson (2000)], or experiencing a reduction of at least 70% in benefit payments over a three-month period (the criterion for a paid outcome from Intensive Assistance).

198. As noted previously, if measured from the start of programme participation, programme net impacts for most Working Nation programmes may have been quite strongly negative. Even for programmes like Intensive Assistance, there is a risk that the process of starting in the programme and waiting to receive expected services (*e.g.* counselling or training) may divert attention from job search, whereas a control group – particularly when subject to job-search reporting and other (*e.g.* Mutual Obligation) requirements – is not distracted in this way.

199. Although published evaluation studies have focused on status three months after leaving assistance, DEWRSB has been tracking the income support status of participants for many years. Information on the declared part-time work status of those remaining on income support only became available in DEWRSB's administrative systems in July 2000 [*cf.* DEWRSB (2000*l*, p. 3)]. The employment status of those who have left income support is not known in detail, because the PPM surveys only provide employment, education and other status information at one point in time after leaving, and for some client groups.

200. Advice to the OECD from DEWRSB.

201. Rowlands (2000) remarks that the technological change of recent years seems to leave the social security system as a whole less rather than more easy to change in response to policy decisions by ministers. This may be partly true for Job Network, which depends heavily upon information flows in DEWRSB computer systems.

202. The description of the Community Support Program is based partly on a DEWRSB (2000*d*) and a DEWRSB web page (www.dewrsb.gov.au/employment/programmesand services/).

203. The description of the JET programmes is based partly on FaCS (2000*a*) and the DSS Annual Report 1997/98 (www.facs.gov.au/annualreport/ar2-4009.htm), which states that in 1997/98 JET cost $11 million, but reduced income support outlays by an estimated $121 million.

204. The description of the Return to Work programme is based on DEWRSB programmes and services pages (www.dewrsb.gov.au/employment/programmesandservices/), which see for further details.

205. The description of the Regional Assistance Plan is based on DEWRSB's web page for the programme (www.dewrsb.gov.au/employment/programmesAndServices/Rap/default.asp) and a description of the core functions of Area Consultative Committees (www.ac.gov.au/corefunctions.htm).

206. The federal government may enact legislation only when there is an enumerated power in the Constitution. Those most relevant for labour legislation are the "conciliation and arbitration power" and the "corporations power". The "external affairs power" can also be used, for example, for legislation meant to comply with international instruments, such as ILO Conventions. It is possible that federal and state law attempt to regulate the same subject matter, but in the event of conflicting requirements, the federal law will invalidate state regulations.

207. Niland (1978, p. 19*f*) identified four elements of compulsory arbitration in Australia: (1) the parties are forced to appear before a tribunal either because the tribunal so ordains or because one of the parties seeks an arbitrated settlement; (2) a settlement is determined by the tribunal without the parties' prior agreement to accept and abide by it; (3) penalties are imposed for non-compliance; and (4) the penalties imposed are implemented and fines collected. However, in recent decades the third

315

and fourth elements have not been invoked, which means that arbitration has lost much of its compulsory character.

208. Thus, the Australian arbitration practice did not fully respect the principle of trade union pluralism. Although historically Australian workplaces have been characterised by multiple unions demarcated by craft or occupation, once a union had registered and its coverage was recognised by the Commission, it was protected from the encroachment of other unions in the particular occupation or sector. This, to some extent, inhibited the development of new unions or made it difficult for them to extend their coverage [see Curtain (1992)].

209. According to the 1995 Australian Workplace Industrial Relations Survey, of all workplaces with 20 or more employees, 18% were covered by both federal and state awards. Of workplaces with 500 or more employees, over a quarter were covered by both types of awards [Morehead et al. (1997)].

210. On the other hand, the compulsory arbitration system formally constrained union recourse to collective action.

211. Household surveys tend to show slightly lower rates.

212. The AWIRS (1995) survey shows that unions at the time were trying to develop a more extensive workplace presence. As one measure of shop steward activity, over two-thirds of them spent an average of two hours or less per week on trade union business.

213. The minimum membership was reduced again by the federal Labor government in 1994, in response to an adverse report by the International Labour Organisation (ILO) that the requirement did not conform with Convention 98 on the Right to Organise and Collective Bargaining.

214. According to Peetz (1998, p. 134), ACTU members themselves felt that Australia's fragmented union structure "... had led to a poor response to the structural shift in jobs, under-resourced unions, inadequate services to members, insufficient training of officials, damaging conflict within union ranks and failure to seek new members in poorly organised sectors ..."

215. For example, trade unions in the manufacturing sector in Victoria have undertaken the "Campaign 2000/2001" to reach identical collective agreements through pattern bargaining – something not very common in the current context of labour relations and actively discouraged by the federal government.

216. There were important exceptions. For example, certain awards attempted to determine aspects of work organisation, such as manning levels. Also, awards tend to prescribe rules and procedures to be followed in case of redundancy.

217. State chambers may themselves present claims to the federal AIRC, representing the interests of both the national and other state chambers. This happened, for example, in 1999 when the Victoria chamber filed a counter-claim to the ACTU's wage demands in the annual safety-net review.

218. All instances of bargaining and all agreements reached have to be registered with the Commission in order to be legally protected.

219. In addition to the AIRC, there are over 300 permanent industrial tribunals in Australia charged with regulating various aspects of labour relations. 15 of these operate in the Commonwealth jurisdiction (for example, Coal Industry Tribunals, an Academic Salaries Tribunal or a tribunal dealing with Employment Discrimination), the rest at state level.

220. According to evidence gathered at the ILO, the proportion of total unfair dismissal cases to the total number of employees seems to be higher in Australia than in Canada, New Zealand and the United States, but much lower than in France, Germany or Spain (data referring to 1995) (Cazes *et al.* 1999).

221. There were eight versions of the Accord between 1983 and 1995 which have been extensively discussed in the literature [see, *inter alia*, ALP/ACTU (1983); Curtain (1992); Isaac (1994); Dabscheck (1995); OECD (1997*a*)].

222. It is fair to say that this general priority was also included in the Keating government's Working Nation program, which envisaged that, over time, "the vast bulk of the workforce will turn to locally negotiated enterprise agreements, rather than depending on [...] awards for increases in pay" [Commonwealth of Australia (1994)].

223. New Zealand's Employment Contracts Act abolished all industrial arbitration tribunals and was designed to replace the predominant pattern of multi-employer and occupational awards with individual or collective contractual arrangements at the enterprise or workplace level. After a change in government, the ECA was replaced by the Employment Relations Act (ERA) in October 2000. Importantly, the ERA does not represent a return to the highly centralised wage-setting system of the 1980s. However, it introduced a number of modifications to the industrial relations framework, including a renewed focus on the multi-employer bargaining level [OECD (1997*b*, 2000*c*); Honeybone (1997); Bray and Walsh (1998)].

224. The WRA, Part I, lists among its objectives "enabling employers and employees to choose the most appropriate form of agreement for their particular circumstances".

225. Certain enterprises, such as key mining companies, have offered individual contracts to their employees in an attempt to break "job control" unionism. The courts do not necessarily side with the government view when AWAs conflict with traditional bargaining contracts. For example, in April 2000 the Federal Court upheld a lower court injunction stopping the mining company BHP from offering individual contracts which it considered were inducing its employees to quit their union.

226. The twenty allowable matters laid down in the WRA refer to: skill classifications and career paths; working hours and work-time scheduling; ordinary and junior rates of pay; piece rates and bonuses; annual leave; long service leave; multiple forms of personal and carer's leave; parental and maternity leave; public holidays; allowances; loadings for overtime, casual and shift work; penalty rates; termination notice and redundancy pay; stand down provisions; dispute setting procedures; jury service; type of employment (full-time, casual etc.); superannuation; pay and conditions for outworkers; and provisions incidental to the allowable matters.

227. While about 1 500 awards have ceased operation, new awards continue to be created. In addition, there are about 2 000 awards in operation in the state jurisdictions.

228. See OECD (1994*b*) for an overview of union security arrangements. Reflecting – and perhaps accelerating – recent declines in trade union density, there seems to be a growing consensus that freedom of association includes the freedom *not* to associate. In this context, it should nevertheless be noted that proposals to include the "right not to join" trade unions in ILO Conventions 87 and 98 were rejected on several occasions at the International Labour Conference [Creighton (1990)].

229. For example, it is not necessary for an enterprise union to be capable of engaging in interstate industrial action to be registered at the federal level. Despite such legal encouragement, there has been only one successful application for registration by an

enterprise union. In response to this, the government has proposed amendments to facilitate the registration of enterprise unions, such as lowering the minimum number of members to 20.

230. It is often claimed that "the locus of bargaining is shifting downward" [Katz (1993)]. However, as comparative analyses by the OECD (1994b; 1997c) and ILO (1998b) have shown, current trends are not so unequivocal. Evidence cited for decentralisation often refers less to wage negotiations, but to issues like working hours or work restructuring. By contrast, in a majority of OECD countries (particularly in Europe), the sectoral level has remained the principal arena for wage determination, although increasingly supplemented by some additional wage negotiation at workplace or enterprise level.

231. Previous surveys have identified up to 20% of employees in this category [ABS (1990); DEWRSB (1999a)].

232. Another grouping within this category are working proprietors who set their own rate of pay.

233. These data do not differentiate between coverage of employees at the state and at federal level. Latest estimates submitted by DEWRSB indicate that after the transfer of Victoria's industrial relations powers to the Commonwealth, 50% of Australian workers are now covered by federal awards and agreements, 36% by state awards and agreements, while 14% are award- and agreement-free.

234. Although there is a definite trend, changes have been gradual and, as noted by Wooden (2000), are perhaps less dramatic than often assumed, as unregistered agreements and overaward pay have always been important elements of wage determination in Australia.

235. Statistics on industrial disputes in Australia relate to disputes which involve time loss of ten working days or more for the establishment concerned and include unauthorised stopwork meetings, unofficial strikes, political or protest strikes and lockouts. International comparisons of strikes statistics need to be interpreted with caution, as countries apply varying criteria for inclusion of strikes and lockouts in national statistics.

236. That there is a link between declining trade union density and declining strike rates in Australia seems confirmed by the finding from a re-analysis of the 1995 AWIRS data set, according to which "the share of union members at a workplace is positively associated with some type of industrial action having taken place in the past year" [Loundes (2000, p. 18)].

237. Several researchers have tried to estimate the impact of the ALP/ACTU Accord, which lasted from 1983 to 1996, on the evolution of strike rates. The latest analysis concluded that the Accord reduced strike activity by approximately 38% over and beyond what could have been explained by other factors, such as wage developments or declines in union membership [Morris and Wilson (1999)]. However, when comparing strike rates in 1983 and 1996, the decline was not greater in Australia than in the OECD area as a whole. Alternatively, the fact that the latest decline started in 1991, may be more suggestive of a link to the acceleration in enterprise bargaining in the early 1990s.

238. Minimum rates were raised by $8 in the 1993 to 1995 reviews, which did not keep up with inflation. Later increases were between $10 and $14, and the 2000 and 2001 safety-net reviews awarded a $15 and a staggered $13/15/17 raise (about 3 1/2% nominally). State commissions or legislatures can set their own minimum wage rates,

which can differ somewhat from the federal rate. According to the 2000 EEH survey, about 2% of Australian full-time adult non-managerial employees had earnings below the federal minimum (which was at $400.40 per week at the time).

239. When employment status is not known directly from administrative systems, providers might be paid the value of known reductions in benefit payments conditional on providing documentary evidence at intervals that the person is actually in work. Such a mechanism is already used for Intensive Assistance (the secondary employment outcome fee is payable when benefits are reduced by at least 70% on average over a three-month period).

240. Worker utility considerations can justify paying providers a bonus related to such factors as jobseeker satisfaction and the wage level of jobs obtained for clients.

241. Allowing an easy-to-place person to remain unemployed for a year (and thus become long-term unemployed) is likely to be just as costly from a social welfare point of view as allowing an already-disadvantaged person to stay unemployed for another year. Also, it is unlikely that devoting relatively little effort to placing less-disadvantaged people improves prospects for more-disadvantaged people. In practice, employment service resources (which include job vacancies as well as financial and human resources) can only be effectively concentrated on severely disadvantaged people when total unemployment is kept low. For these reasons it seems hard to see any justification in social welfare terms for Australia's policy of paying less (at the margin) for IA level A outcomes than for level B outcomes. This is a particular concern given that levels of service provision, and their impact on outcomes, should normally be highest for jobseekers with intermediate levels of employability.

242. More-disadvantaged clients enter work relatively slowly if they are initially unemployed, but also return to unemployment relatively rapidly if they are initially employed. For example, three months after a Job Matching placement, employment rates were 75% for jobseekers who had been unemployed for less than six months but below 50% for jobseekers who had been unemployed for over five years [DEWRSB (2001b), Table 4.2]. (An asymmetric fee – a payment for months employed after exit from case management, but made only in respect of jobs started before exit from case management – would need to be higher for relatively disadvantaged workers, but this is a special case.)

243. Upon exit from case management, clients transfer to some other form of employment assistance. This makes it difficult to envisage paying providers for entries to employment that occur after a client has left them. Given that there is a lag between service provision and employment outcomes, there is a risk that the incentive for service provision will decline towards the end of a client's participation [this issue is discussed in DEWRSB (2001b)]. To maintain incentives, final payments need to be quite large but only relatively *ad hoc* methods for defining them appear to be available. Final payments might include a component based on estimates of the provider's contribution to employment outcomes that arise after exit from case management, and indicators of whether service provision is maintained towards the end of participation and whether services such as training which have a long-term impact have been delivered.

244. Kelly *et al.* (1999) report that every JN member surveyed considered the Flex 3.1 outcome payment for Intensive Assistance (which had a maximum value of $2 700) to be adequate (this is no doubt based on the expected average cost of the assistance provided). All parties involved should pay close attention to the economic principles,

outlined here, which indicate a need for outcome fees to be higher at the margin, although not necessarily on average.

245. There may also be positive externalities to services provision within Intensive Assistance. If jobseekers realise that IA providers are likely to place them in a job rapidly, "compliance" effects – whereby jobseekers find work themselves before starting in Intensive Assistance – may be increased.

246. Provider efforts to capture exclusive access to vacancies could involve long-run externalities: this is an argument for enforcing transparency in job matching procedures. PES arrangements where employment services face a budget constraint on counselling staff, yet can refer clients to labour market programmes (financed through other channels) at zero cost, are quite common. Possible reasons for this are (a) an employment office with a local monopoly may internalise short-run externalities and consequently make a generally suboptimal level of placement effort (subsidising inputs is one way of compensating for this); (b) placement efforts may be subject to some negative externalities while employability measures are not; and (c) employability measures have effects in the long run, beyond the time-scale of outcomes that easily be credited to individual counsellors or employment offices.

247. When a jobseeker expresses a preference for a particular provider, it might often be possible to meet that preference within the terms of block contracts to supply referrals with a given disadvantage (JSCI) profile. Other possibilities would be to require providers to accept such referrals at the estimated market price for the jobseeker's profile (as determined by government), or for the government to top up that provider's bid for the referral by a certain amount, resulting in jobseekers usually (but not always) being allocated to their preferred provider.

248. If there are short-run but not long-run negative externalities to employment service provision, competitive behaviour (which ignores externalities) ensures an optimal level of service. By granting a monopoly to a single provider the government could gain financially in the short term (to the extent that the monopoly provider internalises short-term externalities and makes reduced placement efforts) but this would not be long-run optimal.

249. For clients with problems such as drug addiction or mental disturbances, who are unlikely to enter employment, assistance should be provided to improve the person's general welfare or ability to cope, but it should be separately funded as a social service, like CSP. In the model here, participation in non-employment services need not be mutually exclusive with participation in employment services. (In the JN model the government has been reluctant to fund an individual for IA as well as for CSP.)

250. For easy-to-place clients, providers would have to operate a relatively cheap and traditional placement strategy, without systematically using expensive measures such as hiring subsidies, because for these clients placement assistance can only accelerate entry to employment by a few weeks. But outcome fees of up to $24 000 would give providers a more incentive to use labour market programmes, which can cost about $10 000 per net employment impact [see Chapter 5] in targeted cases with intermediate levels of employability.

251. Currently, IA payments average roughly $1 400 in commencement fees and $700 in outcome fees per client. In a theoretically optimal model, net fee income might be the equivalent of a $24 000 outcome fee, but paid only in respect of 10% of clients (corresponding not to the gross outcome rate but to the increase in outcome rate from 15% to 30% that may result from service provision, marked down because not all

outcomes attract a maximum fee). This rough guess indicates how total net fee income could remain similar to its current level if results were similar to current results – but could go higher if better results were obtained, as intended. Total net fee income would depend heavily upon the activation strategies available to providers. If the government decided to make jobseeker participation in employment assistance optional, the total impact of assistance might fall sharply, and competitive mechanisms would operate to achieve a corresponding fall in net fee income for the sector.

252. Strictly speaking, the linear schedule which relates net fee income to the employment outcomes achieved needs to be tangential (at the optimum point) to the non-linear function which relates employment outcomes to spending on service provision. (Variations in outcomes either side of their actual average level are relevant: the case where no services at all are provided is typically not observed.) Contracted threshold employment rates would be somewhat higher than the employment rates that would occur if there were truly no service provision.

253. In the first JN contract period, good and bad IA provider performance seem to have been related to service levels and strategies, more than to good or bad luck with the external environment.

254. For employment services the main gains from competition are likely to derive from the market's ability to experiment with higher and lower levels of spending on services and identify the most effective placement strategies. Incentives for great effort by those managers and shareholders who receive the after-tax profits from an IA business are unlikely to make a critical difference. In this case, the taxation of profits can handle risk without any major negative effects on market operation.

255. When costs are subsidised, spending needs to be audited to prevent profitable providers from distributing profits as supernormal salaries, or using subsidised inputs for the benefit of parent or associate companies. This probably involves restrictions on the subsidisation of labour costs (i.e. regular rates of pay would be subsidised, but not supernormal wage increases or bonus payments). Such arrangements involve additional supervision and auditing by the government (or a third-party regulator). Thus Japanese companies often allow their subcontractors to pass on increases in materials costs (over which the subcontractor has little influence) but not labour costs (which the subcontractor can influence through discipline in wage negotiations), and to check the implementation of such contracts the procuring company regularly inspects suppliers' production lines and accounts [McMillan (1992)]. Laffont and Tirole (1993, p. 188) report that "external accounting of subcost is routine in procurement in which firms often produce for the government and at the same time engage in commercial activities with steeper incentives", and they devote a chapter to "cost padding, auditing and collusion". In a competitive employment services market with input cost subsidisation, "cost padding" could not persist in equilibrium: a provider that persistently reported costs exceeding income from outcome fees (the true value of the latter being known to government with certainty) would be an immediate target for auditing.

256. Switzerland tracks the unemployment outcomes of clients directly for up to two years (the duration of insurance benefits), and although the long-term stability of employment outcomes is not directly recorded it is measured indirectly (in terms of the rate at which jobseekers return to unemployment after they have been placed). With only one provider in each employment service region, Switzerland assesses the relative performance of different employment service offices by an econometric

321

method (as outlined here for thin markets) rather than through market mechanisms [OECD (2001*b*)].

257. The description of the Jobs Pathway Programme here is based on the JPP website (jpp.detya.gov.au/default.asp), particularly the 2000/01 Programme Guidelines, Kellock with Bruce (2000), and advice from Australian authorities.

258. However, according to Kellock with Bruce (2000), school staff are in a position to determine whether young people access the service and the level of the service they will receive, and this can range from every student in a senior school being assisted by JPP to schools in which there is no JPP presence.

259. Information on the JPET programme comes mainly from the DETYA website (jpet2000.detya.gov.au/default.asp).

260. Ball and Robinson (1998) give statistics for apprenticeship commencements in 1989/90, 1995 and 1996, but in the main official series [Ainley *et al.* (1997), Table 9; NCVER (2000), Table 1] figures are different and the last year shown is 1994/95.

261. Statistics for training of more than two years' duration to Certificate III level or higher, which is roughly equivalent to apprenticeship training, indicate that such commencements had by 1998/99 approximately regained their 1989/90 peak level. Numbers in apprenticeship-type training remained somewhat below their former peak level suggesting that the average duration of this type of training has fallen slightly.

262. Basic information on New Apprenticeship processes can be found on www.newapprenticeships.gov.au, particularly the employer page, and South Australia's guide to employing a New Apprentice (www.tafe.sa.edu.au/vet_div/trb/newapprentices/steps.htm).

263. Courses are generally accredited under Australian Qualification Framework (www.aqf.edu.au/cert.htm) but in other cases states, responsible for many aspects of vocational training, can issue a Certificate of Competency (www.tafe.sa.edu.au/vet_div/trb/newapprentices/steps.htm).

264. On-the-job training is complemented by formal off-the-job training in most cases but not always. Schofield (2000) reported that in Victoria, the main training provider was in-house for about 10% of apprentices and nearly 30% of trainees. The monitoring of on-the-job training and assessments of apprentices by Registered Training Organisations was found to be ineffective in some areas. However off-the-job training was also found to be generally of low intensity, and demotivating for many participants. There was also a risk that existing workers, employees and training organisations would collude in applying lax standards for Recognition of Prior Learning, so as to justify granting qualifications after reduced hours of training.

265. The description of the Group Training scheme here is based on OECD (1997*e*) and OECD (2000*f*).

266. In May 2000, Minister Kemp announced spending over the next four years of $342 million for New Apprenticeship Centres, $1 500 million for the incentive payments to employers, and $79 million for the New Apprenticeships Access programme.

267. The description of the Adult Migrant Education Program is based on the Department of Immigration and Multicultural Affairs pages (www.immi.gov.au/amep/index.html), which see for further details.

268. Information on indigenous programmes is based partly on the indigenous employment service site (jobsearch.gov.au/indigenous/), fact sheets from the Department of Foreign Affairs and Trade (www.dfat.gov.au/australia/2000/) and DEWRSB (www.dewrsb.gov.au/department/factsheets/), and Issue Briefs and other material from the CAEPR at the Australian National University, which see for further details.

269. ABS (2000e) reports the number of CDEP communities and participants for 1981, 1986, 1991 and each year from 1994, and explains why individual participants are defined as being employed even though they are paid from funds originating as unemployment benefits.

270. CDEP participants have been allowed to earn up to twice the average per participant (APP) rate of the block grant to the CDEP grantee organisation from within the scheme and a similar amount again from part-time work outside the scheme, without losing eligibility. Many individuals have participated for over a decade [Altman (2000); Altman et al. (2000)].

271. CDEP participation is voluntary in the sense that participants can opt out at the end of each quarter. However when a person who has agreed to participate in the project for a given quarter leaves before the end of that quarter, a sanction for voluntary unemployment may be applied (www.facs.gov.au/guide/ssguide/381080.htm)

272. Sanders (2000) remarks that "it would be very difficult to encourage people off the [CDEP] scheme onto social security payments because they are not working" and asks whether there are not "some old and thorny issues about working and not working within the scheme pottering on unchanged?". The 1998 budget measures which promote greater awareness of income support benefits to which CDEP participants would be entitled, as well as flows of information between ATSIC and Centrelink systems concerning individual entitlement to the CDEP participant supplement, have enabled greater mobility of participants from CDEP to income support and have also allowed movement between the two systems to be clearly distinguishable.

273. These estimates are given by Altman et al. (2000), who also report that the median income of CDEP employed in 1994 was $217 per week, only 49% of the $442 per week for mainstream employed indigenous persons. But if the bottom third of the distribution were excluded (in the light of Spicer's estimate that up to a third of CDEP employees do not work), the median for CDEP employees who are working might have been close to that for mainstream employed.

274. CDEP projects are audited regularly and there are also spot checks. The emphasis is on bringing projects up to standards of accountability. Where there are shortfalls, assistance in management is provided and project managers sometimes receive training themselves. ATSIC is developing a training package to help build CDEP project board management competencies. In 1999, six of the 270 CDEP projects were suspended because of accountability issues.

275. The subsections on the early years and the 1980s are mainly drawn from Lindsay (1996).

276. The comment cited, from the Handicapped Programs Review (1985), resembles the evaluation finding that the decentralisation of the public employment service in the Netherlands led to "unequal chances for the same groups in different regions" [OECD (2001b)].

277. The 1992 Disability Discrimination Act recognises the right of people with disabilities to equality before the law and prohibits discrimination on the grounds of disability,

both to the person with a disability and their associates such as family members, carers and friends. It defines disability broadly and covers many areas of life including employment, education, access to premises, administration of Commonwealth laws and programs, and the provision of goods, services and facilities.

278. Under the second CSDA, which expires in June 2002, the total funding for the five years is $10.8 billion This includes extra funding in the order of $510 million for the final two years by both Commonwealth and State governments to address unmet need in the areas of accommodation, respite and day activities.

279. A Disability Wages Supplement was introduced for employees on reduced rates, but conditions appear to have been unattractive compared to those available under the regular Disability Support Pension (subject to a free area and income taper, see Chapter 4) and in 1997 it was abolished.

280. A Mobility Allowance (together with a Rehabilitation Allowance for basic income support, which in 1991 was incorporated into DSP) was introduced in 1983. It is a fixed fortnightly amount for disabled people who are seeking work or in vocational training or employment of at least eight hours per week, and who are unable to use public transport unaided (and have not received separate assistance to purchase a motor vehicle). It was paid to about 35 000 people in the year 2000.

281. The description of rehabilitation services here is taken in part from the Commonwealth Rehabilitation Services website (www.crsrehab.gov.au).

282. For further information on open employment services see the websites of FaCS, ACROD, DICE and the "Workright" network.

283. The information on supported employment service is partly based on Carmody et al. (2000).

284. Low wages in supported employment appear to reflect not only low productivity but also "strong perceptions… among parents and people with disabilities that the payment of DSP and its associated benefits are more advantageous than the receipt of additional wages" [Carmody et al. (2000), p. 22].

285. The vast majority of Business Service employees have been employed for over five years [Carmody et al. (2000), p. 18].

286. Carmody et al. (2000) propose that Business Services should be marketed to people with disabilities as a "quality employer" (Recommendation 43) and "a real and viable employment option" (p. 30). At the moment although supported employment services are heavily subsidised they are quantity constrained, i.e. there is no expectation that a new or expanding operation will be funded to the same level as existing operations. Such a constraint would be lifted in a model where funding follows the client. Average disability levels are higher in supported employment than in open employment: in 1998, 77% had an intellectual disability and 38% had two or more disabilities, compared with 41% and 20%, respectively, for clients receiving open employment services [FaCS (1999b)].

287. DIRG (1999) reported a "relatively high rate of drop out of jobseekers with disabilities who do not follow up referral advice". Participation is voluntary for jobseekers on Disability Support Pension, but the report recommended that Centrelink Disability Officers should provide more assistance with choice of provider and, with agreement of the jobseeker, actually make an appointment with at least one of the services.

288. The Disability Services Standards can be accessed at www.workright.org.au/archive/dstoc.htm.

Bibliography

Web references cited in this bibliography were checked as valid in May 2001.

AARTS, L. and DE JONG, P.R. (1992),
Economic Aspects of Disability Behaviour, North Holland, Amsterdam.

ABBOTT, T. (1999*a*),
"Beyond the Unemployment Pieties", Speech to CEDA, 30 June (www212.pair.com/bdavies/Unemployment%20Pieties.htm).

ABBOTT, T. (1999*b*),
"Intensive Assistance and Training", *Job Network Bulletin*, Issue 23, 9 November (www.jobnetwork.gov.au/bulletin/archive/default.asp).

ABBOTT, T. (2000),
"Mutual Obligation and the Social Fabric", Bert Kelly lecture to the Centre for Independent Studies, August (www212.pair.com/bdavies/Bert%20Kelly%20Lecture.htm).

ABBOTT, T., ANDERSON, J., and KEMP, D. (2000),
"$6.5 Million Funding for Regional Jobs", joint media release (www.dewrsb.gov.au/ministers/mediacentre/default.asp).

ABELLO, D., and EARDLEY, T. (2000),
Is the Job Network Benefiting Disadvantaged Job Seekers?, SPRC Newsletter, No. 77, Social Policy Research Centre, October.

ABS (Australian Bureau of Statistics) (1990),
Award Coverage Australia, Catalogue No. 6315.0.

ABS (1994),
Australian Social Trends 1994, Catalogue No. 4102.0.

ABS (1998*a*),
Australian Social Trends 1998; Income & Expenditure – Income Distribution: Poverty: Different Assumptions, Different Profiles, Canberra (www.abs.gov.au/ausstats/abs@.nsf/Lookup/NT00007CBE).

ABS (1998*b*),
Multiple Jobholding, Catalogue No. 6126.0, Canberra.

ABS (1999*a*),
Job Search Experience of Unemployed Persons, Catalogue No. 6222.0, Canberra.

ABS (1999*b*),
Transition from Education to Work, Catalogue No. 6227.0, Canberra.

ABS (1999*c*),
Year Book Australia, 1999, Number 81, Catalogue No. 1301.0, Canberra.

ABS (2000*a*),
Australian Social Trends 2000, Catalogue No. 4102.0, Canberra.

ABS (2000*b*),
Employment Services Australia, Catalogue No. 8558.0, Canberra.

ABS (2000*c*),
Forms of Employment, Catalogue No. 6359.0, Canberra.

ABS (2000*d*),
Household Income Account, Current Prices, Catalogue No. 5204.0, Canberra.

ABS (2000*e*),
Labour Force Characteristics of Aboriginal and Torres Strait Islander Australians: Experimental Estimates from the Labour Force Survey, ABS Occasional Paper, Catalogue No. 6287.0, Canberra.

ABS (2000*f*),
Labour Mobility, Australia, Catalogue No. 6209.0, Canberra.

ABS (2000*g*),
Population by Age and Sex, Catalogue No. 3201.0, Canberra.

ABS (2000*h*),
The Dynamics of Labour Market State and Benefit Receipt: An Application Using the 1994-1997 Survey of Employment and Unemployment Patterns, Catalogue Nos. 6293.0.00.004, Canberra.

ABS (2000*i*),
Year Book Australia, 2000, Number 82, Catalogue No. 1301.0, Canberra.

ABS (2001*a*),
Employee Earnings and Hours, Australia, Catalogue No. 6306.0, Canberra.

ABS (2001*b*),
Employee Earnings, Benefits and Trade Union Membership, Australia, Catalogue No. 6310.0, Canberra.

ABS (2001*c*),
Industrial Disputes, Australia, Catalogue No. 6321.0, Canberra.

ACCI (Australian Chamber of Commerce and Industry) (2000),
"Legislative Remedies for IR Problems, Making the System Work Better", ACCI Review, No. 68, October.

ACCI/BCA (2000),
"Australia's Private Sector Associations call for Sensible and Balanced Approach to Labour Relations", Media Release, 6 August.

ACOSS (Australian Council of Social Service) (2000*a*),
"Does Work for the Dole Lead to Wages? ACOSS Analysis", ACOSS Info 223 (www.acoss.org.au/media/index2000.htm).

ACOSS (2000*b*),
"Is the Job Network Working? ACOSS Analysis of the First Stage of the Official Evaluation", ACOSS Paper 108, Strawberry Hills, New South Wales, Australia, August (www.acoss.org.au/media/2000/mr000807.htm).

ACOSS (2000*c*),
"Social Security Breaches: Penalising the Most Disadvantaged", ACOSS Info 204 (www.acoss.org.au/media/index2000.htm).

ACTU (Australian Council of Trade Unions) (1997),
  Congress Resolution, ACTU Congress 1997 (www.actu.asn.au).

ACTU (2000),
  Wages, Superannuation and Collective Bargaining, 2000 to 2003 policy, ACTU policy statement (www.actu.asn.au).

AINLEY, J., MALLEY, J. and LAMB, S. (1997),
  "Thematic Review of the Transition from Initial Education to Working Life: Australia Background Report" (www.oecd.org/els/education/tiew/docs.htm).

AIRC (2000),
  Annual Report of the Australian Industrial Relations Commission 1998-99, Melbourne.

ALIGSAKIS, M. (1997),
  "Labour Disputes in Western Europe: Typology and Tendencies", *International Labour Review*, Vol. 136, No. 1, pp. 73-94.

ALP/ACTU (1983),
  Statement of Accord by ALP and ACTU regarding Economic Policy, Melbourne.

ALTMAN, J. (2000),
  "'Mutual Obligation', the CDEP Scheme and Development: Prospects in Remote Australia", draft-only paper for a conference on The Indigenous Welfare Economy and the CDEP Scheme, 7-9 November, Centre for Aboriginal Economic Policy Research, Australian National University (www.anu.edu.au/caepr/iwepapers/Altman.pdf).

ALTMAN, J., GRAY, M, and SANDERS, W. (2000),
  "Indigenous Australians Working for Welfare: What Difference Does it Make?", *Australian Economic Review*, Vol. 33, No. 4, December, pp. 355-62.

ANAO (Australian Audit Office) (1998),
  Management of the Implementation of the New Employment Services Market, Department of Employment, Education, Training and Youth Affairs, Audit Report No. 7, Canberra (www.anao.gov.au).

ANAO (2000)
  Management of Job Network Contracts: Department of Employment Workplace Relations and Small Business, Audit Report No. 44, Canberra, May (www.anao.gov.au).

ANAO (2001),
  Contract Management, Better Practice Guide, Canberra, February (www.anao.gov.au).

ARGYROUS, G. and NEALE, M. (2000),
  "Labour Market Disability: Implications for the Unemployment Rate", paper for the 7th National Conference on Unemployment: Unemployment and Labour Market Policies, University of Western Sydney.

ATKINSON, A., RAINWATER, L., and SMEEDING, T. (1995),
  Income Distribution in OECD Countries: Evidence from the Luxembourg Income Study, Social Policy Studies No. 18, OECD, Paris.

ATSIC (Aboriginal and Torres Strait Islander Commission) (2000),
  1999-2000 Annual Report, Commonwealth of Australia.

BALDOCK, C. (1994),
  "The Family and the Australian Welfare State", *Australian Journal of Social Issues*, Vol. 29, No. 2, pp. 105-17.

BALL, C. (1996),
"Ways That Work: Good Practices in Dealing with Unemployed People", National SkillShare Association Limited, Victoria.

BALL, K. and ROBINSON, C. (1998),
"Young Peoples' Participation in and Outcomes from Vocational Education and Training", in Dusseldorp Skills Forum, *Australia's Youth: Reality and Risk*, Sydney.

BAUME, P. and KAY, K. (1995),
Working Solution. Report of the Strategic Review of the Disability Services Program, AGPS, Canberra (www.workright.org.au/archive/toc00.htm).

BCA (Business Council of Australia) (2000a),
Submission to Senate Employment, Workplace Relations and Small Business and Education Legislation Committee, *Inquiry Into Workplace Relations Amendment Bill*, 2000.

BCA (2000b),
Submission to Senate Employment, Workplace Relations and Small Business and Education Legislation Committee, *Inquiry into Workplace Relations Amendment (Termination of Employment) Bill*, 2000.

BCA (2000c),
Business in the National Interest, Melbourne.

BLMR (Bureau of Labour Market Research) (1984),
Public Sector Job Creation: Interim Report on the Wage Pause Program, Canberra, AGPS.

BORLAND, J. (1999),
"Earnings Inequality in Australia: Changes, Causes and Consequences", *The Economic Record*, Vol. 75, June, pp. 177-202.

BOTSMAN, P. (1995),
"Practical Egalitarians: Australia's Labour Market Institutions, Unions and the Minimum Wage", Evatt Foundation, www.labor.org.au/evatt/mwage.html (December 2000).

BOURK, M. (2000),
"Universal Service? Telecommunications Policy in Australia and People with Disabilities" (www.tomw.net.au/uso).

BRADBURY, B. (1995),
"Added, Subtracted or Just Different: Why do the Wives of Unemployed Men Have Such Low Employment Rates?", *Australian Bulletin of Labour* 21, No. 1, pp. 48-70.

BRAY, M. and WALSH, P. (1998),
"Different Paths to Neo-liberalism? Comparing Australia and New Zealand", *Industrial Relations*, Vol. 37, No. 3, pp. 358-87.

BREDGAARD, T. (2000),
"Temporary Subsidised Employment in the Public and Non-Profit Sector", National Report for the MESANOM Project (www.socsci.auc.dk/~thomas/the_MESANOM_report.pdf)

BROOKS, B. (1994),
"Australia", *International Encyclopedia of Labour Law and Industrial Relations*, Kluwer, Deventer.

BURGESS, J., MITCHELL, W., O'BRIEN, D. and WATTS, M. (1999),
"The Developing Workfare System in Australia and New Zealand", Current Research in Industrial Relations, Vol. 2, paper presented to Air AANZ Conference, Adelaide (www.mngt.waikato.ac.nz/depts/sml/airaanz/conferce/adelaide1999/nonrefabstracts.htm).

CALMFORS, L. and DRIFFILL, J. (1988),
"Bargaining Structure, Corporatism and Macroeconomic Performance", *Economic Policy*, April, pp. 14-61.

CARMODY, M., CLARK, N. and SUMNER, M. (2000),
A Viable Future: Strategic Imperatives for Business Services, report prepared by KPMG Consulting on behalf of the Department of Family and Community Services and ACROD (www.facs.gov.au/internet/facsinternet.nsf/whatsnew/bsrdisab.htm).

CASS, B. (1988),
Income Support for the Unemployed: Towards a More Active System, Social Security Review, Issues Paper No. 4.

CASTLES, F. (1985),
The Working Class and Welfare: Reflections on the Political Development of the Welfare State in Australia and New Zealand, Allen & Unwin, Wellington.

CAZES, S., BOERI, T. and BERTOLA, G. (1999),
Employment Protection and Labour Market Adjustment in OECD Countries: Evolving Institutions and Variable Enforcement, Employment and Training Papers 48, International Labour Office, Geneva.

CCF (Constitutional Centenary Foundation) (1999),
The Australian Constitution (www.centenary.org.au/about_constitution.html).

CENTRELINK (2000),
Annual Report 1999-2000, Commonwealth of Australia, Canberra.

CHAPMAN, A. (2000),
"Industrial Legislation in 1999", *Journal of Industrial Relations*, Vol. 42, No. 1, March, pp. 29-40.

CHATRIK, B., CONVERY, P. and PROSSER, J. (1999),
Unemployment and Training Rights Handbook, Unemployment Unit & Youthaid, Bristol.

COLEBATCH, T. and SALTAU, C. (1999),
"Push to Make More Jobless Work for the Dole", *The Age*, 18 December.

COMMONWEALTH OF AUSTRALIA (1994),
Working Nation: Policies and Programs, Canberra, May.

CONNOLLY, G. (1999),
"The Relationship between the ABS Estimate of Unemployment and the Number of Unemployment Allowees", a paper presented to the 28th Conference of Economists, La Trobe University, Melbourne, 27-29 September.

CREIGHTON, B. (1990),
"Freedom of Association", in Blanpain, R. (ed.), *Comparative Labour Law and Industrial Relations in Industrialised Market Economies*, Vol. 2, Chapter 17, pp. 19-44.

CROWLEY, S. (2000),
"Government Policy, What have Literacy Learners to Say? The Impact of May Day 1998", Proceedings of the Australian Council for Adult Literacy's Year 2000 Lens on Literacy Conference, Perth, 21-23 September (www.cleo.murdoch.edu.au/confs/acal/acal.html).

CULLY, M. (1999),
"The Booming Australian Labour Market: State Variations", *The Australian Bulletin of Labour*, Vol. 25, No. 3, September.

329

CURTAIN, R. (1992),
"Emergence of Workplace Bargaining within a Centralised Wage System: The New Industrial Relations in Australia", in OECD, *New Directions in Work Organisation. The Industrial Relations Response*, Paris.

CURTAIN, R. (2000),
Mutual Obligation: Policy and Practice in Australia Compared with the UK, paper prepared for the Dusseldorp Skills Forum (www.dsf.org.au/papers/ol/MutualObligation/Mutual Obligation.html).

DABSCHECK, B. (1995),
The Struggle for Australian Industrial Relations, Oxford University Press, Sydney.

DANIELS, D. (1999),
Social Security Payments for the Aged, those with Disabilities and Carers 1909 to 1998, Parliamentary Library Research Paper 11, 1998/99 (www.aph.gov.au/library/pubs/rp/1998-99/99rp11.htm).

DAVIES, R., ELIAS, P. and PENN, R. (1992),
"The Relationship between a Husband's Unemployment and his Wife's Participation in the Labour Force", *Oxford Bulletin of Economics and Statistics*, No. 54, pp. 145-71.

DAVIS, E.M. and LANSBURY, R.D. (1998),
"Employment Relations in Australia", in Bamber, G. and Lansbury, R. (eds.), *International and Comparative Employment Relations*, Sage Publications, London.

DEETYA (Department of Employment, Education, Training and Youth Affairs) (1996),
Working Nation: Evaluation of the Employment, Education and Training Elements, Evaluation and Monitoring Branch, EMB Report 2/96, Canberra, July.

DEETYA (1998a),
Job Seeker Classification Instrument (JSCI), Canberra, April.

DEETYA (1998b),
"The Early Identification of Jobseekers who are at Greatest Risk of Long-Term Unemployment in Australia", in Fay, R. (ed.), *Early Identification of Jobseekers at Risk of Long-Term Unemployment: the Role of Profiling*, OECD Proceedings, OECD, Paris.

DETE (Department of Education, Training and Employment of South Australia) (1999),
"Employing a New Apprentice in South Australia" (www.tafe.sa.edu.au/vet_div/trb/newapprentices/).

DEWRSB (Department of Employment, Workplace Relations and Small Business) (1997),
Changes in Federal Workplace Relations Law – Legislation guide, Canberra, mimeo.

DEWRSB (1998),
More Jobs, Better Pay, Canberra.

DEWRSB (1999a),
Award and Agreement Coverage Survey 1999, A Summary of the Main Findings, Canberra.

DEWRSB (1999b),
Evaluation of the Work for the Dole Pilot Programme, Evaluation and Monitoring Branch (www.dewrsb.gov.au/employment/publications/workForDoleEvaluation/wfd.pdf).

DEWRSB (1999c),
General Information and Service Requirements for the Employment Services Request for Tender 1999, Canberra, June (www.jobnetwork.gov.au/tenders/jn/jn/rftcservice require99.pdf).

DEWRSB (1999d),
Job Network Bulletin Issue 25, 22 December (www.jobnetwork.gov.au/bulletin/archive/default.asp).

DEWRSB (1999e),
"Job Network Member Performance Information as at 31 October 1999" (www.jobnetwork.gov.au/bulletin/archive/default.asp).

DEWRSB (1999f),
The Members Information Guide, Section 11, Intensive Assistance, Canberra, May.

DEWRSB (2000a),
Agreement Making in Australia under the Workplace Relations Act, 1998 and 1999, Canberra.

DEWRSB (2000b),
Annual Report 1999-2000, Canberra (www.dewrsb.gov.au/department/keycorporate documents/annualreport/9900/default.asp).

DEWRSB (2000c),
Job Network Bulletin Issue 29, 20 April (www.jobnetwork.gov.au/bulletin/archive/default.asp).

DEWRSB (2000d),
Job Network Evaluation. Stage One: Implementation and Market Development, Evaluation and Program Performance Branch Report 1/2000, Commonwealth of Australia, Canberra, February (www.dewrsb.gov.au/employment/publications/JobNetworkEval/stage1/default.asp).

DEWRSB (2000e),
Job Network Evaluation: Key Findings from the 1999 Employer Survey, Canberra, July.

DEWRSB (2000f),
Labour Market Assistance Outcomes, Canberra, various issues.

DEWRSB (2000g),
Labour Market Policies in Australia, DEWRSB submission to OECD questionnaire, Canberra, December.

DEWRSB (2000h),
Labour Market Review of Australia: Background Paper for the OECD Review Team, Canberra, August.

DEWRSB (2000i),
Performance of the Job Seeker Classification Instrument, www.jobnetwork.gov.au/general/services/jsci.htm (December 2000).

DEWRSB (2000j),
Safety Net Review – Wages 1999-2000, Joint Governments' Submissions, Canberra.

DEWRSB (2000k),
Sponsor Booklet (on the official Work for the Dole website: www.dewrsb.gov.au/wfd/default.asp).

DEWRSB (2000l),
Work for the Dole: a Net Impact Study, Evaluation and Program Performance Branch (www.dewrsb.gov.au/employment/publications/workForDoleEvaluation/netImpact/default.asp).

DEWRSB (2001a),
Job Network: a Net Impact Study, Evaluation and Program Performance Branch, Report 1/2001, Commonwealth of Australia, April (www.dewrsb.gov.au/employment/publications/JobNetworkEval/Net_Impact/default.asp).

331

DEWRSB (2001*b*),
>   *Job Network Evaluation. Stage Two: Progress Report*, Evaluation and Program Performance Branch Report 2/2001, Commonwealth of Australia, Canberra, February (www.dewrsb.gov.au/employment/publications/JobNetworkEval/Stage2/JN2report.asp).

DEWRSB (2001*c*),
>   *Job Network Member Performance Ratings as at* 31 January 2001 (www.jobnetwork.gov.au/reports/performance/pr01/JNMratings.doc).

DEWRSB (2001*d*),
>   "The Future Purchasing of Job Network Service", Discussion Paper (www.jobnetwork.gov.au/tenders/jn3/discussionc3.doc).

DEX, S., GUSTAFSSON, S., SMITH, N. and CALLAN, T. (1995),
>   "Cross-National Comparisons of the Labour Force Participation of Women Married to Unemployed Men", *Oxford Economic Papers*, No. 47, pp. 611-35.

DIRG (Disability Industry Reference Group) (1999),
>   *Report of the Disability Industry Reference Group* (www.facs.gov.au/disability/ood/publis.htm).

DOCKERY, M. and STROMBACK, T. (2000*a*),
>   "Devolving Public Employment Services: the Australian Experiment", paper presented at the PhD Conference in Economics and Business, Australian National University, 15-17 November, Canberra.

DOCKERY, M. and STROMBACK, T. (2000*b*),
>   "Evaluation of Labour Market Programs: an Assessment", paper prepared for the 29th Annual Conference of Economics, Gold Coast, 3-6 July 2000.

EARDLEY, T., ABELLO, D. and MACDONALD, H. (2001),
>   "Is the Job Network Benefiting Disadvantaged Jobseekers? Preliminary Evidence from a Study of Non-profit Employment Services", Social Policy Research Centre, Discussion Paper, No. 111, Sydney, January (www.sprc.unsw.edu.au).

EARDLEY, T., SAUNDERS, P. and EVANS, C. (2000),
>   "Community Attitudes towards Unemployment, Activity Testing and Mutual Obligation", Social Policy Research Centre Discussion Paper No. 107 (www.sprc.unsw.edu.au/dp/index.htm).

EARDLEY, T., BRADSHAW, J, DITCH, J, GOUGH, I. and WHITEFORD, P. (1996*a*),
>   *Social Assistance in OECD Countries: Synthesis Report*, Department of Social Security Research, Report No. 46, HMSO, London.

EARDLEY, T., BRADSHAW, J., DITCH, J., GOUGH, I. and WHITEFORD, P. (1996*b*),
>   *Social Assistance in OECD Countries: Country Reports*, Department of Social Security Research, Report No. 47, HMSO, London.

EBBINGHAUS, B. and VISSER, J. (2000),
>   *Trade Unions in Western Europe since* 1945, Macmillan, London.

ELMESKOV, J., MARTIN, J.P. and SCARPETTA, S. (1998)
>   "Key Lessons for Labour Market Reforms: Evidence from OECD Countries' Experiences", *Swedish Economic Policy Review*, pp. 205-52.

ESC (Select Committee on Education and Employment) (1999),
>   *Active Labour Market Policies and their Delivery: Lessons from Australia*, Session 1998-99 First Report (www.publications.parliament.uk/pa/cm199899/cmselect/cmeduemp/cmeduemp.htm).

ETUI (European Trade Union Institute) (1990),
>   *The Role of Economic and Social Councils in Western Europe*, Brussels.

EWRSBE (Senate Employment, Workplace Relations, Small Business and Education Reference Committee) (2000),
Aspiring to Excellence: Report into the Quality of Vocational Education and Training in Australia (www.aph.gov.au/senate/committee/eet_ctte/).

FaCS (Department of Family and Community Services) (1999a),
Annual Report 1998-1999, Canberra (www.facs.gov.au).

FaCS (1999b),
Disability Services Census 1998.

FaCS (1999c),
"Unemployed People on Newstart Allowance or Youth Allowance", Fact Sheet 2 on The Future of Welfare in the 21st Century (www.facs.gov.au/internet/facsinternet.nsf/whatsnew).

FaCS (2000a),
Annual Report 1999-2000, Canberra (www.facs.gov.au).

FaCS (2000b),
"Government Response" (www.facs.gov.au – Welfare Reform, Government Response to Final Report).

FAY, R. (1997),
Making the Public Employment Service More Effective through the Introduction of Market Signals, Labour Market and Social Policy Occasional Papers, No. 25, OECD, Paris.

FINN, D. (1997),
Working Nation: Welfare Reform and the Australian Job Compact for the Long term Unemployed, Australian Council of Social Service, NSW, Darlinghurst and Unemployment Unit, London.

FINN, D. and BLACKMORE, M. (2001),
"Activation: The Point of View of Clients and 'Front line' Staff", in OECD (2001b), pp. 293-307.

FINN, D, BLACKMORE, M. and NIMMO, M (1998),
Welfare-to-Work and the Long-term Unemployed: They're Very Cynical, Unemployment Unit & Youthaid, London.

FÖRSTER, M., assisted by PELLIZZARI, M. (2000),
"Trends and Driving Factors in Income Distribution and Poverty in the OECD Area", Labour Market and Social Policy Occasional Papers, No. 42, OECD, Paris.

FREELAND, J. (1998),
"Employment and Training Policy and Programs: Past, Present and Future", Working 2001 Employment Futures Conference (www.training.wa.gov.au/w2001/employ.htm).

FREELAND, J. (1999),
"Young People: Mutual Obligation of Active Citizenship?", ACAL Occasional Paper (www.acal.edu.au/pubs.html).

GOLIGHTLY, M., THURLEY, A., KELSHIKER, M. and CLARKE, B. (1996),
Implementation of Competition in Case Management, The Auditor-General Performance Audit, Audit Report No. 30, 1995-96, Australian National Audit Office.

GOODGER, K. and LAROSE, P. (1998),
"Changing Expectations: Sole Parents and Employment in New Zealand", paper for the 6th Australian Institution of Family Studies Conference (www.aifs.org.au).

333

GREENWOOD, J. and VOYER, J-P. (2000),
"Experimental Evidence on the Use of Earnings Supplements as a Strategy to 'Make Work Pay'", OECD *Economic Studies*, No. 31, Paris, pp. 43-68.

GREY, K., BESWICK, W., and O'BRIEN, C. (1999),
Traineeship Non-Completion, Research and Evaluation Branch Report 1/99, Department of Education, Training and Youth Affairs, Canberra.

GRIMES, D. (1992),
Meares Oration, *Australian Disability Review*, Macquarie University, NSW, pp. 1-15.

GRUBB, D. (2001),
"Eligibility Criteria for Unemployment Benefits", in OECD (2001*b*), pp. 187-216.

HAMPSON, I. and MORGAN, D.E. (1998),
"Continuity and Change in Australian Industrial Relations", *Relations Industrielles*, Vol. 53, No. 3, pp. 564-89.

HANDICAPPED PROGRAMS REVIEW (1985),
New Directions: Report of the Handicapped Programs Review, AGPS, Canberra.

HANNAN, E. (2000),
"Revealed: Plan to Fund 27,000 New Jobs", *The Age*, 17 April.

HARDING, D. (1998),
"What Incentives Does Job Network Create?", *Mercer-Melbourne Quarterly Bulletin of Economic Trends*, No. 4.

HEINRICHS, P. (2000),
"How the Homeless are Punished: the Welfare Trap", *The Age*, 9 December (www.theage.com.au/news/2000/12/09/FFXPMGS5IGC.html)

HONEYBONE, A. (1997),
"Introducing Labour Flexibility: The Example of New Zealand", *International Labour Review*, Vol. 136, No. 4.

HORIN, A. (1999),
"The Burden of Disability", *Sydney Morning Herald*, 14 December.

HUGO, G. (2001),
"International Migration and the Labour Market in Australia", in *International Migration in Asia: Trends and Policies*, OECD Proceedings, OECD, Paris.

ILO (International Labour Office) (1998*a*),
Report of the Committee of Experts on the Application of Conventions and Recommendations, Geneva.

ILO (1998*b*),
World Labour Report 1997-98, Geneva.

ILO (2000),
Report of the Committee of Experts on the Application of Conventions and Recommendations, Geneva.

ISAAC, J.E. (1994),
"Australia", in Trebilcock, A. *et al.* (eds.), *Towards Social Dialogue: Tripartite Co-operation in National Economic and Social Policy-making*, International Labour Office, Geneva, pp. 67-100.

JOBS AUSTRALIA (1999),
"Jobs Australia Submission", Submission to the Reference Group on Welfare Reform (www.facs.gov.au – Welfare reform, Background information, Public submissions, Submission No. 332).

KATZ, H. (1993),
"Decentralisation of Collective Bargaining: A Literature Review and Comparative Analysis", *Industrial and Labour Relations Review*, Vol. 47, No. 1, pp. 3-22.

KELLY, R., LEWIS, P., MULVEY, C., NORRIS, K., DOCKERY, M. (1999),
"The Job Network: Is It Working?", CEDA Information Paper No. 64, CEDA and Centre for Labour Market Research (www.murdoch.edu.au/bitl/clmr/wp/jnreport.pdf)

KELLOCK, P. in association with BRUCE, C. (2000),
"A Window into the Future: Lessons from the Jobs Pathway Programme". A Report to the Dusseldorp Skills Forum (www.dsf.org.au/papers/dl/jpp0800/jpp3-case_studies.pdf).

KEMP, D. (1999a),
"Government Tightens Literacy Requirement for Unemployed", media release 28 January (www.detya.gov.au/ministers/Kempm+s.htm).

KEMP, D. (1999b),
"Government Tightens Eligibility Criteria for Re-Skilling Existing Worker Incentive Payments", media release 21 May (www.detya.gov.au/ministers/Kempm+s.htm).

KEMP, D. (2000a),
"Questions and Answers: Mutual Obligation", Minister Archive Media Release (www.detya.gov.au/archive/ministers/kemp/kqa_mo.htm).

KEMP, D. (2000b),
"Record Numbers Put at Risk by Labor States", media release 28 June (www.detya.gov.au/ministers/Kempm+s.htm).

LAFFONT, J.-J. and TIROLE, J. (1993),
A *Theory of Incentives in Procurement and Regulation*, MIT Press, Cambridge.

LAMB, S., DWYER, P., and WYN, J. (2000),
Non-completion of School in Australia: The Changing Patterns of Participation and Outcomes, LSAY Research Report Number 16, Australian Council for Educational Research, Camberwell, Victoria, October.

LANDT, J. and PECH, J. (2000),
"Work and Welfare in Australia: the Changing Role of Income Support", paper for the 7th Australian Institute of Family Studies Conference, Sydney, July (www.aifs.org.au).

LINDSAY, M. (1996),
"Commonwealth Disability Policy 1983-1995", Parliamentary Library Background Paper No. 6 (also listed as Paper 2), 1995/96 (www.aph.gov.au/library/pubs/bp/1995-96/96bp06.htm).

LIST, D. (1996),
Working Agreements, National Skillshare Association, Carlton South.

LOUNDES, J. (2000),
"Management and Industrial Relations Practices and Outcomes in Australian Workplaces", Melbourne Institute, Working Paper No. 12/2000, University of Melbourne.

MACDERMOTT, T. (1997),
"Industrial Legislation in 1996: The Reform Agenda", *Journal of Industrial Relations*, Vol. 39, No. 1, pp. 52-76.

MACDONALD, H. in association with JOPE, S. (2000),
"Getting Back on Your Feet: an Evaluation of the Community Support Program", Fitzroy, Victoria, Brotherhood of St. Lawrence.

MADIGAN, N. (1999),
"Social Security Reform in the Netherlands and the Dutch Miracle: an Overview", *Australian Social Policy*, No. 2, pp. 53-74.

MÆRKEDAHL, I. (2001),
"The Active Labour Market Policy in Denmark", in OECD (2001*b*), pp. 263-74.

McINTYRE, S. and MITCHELL, R. (eds.) (1989),
Foundations of Arbitration, Oxford University Press, Melbourne.

McKENNA, R. (2000),
"Adult Literacy and Numeracy Provision: the Facts", Impact magazine, Australian Council of Social Service's online library (www.acoss.net.au/pubs/allpubs/11457.html).

McMILLAN, J. (1992),
Games, Strategies and Managers, Oxford University Press.

MILLER, P. (1997),
"The Burden of Unemployment on Family Units: an Overview", *Australian Economic Review*, Vol. 30, No. 1, pp. 15-30.

MITCHELL, R. and SCHERER, P. (1993),
"Australia: the Search for Fair Employment Contracts through Tribunals", in Hartog, J. and Theeuwes, J. (eds.), *Labour Market Contracts and Institutions. A Cross-national Comparison*, North Holland, Amsterdam.

MOREHEAD, A. *et al.* (1997),
Changes at Work. The 1995 Australian Workplace Industrial Relations Survey, Longman, Melbourne.

MORRIS, A. and WILSON, K. (1999),
"Strikes and the Accord: The Final Word?", *Australian Bulletin of Labour*, Vol. 25, No. 1, March.

MOSES, J. and SHARPLES, I. (2000),
"Breaching – History, Trends and Issues", paper for the 7th National Conference on Unemployment: Unemployment and Labour Market Policies, Employment Strategies Section, Department of Family and Community Services, mimeo.

MURTOUGH, G., and WAITE, M. (2000*a*),
The Diversity of Casual Contract Employment, Staff Research Paper, Productivity Commission, Canberra.

MURTOUGH, G. and WAITE, M. (2000*b*),
The Growth of Non-traditional Employment: Are Jobs Becoming More Precarious, Staff Research Paper, Productivity Commission, Canberra.

NCVER (2000*a*),
Apprentices and Trainees in Australia 1985 to 1999, Leabrook, South Australia, NCVER (www.ncver.edu.au/statistics/aats/series8599/).

NCVER (2000*b*),
Australian Apprentice and Trainee Statistics, October-December Quarter.

NCVER (2001),
Australian Apprenticeships: Facts, Fiction and Future, Leabrook, South Australia, NCVER (www.ncver.edu.au/apprentices.htm).

NEWMAN, J. (1999),
   The Challenge of Welfare Dependency in the 21st Century (www.facs.gov.au – Welfare reform, Background information, Government's discussion paper).

NILAND, J. (1978),
   Collective Bargaining and Compulsory Arbitration in Australia, New South Wales University Press, Kensington.

NORRIS, K. and MCLEAN, B. (1999),
   "Changes in Earnings Inequality 1975 to 1998", Australian Bulletin of Labour, Vol. 25, No. 1, March.

O'BRIEN, M. (2000),
   "Older Workers and Government Policy in Australia", paper for the 7th National Conference on Unemployment: Unemployment and Labour Market Policies, University of Western Sydney.

O'DONNELL, A. (2000),
   "The Public Employment Service in Australia: Regulating Work or Regulating Welfare?", Centre for Employment and Labour Relations Law and Centre for Public Policy, University of Melbourne, mimeo.

OECD (1988),
   Structural Adjustment and Economic Performance, Chapter 3: "The Labour Market and Industrial Relations", Paris.

OECD (1991),
   Employment Outlook, Chapter 4: "Trends in Trade Union Membership", Paris.

OECD (1993),
   The Labour Market in the Netherlands, Paris.

OECD (1994a)
   Employment Outlook, Paris.

OECD (1994b),
   The OECD Jobs Study, Evidence and Explanations, Part II, Paris.

OECD (1994c),
   The OECD Jobs Study: Facts, Analysis, Strategies, Paris (www.oecd.org/sge/min/job94/tabcont.htm).

OECD (1995a),
   Economic Surveys: Australia, Paris.

OECD (1995b),
   Employment Outlook, Paris.

OECD (1996),
   Enhancing the Effectiveness of Labour Market Policies, Paris.

OECD (1997a),
   Economic Surveys, Australia, Paris.

OECD (1997b),
   Economic Surveys, New Zealand, Paris.

OECD (1997c),
   Employment Outlook, Paris.

337

OECD (1997d),
Enhancing the Effectiveness of Active Labour Market Policies: A Streamlined Public Employment Service, OECD General Distribution Document [OCDE/GD(97)61], Paris.

OECD (1997e),
"Thematic Review of the Transition from Initial Education to Working Life: Australia Country Note" (www.oecd.org/els/education/tiew/docs.htm).

OECD (1997f),
The OECD Jobs Strategy, Making Work Pay, Paris.

OECD (1998a),
Economic Surveys, Australia, Paris.

OECD (1998b),
Employment Outlook, Paris.

OECD (1998c),
Income Distribution and Poverty in Selected OECD Countries, Economics Department Working Paper No. 189, Paris.

OECD (1998d),
The Battle Against Exclusion: Social Assistance in Australia, Finland, Sweden and the United Kingdom, Paris.

OECD (1998e),
The Battle Against Exclusion: Social Assistance in Belgium, the Czech Republic, the Netherlands and Norway, Paris.

OECD (1998f),
The Public Employment Service: Greece, Ireland, Portugal, Paris.

OECD (1999a),
A Caring World: The New Social Policy Agenda, Paris.

OECD (1999b),
Benefit Systems and Work Incentives, Paris.

OECD (1999c),
Economic Surveys, Australia, Paris.

OECD (1999d),
Employment Outlook, Paris.

OECD (1999e),
The Public Employment Service in the United States, Paris.

OECD (2000a),
Economic Outlook, No. 68, Paris, December.

OECD (2000b),
Economic Surveys: Australia, Paris.

OECD (2000c),
Economic Surveys, New Zealand, Paris.

OECD (2000d),
Education at a Glance, Paris.

OECD (2000e),
Employment Outlook, Paris.

OECD (2000f),
From Initial Education to Working Life: Making Transitions Work, Paris.

OECD (2000g),
OECD in Figures, Paris.

OECD (2000h),
Pushing Ahead with Reform in Korea, Paris.

OECD (2001a),
Education Policy Analysis: 2001, Paris.

OECD (2001b),
Labour Market Policies and the Public Employment Service, Paris.

OECD and Statistics Canada (1995),
Literacy, Economy and Society, Paris and Ottawa.

O'LOUGHLIN, T. (2000),
"Centrelink Ultimatum to Jobless: Try Harder or We Cut Your Dole", Sydney Morning Herald, 27 January.

O'NEILL, S. and SHEPHERD, B. (2000),
The Role of Safety Net Awards, Resource Guides, Parliamentary Library, Parliament of Australia (www.aph.gov.au/library/intguide/econ/safetybody.htm).

PEETZ, D. (1998),
Unions in a Contrary World, Cambridge University Press, Cambridge.

PRODUCTIVITY COMMISSION (1999),
Microeconomic Reforms and Australian Productivity: Exploring the Links, Commission Research Paper, Melbourne.

QUIGGIN, J. (1993),
Socially Useful Employment, Centre for Economic Policy Research, Australian National University, Canberra, November (www.ecocomm.anu.edu.au/quiggin/Submissions/ASSA93.html).

RAHMANI, Z. (2000),
"Literacy and Numeracy Training for the Unemployed", Proceedings of the Australian Council for Adult Literacy's Year 2000 Lens on Literacy Conference, Perth, 21-23 September (www.cleo.murdoch.edu.au/confs/acal/acal.html).

RÄISÄNEN, H. (2001),
"Implementation Issues in Finland: Experiences, Developments and Context of Labour Market Policy Measures", in OECD (2001b), pp. 337-62.

RAPER, M. (1999),
"Work, Wages, Welfare: Where is Australia Heading?", Address to the ACROD Employment Forum, 19 July (www.acrod.org.au/employment/keynote.htm).

RAY, D., BESWICK, W., LAWSON, C., O'BRIEN, C., AND MADIGAN, S. (2000),
Attrition in Apprenticeships: An Analysis of Apprentices Commencing Between July 1994 and June 1996, Research and Evaluation Branch Report 1/00, Department of Education, Training and Youth Affairs, Canberra.

REDMOND, G. (1999),
"Tax-Benefit Polices and Parents' Incentives to Work: the Case of Australia 1980-1997", Social Policy Research Centre, Discussion Paper No. 104 (www.sprc.unsw.edu.au/dp/index.htm).

REITH, P. (1999),
The Continuing Reform of Workplace Relations: Implementation of More Jobs, Better Pay, Ministerial Discussion Paper, DEWRSB, May.

RGWR (Reference Group on Welfare Reform) (2000a),
Interim Report of the Reference Group on Welfare Reform: Technical and Other Appendices (www.facs.gov.au – Welfare Reform, Interim Report Technical Appendices).

RGWR (2000b),
Participation Support for a More Equitable Society: Final Report of the Reference Group on Welfare Reform, Canberra, July (www.facs.gov.au – Welfare Reform, Final Report).

RICHARDSON, L. (2000),
"Impact of the Mutual Obligation Initiative on the Exit Behaviour of Unemployment Benefit Recipients: The Threat of Additional Activities", paper for the 7th National Conference on Unemployment: Unemployment and Labour Market Policies, University of Western Sydney.

RIGGS, L. (2001),
"Introduction of Contestability in the Delivery of Employment Services in Australia" in OECD (2001b), pp. 363-92.

ROWLANDS, D. (2000),
"Purchaser-Provide in Social Policy: How Can We Evaluate the Centrelink Arrangements?", Australian Social Policy 2000/1.

ROY MORGAN RESEARCH (2000),
"Community Attitudes towards the Unemployed of Workforce Age", report to the Department of Family and Community Services (www.facs.gov.au/internet/facs internet.nsf).

SANDERS, W. (1997),
"How Does (and Should) DSS Treat CDEP Participants? (What are these Allegations of Racial Discrimination?)", Centre for Aboriginal Economic Policy Research Discussion Paper No. 149/1997, Australian National University (www.anu.edu.au/caepr/1997/1997.html).

SANDERS, W. (2000),
"Adjusting Balances: Reshaping the CDEP Scheme after Twenty Good Years", paper for a conference on The Indigenous Welfare Economy and the CDEP Scheme, 7-9 November, Centre for Aboriginal Economic Policy Research, Australian National University (www.anu.edu.au/caepr/iwepapers/Sanders.pdf).

SCHOFIELD, K. (2000),
Delivering Quality: Report of the Independent Review of the Quality of Victoria's Apprenticeship and Traineeship System, Melbourne, Victoria, Office of Post Compulsory Education Training and Employment (www.otfe.vic.gov.au/publi/qualityreview/).

SIHTO, M. and MYSKYLÄ, M. (2000),
"Erilaisia työttömiä erilaisissa tilastoissa" (different kinds of unemployed people in different kinds of statistics), Finnish Economic Journal, Vol. 96, No. 4, pp. 539-51.

SLOAN, J. (1993),
"Some Policy Responses to Long-Term Unemployment", Australian Economic Review, No. 102.

SPICER, I. (1997),
"Independent Review of the Community Development Employment Projects (CDEP) Scheme" (www.atsic.gov.au/programs/noticeboard/CDEP/Spicer_Report/contents.asp).

STRAUSS, G. (1988),
"Australian Labour Relations through American Eyes", *Industrial Relations*, Vol. 27, No. 2, pp. 213-35.

STROMBACK, M. and DOCKERY, A. (2000),
"Labour Market Programs, Unemployment and Employment Hazards: an Application Using the 1994-1997 Survey of Employment and Unemployment Patterns", ABS *Occasional Paper*, Catalogue No.6293.0.00.002, Australian Bureau of Statistics, Canberra.

SUSHAMES, L. and GOODWILL, C. (2000),
"LANT in Focus: an Experimental Report on the Context and Delivery of the Literacy and Numeracy Training Program for Centrelink Clients", Proceedings of the Australian Council for Adult Literacy's Year 2000 Lens on Literacy Conference, Perth, 21-23 September (cleo.murdoch.edu.au/confs/acal/acal.html).

TAYLOR, J. and HUNTER, B. (1998),
The Job Still Ahead: Economics Costs of Continuing Indigenous Employment Disparity, ATSIC Office of Public Affairs (www.atsic.gov.au/issues/employment/contents.htm).

THATCHER, C. (2000),
"Towards a Unitary National Workplace Relations System", Business Council of Australia, *The Workplace*, Vol. 2, No. 1, April.

TREBILCOCK, A. *et. al.* (1994),
Towards Social Dialogue: Tripartite Cooperation in National Economic and Social Policy-Making, ILO, Geneva.

VAN BASTELAER, A., LEMAÎTRE, G., and MARIANNA, P. (1997),
"The Definition of Part-time Work for the Purpose of International Comparisons", *Labour Market and Social Policy Occasional Papers*, No. 22, OECD, Paris.

VANSTONE, A. (1996a),
"Plans for Labour Market Program Funding", media release, 28 June (www.detya.gov.au/archive/ministers/vanstone/vm28_6.htm).

VANSTONE, A. (1996b),
Reforming Employment Assistance: Helping Australians into Real Jobs, Ministerial Statement by the Minister for Employment, Education, Training and Youth Affairs, Canberra.

VROMAN, W. (2000),
"Unemployment Insurance and Unemployment Assistance: a Comparison", report prepared for presentation at a World Bank seminar on Income Support Programs for the Unemployed, 13 June (www.urban.org/employment/ui_and_ ua.html).

WARBURTON, M., MARTIN, P., READ, A. and VUONG, L. (1999),
"Incapacity among Unemployed Customers: a Statistical Analysis", *Australian Social Policy*, No. 2, pp. 75-90.

WARBURTON, M., OPOKU, A. and VUONG, L. (1999),
"Long-term Unemployment: a Statistical Analysis of FaCS Customers", *Australian Social Policy*, No. 2, pp. 33-52.

WARBURTON, M., VUONG, L. and EVERT, H. (1999),
"An Evaluation of the Working Nation Income Test Changes for Unemployed People", Labour Market Analysis Section, Department of Family and Community Services, July, mimeo.

WARING, P. and de RUYTER, A. (1999),
"Dismissing the Unfair Dismissal Myth", *Australian Bulletin of Labour*, Vol. 25, No. 3, September.

WDI (World Development Indicators) (2000),
CD-ROM, World Bank, Washington, D.C.

WEBSTER, E. and HARDING, G. (2000),
"Outsourcing Public Employment Services: The Australian Experience", *Melbourne Institute Working Papers*, March.

WHITEFORD, P. (1998),
"Is Australia Particularly Unequal? Traditional and New Views", in Smyth, P. and Cass, B. (eds.), *Contesting the Australian Way: States Markets and Civil Society*, Cambridge University Press, New York.

WHITEFORD, P. (2000),
The Australian System of Social Protection – an Overview, Department of Family and Community Services Policy, Research Paper, No. 1 (www.facs.gov.au – Publications, Policy Research Paper Series).

WOODEN, M. (2000),
The Transformation of Australian Industrial Relations, Federation Press, Sydney.

WOODEN, M. and HARDING, D. (1998),
"Recruitment Practices in the Private Sector: Results from a National Survey of Employers", *Asia-Pacific Journal of Human Resources*, Vol. 36, No. 3, pp. 73ff.

WRIGHT, T (1999),
"PM Tells Jobless to Study", *The Age*, 29 January (www.theage.com.au/daily/990129/news).

YEEND, P. (2000),
"Mutual Obligation/Work for the Dole", Parliamentary Library e-brief (www.aph.gov.au/library/intguide/hotissues.htm).

Glossary

ABS   Australian Bureau of Statistics
ACC   Area Consultative Committee
ACCI   Australian Chamber of Commerce and Industry
ACOSS   Australian Council of Social Service
ACROD   Australian Council for Rehabilitation of the Disabled
ACT   Australian Capital Territory
ACTU   Australian Council of Trade
AEMP   Advanced English for Migrants Program
AIRC   Australian Industrial Relations Commission
AJS   Australian Job Search
ALFS   Australian Labour Force Survey
ALMP   Active Labour Market Policies
AMEP   Adult Migrant English Program
ANAO   Australian National Audit Office
APP   Average per Participant
APW   Average Production Worker
ASTF   Australian Student Traineeship Foundation
ATSIC   Aboriginal and Torres Strait Islander Commission
AWAs   Australian Workplace Agreements
AWIRS   Australian Workplace Industrial Relations Survey
BCA   Business Council of Australia
BLMR   Bureau of Labour Market Research
BPA   Business Partnership Arrangements
CAs   Certified Agreements
CAI   Confederation of Australian Industry
CCMs   Contracted Case Managers
CDEP   Community Development Employment Projects
CEACR   Committee of Experts on the Application of Conventions and Recommendations
CES   Commonwealth Employment Service
CETP   Competitive Employment, Training and Placement
CFA   Committee on Freedom of Association
CPS   CDEP Participant Supplement
CRS   Commonwealth Rehabilitation Service
CSP   Community Support Program
CWCs   Community Work Coordinators
DARES   Direction de l'animation de la recherche, des études et des statistiques
DEAP   Disability Employment Assistance Program
DEETYA   Department of Employment, Education, Training and Youth Affairs
DETYA   Department of Education, Training and Youth Affairs

343

DEWRSB	Department of Employment, Workplace Relations and Small Business
DIRG	Disability Industry Reference Group
DOI	Declaration of Intent
DPI	Disability Pre-Employment Instrument
DRP	Disability Reform Package (1991)
DSA	Disability Services Act
DSP	Disability Support Pension
DSS	Department of Social Security
EAA	Employment Assistance Australia
ECCs	Employer Contact Certificates
ECEF	Enterprise and Career Education Foundation
EPL	Employment Protection Legislation
ERA	Employment Relations Act (New Zealand)
ESRA	Employment Services Regulatory Authority
FaCS	Department of Family and Community Services
GDP	Gross Domestic Project
IA	Intensive Assistance
IALS	International Adult Literacy Survey
IASP	Intensive Assistance Support Plan
IES	Integrated Employment System
ILO	International Labour Office
JET	Jobs, Education and Training
JM	Job Matching
JN	Job Network
JPET	Job Placement, Employment and Training
JPP	Jobs Pathway Program
JSCI	Job Seeker Classification Instrument
JSD	Jobseeker Diary
JSI	Jobseeker Screening Instrument
JST	Job Search Training
KPI	Key Performance Indicators
LANT	Literacy and Numeracy Training
LAP	Labour Adjustment Packages
LEAP	Landcare and Environmental Action Program
MAA	Mature Age Allowance
MAATS	Modern Australian Apprenticeship and Traineeship System
MTIA	Metal Trades Industry Association
NAAP	New Apprenticeships Access Program
NACs	New Apprenticeship Centres
NEIS	New Enterprise Incentive Scheme
NESA	National Employment Services Association
NLCC	National Labour Consultative Council
NNA	National New Enterprise Incentive Scheme Association
NSA	Newstart Allowance
NTS	New Tax System
NTW	National Training Wage
NWO	New Work Opportunities
PES	Public Employment Service
PfWA	Preparing for Work Agreement
PPM	Post Program Monitoring

PPS	Parenting Payment (single)
PPP	Parenting Payment (partnered)
RAP	Regional Assistance Program
RGWR	Reference Group on Welfare Reform
SEUP	Survey of Employment and Unemployment Patterns
SIHC	Survey of Income and Housing Costs
SNA	Special Needs Assessment
SSP	Self-Sufficiency Project
STA	State/Territory Training Authority
STEP	Structured Training and Employment Program
TAFE	Training and Further Education
WAT	Work Ability Tables
WELL	Workplace English Language and Literacy
WfD	Work for the Dole
WDI	World Development Indicators
WRA	Workplace Relations Act
WRG	Welfare Reference Group
YTI	Youth Training Initiative

OECD PUBLICATIONS, 2, rue André-Pascal, 75775 PARIS CEDEX 16
PRINTED IN FRANCE
(81 2001 11 1 P) ISBN 92-64-18735-9 – No. 51977 2001